CHILDREN'S COGNITIVE AND LANGUAGE DEVELOPMENT

EDITORS

VICTOR LEE AND PRAJNA DAS GUPTA

The Open University

BLACKWELL
Oxford UK & Cambridge USA

First published 1995 by Blackwell Publishers in association with The Open University

The Open University
Walton Hall
Milton Keynes MK7 6AA
UK

Blackwell Publishers Ltd
108 Cowley Road
Oxford OX4 1JF
UK

Blackwell Publishers Inc.
238 Main Street
Cambridge, Massachusetts 02142
USA

Cover illustration
Joan Eardley, *Children and Chalked Wall*, c. 1961, oil/collage on canvas, $23\,^3/_4 \times 29$ ins, reproduced by kind permission of the artist's estate.

A catalogue record for this book is available from the British Library .

Library of Congress Cataloguing-in-Publication data
Children's cognitive and language development / editors,
    Victor Lee and Prajna Das Gupta.
        p. cm. — (Child development: 3)
    Includes bibliographical references and indexes.
    ISBN 0-631-19427-4 (alk. paper). — ISBN 0-631-19428-2 (pbk.: alk. paper)
1. Cognition in children. 2. Human information processing in children.
    3. Children—Language.   I. Lee, V. J. (Victor J.)   II. Das Gupta, Prajna.
    III. Series: Child development (Cambridge, Mass.); 3.
    BF723.C5C497   1995
    155.4'13—dc20   94-33968
                                                  CIP

Edited, designed and typeset by The Open University

Printed in the United Kingdom by The Alden Press Limited.

This book is printed on acid-free paper

CHILDREN'S COGNITIVE AND LANGUAGE DEVELOPMENT

THE UNIVERSITY OF
WINCHESTER

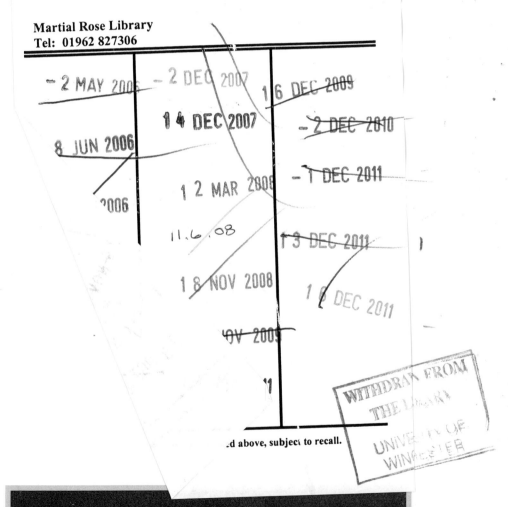

Children's Cognitive and Language Development forms part of the
Open University course ED209 *Child Development*. The icons that appear in
the margin of this text refer to other elements in the course such as television
programmes, study guides and a methodology handbook. For further
information about this course, please write to Open University Educational
Enterprises Limited, 12 Cofferidge Close, Stony Stratford, Milton Keynes
MK11 1BY, United Kingdom. Other titles in the series are:

CONTENTS

INTRODUCTION

Victor Lee and Prajna Das Gupta

The emergence and development of the ability to communicate through speech and the ability to move beyond the here-and-now through thinking are among the most striking achievements of childhood – for they are not only the most distinctly human capacities, but are also at the very centre of psychological development. The connections between these two key characteristics continue to intrigue and excite psychologists. There is no shortage of theoretical ideas about the development of these capacities or about their interrelationships, and this book reviews the more significant theoretical and empirical contributions to this field.

A further organizing theme concerns the significance of culture for the development of language and thinking. Several of the chapters focus on the role that social relationships play in directing both the form and content of language and thought.

Chapter 1, 'Theories of cognitive development', provides a conceptual framework for the book as a whole. In this chapter, four major theories of cognitive development are discussed: constructivism, social constructivism, nativism and connectionism. Although these theories inform much of the conceptual framework, there is no following of any one pattern in the detail of the treatment. For example, connectionism appears in the first four chapters of the book, but is described in greatest detail in Chapter 3, 'Models of memory development'. On the other hand, Chapter 6, 'Mathematical and scientific thinking', deals with the development of cognition in particular contexts, and constructivist and social constructivist explanations are stressed.

Several themes link the chapters. For example, questions about mental representation are dealt with throughout the book, and the differences between everyday understandings and psychological concepts of this process are discussed in various chapters.

In any academic discipline there are some researchers who make an outstanding contribution. Jean Piaget is one such figure in developmental psychology, and his theory of cognitive development is one of the focal points of Chapter 1. Piaget's claim that children pass through four sequential *stages* of thinking is described and evaluated, as are other central concepts of his theory. Another key figure introduced in this chapter is the Russian psychologist, Lev Vygotsky. Both Piaget and Vygotsky see children as active participants in their own development, but Vygotsky puts more stress on the importance of social context. As well as discussing recent developments in the Piagetian tradition, the chapter also considers some other recent theories of development.

Chapter 2, 'Language development', starts with a discussion of the nature of language and communication. Brief reviews of the major theoretical explanations of language set the context for the chapter, and concern matters such as the development of sounds, vocabulary and grammar in the young child. However, such distinctions are not without their problems. For example, a common way of assessing a child's language development is to measure the 'mean length of utterance', but deciding what constitutes an utterance is not as straightforward as it may seem. Indeed, even the definition of basic units, such as a word, can be problematic. The chapter explores evidence suggesting that many conversation-related skills are developed before children produce their first words, and uses jokes as an instance of sophisticated language use, of 'putting it all together'.

Very few of us remember much of our first five years or so. Infantile amnesia is the starting point for Chapter 3, 'Models of memory development', which discusses how memory is organized and how it develops. Much of the work on human memory has been conducted within an information-processing framework, although the chapter also considers a recent and significant development: the connectionist approach. The strengths and weaknesses of the various models are critically evaluated. One of the problems with much of this research is that it is laboratory-based, ignoring the everyday contexts in which memory operates, and the chapter includes a discussion of everyday and autobiographical memory, noting the advantages of dealing with real-life situations and the accompanying difficulties associated with measurement.

How do children learn to make sense of the world around them? How do they categorize experience and develop concepts? Both processes are central to Chapter 4, 'Categorization, concepts and reasoning'. Early work suggested that children's concepts are different in kind from those of adults, but there is now a growing body of evidence that suggests that the differences are quantitative, not qualitative. Nowhere is the link between language and cognition more salient than in a discussion of the Sapir–Whorf hypothesis, which suggests that language determines or influences thinking. The chapter starts with the idea of the concept as a means by which the child organizes the world, and concludes with a consideration of the child's ability to manipulate concepts as part of the reasoning process.

Chapter 5, 'The development of intelligence', deals with a subject on which everyone has an opinion. The chapter opens with a discussion of intelligence as an everyday concept. A brief consideration of the history of the idea of intelligence is then followed by a detailed examination of the psychometric and cognitive perspectives. The psychometric approach, with its emphasis on the measurement of intelligence, is traced from its origins with Sir Francis Galton in the nineteenth century. The work of Alfred Binet and the growth of IQ testing are considered, as are the problems associated with testing. The cognitive approach, with its attempt to look at intelligence in terms of actual knowledge and reasoning processes, is also discussed in some detail, including Howard Gardner's theory of multiple intelligences and Piaget's theory of cognitive development. The chapter ends with a section on intelligence as a social construct, created through social activities, rather than as a fixed entity within the individual.

Chapter 6, 'Mathematical and scientific thinking', opens with a discussion of the nature of mathematical and scientific knowledge. This is followed by sections on the development of mathematical and scientific concepts. The discussion of the development of mathematical concepts includes both Piagetian and post-Piagetian views. The post-Piagetians stress the importance of social situations and cultural practices – for example, the oral arithmetic of young street vendors in Brazil is much more efficient than their written arithmetic in a school-like situation. In the section on the development of scientific concepts, the differences between scientific and everyday concepts of the world are examined by looking at how experts and novices behave. There is a growing body of evidence suggesting that knowledge and reasoning skills are both important in scientific problem-solving. The issue of the relationship between the acquisition of mathematical and scientific concepts and general cognitive development is then debated. How can children be persuaded to embrace a scientific, as opposed to an everyday, way of thinking? Traditional teaching, seen as a didactic passing-down of information, is judged to have been unsuccessful in this regard. A Piagetian alternative is explored, based on the expectation that cognitive change will occur if the student is actively engaged in the learning process. Piaget's hypothesis regarding cognitive change has been translated into a teaching style called 'discovery learning'. In its early days, discovery learning stressed the importance of the individual as a 'lone learner', but later developments and other theorists have emphasized the role of interactions in a social world in effecting cognitive change.

Most children draw spontaneously, and how and what they draw interest psychologists for a number of reasons. Chapter 7, 'Development in drawing', introduces some of the ways in which drawings have been studied in a search for a 'window' into the cognitive and emotional worlds of children. Are drawings a source of insight into children's intelligence? Are the features of the characters and the composition of the picture valid and reliable clues to the artist's emotional state? The conclusions are cautious and limited. More progress has been made in studies of how children deal with the problems of representing a three-dimensional world in a two-dimensional form. In some instances, the nature of the development of 'free' drawings themselves is of significance; in others, the variations in children's graphic responses to a particular problem of order or organization can prove revealing. However, these experimental investigations need to be viewed against a more extensive cultural backdrop, and the chapter's account of some of the cross-cultural variety in the content and nature of children's drawings raises questions about what can really be inferred from this fascinating subject.

Complementary to the development of a non-verbal area, such as drawing, is the development of a verbal area, such as reading, and this is the subject of the concluding chapter, 'Development in reading'. This chapter starts by examining some of the skills involved in learning to read, and includes a theoretical model of the stages children pass through. Which skills are essential for the beginning reader? Which skills develop as the child starts to read? The relationship between phonological skills and reading development is discussed, with the conclusion that it is not a case of 'either ... or', as each can influence the other. The chapter also includes an evaluation of the methods used to teach children to read, and the relative importance of the spoken word and context in learning to read is also considered. The chapter closes with an evaluation of the skills needed in comprehension, and an assessment of some of the difficulties children may encounter.

Prajna Das Gupta and Ken Richardson

CONTENTS

OBJECTIVES

After you have studied this chapter, you should be able to:

1 describe the major divisions in theories of cognitive development;

2 describe the main principles of Piaget's theory of cognitive development including its theoretical foundations and main stages of development;

3 explain why Piaget's theory has been criticized in recent years yet still remains the dominant theory of cognitive development;

4 describe the main principles of Vygotsky's theory of development, and how they contrast with those of Piaget;

5 explain why Vygotsky's theory has become popular in recent years;

6 describe some of the 'contextualist' theories stemming from Vygotsky's theory;

7 describe in outline recent theories based on the assumption of 'modular' and 'domain-specific' principles of cognitive development, and explain what these terms mean;

8 understand how these are based on nativist (or rationalist) principles;

9 understand how recent 'connectionist' theories are based on 'associationist' principles;

10 understand that various amalgamations of these different sets of principles are possible.

1 INTRODUCTION

In the following scenario, Jonathan (3 years 9 months) and his father are playing with a large plastic bowl full of water, a toy boat and various other objects.

D: What's happened to the boat now we've put it in the water?
J: *It's splashed.*
D: Yes – and what's it doing on top of the water?
J: *Floating.*
D: And why is it floating?
J: *Because the water is too little ... shall I see if this crayon works?*
D: What's happened to the crayon?
J: *It's floated! (laughs).*
D: No it hasn't – what's happened to it? Why do you think the boat floats but the crayon goes to the bottom? Think carefully ...
J: *Because ... I don't know why.*
D: Let's try this stone: has it floated?
J: *No.*
D: Why has the stone gone to the bottom?
J: *Because it doesn't float.*
D. Why does the boat float?
J: *Because it's big ... shall I see if this [button] does?*
D: Has that floated?
J: *No, it's sinked on the stone poor button.*
D: Why do you think the button's not floating?
J: *Because it's a stone in.*

(Berryman *et al.*, 1991, p. 109).

You have just *read* something, *understood* it and, if asked, you could *remember* what the scenario was about. Probably you also engaged in *problem-solving* by trying to work out for yourself what would float and used *knowledge* to do so. At the moment you may be *evaluating* the relevance of this material to this chapter. You have just been involved in a series of cognitive processes. (And later, in Activity 3, we will return to this scenario to involve you in a few more!)

Cognition is a collective term for the processes involved in organizing, handling and using knowledge, and refers to all the processes and products of the human mind that lead to knowledge. All types of mental activity – remembering, understanding, problem-solving, relating, imagining, creating, fantasizing, using symbols and so on – are part of cognition.

Jonathan's responses also illustrate wide differences between children and adults. *Cognitive development* is the term used to cover the acquisition and development of knowledge and cognitive processes such as language, memory, problem-solving and drawing. Most theories of cognitive development have been based on children's responses to questions around tasks devised by investigators. The 'conservation task' shown in Research Summary 1 is a classic example.

RESEARCH SUMMARY 1
CONSERVATION TASKS

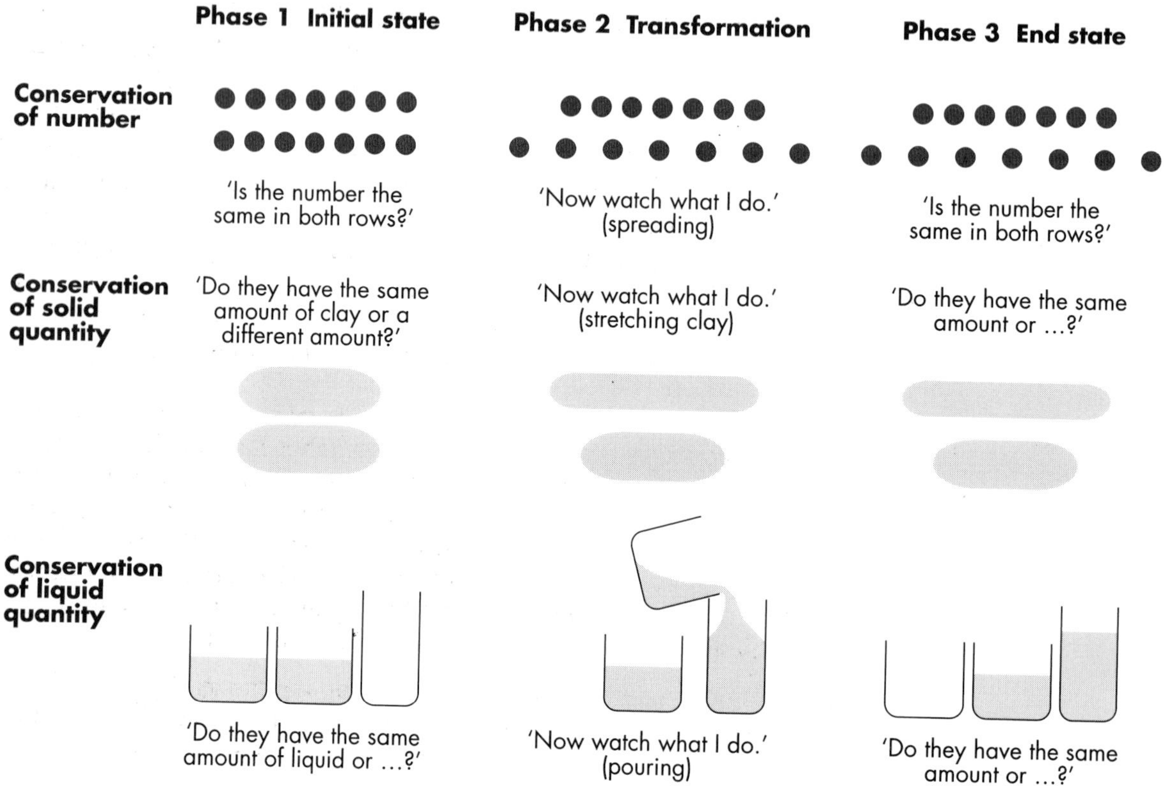

Phase 1 Initial state	Phase 2 Transformation	Phase 3 End state

Conservation of number

'Is the number the same in both rows?'

'Now watch what I do.' (spreading)

'Is the number the same in both rows?'

Conservation of solid quantity

'Do they have the same amount of clay or a different amount?'

'Now watch what I do.' (stretching clay)

'Do they have the same amount or ...?'

Conservation of liquid quantity

'Do they have the same amount of liquid or ...?'

'Now watch what I do.' (pouring)

'Do they have the same amount or ...?'

FIGURE 1 Examples of conservation tasks.

In conservation tasks, three of which are illustrated in Figure 1, children are first shown two or more identical objects, or sets of objects (e.g. counters, clay, glasses of water). After the children have agreed that the two are equal (e.g. there is the same amount of liquid in both glasses, or the same number of counters in the two rows), one of the sets of objects is 'transformed' in such a way that its appearance changes (water is poured into a different shaped container, the row of counters is elongated, etc.). Finally, the children are asked if the feature of interest (quantity of liquid, number of counters) which they said was equal earlier is still equal after the transformation. As adults, we find such questions trivial – of course the answer is 'yes'! Surprisingly, almost all 5 year olds fail these conservation problems when posed in this way, while 7 to 8 year olds are more likely to be correct.

ACTIVITY 1
Allow about 5 minutes

THINKING AND ITS DEVELOPMENT

Before looking at our suggestions below, write down what you think a child must 'do', mentally, to solve the conservation tasks shown in Research Summary 1.

Comment

Here are three things the child must do at the very least:

1. mentally represent and 'hold' the transformation (pouring or remoulding) imposed on the materials;

2. consider not just how each single dimension (height or width of liquid; length or thickness of clay etc.) has changed independently, but also how they have changed *together* (i.e. how the dimensions are *co-ordinated*);

3. compare the consequences of the transformation with the earlier state of the material.

It can be argued that all of these abilities must develop for the 5 year old to solve the task. It then follows that the average 5 year old has failed to develop at least one of them. As we shall see, whether or not this is true is a major theoretical and empirical issue.

Such studies present us with some of the core questions that theories of cognitive development attempt to answer. What has developed in the child so far; and what must further develop for 'mature' responses to be achieved? Finally, how does that development occur? Different theories offer different answers to such questions. Most of this chapter will give an overview of the ideas of two key theorists. The first is Jean Piaget's theory of cognitive development, probably the most comprehensive theory produced so far. This is dealt with in Section 2.

In Section 3 we give an overview of another key theory, that of L. S. Vygotsky. This section also looks at studies that have offered important critiques of Piaget's theory, some of which have been influenced by Vygotsky's ideas.

Both Piaget and Vygotsky were *constructivist theorists*. Such theories assume the active building-up of knowledge and cognitive processes from very simple starting points (Das Gupta, 1994). In the final sections of this chapter, therefore, we consider some alternatives offered by developmental psychologists today, based on different theoretical assumptions. Some of these modern approaches will be discussed in greater detail throughout this book in chapters about the development of specific abilities such as number and drawing (Chapters 6 and 7) or more general processes such as memory and conceptual representation (Chapters 3 and 4).

SUMMARY OF SECTION 1

- Cognitive development refers to the emergence of knowledge and the mental processes associated with it.

- Much research into cognitive development has consisted of the administration of very simple tasks (together with sets of questions) to children of different ages.

- There are widely different theories about what develops, cognitively, and about how development occurs.

2 PIAGET: THE CHILD AS A SOLITARY THINKER

Jean Piaget was born in 1896, in Neuchatel, Switzerland. Piaget became famous for his claim that children take the long journey to adult knowledge and thinking through stages that are qualitatively different from each other. Before Piaget, studies of learning and development were dominated by the idea that an accumulation of simple associations explained mental development. The prevailing view was that the only difference between children's and adults' cognitive processes was that the latter were more efficient. In that context Piaget's claim – that the infant and the child learn and think in a qualitatively different way from each other and from the adult – was a revolutionary one!

Piaget believed that the child's own actions on the world were crucial to development. He believed that the social context was important for development, but the bulk of his work emphasizes the important role that individuals play in their own development. In this sense, the individual is seen as developing in isolation, behaving like a little scientist, making and testing hypotheses in order to construct an understanding of the world. As we shall see later, Vygotsky's theory is based on quite different assumptions.

2.1 Piaget's constructivist theory

Piaget sought to describe and explain the development of *intelligence* in the individual as a form of *adaptation* to the environment. Piaget used some terms idiosyncratically. By *intelligence*, Piaget meant something more general than the quality measured by intelligence tests (see Chapter 5). According to Piaget, intelligence influences all acts of thinking – perception, language, number and morality, to name a few. Intelligence includes not only responses to particular situations, but also the understanding of basic concepts.

Piaget's ideas about *adaptation* were influenced by biology. He saw the development of intelligence as an evolutionary process, and argued that the acquisition of knowledge proceeds in a manner analogous to the evolution of species (Butterworth and Harris, 1994, p. 18). As Butterworth and Harris put it, later stages succeed earlier stages because they are more adaptive, that is, more adequate to the demands of reality.

Piaget called his approach *genetic epistemology*, using the term 'genetic' to refer to growth and development, and not to the action of genes. 'Epistemology' is a philosophical term for the study of knowledge.

Knowledge and cognition, Piaget argued, evolve through a series of stages which are qualitatively different. Changes from stage to stage are accomplished by a set of developmental processes.

It is important to realize, though, that the characteristics of these stages do not constitute a complete description of development itself, so much as *symptoms* of what is developing. The latter, according to Piaget, consist of the increasingly complex representations in the mind of co-ordinations found in activity and experience. By *co-ordinations* Piaget meant the relationships by which some things *change together*. In perception, for example, the height and width of a volume of liquid change together as it is passed from one glass to another (see Activity 1). In grasping objects, a host of muscle contractions and sensations in the infant's grip become co-ordinated with the size and shape of the object, as well as its visual appearance. In later development, co-ordinations appear in *thought*, as well as perception and action – examples are as in arithmetic operations or planning a scientific investigation (thought becomes logical). The nature of these co-ordinations, and the benefits to be derived from 'internalizing' them, are discussed briefly in Section 3.5 of Chapter 5. You may find it helpful to skim through that section now, before turning to the further discussion below of the stages and processes of development postulated by Piaget.

2.2 The stages of development

Piaget described four main stages of development (see below). He believed that all children go through these stages, or *periods* as he called them, and they do so in the same order (e.g. sensorimotor first, followed by preoperational, and so on). Some of the terms used by Piaget sometimes seem difficult to understand – you might ask, for example, 'What are operations?' Most of these terms will be further explained at appropriate points in the text; see Reading A, in particular.

> **I   The sensorimotor stage: from birth to about 2 years**
> The child comes to know the world in terms of the physical actions she can perform. The stage ends with the acquisition of thought and language.
>
> **II   The preoperational stage: from 2 to about 7 years**
> So-called because, according to Piaget, the pre-school child has yet to acquire fully logical [operational] thinking.
>
> **III   The concrete operational stage: from 7 to about 12 years**
> Typical of primary school age child who can think logically about 'concrete' problems in the here and now. With the acquisition of concrete operations, [co-ordinations become represented mentally, and] thought becomes reversible.
>
> **IV   The formal operational stage: from 12 years onwards**
> A form of thought acquired by adolescents … who can think about abstract or hypothetical problems, especially in the realm of scientific reasoning, proceeding by systematic deductions from hypotheses.

(Butterworth and Harris, 1994, p. 19)

READING

At this point you should study 'Features of Piaget's stages II to IV' (Reading A at the end of this chapter).

This reading from Miller (1989) describes the main features of the three stages covering ages 2–12 years onwards, that is after completion of the sensorimotor stage. The sensorimotor stage is one in which the child starts from basic reflexes and develops complex co-ordinations about the physical world and personal actions upon it (so-called 'action schemes'). However, the co-ordinations developed in this stage are still, as it were, in the senses and muscles, and appear (to Piaget at least) to have no representation at the conscious level. This is why, as Miller puts it, the child now has to start all over again.

Some of the technical language in Miller's account may be a little off-putting. All you need to grasp is the idea that relations or co-ordinations are developing *at the level of mental representation* throughout the three stages, but for a long time this development is incomplete. For example, in the preoperational stage there is still egocentrism and a focus on states rather than relations and transformations; this shows lack of co-ordination between objects (including people) and between situations. Similarly, centration and lack of reversibility suggest lack of co-ordination between specific dimensions or variables (e.g. the height and width of the liquid in the glass in the conservation task). You need to understand the terms 'function', 'regulation' and 'identity' only as aspects of the development of how such co-ordinations are represented.

2.3 What develops: operations

We can now see that, according to Piaget, development is a slow progression in the construction of self-contained operations. In stage I, children physically act on the environment; by stages II and III they are forming internal representations, and in stage IV these can be manipulated flexibly and productively, detached from concrete objects or situations.

ACTIVITY 2

Allow about 5 minutes

PROPERTIES OF OPERATIONS

Now look back to the description of the conservation tasks in Activity 1. Try to describe in your own words in what way children who fail the tasks appear to lack co-ordination and reversibility in their representations (and thus may be said to lack operations).

Comment

Prior to the concrete operational stage, children seem to focus on only one dimension at a time, rather than the interrelations between them, and fail to appreciate that a transformation is reversible. For example, a 5 year old will usually say there is more water or clay in phase 3 (Figure 1), because the water in the new glass is higher or the clay sausage is longer (i.e. without reference to the other dimensions). However, 8 year olds say that amounts in phases 1 and 3 are the same. When asked to explain why, they not only mention the transformation (e.g. 'You just poured it'), but they are also able to point out the reversible nature of the operation – 'If you pour it back it will be the same' (Inhelder and Piaget, 1958). Also, they usually refer to the related dimensions (e.g. 'The water is higher but the glass is narrower').

2.4 How does the development occur?

How do children move from one stage to another? Piaget suggested three processes that enable the transition: assimilation, accommodation, and equilibration, as explained in the next reading.

READING

Now read 'Developmental processes' (Reading B at the end of this chapter). Siegler describes the three processes used by Piaget to explain developmental change. Note that the process of equilibration implies that conflict is necessary for cognitive change – it is only when children become dissatisfied with 'shortcomings' in their thinking that the resulting disequilibrium prompts change.

2.5 Piaget's stages and the nature of development

Piaget's concept of stages includes a number of assumptions about the nature of development (Crain, 1992). First, Piaget argues that people pass through stages at different rates, and therefore the ages attached to them are not very important. But everyone progresses through the stages in a fixed order or *invariant sequence*.

An invariant sequence of stages, though, does not necessarily mean that they are programmed by the genes, or that stages unfold according to an inner timetable (a maturationist view; see Das Gupta, 1994, and Richardson, 1994). Far from thinking that stages are genetically determined, Piaget saw them as reflecting increasingly complex ways of thinking, which children construct in trying to make sense of their environment.

Secondly, the stages do not only imply qualitatively different periods; for Piaget, the process of thinking itself at each stage is qualitatively different. As we saw, thinking at stage II, because it lacks 'operations', is qualitatively different from thinking at stage III, where operations are present. In the same way, thinking at stage III, although logical, is still tied to concrete objects and lacks the truly abstract and hypothetical qualities of stage IV thinking.

Thirdly, Piaget believed that stages refer to general characteristics, rather than specific competencies. For instance, a 4 year old cannot copy a diamond, but a 5 year old can. Can we say the latter is at a diamond-copying stage? If we called each specific achievement a stage we would have innumerable stages, so it may be more appropriate to say that a child of 5 has reached a new *general* stage that allows him or her to do new things, including copying diamonds. Piaget's stages, too, refer to general patterns of logical thinking, and he argued that a child at a particular stage should perform similarly on a wide range of tasks.

Fourthly, Piaget believed that lower stages never disappear, they become integrated into the new stage (hierarchic integration) (Inhelder and Piaget, 1958). We all continue to use the co-ordinations of sensorimotor knowledge in everyday activities like playing games such as tennis without having to think about them too much. However, we can also represent those co-ordinations at a concrete operational level by describing specific rallies and consequences in drawings or words. Finally, we can operationalize them in formal terms by working out (predicting) consequences *given* certain hypothetical factors such as the strength of players, direction of volley, hardness of court and so on – and stating how the importance of each factor could be checked. In Piaget's terms we can 'operate on our operations'.

Finally, Piaget held that stages unfold in the same sequence across cultures. The specific beliefs and ideas of different cultures may vary, but Piaget believed that the underlying cognitive capacities are universal.

2.6 A general evaluation of the theory

Are there stage sequences?

Many of the early experiments on children's thinking were conducted using similar methods to Piaget's, but on larger samples of children, and often using more standardized versions of tasks. In the 1960s and 1970s large samples of children from different countries (America, Africa, Britain, China) showed the same stages of thinking reported by Piaget's small sample of Swiss children in the 1920s and 1930s (Goodnow, 1969). Children from non-industrial societies seemed to reach the stages of reasoning later than North American or British children, but all children did seem to reach the concrete operational period (Dasen, 1975). Formal operational reasoning, however, was only reached by a minority of adolescents and adults, even in industrial societies, especially on scientific reasoning problems (King, 1985).

Other studies, however, have suggested that performance on Piagetian tasks does vary from culture to culture, and may depend on a number of variables such as whether children go to school. Indeed, it has been suggested that the whole format of such tasks is culture bound, and that the 'reasoning' performances required 'reflect the cognitive style demanded by Western (industrialized) society' (Butterworth and Harris, 1994, p. 170).

The notion of stage-like development has also been challenged by studies that have modified Piagetian tasks. For example, a child may appear to understand a specific concept when tested with one type of material but not another. When Uzgiris (1964) tested conservation of substance using a variety of materials (Plasticine, wire coils and plastic wire) children demonstrated conservation on some material but not others. Subtle changes in task demands have also revealed logical thinking in pre-schoolers that was not apparent in the traditional tasks.

In the next section we will consider arguments that have questioned Piaget's conclusions by modifying his tasks.

Are there general modes of thought particular to each stage?

There is little support for Piaget's claim that stages reflects general modes of thought (or ways of thinking). For instance a child who can conserve liquids may fail at a class-inclusion task, another ability associated with the concrete operations stage. Even on conservation tasks, conservation of weight develops a year or two after conservation of substance.

Piaget himself recognized this unevenness in development (children master different tasks at different rates) and called it *horizontal décalage*. This unevenness, however, is problematic for Piaget's stage theory because he argued that the mental operations underlying a concept should be identical and content-free, so that the operations apply over a large number of cases and materials.

Finally, child prodigies, whose development in a particular area (e.g. maths) is more advanced than in other areas of thinking, challenge Piaget's theory. He does not explain how structures limited to one domain can be isolated from the child's overall cognitive structure at a particular stage of development (Miller, 1989).

Some contemporary psychologists have argued that we should abandon the notion of stages in development altogether. They argue that children do not go through any general stages of development; rather, they develop a repertoire of task-specific skills and strategies. This issue is further explored in Section 4.

Do people reach the highest stages?

In general, the answer to this question is no. Most adults do not demonstrate the highest stages of formal operations on Piaget's tasks (King, 1985). Piaget accounted for these findings by suggesting that most people attain some kind of formal operational thinking but they only use it in areas of specialization. A car mechanic might not use formal operations for solving a philosophical problem but may do so in order to work out what is wrong with a car. Similarly, when Kalahari bush people discuss animal tracking they use hypothetical thinking in ways that tax the best inferential and analytical capacities of the human mind, but fail on classical Piagetian formal operations tasks. The 'context-dependence' of thinking is another area we will return to below.

Do children really learn on their own?

Piaget argued that cognitive development is a spontaneous process. Cognitive structures develop without any direct teaching from adults. Many psychologists, including Vygotsky, disagree with this idea. On the other hand, a number of training studies have been conducted to teach concepts like conservation to 4- and 5-year-old children. The overall conclusion of these studies has been that conservation is surprisingly difficult to teach. Conservation can be taught, as demonstrated by Gelman (1969), but the procedure is laborious: her training lasted two days, consisted of 192 trials, and there are some doubts about whether the effects were permanent.

Piaget suggested that the idea of spontaneous development is unpopular because of its slowness, whereas direct teaching seems desirable because it can speed up development. However, he argued that slowness may be one of the signs of fruitful invention (Crain, 1992) and speculated that by virtue of differences in activity/experience alone, individual differences in rates of development are bound to emerge.

SUMMARY OF SECTION 2

- Piaget's theory is a constructivist theory, based on analogies with biological evolution and adaptation.
- As such, it postulates highly complex cognitive structures and functions being built up from very simple initial processes in conjunction with personal action and experience.
- The main content of these structures consists of the progressive internalization of the external co-ordinations (and co-ordinations within co-ordinations) revealed by action on the world.
- The resulting structures and functions are called the mental operations.
- The internalization and representation of these is reflected in distinct stages, from sensorimotor knowledge to formal operations, each stage being characterized by distinct abilities or inabilities.
- The operations develop by processes of equilibration, assimilation and accommodation.
- Evaluations of the theory from the mid 1970s or so question: the universality of the stages; whether children develop such 'general' operations (as opposed to abilities related to specific tasks); the extent to which the final ('formal') operations are to be found in fully developed humans (i.e. adults); and the extent to which children can actually develop in the absence of overt teaching.

3 VYGOTSKY: THE CHILD IN SOCIETY

Vygotsky was born in 1896 – the same year as Piaget – in Gomel in Russia. Vygotsky much admired Piaget's work, but argued that the latter had overlooked the impact of cultural context on development. According to Vygotsky, interactions with adults and peers, as well as instruction, are essential for cognitive development. This view was deeply influenced by the Marxist ideas which prevailed in the Soviet Union at the time (the 1930s) of Vygotsky's main psychological writings.

According to this view, human cognitive capacities themselves change as a result of historical development, especially technological development. Human history consists of the development of new 'cultural tools' for dealing with the world – new ways of co-operating, organizing, planning, communicating, calculating (i.e. new *psychological* tools), as well as new technological tools. Both technological tools (because they affect the way people co-operate and act) and psychological tools determine people's cognition. The latter will go on changing so long as the former do.

In general, Vygotsky opposed Piaget's image of human development as a lone venture in the world. For Vygotsky, the major task of a theory of development is to understand how cultural tools are acquired by the child. He argued that concepts, language, voluntary attention and memory are functions which originate in culture (i.e. in the interactions between people) and are acquired through development in interaction between the child and another person. Each of these functions appears first as an interpersonal process before it appears within the child as an intrapersonal process (Vygotsky, 1988). To take the hypothetical example given in Richardson (1994): When young children first attend nursery many are highly emotionally motivated. But collective play around objects and equipment requires regulation of group feelings and activities, and 'tools' of regulation (such as queuing or prioritizing) among participants soon emerge. Later, individual children may internalize these patterns and use them to order their *own* emotions in other situations. What was an interpersonal behaviour pattern has become an intrapersonal cognitive process.

Vygotsky argued that although children might develop some concepts on their own through everyday experience, they would not develop purely abstract modes of thought without instruction in abstract sign systems. The child had a *zone of proximal development* ('proximal' meaning 'next'), which was achievable only with the help and support of an adult. This emphasis on the role of the adult as 'teacher' in Vygotsky's theory stimulated research into the role of teaching on development. The zone of proximal development (ZPD):

> may be defined as the difference between what a child can achieve unaided in problem solving and what can be achieved with the help of adults or with the peer group. A simple example is the difference between how an 18-month-old child might attempt to stack a set of beakers when there is no older person there to assist and how she might attempt the same task with the assistance of an adult or

older child. Vygotsky's important contribution was to point out that the child's own knowledge develops through experience of adults guiding the child towards a more sophisticated solution to a task. In the case of the beaker play, for example, the adult might guide the child towards a systematic selection of beakers on the basis of size.

(Butterworth and Harris, 1994, p. 22)

Although Vygotsky gives equal importance to intrinsic (within individual) and external (cultural) forces in his theory, in practice his investigations focused on the impact of culture on the child.

Vygotsky's theory, too, is a stage theory. Both Piaget and Vygotsky agreed that human development is made up of both continuous and discontinuous changes, and that transitions in development are the result of changes in the organization of mental structures (through the development of operations or reconstruction, for example). However, Vygotsky believed that instruction is essential to reach the highest levels of thinking. He argued that purely abstract levels of thinking are only prevalent in technologically advanced societies which emphasize formal instruction.

In the following sections we will bring out some of these characteristics further by comparing them a little more closely with Piaget's theory.

3.1 The role of social interaction

Although Piaget did occasionally refer to social interaction as a factor in development, it is worth repeating (as critics usually do) that he neglected it. Some recent supporters of Piaget have been keen to demonstrate, in fact, how social interaction can promote cognitive development by presenting the child with new 'disturbances', or points of view, to which his or her existing schemes are forced to re-equilibrate (Doise, 1988).

This is not to imply, however, that followers of Vygotsky have simply restored the balance with a renewed emphasis on social interaction. It is important to point out that Vygotsky conceived of a qualitatively different role for social interaction compared with Piaget. Rather than merely 'assisting' a pattern of cognition within the child to develop independently, in Vygotsky's view the pattern of social interaction *determines* the structure and pattern of internal cognition: 'the very mechanism underlying higher mental functions is a copy from social interaction; all higher mental functions are internalized social relationships' (Vygotsky, 1988, p. 74).

The role of instruction

The distinctive thread in Vygotsky's theory becomes focused around the role of instruction in development.

Our disagreement with Piaget centers on one point only, but an important point. He assumes that development and instruction are entirely separate, incommensurate processes, that the function of instruction is merely to introduce adult ways of thinking, which conflict with the child's own and eventually supplant them. Studying child thought apart from the influence of instruction, as Piaget did, excludes a very important source of change ...

(Vygotsky, 1962, pp. 116–17)

This source of developmental change, especially its operation in the ZPD, has become a major target of research in the last few years. It has been demonstrated in a large number of naturalistic and institutional and experimental settings, and a number of implications for institutionalized education have been drawn in recent years.

One example in a naturalistic setting is the teaching of weaving among the Zinacantecon of southern Mexico (Childs and Greenfield, 1982). The novice (usually a child) has to learn six main steps, from setting up the loom to finishing off the garment. As each new step is tackled the 'teacher's' intervention is, at first, frequent and detailed. But it reduces rapidly with practice: from 93 per cent of the time with the child's first garment, through 50 per cent with the second garment, and so on.

In an experimental setting, Wood and Middleton (1975) devised a special set of wooden blocks which could only be put together by 4 year olds with considerable help from an adult (usually the mother). In observing mother–child pairs it became clear that the 'instruction' tended to take the form of 'guided arrangement', the level of parental control in which gradually diminished as it became taken over by the child. For example, as we move *up* Table 1, the examples show *reduced* levels of control.

TABLE 1 Levels of control in parent–child interactions.

Level	Example
1 General verbal prompts	'Now you make something'
2 Specific verbal instructions	'Get four big blocks'
3 Indicates materials	Points to blocks needed
4 Prepares for assembly	Orients pairs so hole faces peg
5 Demonstrates	Assembles two pairs

(Source: Wood, 1991, p. 104.)

In such observations it is clear that instruction takes place by a method of 'arranging experience' rather than didactic teaching. Wood, Bruner and Ross (1976) used the term 'scaffolding' to describe the support through which the child can extend or construct current skills to higher levels of competence and control, during which progression the scaffolding is slowly removed. Research into language development has provided a number of examples of the process, and some of these are discussed in Chapter 2.

Language and thought

In explaining the onset of language in the second year, Piaget pointed to the completion of general sensorimotor development at this age and the onset of symbolic functions. Language does not appear earlier because it is part of the development of symbolic functions which provides the capacity for mental representation, imagery, imitation and pretend play as well as spoken language. Language is thus a *product* of this exciting period of cognitive development.

Vygotsky and his followers take a different view: language develops first in social interactions with adults or peers with the sole objective of communicating. As it is mastered it is 'internalized' to support thought and 'inner speech' dialogues: that is, thought is largely the product of language, not vice versa. Vygotsky (e.g. 1962) wrote much about the relations between 'inner speech' and 'external speech', and these matters are taken up further in Chapter 2.

In the next section we shall describe the work of some psychologists who questioned Piaget's interpretation of evidence, particularly the cognitive incompetence that Piaget ascribes to young children. Some of this criticism has been significantly influenced by Vygotsky's theory. In discussing these developments of Piaget's and Vygotsky's ideas we shall focus on the preoperational and concrete operational stages, since the majority of studies on cognitive development involve these periods.

ACTIVITY 3

Allow about 10 minutes

COMPARING PIAGET AND VYGOTSKY

You have now covered the main concepts in both Piaget's and Vygotsky's theories. Now look back to the scenario given on the first page of this chapter in which a father and son are playing with toys in water. First try to interpret the scene from a Piagetian perspective (it is probably best to focus on the responses of the child for this). Write down what you would draw attention to if you were such a theorist. Then try to interpret it from a Vygotskian perspective (it is probably best to look at the whole interaction, including the father's questions, for this). Again write down what you might draw attention to. *Note that you will be able to do this in very general terms only* – but the exercise should still help sharpen some of the distinctions we have just been making.

Comments

A Piagetian might draw attention to:

- the 'semilogical' thinking of the child evident in most responses;
- centration on one prominent dimension (the size of the boat);
- assimilation of the action of one object to the (albeit immature) schema of another (as when the button is likened to a stone);
- the absence of an operational structure for predicting or explaining flotation (i.e. the co-ordination between weight and size in the concept of density).

A Vygotskian might draw attention to the following points:

- Rather than trying to teach a concept directly, the adult is concerned to arrange experience for the child, sensitively scaffolding trials and questions within a perceived zone of proximal development;

- part of this arrangement consists of attempts to draw the child's attention to key variables or differences between the objects (e.g. boat versus stone);
- there are prompts for explanations;
- there is the high level of parental intervention appropriate to a difficult concept – mainly in the form of demonstrations and highly specific questions (see Table 1, from Wood's study);
- Overall, the impression is given that density/flotation are defined socially as 'important concepts', which the father is assuming some responsibility for transmitting; and that they will be best acquired by this process of social interaction around objects and the development of shared understanding.

3.2 Making sense – cognition in context

The Scottish psychologist Margaret Donaldson argued that young children might fail Piagetian tasks because the tasks selected made little sense to them, and because they could not understand what the adult actually meant when they asked children a question (for example, what does it mean if an adult shows you a transformation such as making a lump of clay longer, and then asks you whether the amount of clay has changed?). Donaldson argued that most reasoning is embedded both in a particular context and in the knowledge we have already; and that interpreting language is more than a matter of interpreting word meaning – we almost always need to add something of our own knowledge and thought as well.

> There is a story – a true story – about a robot called Freddy which illustrates the point well. Freddy was once given the task of putting all the objects on a table into a big box. The operation ran smoothly and successfully until the very end, but then Freddy did something that no human being would ever do. He tried to put the box in the box. Or, if that is to speak too humanly, he picked the box up and put it down again, and picked it up and put it down again – and presumably would have gone on doing so indefinitely. He had been instructed to put 'all the objects on the table' into the box and, after all, the box was one of the objects on the table.
>
> Human beings, however, have a powerful urge that was lacking in Freddy. They have an urge to make sense of what they hear – or read. So in this case they would add to the instruction, without even noticing what they were doing, the crucial phrase 'except the box itself'. Then the instruction 'makes sense' in relation to the world we know and to purposes we can understand, and all seems well.
>
> (Donaldson, 1987, p. 105)

Inspired by this perspective many researchers over the last decade or so have demonstrated that, when the task and its context are made clear to children, they may be able to exhibit 'logical' thought and understanding well before the ages which Piaget had suggested as a lower limit.

READING

Now read Reading C, an extract from Butterworth (1992), 'Context and cognition in models of cognitive growth'. This brief overview extends points just made above, and others will be developed further in other chapters of this book, especially Chapters 5 and 6. In it Butterworth begins to ask *in what ways* reasoning and context and background knowledge may be connected.

One line of research discussed by Butterworth has suggested that knowledge 'works' in reasoning because mental representations reflect the structure of reality as experienced. Thus a social concept such as that of 'obligation' 'actually exists in a social reality, it is not a mere abstraction'. Everyday reasoning appears to be based on such structures, and context 'works' by evoking the appropriate representation. A problem in an unfamiliar context that evokes no suitable mental representation can make any one of us appear cognitively undeveloped! This appears to be the case with Raven's matrices (a well-known IQ test) and Wason's selection problem (a well-known research task), both of which are mentioned near the end of Reading C. Success on these problems may simply depend on children having particular kinds of cultural–contextual experience, rather than abstract cognitive ability as such. These matters are considered further in Chapter 5.

As Butterworth warns us, though, it is still unclear how context and background knowledge are involved in these processes in most cases of reasoning and its development. Research Summary 2 is about one attempt at clarification.

Why is direct experience more effective in the development of conceptual knowledge than passive observation? Hatano and Inagaki (1992) suggest that conceptual knowledge consists of a kind of 'mental model'. Similarities between the model and a new target object allow for hypotheses or predictions to be made about the latter, even though this is sometimes inappropriate, as when young children, on the basis of their mental model of humans, might attribute feelings to plants, or the sensations of pain to insects. In the process of extending one model, a new model (of the target) is being created.

They argue that humans have an intrinsic motivation for understanding or comprehension. Incongruity in experience leads to 'comprehension activity', including seeking further information, making and testing predictions, and so on. Children directly involved in the care of animals are likely to experience more variability in their behaviour, more inconsistency or incongruity arising from it, and thus greater motivation for mental model creation. This process may be further enhanced by 'dialogue interaction'. Communicating about something requires that implicit ideas be made explicit, and thus opens up comprehension activity to alternative views. They also point to evidence that comprehension activity is far more effective when carried out for intrinsic reasons (i.e. greater comprehension itself) than for external rewards, and when valued by the learners' 'reference group' (such as

RESEARCH SUMMARY 2
ROUTINE KNOWLEDGE AND CONCEPTUAL KNOWLEDGE

Like most theorists Hatano and Inagaki (1992) make a distinction between 'routine' knowledge which is restricted to specific situations and 'conceptual' knowledge which is transferable across different situations. They compared the knowledge of pre-school children who had experience of caring for goldfish at home with that of other children who had no such experience. This was done by asking various questions, not only about the fish, but about a new target animal, like a frog. The questions concerned the consequences of over-feeding, whether the animals had hearts and blood and whether they excreted.

They found that the experienced children tended to use their knowledge of goldfish as an analogy for making reasonable predictions and explanations about frogs as well – i.e. they had developed conceptual knowledge that was transferred to another situation. This tendency was more advanced than that of children who merely *observed* their teachers in kindergarten carrying out caring procedures with animals, but had no direct experience themselves.

peers). They conclude that although primary experience is necessarily tied to particular situations, given certain conditions that very experience impels development to more conceptual, context-free, levels.

If you are beginning to think that ideas like 'comprehension activity' sound a bit like Piaget's equilibration, or others like 'dialogue interaction' sound like Vygotsky's social constructivism, then you could have a point. They could illustrate how the two views are converging in some recent theoretical work. The important implication, though, is that the development of 'abstract' or 'disembedded' thinking, so much the aim of learning in schools, is actually best fostered in real-life contexts: 'The paradoxical fact is that disembedded thinking, although by definition it calls for the ability to stand back from life, yields its greatest riches when it is conjoined with doing' (Donaldson, 1978, p. 83).

SUMMARY OF SECTION 3

- Vygotsky's theory stresses the role of social interaction as the 'motor' of cognitive development.
- This occurs to a large extent through the internalization of 'cultural tools' – a process that shapes personal knowledge and thought.
- This process is heavily dependent on instruction or teaching by adults or peers.
- Vygotsky's theory contrasts with Piaget's in terms of the importance of social interaction and instruction and the relations between language and thought.
- More recent 'Vygotskian' theorists have drawn further attention to the importance of context and background knowledge when children are asked to deal with specific problems or learn specific things.

4 RECENT NATIVIST AND ASSOCIATIONIST THEORIES

As mentioned earlier, the theories we have just been discussing are essentially constructivist. Other recent theories have invoked either nativist (rationalist) or associationist (empiricist) principles. (This distinction and these terms are explained in Das Gupta, 1994). We will take a brief look at the principles underlying these theories.

4.1 Modules and domains

As described in Oates (1994), many theorists have argued that our knowledge and cognitive processes are, in all essential respects, 'wired in' on the basis of genetic information. Development – i.e. growth or maturation – is then simply the expression of a kind of genetic program. One of the strongest statements regarding genetic programs is that of Noam Chomsky on language development, which is looked at in the next chapter (see also Richardson, 1994).

In the area of cognitive development, Jerry Fodor (e.g. 1983) has argued that there is little evidence for qualitative or structural changes in development at all. Instead, he suggests that we are all born with identical representational and computational systems, which are genetically pre-structured to allow us to make sense of the world in which humans evolved. Although the basic idea is far from new, it has been taken up by many theorists in the last decade or so. Recent theory based on this idea involves the concepts of *module* and *domain*.

Modules are different subsets of our neural networks which are genetically pre-structured for processing different kinds of input information: for example, language information, or musical or mathematical information. The 'architectures' and processes in these specialized sets don't change with age and experience. Rather their task is to pass on the information they have processed to a 'central executive' in the form of a common 'language of thought'. On this basis the executive builds up information in memory, and can generate new hypotheses about the world, make decisions and so on.

A *domain* is the set of representations on which a particular kind of knowledge and the cognitive processes associated with it are based. Some authors will apply their definition of domain to quite wide areas of knowledge such as 'language', 'physics', and so on. Others apply it much more narrowly to include 'microdomains' such as gravity in physics or pronoun knowledge in the area of language (Karmiloff-Smith, 1992). Either way, development is spoken of as being 'domain-specific' – that is, development (or maturation) in one domain is independent of development (or maturation) in other domains. Thus children may progress in language or drawing while being backward in mathematics. Indeed, the existence of such children (see Chapter 7) is often taken as strong evidence that development is domain-specific, and thus modular.

There is, inevitably, some debate about this. Modularity implies 'domain-specificity' in development. But 'domain-specificity' (that is, development in one area independently of others) does not necessarily imply a modular system. For example, a child might apply general cognitive processes to become an expert in chess or computer games, but this doesn't necessarily mean that specialized modules have been involved. More generally, you should be able to see how 'domain-specific' theories, modular or otherwise, contrast with that of Piaget as discussed above. The latter is a 'domain-general' theory, in that development in particular domains arises from the application of the same general processes to different knowledge areas.

Fodor's (and Chomsky's) theories, of course, revive ideas which have been expressed many times before in the history of psychology (see Das Gupta, 1994, for a brief historical discussion of these ideas). And these ideas have found expression in a number of related theories recently. Chapter 5 considers how different modules have been treated as different kinds of 'intelligence' by Gardner (1984), each developing in its own independent manner. Some have followed Chomsky in arguing that, for example, infants are born with specific information processors which enable them to parse, or segregate, a continuous sound-stream into constituent letters or phonemes and different clauses or parts of sentences (see Chapter 2). Others have argued that domain-specific, pre-structured, cognitive processes prepare the infant for identifying objects, and building up object concepts; for recognizing the basic number concepts underlying mathematics; recognizing and attending to specific social cues in interactions with adults and peers; distinguishing faces from non-faces; and so on (see Oates, 1994; an exhaustive contemporary review is given in Hirschfeld and Gelman, 1994).

Note that the term 'constraints' is used more or less loosely, and not always clearly, by these theorists. To some it means the rigid application of highly specific modular processes (for example, attention to face-like stimuli in preference to random dots); to others it means rather looser 'guides' to processing (using contextual information as well). Acceptance of this looser interpretation opens the door to the influence of other factors – i.e. other than genetically-specified ones – in development.

Note how Karmiloff-Smith's theory, described in Research Summary 3, is an interesting amalgamation of both nativist and constructivist principles. Clearly, the interplay of these ideas can yield a rich variety of theoretical permutations, and this explains why the area is a very exciting one at the present time.

RESEARCH SUMMARY 3
MODIFIABLE MODULARITY

Karmiloff-Smith (1992) has proposed a theory in which infants are born with a number of domain-specific processing constraints which help give the child a 'flying start' in the world. The representations initially formed, however, become progressively 're-described' (or reformatted) in the light of further experience. Such 'representational re-description' is suggested, according to Karmiloff-Smith in the results of an experiment shown in Figure 2.

Five to seven year olds were asked to draw a model railway line, which they did quite easily. Then they were asked to build a similar circuit by asking the experimenter for the parts. When they were asked to draw that circuit, however, the resulting drawing was different from the first.

This suggests that after having to ask for the pieces of track using a linguistic code the separate elements became represented differently (i.e. more explicitly). It is these new representations that then appear in the second drawing.

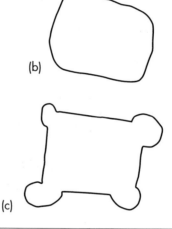

(b)

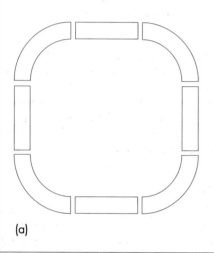

(a)

(c)

FIGURE 2 (a) The original railway circuit; (b) the first drawing; (c) the second drawing, following the circuit construction. (From Karmiloff-Smith, 1992.)

READING

Now study Reading D, 'Beyond modularity'.

In these extracts Karmiloff-Smith (1992) describes some of the principles of 'modularity' and suggests why they need to be revised. Three points in particular are worth noting: first, what development from a 'domain-specific' perspective is like compared with development from a 'domain-general' point of view; second, the crucial point about the inflexibility of modular processes and its disadvantages; third, why this limitation requires the kind of revision she suggests. Instead of completely pre-specified structures she suggests that weaker innate 'predispositions' permit the *development* of better-adapted modules (i.e. modularization) along constructivist lines.

4.2 Connectionism and development

The theory that knowledge and mental processes are based on 'associations' between stimulus inputs, between stimuli and responses, and/or between mental 'ideas', is discussed briefly by Das Gupta (1994). The view has long been known as 'associationism'.

In the last decade or so another version of associationism has arisen, one which has been brought to bear more specifically on questions of cognitive development. According to such theory the initial state of development is the existence in the human brain of many thousands of highly interconnected units or cells, each of which is responsive to only very rudimentary information such as lines of particular orientation or sounds of particular frequency. Such is the interconnectedness in the network, however, that, over many experiences, 'emergent' patterns of activity are created that can represent highly complex objects, relations and events, such as the grammatical rules of language or complex object concepts. In this process the network is acting as a 'self-organizing' system that creates representations in interaction with structured information in its environment (Plunkett and Sinha, 1992). The changes of structures and complexity in such representations are seen as the essence of cognitive development.

These 'connectionist' theories are dealt with in greater detail in Chapters 2 and 3, so will not be described any further here. It is worth noting from a theoretical point of view, however, that some connectionist theorists claim that the 'development' of representational networks takes an essentially 'constructivist' form, thus presenting an amalgamation of associationist and constructivist perspectives. Whether or not such a position can be sustained remains to be seen.

ACTIVITY 4

Allow about 10 minutes

FIGURE 3 Three theoretical frameworks. (Keil, 1990, pp. 148–9.)

COGNITIVE STRUCTURES

Figure 3 is taken from Keil (1990). Each part of the figure is meant to illustrate the development of cognitive structures according to each of the main theoretical frameworks we have just been talking about: a domain-general, constructivist, view of development; a domain-specific, nativist view; and an associationist view. See if you can identify the theoretical framework shown in each diagram before looking at the explanation below.

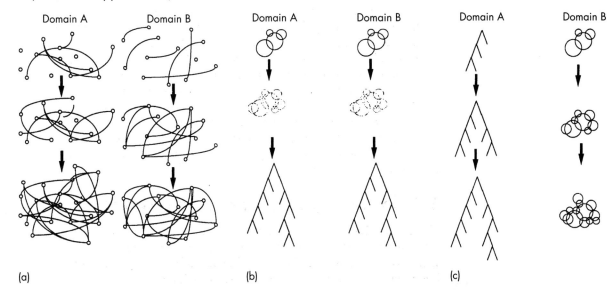

(a)　　　　　　　　　　　(b)　　　　　　　　　　　(c)

Comment

(a) is the associationist view. Development consists of the progressive elaboration of associations between features, objects and events (the small circles in the diagram) 'copied' from experience. Different domains have different patterns of associations.

(b) is the constructivist, domain-general view. Note how initial representations, which do not vary across domains, undergo periodic transformations, to different, more elaborate, but still general, representations.

(c) is the nativist, domain-specific view: initial representations vary according to domain, and mature into progressively more elaborate representations, each still tied to a particular domain.

SUMMARY OF SECTION 4

- Theories of cognitive development based on both nativist and associationist assumptions have gained in popularity in recent years.

- Most recent nativist theories have suggested the role of genetically specified 'modules' committed to the processing and accumulation of specific kinds of information ('domains').

- Development is thus said to be 'domain-specific' in contrast to the 'domain-general' development proposed in theories like that of Piaget.

- The inflexibility of rigid modules can, however, be a disadvantage in a changeable world, so some theories have suggested innate modules modifiable to some extent by constructivist developmental processes.

- Most recent associationist theories of development have proposed changes in connections among highly interconnected processing units. Such changes, it is claimed, can lead to the emergence (development) of highly sophisticated mental structures.

---

5 CONCLUSION

It is a cliché to suggest that this is an exciting period in the area of language and cognitive development. This brief overview of theories ought to show, however, that we are currently witnessing a highly fertile production and exchange of ideas, some old, some new. Many key issues are being brought into clearer focus; and the daunting nature of the task ahead is becoming clearer, too. The chapters which follow offer accounts of the expression of these ideas in particular areas of language and cognitive development. We hope you will approach them, however, with one particular lesson from the overview just given. This is that the construction of a comprehensive theory such as Piaget's is a phenomenal achievement; but it is only by being prepared to identify and criticize underlying assumptions that dogma is avoided and progress gained. To borrow the ideas of Hatano and Inagaki (1992), we hope these chapters will engage you in the kind of 'comprehension activity' that will excite your own interest in this highly important area.

FURTHER READING

In further defence of Piaget:

DEMETRIOU, A., SHAYER, M. and EFKLIDES, A. (eds) (1994) *Neo-Piagetian Theories of Cognitive Development: implications and applications for education*, London, Routledge.

On Vygotskian perspectives and cognition in context:

VAN DER VEER, R. and VALSINER, J. (eds) (1994) *The Vygotsky Reader*, Oxford, Blackwell.

On domain-specific and modular theories:

HIRSCHFELD, L. A. and GELMAN, S. A. (eds) (1994) *Mapping the Mind: domain specificity in cognition and culture*, Cambridge, Cambridge University Press.

On connectionism and cognitive development:

KARMILOFF-SMITH, A. (1992) *Beyond Modularity: a developmental perspective on cognitive science*, Chapter 10, Cambridge (Mass.), MIT Press.

REFERENCES

BERRYMAN, J. C., HARGREAVES, D., HERBERT, M. and TAYLOR, A. (1991) *Developmental Psychology and You*, Leicester, BPS Books (The British Psychological Society), in association with Routledge.

BUTTERWORTH, G. (1992) 'Context and cognition in models of cognitive growth' *in* LIGHT, P. and BUTTERWORTH, G. (eds) *Context and Cognition*, pp. 1, 2–7, 10, 13, London, Harvester.

BUTTERWORTH, G. and HARRIS, M. (1994) *Principles of Developmental Psychology*, Hove, LEA.

CHILDS, C. P. and GREENFIELD, P. M. (1982) 'Informal modes of learning and teaching: the case of Zinacanteco learning' *in* WARREN, N. (ed.) *Advances in Cross-cultural Psychology*, London, Academic Press.

CRAIN, W. (1992; 3rd edn) *Theories of Development: concepts and applications*, Englewood Cliffs (N.J.), Prentice-Hall.

DAS GUPTA, P. (1994) 'Images of childhood and theories of development' *in* OATES, J. (ed.) *The Foundations of Child Development*, Oxford, Blackwell/The Open University (Book 1 of ED 209).

DASEN, P. (1975) 'Concrete operational development in three cultures', *Journal of Cross-cultural Psychology*, **6**, pp. 156–72.

DOISE, W. (1988) 'On the social development of the intellect' *in* RICHARDSON, K. and SHELDON, S. (eds) *Cognitive Development to Adolescence*, Hove, Erlbaum.

DONALDSON, M. (1978) *Children's Minds*, London, Fontana.

DONALDSON, M. (1987) 'The origins of inference' *in* BRUNER, J. and HASTE, H. (eds) *Making Sense: the child's construction of the world*, London, Methuen.

FODOR, J. (1983) *The Modularity of Mind*, Cambridge (Mass.), MIT Press.

GARDNER, H. (1984) *Frames of Mind: the theory of multiple intelligences*, London, Heinemann.

GELMAN, R. (1969) 'Conservation acquisition: a problem of learning to attend to relevant attributes', *Journal of Experimental Child Psychology*, **7**, pp. 167–87.

GELMAN, R. and BAILLARGEON, R. (1983) 'A review of some Piagetian concepts' *in* FLAVELL, J. H. and MARKMAN, E. M. (eds) *Handbook of Child Psychology: vol. 3, Cognitive development* (4th edn), pp. 167–230.

GOODNOW, J. J. (1969) 'Problems in research on culture and thought' *in* ELKIND, D. and FLAVELL, J. (eds) *Studies in Cognitive Development: essays in honour of Jean Piaget*, Oxford, Oxford University Press.

HATANO, G. and INAGAKI, K. (1992) 'Desituating cognition through the construction of conceptual knowledge' *in* LIGHT, P. and BUTTERWORTH, G. (eds) *Context and Cognition*, London, Harvester.

HIRSCHFELD, L. A. and GELMAN, S. A. (1994) *Mapping the Mind: domain specificity in cognition and culture*, Cambridge, Cambridge University Press.

INHELDER, B. and PIAGET, J. (1958) *The Growth of Logical Thinking from Childhood to Adolescence*, London, Routledge and Kegan Paul.

KARMILOFF-SMITH, A. (1992) *Beyond Modularity: a developmental perspective on cognitive science*, Cambridge (Mass.), MIT Press.

KEIL, F. C. (1990) 'Constraints on constraints: surveying the epigenetic landscape', *Cognitive Science*, **14**, pp. 135–68.

KING, P. M. (1985) 'Formal reasoning in adults: a review and critique' *in* MINES, R. A. and KITCHENER, K. S. (eds) *Adult Cognitive Development*, New York, Praeger.

MILLER, P. H. (1989; 2nd edn) *Theories of Developmental Psychology*, New York, Freeman.

OATES, J. (1994) 'Sensation to perception' *in* OATES, J. (ed.) *The Foundations of Child Development*, Oxford, Blackwell/The Open University (Book 1 of ED 209).

PLUNKETT, K. and SINHA, C. (1992) 'Connectionism and developmental theory', *British Journal of Developmental Psychology*, **10**, pp. 209–54.

RICHARDSON, K. (1994) 'Interactions in development' *in* OATES, J. (ed.) *The Foundations of Child Development*, Oxford, Blackwell/The Open University (Book 1 of ED 209).

SIEGLER, R. S. (1991) *Children's Thinking*, Englewood Cliffs (N.J.), Prentice-Hall.

UZGIRIS, I. C. (1964) 'Sustained generality of conservation', *Child Development*, **35**, pp. 831–41.

VYGOTSKY, L. S. (1962) *Thought and Language*, Cambridge (Mass.), MIT Press.

VYGOTSKY, L. S. (1988) 'The genesis of higher mental functions' *in* RICHARDSON, K. and SHELDON, S. (eds) *Cognitive Development to Adolescence*, Hove, Erlbaum.

WOOD, D. (1991) 'Aspects of teaching and learning' in LIGHT, P., SHELDON, S. and WOODHEAD, M. (eds) *Learning to Think*, London, Routledge/The Open University.

WOOD, D. J. and MIDDLETON, D. J. (1975) 'A study of assisted problem-solving', *British Journal of Psychology*, **66**, pp. 181–91.

WOOD, D. J., BRUNER, J. S. and ROSS, G. (1976) 'The role of tutoring in problem-solving', *Journal of Child Psychology and Psychiatry*, **17**, pp. 89–100.

READINGS

Reading A   Features of Piaget's stages II to IV

P. H. Miller

Preoperational period (roughly 2 to 7 years)

Ending the first period and beginning the next can be likened to climbing a mountain, only to discover that it is merely a foothill to Mt Everest. The achievements of the sensorimotor period, although monumental, are also preparation for what is to come. In a sense, the child starts all over again. What he has achieved in the realm of actions on the world is redeveloped, now in the realm of mental representations. He transfers notions about objects, relations, causality, space, and time to a new medium (mental representation) and a more highly organized structure.

[…]

Although thinking through symbols and signs is a tremendous advance over sensorimotor thought, such thinking is limited in a number of ways. As the term *preoperational* suggests, children in this period have not yet acquired reversible mental operations, which characterize the thinking of the next period, called concrete operations.

[…]

The main characteristics of preoperational thought are egocentrism, rigidity of thought, semilogical reasoning, and limited social cognition.

1. Egocentrism

Egocentrism does not refer to selfishness or arrogance, and Piaget does not use it in a derogatory way. Rather, the term refers to (a) the incomplete differentiation of the self and the world, including other people, and (b) the tendency to perceive, understand, and interpret the world in terms of the self. One implication is that the child cannot take another person's perceptual or conceptual perspective. For example, the preoperational child does not realize that a person viewing a display from a position different from his own sees the display from a different perspective. A child holding a book upright points to a picture and asks, 'What is this?' He is unaware that his mother, who is facing him, can see only the back of the book. Egocentrism makes it difficult to take the role or point of view of another person.

[…]

Egocentric speech is rampant in children's play groups. Children who apparently are talking while playing in a group may actually be talking, but not necessarily together. Each child's remarks are unrelated to anyone else's. There is a collective monologue, of sorts, rather than a conversation. For example, one child's statement, 'I think I saw Superman in a phonebooth yesterday', might be followed by 'this sweater makes me itch' from another child.

Although the preoperational child is considered to be egocentric, he is less egocentric than he was in the sensorimotor period. Early sensorimotor functioning reflects a lack of differentiation between one's own actions and properties of objects. After the preoperational period, egocentrism continues to decline, but never disappears completely, even in adulthood.

2. Rigidity of thought

Piaget characterizes preoperational thought as frozen. One example is *centration*, the tendency to attend to or think about one salient feature of an object or event and ignore other features. If two identical containers have equal amounts of water and the contents of one container are poured into a taller, thinner container, the child centers on the heights of the liquids, while ignoring their widths. Consequently, he erroneously concludes that there is now more liquid because the water is higher. Centration and egocentrism are similar in that they both reflect an inability to deal with several aspects of a situation at the same time and that they both cause a biased view of the world.

We also find a rigidity, or lack of flexibility, of thought in the tendency to *focus on states* rather than on the transformations linking the states. When faced with the task concerning quantity of liquid in the containers, the child thinks about the 'before' and 'after' states, but ignores the process of changing from A to B as the liquid is poured.

Perhaps the clearest example of the rigidity of thought is its *lack of reversibility*. The preoperational child cannot mentally reverse a series of events, transformations, or steps of reasoning. For example, he is unable to return the poured liquid to its original container mentally. His ability to internalize action is not yet complete because it is not bidirectional.

Toward the end of the preoperational period, we begin to see 'the great thaw', as the child partially corrects the tendency of thought to be centrated, focused on states, and irreversible. We now see three positive achievements of the preoperational period: function, regulation, and identity.

A *function* is the notion that there is a covariation between factors, as expressed in the equation, $y = f(x)$. For example, the more one pulls a curtain, the farther a curtain opens. Or when the rope on a pulley is pulled, there is an increase in the length of one section of rope as the other section decreases in length. However, the child cannot yet work out the precise and quantitative nature of the relationship.

A *regulation* is a mental act that is partially decentered. Again using the test of liquid quantity, we find that the child switches back and forth between using liquid height and width to make his judgments about quantity. A glass may contain more than another glass because it has a higher water level, or it may contain less because it is thinner.

The third achievement, *identity*, is the notion that an object can change its appearance without changing its basic nature, or identity. Water may look different after it is poured from one container to another, but it is the same water. Putting on a Halloween mask does not change a person into a witch, contrary to belief of younger children. Thinking has become less rigid because a concept can be maintained despite superficial physical changes.

3. Semilogical reasoning

As a young psychologist, Piaget questioned children about their beliefs concerning the world. These interviews revealed various fascinating characteristics of preoperational reasoning. The conversations provide many examples of egocentrism and rigidity of thought. We treat them separately because they demonstrate some specific, somewhat surprising, properties of semilogical reasoning.

The following protocol illustrates several facets of semilogical reasoning in a 6-year-old child.

> How did the sun begin? – *It was when life began.* – Has there always been a sun? – *No.* – How did it begin? – *Because it knew that life had begun.* – What is it made of? – *Of fire.* – But how? – *Because there was fire up there.* – Where did the fire come from? – *From the sky.* – How was the fire made in the sky? – *It was lighted with a match.* – Where did it come from, this match? – *God threw it away.* … How did the moon begin? – *Because we began to be alive.* – What did that do? – *It made the moon get bigger.* – Is the moon alive? – *No …Yes.* – Why? – *Because we are alive.*
>
> [Piaget, 1926/29, pp. 258–9]

The child tries to explain the mysterious natural events in terms of everyday life. One solution is to explain natural events in terms of human behaviour. The sun and moon, like people, are alive, are created by a humanlike action (a god lighting a match) and are tied to human activities (the moon began because people began to exist). Similarly, a preoperational child may assert that snow is made for children to play in and clouds move because they are pulled when people walk.

Thoughts are often linked together in a loose way rather than in a logical relationship. For example, one afternoon when Lucienne had no nap, she reasoned that it could not be afternoon because she had not had her nap. Or a child might say that his friend fell down because he got hurt. The child reasons from the particular to the particular.

4. Limited social cognition

Piaget argues that his description of thought applies to social objects and events as well as physical ones. Our description of preoperational thought hints at this parallel between the physical and the social realms. Examples are deficits in role taking and communication resulting from egocentrism, confusions between natural events and human events, and notions about the identity of persons when physical appearances are changed. In addition, Piaget specifically examines social thought in his work on moral judgments. A preoperational child judges the wrongness of an act according to external variables, such as how much damage was done and whether the act was punished. He ignores internal variables, such as the person's intentions. Thus, the boy who breaks fifteen cups while trying to help his mother set the table is considered to be more guilty than the boy who breaks only one cup while trying to steal cookies from the cabinet.

Concrete operational period (roughly 7 to 11 years)

Piaget sometimes combines ages 2 to 11 and labels this period as 'preparation for and achievement of concrete operations'. Despite the considerable accomplishments in the preoperational period, in many ways the period is simply preparation for the pinnacle of cognitive development: the operation. Regulations, functions, and identities turn into operations as they become more complete, differentiated, quantitative, and stable. Let us now turn to these operations.

An *operation* is an internalized action that is part of an organized structure. With the ability to use these concepts, the child's representations are no longer isolated or simply juxtaposed, as in the preoperational period. They are brought to life.

We can most easily see operations at work in Piaget's famous *conservation* task, which we described as the problem of liquid quantity. Let us consider this task in more detail. The child sees two identical containers equally filled with water and judges them to contain the same amount of water. As the child watches, one container is poured into a container with different dimensions or into several small containers. A 'nonconserver' claims that the amount has changed, usually because the water level has changed. Since the water rises higher in a taller, thinner container, the child concludes that the amount has increased. In contrast, a 'conserver' believes that the amount has not changed. He realizes that quantity remains the same despite changes in appearance. Piaget usually requires the child to give a logical explanation for this judgment before he considers the child to be a true conserver.

Both the nonconserver and the conserver have a basis for their answers. Both think their conclusions are quite reasonable. In fact, if a tester happens to test the same child twice – once when the child is a nonconserver and later when she is a conserver – he may face the child's scorn on both occasions. The child on both occasions is likely to think that the tester is dumb to ask a question when the 'correct' answer is so obvious.

Conservation is an important concept because it gives a certain stability to the physical world. In addition, Piaget assigns a great deal of importance to the conservation task because it reveals the presence or absence of mental operations. It is a diagnostic tool that probes the cognitive structures. Piaget asserts that a child cannot conserve unless he has certain mental operations. These operations can be illustrated by the explanations the children give:

'If you pour it back where it was, they will have the same amount.' (*reversibility*)

'The water goes up higher, but the glass is thinner.' (*compensation*)

'You didn't add any water or take any away.' (*addition – subtraction*)

The preoperational child who lacks these operations centers on states, especially the water level.

Other examples of operations are the common mathematical operations of multiplying, dividing, ordering (greater than, less than), and substituting (one thing equals another thing). Each operation is related to and obtains its meaning from the entire structure of which it is a part. Thus, addition is co-ordinated with subtraction, multiplication, and division to form a system of mental actions. Piaget's interest in logic and mathematics appears in his attempt to describe these systems of operations in terms of logicomathematical structures. These structures serve as a model for characterizing concrete operational thought. ...

[...]

Operations apply not only to classes but also to *relations*. If a concrete operational child knows that John is taller than Bill, and Bill is taller than Henry, she can infer that John has to be taller than Henry. In addition, she can order a row of dolls according to height and give the dolls sticks ordered according to length.

Operations are also applied to *temporal–spatial representations*. For example, a preoperational child draws liquid in a container in such a way that it remains parallel to the base or a side [as in Figure 4]. Her perceptions are influenced by the immediate surroundings. In contrast, a concrete operational child keeps the liquid parallel to the larger context, the surface of the earth.

FIGURE 4 A typical error on the water-level problem occurs during the preoperational period (Miller, 1989, Figure 1.1, p. 64).

We have seen the child move from an understanding of the world based on action schemes, to one based on representations, to one based on internalized, organized operations. Thought now is decentered rather than centered, dynamic rather than static, and reversible rather than irreversible. For the first time, the lawful nature of the world seems to be reflected in a logical system of thought. Thought is in tune, in equilibrium, with the environment. However, the concrete operations are still 'concrete'. They can be applied only to concrete objects – present or mentally represented. They deal with what 'is' rather than what 'could be'. The final step is to apply the operations to purely verbal or logical statements and to the possible as well as the actual. This story unfolds as we turn to formal operations.

Formal operational period (roughly 11 to 15 years)

During the concrete operational period, mental operations are applied to objects and events. The child classifies them, orders them, and reverses them. During formal operations, the adolescent carries concrete operations one step further. He can take the results of these concrete operations and generate hypotheses (propositions, statements) about their logical relationships. Thus, we now have operations on operations: thought has become truly logical, abstract, and hypothetical.

Formal operational thought resembles the kind of thinking we often call the scientific method. The child formulates a hypothesis about a present or potential event and tests this hypothesis against reality. If necessary, he can generate all possible outcomes or all possible combinations at the beginning. Piaget typically presents a problem from physics or chemistry and observes how the adolescent goes about solving it. The problem-solving process, rather than the correct answer itself, is what is of interest.

A prototypic task is the pendulum problem. An adolescent observes an object hanging from a string and attempts to discover what determines how fast the object swings. He is shown how to vary the length of the string, the height from which the pendulum is released, the force of the push on the pendulum, and the weight of the object. One or several of these variables could control the speed of the swing. A concrete operational child experiments with the variables and may even arrive at the correct answer, but his approach is haphazard; he has no overall plan. He does not vary one factor while holding the other factors constant. For example, he may compare a long, light pendulum with a short, heavy one and conclude that both factors are important. In fact, the length of the string is the main determinant of the rate of oscillation.

In contrast to the concrete operational child, the formal operational adolescent imagines all possible determinants of the rate of oscillation before he begins, systematically varies the factors one by one, observes the results correctly, keeps track of the results, and draws the appropriate conclusions (identifies which factor controls the rate of oscillation). He has systematically isolated the critical factor and dealt all the while with propositions, not objects. By testing predictions from each hypothesis, he has demonstrated hypothetico-deductive thought …

[…]

The ability to consider abstract ideas, the future, and various possibilities is evident in the adolescent's social world. She dreams about her future and imagines herself in various occupational and social roles. She may experiment with some of these roles just as she experiments with hypotheses about physical events. She is concerned with the world of ideas. In sessions with friends, she debates various moral and political issues, such as whether wars can ever be moral, whether abortions should be legal, whether there are basic inalienable human rights, and what an ideal community would be like. She can consider these issues from a number of different perspectives and see how the issues are related to a larger set of social relationships. However, there is still a lingering egocentrism. The adolescent is impressed with the power of thought and naively underestimates the practical problems involved in achieving an ideal future for herself or for society. She feels that the sheer force of her logic will move mountains. Piaget notes that this starry-eyed egocentrism is squelched when the adolescent undertakes her first real job!

[…]

By achieving formal operations, the adolescent completes her cognitive structures. The various concrete operational logical systems have been combined to create a single, tightly organized system of thought – a unified whole. Thought is logical, abstract, and flexible. Thinking continues to develop throughout adulthood as the formal operations are applied to more and more content areas and situations. Egocentrism continues to decline as the person broadens her experiences in the world of work and social relationships. However, these changes after age 15 entail a change not in the structure of thought but only in its content and stability.

Reference

PIAGET, J. (1926/29) *The Child's Conception of the World*, New York, Harcourt Brace.

SOURCE: MILLER, P. H. (1989; 2nd edn) Theories of Developmental Psychology, *New York, Freeman, extracts from pp. 56–68.*

Reading B Developmental processes

R. S. Siegler

How do children progress from one stage to another? Piaget views three processes as crucial: *assimilation*, *accommodation*, and *equilibration*.

Assimilation

Assimilation refers to the way in which people transform incoming information so that it fits within their existing way of thinking. To illustrate, when my older son was 2, he encountered a man who was bald on the top of his head and had long frizzy hair growing out from each side. To my embarrassment, on seeing the man, he gleefully shouted, 'Clown, clown'. The man apparently possessed the features that my son believed separate clowns from other people. Therefore, the boy perceived him in that light.

[...]

One interesting type of assimilation that Piaget described is *functional assimilation*, the tendency to use any mental structure that is available. If children or adults have a capacity, they seek to use it, especially when they first acquire it. Illustratively, when my older son was first learning to talk, he spent endless hours talking in his crib, even though no one else was present. He also would turn somersaults over and over again, despite considerable encouragement from his parents to stop. Piaget contrasted this source of motivation with behaviourists' emphases on external reinforcers as motivators of behaviour. In reinforcement, the reason for engaging in an activity is the external reward that is obtained. In functional assimilation, the reason for engaging in the activity is the sheer delight children obtain from mastering new skills.

Accommodation

Accommodation refers to the ways in which people adapt their ways of thinking to new experiences. Returning to the clown anecdote, after biting my lip to suppress a smile, I told my son that the man we had seen was not a clown; that even though his hair was like a clown's, he wasn't wearing a funny costume and wasn't trying to make people laugh. I hope that the experience helped his concept of clowns to accommodate to the concept's generally accepted meaning.

Assimilation and accommodation mutually influence each other; assimilation is never present without accommodation and vice versa. On seeing a new object, an infant might try to grasp it as he has other objects (thus assimilating the new object to an existing approach). However, he also would have to adjust his grasp to conform to the shape of the object (thus accommodating his approach as well). ...

Equilibration

Equilibration encompasses both assimilation and accommodation. It refers to the overall interaction between existing ways of thinking and new experience. It also is the keystone of developmental change within Piaget's system. Piaget saw development as the formation of ever more stable equilibria between the child's cognitive system and the external world. That is, the child's model of the world would increasingly resemble reality.

Piaget also suggested that equilibration takes place in three phases. First, children are satisfied with their mode of thought and therefore are in a state of equilibrium. Then they become aware of shortcomings in their existing thinking and are dissatisfied. This constitutes a state of disequilibrium. Finally, they adopt a more sophisticated mode of thought that eliminates the shortcomings of the old one. That is, they reach a more stable equilibrium.

To illustrate the equilibration process, suppose a girl thought that animals were the only living things. (In fact, Richards and Siegler [1984] found that most 4- to 7-year-olds do think this.) At some point she would hear plants referred to as being alive. This new information might create a state of disequilibrium, in which the girl was unsure what it meant to be alive. After all, plants share few obvious features with animals. Eventually she would discover commonalities between plants and animals that are critical to the meaning of being alive: the ability to grow and to reproduce, in particular. These discoveries would pave the way for a new understanding, in which the girl identified life with the ability to grow and to reproduce. The new understanding would constitute a more stable equilibrium, since further observations would not call it into question (unless the girl later became unusually interested in certain viruses ... whose status as living things continues to be debated by biologists).

References

RICHARDS, D. D. and SIEGLER, R. S. (1984) 'The effects of task requirements on children's life judgements', *Child Development*, **55**, pp. 1687–96.

SOURCE: SIEGLER, R. S. (1991) Children's Thinking, *Englewood Cliffs (N.J.), Prentice-Hall, extracts from pp. 21–3.*

Reading C   Context and cognition in models of cognitive growth

G. Butterworth

Introduction

The study of cognitive development in children has moved through three identifiable phases in the last twenty years. First, there was a shift from a focus on intellectual processes within the individual child, as in the classic research of Piaget, to a concern with social cognition in the 1970s and 1980s very much influenced by the resurgence of interest in Vygotsky. This shift reflects a move away from attempting to explain cognition as a process located solely within the individual, towards an understanding of the interpersonal context of cognitive growth. The shift from 'cold blooded' to 'warm blooded' cognition drew attention to the ways in which thought processes and cognitive growth are socially situated but contextual factors were for the most part seen only as moderators of cognitive growth. Work on cognitive development has recently entered a third phase, in which theorists are beginning to stress an *inextricable* link between contextual constraints and the acquisition of knowledge. Moreover, the physical context is being reunited with the social, within the thought process. The contemporary view tends to be that cognition is *typically* situated in a social and physical context and is rarely, if ever, decontextualized.

[…]

Language and situated cognition

The recent focus on the basis of cognition … helps explain how language itself is understood through the social context. Margaret Donaldson (1978) published a series of influential studies that purported to show that versions of Piaget's tasks which were socially intelligible to pre-school children revealed a previously unsuspected competence in perspective-taking, conservation and class inclusion. In Donaldson's terms, her situated tasks make 'human sense' because they draw on everyday social experience, with which the child is very familiar. Both Donaldson and more recently Michael Siegal (1991) take the view that much of the pre-school child's difficulty in reasoning arises because the child cannot comprehend the adult's specialized language. The argument is quite subtle. It is not just that the child lacks knowledge of language, rather the child's errors arise in an *active* attempt to discover what the adult actually *means* by the questions being asked. … As Donaldson (1978, p. 38) puts it:

> It may turn out to be a very long journey from the primary understanding of what people mean by the words they speak and by their concomitant acts to the ultimate and separate understanding of what *words* mean. Perhaps the idea that words mean anything – in isolation – is a highly sophisticated notion, and a Western adult notion at that.

… Just one well-known example will help to make clear the subtle interplay of perception, language and social interaction which is involved.

McGarrigle and Donaldson (1974) reported a beautiful experiment, which has become known as the 'naughty teddy' study, a variant of Piaget's traditional number conservation task. First of all, the child is asked whether two rows of counters arranged in parallel lines contain the same or a different number. The child readily agrees that the number of counters is the same when the length of the rows is identical and each counter is opposite another. Then, under the control of the experimenter, a glove puppet known as 'naughty teddy' rushes in and lengthens one of the rows of counters, just as in the conservation test. The child is then asked whether the longer row contains the same or a different number of counters than the shorter one. Most children between 4 and 6 years now 'conserve', that is, they give the correct answer that the number of counters has not changed, even though they fail to conserve under the standard testing conditions of the conservation task.

[…]

These demonstrations therefore suggest that the child's difficulties with conservation tasks, at least in part, arise in achieving an understanding of what the adult means. The child in discourse with the adult enters into a relationship of unequal power, where the child takes the adult's behaviour in context as a means to understand what is required. As Goodnow and Warton [1992] point out, the particular class of problems often involved in Piagetian tasks are those amenable to criteria of scientific proof, where a correct answer exists. Different criteria for validation may actually apply to understanding socially relevant events. Typical cognitive developmental testing situations, where experimenters are seeking exact answers, may nevertheless depend on how the child applies judgmental criteria to the *social* interaction.

These new insights into pre-operational reasoning do not rule out entirely Piaget's theory that development also involves a change in the child's underlying logic. By the age of 8 or 9 years, the answer to conservation questions is obvious to the child who has entered the concrete operational stage. It is still possible for Piagetians to argue that the context sensitivity of reasoning, revealed by these recent studies of the pre-school child, gives way to a more generalized understanding, at least with respect to the classic Piagetian tasks. On the other hand, as Girotto and Light [1992] point out, even adults may perform poorly on tasks of hypothetico-deductive reasoning, when the contents of the premises are remote from everyday experience. A completely deductive system of reasoning, context-free and independent of any particular content, seems never to be fully achieved. What may be being highlighted in the current phrase of cognitive developmental research is the progressive reintroduction of the *ecology* into Piaget's *evolutionary epistemology* (Piaget, 1971).

[...]

Defining context

It is surprising how often the definition of 'context' is left implicit in developmental theory ... A commonsense approach might focus on the physical, social or cultural setting of a particular intellectual task. Beyond such general statements, what is meant by context often remains unanalysed. It is possible, however, to proceed through a series of definitions from the most general to the more specific, in an attempt to establish what different theorists may hold in common.

Cole and Cole (1989) elaborate what they call a 'cultural-context' view of development. They point out that the word comes from the Latin *contexere* meaning 'to weave together', 'to join together' or 'to compose'. The context in their definition is the interconnected whole that gives meaning to the parts. Variations in the cultural context may give different meanings to otherwise identical behaviours, through the historical experience of the different cultural groups. Cole and Cole particularly emphasize the manner in which social contexts are differentially 'scripted' in different societies. That is, cultures transmit, through their language and their material structure, generalized guides to action. These are sometimes known as 'pragmatic action schemes' (Cheng and Holyoak, 1985).

Cole and Cole describe several ways in which the culture influences the child's development: they suggest that cultures influence development by arranging the *occurrence* of specific contexts. To give their example, the Bushmen of the Kalahari Desert are unlikely to learn about conservation by taking baths or pouring water from one glass to another; nor are the children growing up in Western cities likely to encounter many contexts which will foster skills in tracking animals. The relative *frequency* with which particular contexts are encountered will foster different skills, such as skiing in snowy countries, or making pottery or weaving in simple subsistence societies (Childs and Greenfield, 1980). These relatively culturally specific activities may be *associated* with other contexts, and with different *responsibilities*, such as selling products, which will in turn foster further culturally specific types of number skills. Furthermore, as Goodnow and Warton [1992] argue, contexts can coexist in such a way that individuals may participate simultaneously in several culturally constrained modes of knowing. Children may be adept at mathematics in the streets and they may also need to perform at maths in the schools. Not only mathematics but also botany, biology, physics and medicine are practised in everyday contexts and these forms of traditional knowledge impact on formal methods of tuition (George and Glasgow, 1988). A pluralist perspective on contextual effects enables an understanding of when approximation is a sufficiently accurate method of reasoning, as when cooks solve problems of quantities in baking by using rough approximation, rather than by exact measurement of proportions. The appropriate context may call up the appropriate strategy.

The argument advanced by Cole and Cole is that reasoning typically involves the ability to call up an appropriate scheme, or content-sensitive rule, derived from experience, in regularly occurring settings. These 'pragmatic reasoning schemes' may be abstracted from everyday social experiences in culturally specific contexts. The correspondence between pragmatic action schemas and logical structures is examined by Girotto and Light [1992] for a number of cases. Examples of a correspondence between the logic of implication and commonly occurring types of social interaction pattern are the 'conditional permission schema' (if one wishes to take a particular course of action then one must satisfy a particular precondition) or the 'obligation schema' (if a particular condition occurs, a particular action must be taken). What is striking about these examples is that the logical structure actually *exists in a social reality*; it is not a mere abstraction, as in more desiccated tests of reasoning. In fact, a recent twist to this argument is that apparently abstract tasks, such as the Raven's progressive matrices test, or the Wason selection problem, may in fact be the most acculturated in the sense that their performance requires extensive experience within a culture which values this type of intellectual performance. Hence such tasks differentiate between members of the population and are the least accessible to the majority because they pose their logical problems in a format that is remote from most of everyday life (Richardson, 1991; Johnson-Laird, 1985). The point is that everyday reasoning is generally based on types of culturally specific knowledge, whose representation is evoked by the appropriate context. On this view the context and content of thought are inseparable from the reasoning process.

[...]

Situated cognition

A realistic formulation, then, helps to situate cognition; it gives reasoning an everyday quality because it draws attention to the different ways in which contexts recruit thinking. It does not require a description of reasoning that begins from the strict rules of formal logic; rather thinking begins in the ecological constraints from which physical problems and social encounters are derived. Hatano (1990) has suggested that situated reasoning includes such 'real world' knowledge as 'intuitive physics', 'intuitive psychology', 'intuitive biology' and 'intuitive mathematics'. These domains help us to understand objects in the physical world and to understand why people behave as they do; they provide a means of understanding the natural and social environment and enable basic rules of inference to be applied. Such knowledge arises through informal, everyday experience but it is analogous to the formal, scientific disciplines taught in schools or universities. Everyday knowledge is based on observation and experiment and it has adaptive, heuristic value. The developmental interface between everyday, situated cognition and more formally acquired knowledge within the same domain is seen as a transition from 'novice' to 'expert'. This may involve apprenticeship, verbal instruction, or schooling before fully conceptual knowledge is acquired. Even then, *transfer* between everyday knowledge and formal knowledge may be incomplete because external constraints continue to exercise an influence on cognitive processes. In some domains, such as intuitive psychology or intuitive biology, the distance between the naive and the expert scientist is arguably less than in other domains, such as physics.

References

CHENG, P. W. and HOLYOAK, K. J. (1985) 'On the natural selection of reasoning theories', *Cognition*, **33**, pp. 285–313.

CHILDS, C. P. and GREENFIELD, P. M. (1980) 'Informal modes of learning and teaching: the case of Zinacanteco learning' *in* WARREN, N. (ed.) *Studies in Cross Cultural Psychology*, vol. 2, New York, Academic Press.

COLE, M. M. and COLE, S. R. (1989) *The Development of Children*, San Francisco, Freeman.

DONALDSON, M. (1978) *Children's Minds*, Glasgow, Fontana.

GEORGE, J. and GLASGOW, J. (1988) 'Street science and conventional science in the West Indies', *Studies in Science Education*, **15**, pp. 109–18.

GIROTTO, V. and LIGHT, P. (1992) 'The pragmatic bases of children's reasoning' *in* LIGHT, P. and BUTTERWORTH, G. (eds) *Context and Cognition*, London, Harvester.

GOODNOW, J. J. and WARTON, P. (1992) 'Contexts and cognitions: taking a pluralist view' *in* LIGHT, P. and BUTTERWORTH, G. (eds) *Context and Cognition*, London, Harvester.

HATANO, G. (1990) 'The nature of everyday science: a brief introduction', *British Journal of Developmental Psychology*, **8**, pp. 245–50.

JOHNSON-LAIRD, P. N. (1985) 'Deductive reasoning ability' *in* STERNBERG, R. J. (ed.) *Human Abilities*, New York, Freeman.

LIGHT, P. H. (1986) 'Content, conservation and conversation' *in* RICHARDS, M. and LIGHT, P. (eds) *Children of Social Worlds*, Cambridge, Polity Press.

McGARRIGLE, J. and DONALDSON, M. (1974) 'Conservation accidents', *Cognition*, **3**, pp. 341–50.

PIAGET, J. (1971) *Biology and Knowledge*, Edinburgh, Edinburgh University Press.

RICHARDSON, K. (1991) 'Reasoning with Raven – in and out of context', *British Journal of Educational Psychology*, **61**, pp. 129–38.

SIEGAL, M. (1991) *Knowing Children*, Hove, Erlbaum.

SOURCE: BUTTERWORTH, G. (1992) 'Context and cognition in models of cognitive growth' in LIGHT, P. and BUTTERWORTH, G. (eds) Context and Cognition, pp. 1, 2–7, 10, 13, London, Harvester.

Reading D Beyond modularity

A. Karmiloff-Smith

Is the initial architecture of the infant mind modular?

Fodor's 1983 book *The Modularity of Mind* (which I later criticize) made a significant impact on developmental theorizing by suggesting how the nativist thesis and the domain-specificity of cognition are relevant to constraints on the architecture of the human mind. For Fodor, the notion of 'architecture' refers to the organization of relatively fixed and highly constrained innate specifications: the invariant features of the human information-processing system. Unlike Bruner (1974–75) and Piaget (1952), who argue for domain-general development, Fodor holds that the mind is made up of genetically specified, independently functioning, special-purpose 'modules' or input systems. Like Fodor, I shall use the terms 'module' and 'input system' as synonyms. Each functionally distinct module has its own dedicated processes and proprietary inputs.

[...]

Each module is like a special-purpose computer with a proprietary database. By 'proprietary' Fodor means that a module can process only certain types of data and that it automatically ignores other, potentially competing input. A module computes in a bottom-up fashion a constrained class of specific inputs; that is, it focuses on entities that are relevant to its particular processing capacities only. And it does so whenever relevant data present themselves – that is, an input system cannot refrain from processing. This enhances automaticity and speed of computation by ensuring that the organism is insensitive to many potential classes of information from other input systems and to top-down expectations from central processing.

Input systems, then, are the parts of the human mind that are inflexible and unintelligent. They are the stupidity in the machine – but they are just what a young organism might need to get initial cognition off the ground speedily and efficiently.

[...]

Prespecified modules versus a process of modularization

Fodor's detailed account of the encapsulation of modules focuses predominantly on their role in on-line processing. There is little discussion of ontogenetic [developmental] change, except to allow for the creation of new modules (such as a reading module). Fodor takes it as demonstrated that modules for spoken language and visual perception are innately specified. By contrast, I wish to draw a distinction between the notion of prespecified modules and that of a process of *modularization* (which, I speculate, occurs repeatedly as the *product* of development). Here I differ from Fodor's strict nativist conception. I hypothesize that if the human mind ends up with any modular structure, then, even in the case of language, the mind becomes modularized *as development proceeds*. My position takes account of the plasticity of early brain development (Neville, 1991; Johnson, 1993). It is plausible that a fairly limited amount of innately specified, domain-specific predispositions (which are not strictly modular) would be sufficient to constrain the classes of inputs that the infant mind computes. It can thus be hypothesized that, *with time*, brain circuits are progressively selected for different domain-specific computations; in certain cases, relatively encapsulated modules would be formed. Thus, when I use the term 'innately specified' ..., I do not mean to imply anything like a genetic blueprint for prespecified modules, present at birth. Rather, ... I argue for innately specified predispositions that are more epigenetic than Fodor's nativism. The view that I adopt ... is that Nature specifies initial biases or predispositions that channel attention to relevant environmental inputs, which in turn affect subsequent brain development.

[...]

Development from a domain-general perspective

Fodor's nativist thesis is in sharp contrast with domain-general theories of learning, such as Piaget's constructivist epistemology, which were once popular in the development literature. Piagetian theory argues that neither processing nor storage is domain specific. Of course, implicitly at least, a Piagetian must acknowledge that there are different sensory transducers for vision, audition, touch, and so forth. They do not accept, however, that the transducers transform data into innately specified, domain-specific formats for modular processing. For Piagetians, development involves the construction of domain-general changes in representational structures operating over all aspects of the cognitive system in a similar way.

[...]

Neither the Piagetian nor the behaviourist theory grants the infant any innate structures or domain-specific knowledge. Each grants only some domain-general, biologically specified processes: for the Piagetians, a set of sensory reflexes and three functional processes (assimilation, accommodation, and equilibration); for the behaviourists, inherited physiological sensory systems and a complex set of laws of association. These domain-general learning processes are held to apply across all areas of linguistic and nonlinguistic cognition. Piaget and the behaviorists thus concur on a number of conceptions about the initial state of the infant mind. The behaviorists saw the infant as a *tabula rasa* with no built-in knowledge (Skinner, 1953); Piaget's view of the young infant as assailed by 'undifferentiated and chaotic' inputs (Piaget, 1955) is substantially the same.

Needless to say, there are fundamental differences between these two schools. Piagetians view the child as an active information constructor, behaviourists as a passive information storer. Piagetians conceive of development as involving fundamental stage-like changes in logical structure, whereas behaviorists invoke a progressive accumulation of knowledge. However, in the light of the present state of the art in developing theorizing, Piagetians and behaviourists have much in common in their view of the neonate's 'knowledge-empty' mind and their claims that domain-general learning explains subsequent development across all aspects of language and cognition.

Development from a domain-specific perspective

The nativist/modularity thesis projects a very different picture of the young infant. Rather than being assailed by incomprehensible, chaotic data from many competing sources, the neonate is seen as preprogrammed to make sense of specific information sources. Contrary to the Piagetian or the behaviourist infant, the nativist infant is off to a very good start. This doesn't, of course, mean that nothing changes during infancy and beyond; the infant has much to learn. But the nativist/ modularity stance posits that subsequent learning is guided by innately specified, domain-specific principles, and that these principles determine the entities on which subsequent learning takes place (Gelman, 1990; Spelke, 1991).

The domain specificity of cognitive systems is also suggested by developmental neuropsychology and by the existence of children in whom one or more domains are spared or impaired. For example, autism may involve a single deficit in reasoning about mental states (theory of mind), with the rest of cognition relatively unimpaired. Williams Syndrome, by contrast, presents a very uneven cognitive profile in which language, face recognition, and theory of mind seem relatively spared, whereas number and spatial cognition are severely retarded. And there are numerous cases of idiots-savants in whom only one domain (such as drawing or calendrical calculation) functions at a high level, while capacities are very low over the rest of the cognitive system. By contrast, Down Syndrome is suggestive of a more across-the-board, domain-general deficit in cognitive processing.

Adult brain damage points to domain specificity, also. It is remarkably difficult to find convincing examples in the neuropsychological literature of an across-the-board, domain-general disorder (Marshall, 1984), although a case might be made for an overall deficit in planning in patients with prefrontal damage (Shallice, 1988). But in many instances, disorders of higher cognitive functions consequent upon brain damage are typically domain specific – that is, they affect only face recognition, number, language, or some other facility, leaving the other systems relatively intact.

So if adults manifest domain-specific damage, and if it can be shown that infants come into the world with some domain-specific predispositions, doesn't that mean that the nativists have won the debate over the developmentalists still ensconced on the theoretical shores of Lake Geneva (Piaget's former bastion of anti-nativism and anti-modularity)? Not necessarily, because it is important to bear in mind that the greater the amount of domain-specific properties of the infant mind, the less creative and flexible the subsequent system will be (Chomsky, 1988). Whereas the fixed constraints provide an initial adaptive advantage, there is a tradeoff between the efficiency and automaticity of the infant's input systems, on the one hand, and their relative inflexibility, on the other. This leads me to a crucial point: *The more complex the picture we ultimately build of the innate capacities of the infant mind, the more important it becomes for us to explain the flexibility of subsequent cognitive development.* It is toward such an end – exploring the flexibility and creativity of the human mind beyond the initial state – that my work in language acquisition and cognitive development has been concentrated, in an attempt to determine both the domain-specific and the domain-general contributions to development. It is implausible that development will turn out to be entirely domain specific *or* domain general. And although I will need to invoke some built-in constraints, development clearly involves a more dynamic process of interaction between mind and environment than the strict nativist stance presupposes.

References

BRUNER, J. S. (1974–75) 'From communication to language: a psychological perspective', *Cognition*, **3**, pp. 255–87.

CHOMSKY, N. (1988) *Language and Problems of Knowledge*, MIT Press.

FODOR, J. (1983) *The Modularity of Mind*, MIT Press.

GELMAN, R. (1990) 'First principles organize attention to and learning about relevant data: number and animate–inanimate distinction as examples', *Cognitive Science,* **14**, pp. 79–106.

JOHNSON, M. H. (1993) 'Constraints on cortical plasticity' *in* JOHNSON, M. H. (ed.) *Brain Development and Cognition: a reader*, Blackwell.

MARSHALL, J. C. (1984) 'Multiple perspectives on modularity', *Cognition,* **17**, pp. 209–42.

NEVILLE, H. J. (1991) 'Neurobiology of cognitive and language processing: effects of early experience' *in* GIBSON, K. R. and PETERSEN, A. C. (eds) *Brain Maturation and Cognitive Development: comparative and cross-cultural perspectives*, Aldine deGruyter.

PIAGET, J. (1952) *The Origins of Intelligence in Children*, International University Press.

PIAGET, J. (1955) *The Child's Construction of Reality*, Routledge and Kegan Paul.

SHALLICE, T. (1988) *From Neuropsychology to Mental Structure*, Cambridge University Press.

SKINNER, B. F. (1953) *Science and Human Behaviour*, Macmillan.

SPELKE, E. S. (1991) 'Physical knowledge in infancy: reflections on Piaget's theory' *in* CAREY, S. and GELMAN, R. (eds) *Epigenesis of the Mind: essays in biology and knowledge*, Erlbaum.

SOURCE: KARMILOFF-SMITH, A. (1992) Beyond Modularity: a developmental perspective on cognitive science, *Cambridge (Mass.), MIT Press.*

Dennis Bancroft

CONTENTS

As language develops it acts like a sculptor, carving into ever sharper relief the features of the objective human world.

(De Laguna, 1927, p. 274)

OBJECTIVES

When you have studied this chapter, you should be able to:

1 identify the major characteristics of language that make it the pre-eminent means of communication;

2 locate the origins of verbal communication in the pre-verbal exchanges between infant and caregiver;

3 trace the development of language from the appearance of the 'first word' to the ability to tell stories and make jokes;

4 discuss three particular theoretical perspectives which attempt to describe how language is learnt;

5 use the information gained from a description of the history of language development to evaluate these theoretical perspectives.

1 INTRODUCTION

To begin with, I shall raise questions about what 'communication' might involve and about the nature of language as a means of communication. There is considerable sophistication embodied in this aspect of human life, and it is easy to take it for granted because language is so familiar to us. On the basis of this discussion I shall describe the development of language in human children to the point at which the children possess sufficient skills to make jokes. I shall conclude with an introduction to connectionism, which offers a novel attempt to account for the development of language.

2 COMMUNICATION AND LANGUAGE

ACTIVITY 1

Allow about 15 minutes

INTERPRETING INFANTS

Make a note of the characteristics of these two brief exchanges between caregiver and child. You are observing a 5-month-old infant and its caregiver. How would you describe the contributions of these two individuals?

CAREGIVER: How are you then?

CHILD: Mmmm.

CAREGIVER: What can I do for you?

CHILD: (waves arm) Uhh.

CAREGIVER: Oh, you want some milk do you?

Comment

In this brief exchange the caregiver is doing all the talking, but is leaving some space for the child to 'reply'. The child's contributions are received by the caregiver and interpreted: perhaps the child would like some milk. In order to make sense of this exchange we need to think carefully about the nature of the process of communication and about the system which humans use as a communicative device.

Lizzy is a 2 year old sitting with her mother. They are talking about a book, but the conversation soon moves on to other things.

M: What's the piggy saying to the rabbit?

L: Ah … writing.

M: He's saying writing is he?

L: Yeh.

M: 'n then what did the rabbit say?

L: Say to ho hi ho 's off to work we go.

M: He sang a song did he?

L: Mm.

M: Like Snow White?

L: Mm.

M: What happened when you went to see Snow White?

L: I fell over.

M: You fell over did you?

L: I got tripped over.

In contrast with the first extract, Lizzy at age 2 is able to respond to her mother's questions by giving answers and refinements, to follow the flow of a conversation and to talk about matters other than the immediate context. Lizzy, in developing language skills, has become a more effective communicator.

One purpose in what follows is to develop some understanding of the terms 'language' and 'communication', so that we may recognize communication when we see it and understand what learning a language must involve. This discussion is intended to be a starting point: it will contain much that is contentious or problematical, and it will certainly not be exhaustive.

A useful starting position on language would be to recognize that languages are made up of symbols, and that these symbols are arbitrary, but must be used systematically. Given a system of this kind, our own experience as users of a language shows that language is capable of an indefinitely large range of expression.

There are several things to notice about this starting point. The first is that language is seen as a *system*. This is important as it means that language is predictable from one occasion of use to the next. Language is systematic at the level of words, and also at the level of how sentences are organized. Languages differ, but in English the systematic ordering of a sentence can inform the listener about who did what to whom. For example, in the sentence 'John kissed Mary', we know that it was Mary who was kissed and that it was John who did the kissing. If the ordering of the sentence is reversed, to make 'Mary kissed John', we see that the meaning of the sentence has changed, even though the same three words are used. It may be that any form of communication has to be systematic in order for understanding to occur.

The second important point is that languages use *symbols*. This means that some sound, other behaviour or image is used to represent an aspect of the world. The form of the symbol is not important. The symbol may be some sound or a gesture or a drawing. When we come to consider the language potential of infants prior to the production of recognizable language, we should be alert to the possibility that symbols can be of many different kinds in addition to those we are familiar with and use ourselves.

The third point to note is that the symbols in the language system are *arbitrary*. The word 'arbitrary' is used here in the sense that there is no *necessary* connection between the symbol, be it word or gesture, and the object or idea to which it refers.

= tree(English) = arbre(French) = Baum(German) etc.

FIGURE 1 Symbols representing a tree

By way of example, Figure 1 shows a number of symbols for 'tree'. The first is a drawing which conveys something of the object represented. This symbol is an *iconic* symbol. It is not arbitrary in the way that the word 'tree' is. It may be that the word 'tree' has a great history and has its origins in the languages of the past – but, if one wanted to construct a new word for 'tree', it could be almost any legitimate combinations of sounds that was not being used for other purposes.

It is sometimes argued that this arbitrariness of language has very important consequences for human thought. In some way, arbitrary representations break or reduce the connection between the symbol and the thing represented. This allows words to be used in novel and imaginative ways and increases the range of ideas that humans are able to express. (As an example, you might consider the use of words in the poetry of Dylan Thomas.)

My initial definition of language has allowed me to identify several important characteristics that a language must possess in order to be a language. This list is not exhaustive and so this is the point to make an additional observation that, in order to be a language in our sense of the word, the arbitrary symbol system must be *shared*. We are accustomed to thinking that all members of a particular community must have access to the language of that community, and that this is what must be meant by a language being shared. However, numbers are not everything, and the minimum number of people who must share a symbol system in order for it to be used for communication is two.

One final addition is bound up with the idea that communication is an *intentional* process. We have the feeling that communication is the process whereby we deliberately set out to make our wishes known or express our intentions. There may be other things that humans do which convey information but which are not deliberately communicative. For example, people sometimes try to hide their feelings or opinions, but there can still be aspects of their behaviour which give them away and reveal their true state of mind.

ACTIVITY 2

Allow about 15 minutes

COMMUNICATIONS?

Make a list of things that humans do which are sometimes said to be communicative. Here are a couple of suggestions.

	Symbolic	Arbitrary	Systematic	Shared	Intentional
1 Use language					
2 Dance					

With our discussion of language in mind, including the additional requirements that at least two people share the system and that its use is intentional, go through your list of communicative behaviours assigning ticks to those which possess some or all of the required attributes.

Comment

Perhaps you began by adding things like 'art' and 'music' to the list of possible communicative behaviours. Perhaps you then thought that a person's appearance ought to be included. But appearance is not systematic, in that particular messages are not conveyed by particular combinations of clothes. So while appearance may have ticks under some headings (arbitrary and symbolic), it nonetheless fails as a *communicative* device since all the characteristics I identified are not present. Many will still feel that appearance should qualify, however, so here are some points in reply.

1   If appearance is to be communicative our table of requirements must be changed. Do these changes let in other, more doubtful, candidates? A definition which includes everything, defines nothing.

2   It is clear that appearance *means something*, but what? A distinction can be made between something which is 'communicative' and something which is 'informative'. 'Communication' involves a shared symbol system; 'information' does not. This distinction is found in the work of Marshall (1970) who considers that animals are capable of informative signalling but not communicative signalling. For example, a person's staggering walk can give *information* about their state of inebriation, but this is not intentional communication. To return to the issue of appearance, people are known to dress for interviews in a way that is intended to convey some particular impression. The interviewee may fail in their attempt to impress, however, since there is no general agreement about what counts as being well or appropriately dressed. In other words, the meaning of appearance is not *systematic*.

3   Appearance can be communicative when there is an agreed understanding of the meaning of various items of clothing. For example, where the clothes in question indicate membership or position within some group or society: examples include the badges of rank and so on worn by military personnel.

SUMMARY OF SECTION 2

- Communication is a process.
- A language is a formal system used for the purpose of communication.
- Communication between humans involves the use of symbols. These symbols can be of any form.
- The symbols involved in communication must be used systematically.
- For communication to happen, at least two people must have access to the symbol system.
- The symbol system is used intentionally to pass some message or create some particular impression.

3   HUMAN LANGUAGE DEVELOPMENT

One of the important characteristics of human language is that it can refer to objects, events and possibilities that are not physically present. This allows humans to speak of the past and learn from it, to imagine the future and predict it. Language functions as a device which frees human imagination from the present and allows planning and reasoning. An extension of this idea is that human language allows its users to imagine and speak of what is imaginary or false. It is possible to fantasize, lie and, of course, make jokes. The development of the ability to reason and plan will be explored in Chapter 4.

The description of development allows us to begin to evaluate some of the alternative theoretical perspectives on language development. Theorizing about the process of language development would take a book of its own to describe, but it is possible to discern three main positions. Having said that, there are not many psychologists who would align themselves with the extreme versions of any of these three positions. With each of the positions outlined below are some suggestions as to what to look out for in the account of language development which follows.

3.1 Theory 1: learning theory

Learning theory has its philosophical roots in the work of the philosopher John Locke (1632–1704), who advanced the view that infants were born with everything to learn. The person they became was the direct result of the learning they had done *and nothing else*. Behaviourist psychologists, who are the scientific descendants of John Locke, consider that language is a behaviour to be learnt just like other behaviours. Behaviourists suggest that the sounds made by infants are 'shaped' by their caregivers until the sounds become words. A short cut is possible: if the children 'imitate' adult words and receive appropriate 'reinforcement', then the words should be retained by the child and be used again in the right circumstances (or 'stimulus conditions'). In the description of development that follows we could look for examples of shaping, imitation and reinforcement. In addition to these, we might also look for examples of things said by children that they *could not* have heard from their parents.

3.2 Theory 2: the nativist view

The person often connected with this position is the American linguist Noam Chomsky (1928–). His studies give him an understanding of the complexities of language as a formal system and, in contrast, a knowledge of the rather messy language use which characterizes adult conversation, which is full of hesitations, repetitions and so on. He takes the view that the language sample which a child might hear from his or her parents and others would not be sufficient to allow the child to deduce the complex rule systems of adult language. In order that a child can learn this complex system it must be the case that human infants are *born* with some of this knowledge. Language knowledge is *innate* and universal. The task for young language learners is to discover which particular language community they are in and then apply the universal rules of language to that particular version. Chomsky produced a devastating critique of the behaviourist position which included the claim that much of a child's speech was composed of original constructions and could not, therefore, have been copied from an adult (for example, 'we wented to the seaside'). While this partial description is almost a parody of Chomsky's insights, it does give us something to look for in the descriptions that follow. We should pay attention to the speech addressed to children to see if it is as messy as most adult speech. We might also look for evidence of originality – for example, for evidence that the children are developing their own rule-based theories of grammar.

3.3 Theory 3: the social interactionist view

The social interactionist view of the development of language is less clearly defined than those described above, although one can discern some main themes. The American psychologist Jerome Bruner (1915–) has pointed to the connections that appear to exist between the pre-verbal exchanges between child and caregiver and later language (Bruner, 1975). For example, it is claimed that many pre-verbal exchanges have the structure of conversations as well as some underlying similarities, such as joint attention to a topic. In this view, language develops as a *more effective means* of making communication, rather than as the *first* means. The most important point is that spoken 'language' is part of a history of shared communications which predates it. In this shared history the child's partner in the communication will make the greatest contribution until the child is able to take a progressively more active role. Put more forcibly, it is thought that pre-verbal exchanges make language development possible. The sorts of evidence which we might look for here could be found in a structural comparison between pre-verbal exchanges and verbal exchanges or be found in functional continuity.

There are many different ways in which one can seek evidence about the development of language. For example, one could focus on the *structural* aspects of language, the way in which words are grouped, first in pairs and then in larger groups, according to the conventions of the language. Alternatively, one might describe the development of a child's understanding of *meanings* from an early idiosyncratic usage of words, to the point at which a child's words mean much the same as an adult's. Structure and meaning are, of course, important aspects of language and will feature strongly in the discussion that follows. However, it is possible that concentrating on these structural aspects of language might obscure the insight that language is used purposively, *to do things* within a social and cultural context. Language is used by humans, among other things, to inform, to request and to amuse.

3.4 Have you heard the one about ... ?

Before we begin our account of the development of language, it may be helpful to have some notion of the complexity of the task facing infants. Language behaviour between adults can function on several levels at the same time. Understanding often requires that speaker and listener have knowledge of each other and of their respective histories, as well as knowledge of the more obvious aspects of language. Adults may wish to persuade, to inform, to deceive, to amuse and so on. Each of these endeavours will require the use of sophisticated communicative skills. This chapter includes a description of children's first attempts to use language to amuse, because to make a joke can require just this kind of complex knowledge. Accordingly, I shall begin with a list of the linguistic and other ingredients which are used in joking.

Jokes are a very sophisticated form of (usually) verbal behaviour. In order to tell a joke one needs to have some skill in all of the following areas of language.

1   *Sounds*. It is helpful to have some skill in articulation since jokes sometimes hang on slight differences and similarities between the sounds of words. For example:

ELEANOR (6 years old):   How many kinds of Madeira are there?

PARENT: I don't know, two I suppose.

ELEANOR: No, three! Madeira cake, Madeira wine and oh m'deara.

2   *Syntax*. An obvious requirement. Listeners to jokes have to be introduced to information in the right order and in a way that they are able to recognize.

3   *Semantics*. Once again, a rather obvious requirement. Many jokes hang on the meaning of words, either in terms of the similarity of the meaning of one word to that of another, or in terms of the various meanings of a single word. For example:

QUESTION: Have you heard the one about the three wells?

ANSWER: Well, well, well.

4   *Pragmatics*. This term refers to the kinds of cultural understanding humans have that enable them to understand ambiguous or confusing language. Listeners add what they *know* to what they *hear* and arrive at an assessment of the intended *meaning*. For example, in the sentence 'Dave and Paul wanted to take the girls to the seaside, but they didn't have any money', we know the word 'they' refers to the boys since, in our culture, it is the inviter who pays.

One should remember that many jokes involve a violation of the expected, so that the listener is led down the garden path until confronted by the punch line. The point to remember is that, in order to be led along like this, one must accept that the storyline is consistent with what humans are expected to do. It is the switch to the unexpected at the end which makes the joke.

5   *Knowledge of the listener*. Sometimes, jokes can be made only when the joker has a good appreciation of what the listener understands or how the listener is thinking. In this case, a remark which means nothing to any other person can cause considerable mirth. This is the case of the private joke. The point here is that knowledge about the structure of the language and the meanings of the words used is not sufficient to allow access to the point of the joke.

'Esoteric? Come now Travis, everybody *knows what that means*.'

There may well be other aspects of joke-making that you can think of in addition to these, but the ones described here will be my starting point. One should not lose sight of the fact that in many forms of adult speech these factors operate in concert, and the sophisticated language user will be able to call upon each in support of the others as the conversational need requires.

3.5 Sounds interesting

Spoken languages, such as our own, make use of a wide range of sounds. Each of these sound sequences may be stressed or unstressed and be delivered in one of a range of intonations. A flexible and controlled vocal system seems to be an essential attribute of spoken language users. During the first year of life, children produce a growing range of sounds and begin to indulge in vocal play. These sounds will become closer and closer to the sounds of their language community (see Example 1).

EXAMPLE 1
STAGES OF VOCAL DEVELOPMENT

1. Reflexive crying and vegetative sounds. This is the first stage of sound production and occurs between birth and 8 weeks of age.

2. Cooing and laughter (from 8 to 20 weeks). Rachel Stark reports that these sounds are produced in comfortable states and in response to smiling and talking by the caregiver.

3. Vocal play (from 16 to 30 weeks). Longer segments of sound are produced which contain variations in pitch and stress as well as other aspects of sound control.

4. Reduplicated babbling (from 25 to 50 weeks). This is defined as a series of consonant–vowel syllables in which the consonant is the same for every syllable. For example, 'dadadadada' or 'nahnahnah'. Reduplicated babbling does not seem to be used in communication with adults, although it may be a part of imitation games towards the end of the first year.

5. Non-reduplicated babbling (from 50 weeks onwards). In this stage, infants may produce vowel–consonant–vowel combinations or consonant–vowel–consonant combinations. The components may vary within each series. Towards the end of this stage, stress and intonation patterns can be imposed on the babbling which give it a language-like 'feel'.

(Stark, 1986)

As the first year proceeds, sound production is evidence of a growing control over the vocal system. Parents get the strong impression that children enjoy making sounds and will do so when no other person is around. Sound production of this kind, in the absence of adult sound-makers, suggests that the infants are internally motivated to make sounds. This seems consistent with the nativist position outlined earlier in this section. In addition to this, intonational contour or pattern, the varying of the pitch of a sound, is a very useful device for language users. If you are unable to speak any French, for example, you should still be able to recognize and distinguish things like 'questions' from other kinds of speech.

ACTIVITY 3

Allow about 5 minutes

SOME SOUND PRACTICE

Words are pronounced with different intonational contours that depend on the purpose for which the words are used. Suppose that you are able to speak only one word of English, and that the word is 'spinach'. You do, however, have good intonational control. Practise saying 'spinach' to convey the following meanings.

1   (As to another person) Would you like some spinach?
2   (With delight on finding spinach on the menu) Oh good, they have spinach here.
3   (With revulsion) Oh no, not spinach again.

You should notice that the following formula seems to work.

Limited vocabulary + Intonational control = Considerable range of expression.

Comment

The point of the exercise is to suggest that the vocal play and other sound developments described by Stark mean a considerable advantage for the infant. Vocabulary is first non-existent, and then very limited. Intonational variation means that this limited vocabulary can have a range of uses and express a range of attitudes, from pleasure to disgust.

3.6 Performatives prior to speech

This was part of the title of a paper written by Elizabeth Bates, Luiga Camaioni and Virginia Volterra in 1975, in which they argued that infants could use their sound control purposively before the first word. Their work was based on the ideas of an Oxford-based philosopher of language, John Austin, and the later work of one of Austin's graduate students, John Searle (see Searle, 1969). Austin and Searle argued that an appropriate way to study language was to think about the *purpose* behind the utterance. Expressions of a language can be seen to have two components. One of the components concerns the facts of the matter, which may be true or false, while the other, and more interesting component, concerns the intention behind the utterance. To illustrate this difference, consider the way in which the same fact (John kissed Mary) can be used variously as a question (Did John kiss Mary?) or as a statement (John kissed Mary). Austin and Searle's central point was that language was for doing things. Bates and her colleagues took this idea and considered whether children, before they had any recognizable language, could express various intentions. The pre-verbal behaviour of infants cannot be described in terms of effective/ineffective or systematic/non-systematic. In their study, the researchers filmed three Italian girls at regular intervals over the space of several months. Their data suggests that before about 10 months of age the children's sounds had an effect on their caregivers, but that this was not intended in a conscious way by the children. The children's cries and other sounds were *interpreted* by the adults as signals of some need, but Bates and her colleagues were of the opinion that the children had not deliberately set out to achieve those effects. Earlier in this chapter I noted that one of the characteristics of communication is that it is intentional behaviour. Non-intentional behaviour is 'informative', or in Bates's terms, represents a 'signal'. By the age of 12 months 7 days Carlotta produced the following sequence which was interpreted as having the force of a command.

> C is sitting in her mother's lap, while M shows her the telephone and pretends to talk. M tries to press the receiver against C's ear and have her 'speak,' but C pushes the receiver back and presses it against her mother's ear. This is repeated several times. When M refuses to speak into the receiver, C bats her hand against M's knee, waits a moment longer, watches M's face, and then, uttering a sharp aspirated sound 'ha', touches her mother's mouth.
>
> (Bates *et al.*, 1975, p. 215)

A second example, also from Carlotta, occurred when she was 9 months and 6 days of age.

> C is in her mother's arms, and is drinking milk from a glass. When she has finished drinking, she looks around at the adults watching her, and makes a comical noise with her mouth ... [a 'raspberry']. The adults laugh, and C repeats the activity several times, smiling and looking around in between. Her parents explain that this behaviour had been discovered earlier in the week, and that C now produces it regularly at eating and drinking times, always expecting some response from the adult.
>
> (Bates *et al.*, 1975, p. 216)

Finally, an example from Marta, aged 1 year, 4 months and 2 days.

> Marta is unable to open a small purse, and places it in front of her father's hand (which is resting on the floor). F does nothing, so M puts the purse in his hand and utters a series of small sounds, looking at F. F still does not react, and M insists, pointing to the purse and whining. F asks, 'What do I have to do?' M again points to the purse, looks at F, and makes a series of small sounds. Finally, F touches the purse clasp and simultaneously says 'Should I open it?' Marta nods sharply ...
>
> (Bates *et al.*, 1975, p. 219)

Elizabeth Bates and her co-workers produced evidence of this kind to support their assertion that children had the means to make their wishes known before speech: they are able to communicate something of their intentions. One motive that children might be said to have for the development of language proper would be the perceived need for a more effective and precise system. Both learning theorists and nativists have a view of young children as 'passive' in the developmental process. The work of Bates and others identifies the young child as an active contributor in early pre-verbal exchanges.

3.7 The communicative context

READING

Study the reading at the end of this chapter by Linda Ferrier, in which she describes something of the linguistic context in which her daughter began to make sense of language. Make a note of those aspects of Ferrier's description which might make the task of developing language a little easier for her daughter. Do you think the description of a home environment given by Ferrier is typical?

Comment

One point you might have noted is that the child is experiencing considerable regularity of context, in that similar scenes are played out each day. It is also widely reported that the speech addressed to children is rather different from that used between adults (see Oates, 1994). Researchers attempting to transcribe adult-to-adult speech find that it contains hesitations, repetitions and incomplete fragments of sentences. In contrast, the speech addressed by caregivers to children seems to be a better sample of speech than that which adults customarily produce to each other. This modification of speech style seems not to be a conscious adaptation by caregivers: they are not apparently taught it, they just do it. Interestingly, there is some evidence that older children modify their speech style when talking to younger children, in just the ways that adults do.

Parental speech to children, because of its clarity and relative simplicity, is sometimes thought to be an advantageous introduction to the rather complex system that constitutes language. Once children are familiar with the system they may have enough experience to work out meanings when the linguistic input is less clear.

3.8 A question of give and take

Language learners have to learn things other than how to produce sounds in order to have a conversation; for instance, they need to know how conversations are organized. Some effort has been devoted to discovering if some of these conversational skills are present in children's behaviour before speech (see Oates, 1994). A fair amount of interest has centred on the apparently ubiquitous 'peek-a-boo' and give-and-take games played between infants and their caregivers. Both of

these games have some of the structural properties of conversations. Versions of 'peek-a-boo' games often involve the use of the pop-up, cone-type toys, but elaborate toys of this kind are not necessary. The game can be played using pieces of paper, hands or any other object which can obscure a face. The game takes the following form.

The parent captures the child's attention. The parent hides his or her face behind a piece of paper and waits. Child gives continued attention. Parent says 'Are you ready?' and waits. Child may shift posture or make some sound or movement. Parent says 'Are you ready?' (at a slightly higher pitch) and waits. Child makes some sound or movement. Parent abruptly removes obscuring object and says 'Boo!'. Child laughs, smiles, gurgles and so on. Parent and child return to starting position and repeat.

Jerome Bruner (1976) has reported a study of give-and-take games that looks at the issue of who is in charge of the game.

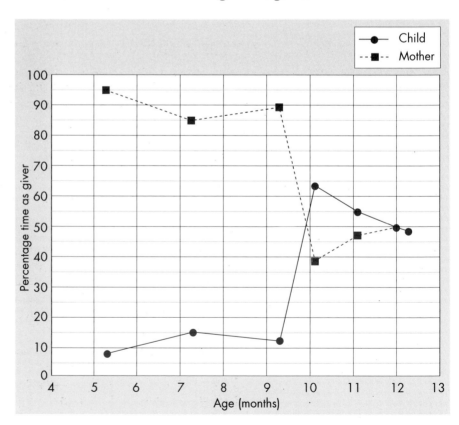

FIGURE 2 The change of control with age through the first year (Bruner, 1976).

Study Figure 2; what can you deduce from it? In the early months, control lies with the caregiver. The caregiver initiates the interaction. The caregiver also controls the pace of the exchange by monitoring the child's responses very closely. Almost any movement or sound from the child can be interpreted as the child's contribution to the sequence. Skilled adults leave space for infant 'replies'. Returning to Bruner's data, we can see that there comes a point at which more responsibility for initiating the game passes to the child. At this point, one can be fairly confident that the child understands the nature of the game and knows how to begin the pleasurable sequence. The last observation to make about Bruner's data is that, towards the end of the record, responsibility for initiating the sequence is shared more equally between the child and caregiver.

Before I move to a discussion of this work, a brief cautionary note is needed. In his writings, Vygotsky (1978) warns against the 'over-intellectualizing' of children's play. The point he is making is that children (and parents) do not appear to play in order to further intellectual or social development. The motive for play sequences and other social exchanges seems to be the pleasure and enjoyment that comes from being involved with another human being. Psychologists should not lose sight of this when speculating on the advantages to be gained from play, whether it is play with language or play with toys.

ACTIVITY 4
Allow about 10 minutes

GAMES AND CONVERSATIONS

In what ways are the games described similar to conversations? There are several points at which a description of the games might also be a description of a conversation.

Comment

1   Each person takes a turn in sequence. At the beginning, the child's behaviour seems to be 'promoted' to the status of a contribution by the caregiver. As the child becomes familiar with the pattern of the game the contribution becomes more obviously intentional.

2   Each person's contribution follows on from the previous contribution and leads on to the next. In other words each contribution is contingent upon the preceding contribution and related to the contribution that follows. (This is what is supposed to happen in conversations, although we all know people who break the rule and switch topics in a conversation without notifying the switch!)

3   A related point is that both participants in an exchange share an understanding about the topic of the exchange. Understanding what the exchange is about allows each participant to make an appropriate contribution.

SUMMARY OF SECTION 3

- Before a child produces a first word there is evidence which suggests that many conversation-related skills are being developed in the context of a specialized and helpful language environment.

- These skills include the progressive mastery of the vocal system until it is capable of producing, under control, the wide range of sounds needed for spoken language.

- Also present in the pre-verbal exchanges between infant and caregiver are some of the properties of conversations, such as turn taking, contingency and topic sharing.

- One might conclude that, by the time an infant produces her first word, she has developed several useful skills which constitute a conversational framework into which the precision of verbal communication will fit.

- A neat story so far, particularly concerning the modification of adult speech to children which seems designed to help a child into language. Much of the work described in this section dates from the 1970s; however, more recent work from the 1980s has muddied the waters somewhat.

4 QUICHÉ MAYAN SPEECH TO CHILDREN

It is helpful to remember that much of the research concerning children's language development has investigated the development of language in middle-class American or English children. There seem to be two reasons behind this state of affairs. Firstly, language development has excited more research interest in the English-speaking world. European psychology, until recently, tended to follow Piaget and was more interested in other aspects of development. The second reason seems to have been that middle-class children (often the children of academics) are available and have parents who are sufficiently interested in issues of development to collaborate with these studies. It may, of course, be the case that such children are like all other children in terms of language development, and that Anglo-Saxon middle-class child-rearing practices are no different from any others. This may not be the case, however, and for this reason, investigations into the language development of children from other cultures can be especially interesting. Clifton Pye (1986) has reported a study of children learning the Mayan language Quiché in South America. He was interested in the idea that the characteristics of adult speech to children, some of which we have already considered in this chapter, make a contribution to language learning. Accordingly, he studied the language addressed to children in this particular Mayan linguistic group. To take one example, it is widely reported that, in western cultures, speech to young children is delivered at a relatively slow rate, is at a higher pitch and has exaggerated intonational contours. Pye used a frequency-intensity analyzer to investigate changes in Quiché maternal speech to infants. He notes that, in contrast to the extensive data previously reported:

> Quiché mothers do not exhibit significant prosodic adjustments when speaking to their children.

(Pye, 1986, p. 88)

> Quiché mothers do use exaggerated intonation, but confine its use to infrequent exclamations to both children and adults.

(Pye, 1986, p. 88)

Pye also describes the findings of the ethnographer Ruth Bunzel, who a quarter of a century before him noted that:

> The Quiché woman is a gentle and solicitous mother, but she never takes time off from serious occupations like weaving to play with her children, or to talk to them. There are no lullabies, no children's tales, no little games which adults play with children.

(Bunzel, 1959, p. 101)

Pye suggests that the idea that maternal speech modification plays an *essential* role in language acquisition cannot be supported, since there are cultures in which language development occurs without the benefit of these modifications. He goes on to make the following important observation.

> I would suggest that the features of speech to children are culturally determined. In the first place, the structural characteristics of each language impose their own limitations on the features of caretaker speech. Secondly, the whole phenomenon of speech to children depends crucially upon cultural concepts about children and conventions for interacting with them.

(Pye, 1986, p. 98)

I have now reached a position at which our young language learner has a level of proficiency in conversational skills and some mastery of the vocal apparatus. In addition, there is evidence that pre-verbal children are already in the business of making their wishes and views known to others. This, then, is the situation that awaits the arrival of the first word.

SUMMARY OF SECTION 4

- As descriptions of the development of language skills in terms of sound control and conversational skills, the observations made earlier in this section still stand.

- What Pye's work has done is alert us to the fact that what has been described is not likely to be causative in the development of language, since there is evidence that other young language learners manage without it.

- There could, however, be an argument that the practices described make some *contribution* to the language development of western children, perhaps in terms of encouraging the development of conversational skills.

5 A WORD IN YOUR EAR

Sooner or later, around the end of the first year of life, children begin to produce words. The problem is that what counts as a word can vary. McCarthy, writing in 1954, listed seven different definitions. Estimates of a child's vocabulary will vary depending on which definition is used. One could use a definition along the lines of 'a word is a recognizable word of the adult language that is produced in a consistent context'. Alternatively, and in the spirit of the theoretical discussion at the beginning of this chapter, one could use another definition: 'any vocalization of the child that is used in a consistent context'. Here I shall adopt the latter definition and add a requirement that, for a 'word' to be used for communication, at least one other person must recognize its import. In order to record the arrival of a child's first word we shall need the assistance of the child's parents, who will be the most likely people to recognize when the criteria for a 'word' have been met.

While it seems very convenient to record the arrival of a child's first words, there is a problem if we want to use this list as an indication of a child's knowledge of language. It is customary to make a distinction between *receptive* language and *productive* language, in order to make a distinction between those words a child can understand and those words a child can produce. Children may understand rather more language than they can produce. Receptive language is much harder to investigate, so, having noted the problem, I shall now focus on children's productive language.

TABLE 1 Brenda's vocabulary at 14 and 19 months.

14 months		19 months[a]	
nau (no)	bear	orange	bone
d di (daddy, baby)	bed	pencil	checkers
d yu (down, doll)	big	write	corder
nene (liquid food)	blue	paper	cut
aw u (want, I don't want)	baby	nice	boat
e (yes)	Brenda	pen	I do
maem (solid food)	cookie	see	met
ada (another, other)	daddy	shoe	Pogo
	eat	sick	Ralph
	at	swim	you to
	(hor)sie	tape	climb
	mama	walk	jump
	mommy	wowow	

Source: adapted from Scollon, 1976, pp. 47 and 57–8.

[a]Brenda did not actually pronounce all these words the way an adult would; I have given the adult version, since that is easier to read.

Look at Table 1; at 14 months Brenda was using about eight 'words', in the sense of expressions with regular and identifiable meanings. Two of these referred to food, one to a person and the others to expressions like 'no', 'yes' and 'another'. By 19 months, Brenda's vocabulary numbers about 38 words. Although rates of vocabulary acquisition vary somewhat, Brenda's progress is about average. Some of the 'words' produced at 14 months are similar to adult words; however, some are not. A learning theory account of language development would find it difficult to explain their appearance and continued use.

Katherine Nelson (1973) investigated the vocabulary development of 18 children in monthly visits, beginning when the children were about 1 year old. Nelson's contribution was to code the children's first 50 words in terms of the kinds of meaning they expressed. She found that just over half the children's first 50 words were what she described as 'general nominals': words which refer to all members of a category, such as 'cars' or 'people'. Nelson included words like 'this' and 'he' in this category. The next most frequent category was 'specific nominals' at 14 per cent. These words refer to one specific thing or individual, such as 'daddy' or 'rover'. With almost the same frequency of occurrence (at 13 per cent) were 'action words' which invite or inhibit some action (for example, 'give' and 'don't'). The other two categories, each contributing about 10 per cent of the total, were described as 'modifiers' (for example, 'hot', 'all gone'), and personal–social words, such as 'bye bye' and 'no'.

'Goodness! How satisfying it must be to form one's own adjectives.'

The bulk of this early vocabulary consists of labels for things and people, but perhaps the most important words are those which allow the child to comment on matters and express needs and opinions. It was argued earlier that mastery of intonational contour could increase the range of comments that can be made. A similar argument is advanced here with respect to Nelson's categories of action words, modifiers and personal–social words.

Within the literature on early language development, one sometimes finds single-word utterances described as 'holophrases'. This specialized term is used to suggest that, for a child, a single word, plus a gesture or the refinement of some specific intonational contour, can make the word do much of the work of a complete sentence. This is a judgement about the function of single-word utterances, however, not the structure.

5.1 Over-extensions

One fact familiar to parents of young children is the habit children have at the beginning of language of using one word to refer to a wide range of objects. An example of this practice is their, occasionally embarrassing, habit of referring to several men as 'dada'. One might suppose that the infant has grasped the major part of the meaning of the term, that is, that it refers to an adult, male, human – but not the fact that it refers to one particular human. Clearly one of the tasks facing early language learners is to refine their use of terms until their usage coincides closely with the usage of the language community. Some aspects of the development of word meaning will be considered in Chapter 4.

Perhaps because children's over-extension of words is so noticeable, it is sometimes thought that over-extension is a major characteristic of single-word utterances. One of Katherine Nelson's students, Leslie Rescorla (1980), has described a study of the over-extensions produced by six children. This longitudinal study used parental records of the children's production of their first 75 words. The records noted the words and the use to which they were put. Of the 445 words produced by the six children, one-third of them (149) were noted in over-extended usage. While a notable percentage, this figure falls short of being a majority. This suggests that most of the words produced are used in circumstances which excite no comment. In other words, they are used in a manner similar to adult usage. Rescorla noted that there were 12 words in particular which seemed to be associated with much of the over-extension. These words were 'baby', 'dada', 'ball', 'cat', 'dog', 'hot', 'apple', 'car', 'truck', 'shoe', 'hat' and 'cheese'.

Rescorla also divided the over-extensions into three types. The most common type of over-extension, *categorical overinclusion*, found in over half the cases, involved the use of some words as though they referred to a higher-order category. For example, oranges and apples are examples of the higher-order category 'fruit'. So when a child refers to an orange using the term 'apple', it is possible that 'apple' is being used as a category term for fruit, rather than as a label for a particular kind of fruit. In using 'dada' to refer to mother, it may be that 'dada' is seen as a general term for humans.

Another category of over-extension described by Rescorla, labelled *analogic over-extension* and found in about 15 per cent of the cases, involved the novel usage of some word on the basis of functional or perceptual similarity. An example of this type of over-extension is the use of the word 'moon' to refer to nail clippings or to the reflection on the surface of a cup of tea.

The final type of over-extension, *predicate statements*, found in about 25 per cent of the cases, was apparently used by the children to indicate some information of a more abstract nature, such as 'absence'. An example given by Rescorla was the use of the word 'doll' when referring to the place in the crib where the doll was normally found. The doll was not there at the time.

The kinds of over-extension found in the early speech of these six children were used to indicate category membership, perceptual or functional similarity, and as a means of drawing attention to some relevant fact about the world. As a final cautionary note on this topic, one should remember that the words that the children produced and the context in which they were produced count as evidence. The interpretation offered to account for this evidence is an attempt to describe the evidence within a consistent framework, it is not itself 'factual'.

SUMMARY OF SECTION 5

- Deciding when children produce their first word depends on some decision about what counts as a word. The position taken here is that the consistent and decodable use of some expression by a child counts as a word, even if the word is not much like any other word found in the language of the community.

- The development of vocabulary is slow at first and varies somewhat between children. Nonetheless, children are likely to have a vocabulary of about 50 words by 18 or 20 months of age.

- The evidence suggests that children understand a much larger vocabulary than they are able to produce.

- Those words that children can produce can each be used to convey a range of meanings, given the judicious use of devices like intonational contour.

- In addition to this, children are able to extract considerable mileage from limited means. One problem with this practice is that the potential for misunderstanding is considerable, given the flexible and varied use of words. Perhaps one 'motive' for the further development of language into combinations of words and for the development of grammar is the precision and reduction of ambiguity offered by these developments.

6 PUTTING WORDS TOGETHER

Children's early word combinations provide useful evidence concerning both the level of children's understanding of language and the characteristics of children as young language learners.

Grammar

As soon as a child begins to combine words to make phrases it becomes possible to investigate the structure and organization of those phrases. It may be that early word combinations are not random assemblages but are systematic. If so, the description of the system used by the child to combine words is called a 'grammar'. This kind of grammar is quite different from the prescriptive sort of grammar sometimes taught in schools. That sort of grammar tells us how things *should* be done, whereas those who study language development are interested in how things *are* done. Based on this idea, it is possible to write a 'grammar' for every stage of a child's language development. By this means one can chart the development of a child's progress towards adult grammar. We now see adult grammar to be only one of the possible ways to organize language. One other reason for studying the structures of early combinations is that it is thought that there is some close relation between those structures and the ways children understand their world. For example, some psychologists have studied children's use of tenses and adverbs in order to find out what young children know of the concepts of time (see Chapter 4).

'Not "fell", Simpkins – "fallen": Mr. Jones has fallen out of the window . . .'

6.1 Stage 1: a first grammar

There is a convention among students of child language which divides language development into two stages. This division is somewhat arbitrary, although it is convenient. In stage 1, children's utterances are generally short, usually consisting of two or three words. Stage 1 utterances are described as 'simple', by which it is meant that grammatical markers are missing. Grammatical markers, or inflections, are the sounds added to words which give precision to the expression. For example, when one refers to objects in the plural one usually adds an 's' to the end of the word, so 'apple' becomes 'apples'.

EXAMPLE 2
CONSISTENCY IN ENGLISH

This is a good point at which to introduce one of the particular problems confronting a learner of English. Although the plural is often signalled by the addition of an 's' to the word, plurality can also be signalled by changing the form of the word ('mouse' becomes 'mice') or by no change at all ('sheep' stays as 'sheep'). A learner of English has to learn the rules – but, in addition, they have to learn the multiplicity of exceptions.

Grammatical markers are absent from a child's speech in stage 1. There will be no plurals, no use of the possessive 's', no tense markers and no auxiliary verbs (like 'is', 'do' and so on). Children in this stage will use nouns, verbs and adjectives, and will also use temporal adverbs (words like 'now', 'soon' and so on). The expression 'telegraphic speech' is often used to describe the language of children in stage 1. All the detail and nicety is stripped away, leaving the essential bones. It is also reported that children's imitations of adult speech have this telegraphic character: for example, asking a child to repeat 'I am playing with the dogs' is likely to be met with 'I play dog'.

However, there is more to this last sample of selective imitation than an example of telegraphic speech. The sentence 'I am playing with the dogs' contains six words, and includes things such as the plural 's' after 'dog', the progressive '-ing' ending to the main verb 'play', and so on. All these refinements are stripped away in the child's imitation. There is also the intriguing question of why these three particular words appear in the child's reply, when only one of them ('I') appears in the adult's sentence. Perhaps you might argue that a child of this age has some memory limit that means only three words can be retained. If this were the case, however, why did the child not remember the first three words? Or the last three? The child's answer supports the view that the child was able to scan the whole sentence and abstract the crucial elements. The child evidently has this ability, even though he or she is unable to duplicate the production of the sentence itself. (This 'scanning' is termed by linguists the parsing of a sentence.)

Novel productions and imitation

Any record of children in stage 1 grammar is likely to contain examples of the following kind.

All gone sticky. = The sweet is finished.
Burny does it. = That is hot.
A more water. = I would like some more water.

The point to note about these examples of language is that they do not appear to be the kind of utterances that the children will have heard an adult say. If this is so, then these utterances cannot be said to be 'imitations'. The meaning of each of the three is clear enough, so they can be described as novel and successful utterances. They are evidently consistent with a view that, even at this early stage of language development, children are being creative. These observations have implications for the theoretical positions already outlined. Do they mean that there is no role for imitation as a means whereby children gain access to language? The answer has to be a guarded 'no'. Almost any parent will have heard their children use expressions which they have copied, complete with intonation, from their parent. This can be embarrassing when the expression imitated reveals an aspect of one's verbal style or vocabulary that one might wish to hide. Clearly, children do imitate, and equally clearly, adults often think that this imitation is a primary route into language. The evidence from children's creative use of language allows us to see imitation as only part of the process.

There have been attempts to describe the formal structures present in the language of the stage 1 child. One criticism which can be levelled is that a purely structural analysis can sometimes underestimate linguistic sophistication. There is a much-cited example in the literature which comes from the work of Lois Bloom (1973). The child that Bloom described used the expression 'mommy sock' on two separate occasions. On one of these occasions the utterance was produced as the child's mother was putting a sock on the child. On the other occasion, the child had picked up one of her mother's socks. The child used the same simple construction on each occasion, but for rather different purposes. The uses seem to have been, firstly, to indicate the mother's role as the person fitting the sock to the child, and secondly, to indicate the ownership of her mother's sock. In order to understand the extent of a child's communicative competence we need to have access to the context in which the utterance is used and hence the range of meanings available to the child.

RESEARCH SUMMARY 1
MEAN LENGTH OF UTTERANCE (MLU)

One very common means of charting the development of a child's language is to measure the child's mean length of utterance (MLU). This is a relatively straightforward process. Over a period of time, the number of words spoken by the child is totalled. This number is divided by the number of times the child has spoken. The resulting number is the child's current MLU. Some researchers count words and inflections separately (so 'jumping' = two 'words', 'jump' and '-ing'). MLU can be a useful indicator of development, but it can also disguise the child's level of sophistication. A child may produce many examples of two-word utterances which vary considerably in meaning. (Look back to the discussion of the expression 'mommy sock' for an illustration.)

6.2 Stage 2: where do rules come from?

The time spent in stage 1 grammar varies widely between children, so it is not helpful to set an age for the onset of stage 2. Stage 2 appears when the child begins to use any of the grammatical inflections that were so obviously absent in stage 1. Just to recap, these include things like the plural 's' and the possessive 's', and tense markers ('-ed' and '-ing'). The appearance of tense markers in English has been a rich source of material for those interested in the development of children's understanding of concepts of time, and, more importantly here, for those interested in language development itself. The sequence of the development of the English tense system, which seems stable over a range of longitudinal studies, is as follows.

1   In stage 1 grammar there are no tense inflections, neither the progressive '-ing' suffix, the '-ed' past-tense ending of regular verbs nor the use of irregular tense forms.

2 First to appear on the scene are the past-tense forms of irregular verbs. For example, one might find both 'sleep' and 'slept' in a child's language. Both of these forms will appear to be used appropriately.

3 At some later point in development the past-tense forms of regular verbs appear. It is only necessary to add the '-ed' suffix to these verbs to make them into the past-tense form.

4 From this moment on, it is reported that *all* references to the past will use verbs with the '-ed' suffix, even those irregular verbs which had been in the child's vocabulary so far. So, for example, 'sleep' becomes 'sleeped'. Actually, the picture seems to be more complex than this, with appropriate and inappropriate usage co-existing for some time before adult usage is established.

An explanation consistent with this set of facts is that, when children begin to use irregular past-tense forms, these words are treated as though they were new words and as not particularly related to the present-tense form. When children begin to use the regular past-tense '-ed' suffix, they have discovered that it is possible to make a great number of past-tense forms by this simple addition. The children, however, do not realise the existence of exceptions to the rule, and thus we see the use of the '-ed' suffix after irregular verbs as well. This gives rise to the widely noted 'comed', 'goed' and 'wented'.

The crucial point is that this language behaviour is consistent with the idea that children are trying to discover the *rules* of language. The rule systems they try out are sensible and plausible, but they are not adult English. The business of discovering or generating rules is a much more sophisticated activity than the rote learning of new words and expressions. One final point on this matter: the child who produces 'comed' and 'goed' is being creative and is definitely not copying an aspect of adult speech.

ACTIVITY 5
Allow about 20 minutes

A PLAY ON WORDS

Here are two transcriptions of a child's speech.

Scene 1: at age 2 years of age

JENNY: I want an ... other one.

MOTHER: Do you? Do you perhaps want to have a bit of one with mummy?

JENNY: Alright then.

MOTHER: Alright then, can daddy peel it? Ask daddy to peel it cos mummy ain't got no nails.

JENNY: Orange.

MOTHER: Mmm, it's a baby orange isn't it? It's a satsuma.

JENNY: Shoos ...

MOTHER: Sats ... suma.

JENNY: Jenny sooma.

MOTHER: Jenny's sooma.

Scene 2: 18 months later

MOTHER: Do you like having your sandpit in the garden then?

JENNY: Yes. Now I want to do a different song now everybody. So … I'm gonna. Now you wait a minute.

JENNY: I'll just get a book … so I can … where's … where the sort of song book?

Using the procedure described in Research Summary 1, work out the MLUs for these two samples of Jenny's language.

Sample 1 MLU

Sample 2 MLU

Is Jenny in stage 1 or stage 2 at the time of these samples? On what do you base your judgement?

Comment

You might notice that in the first sample Jenny's mother attempts to teach the new word (satsuma) by slowing down her delivery and breaking the word up into two parts. In Jenny's response there is first some evidence of imitation, but she reaches a point at which she stops imitating and responds to her mother's efforts on a quite different level.

We have traced the development of vocal skills, the appearance of the first words, and have discussed some aspects of the development of organized, connected speech. Our young language learner knows something of conversational skills and that it is possible to amuse with language. This brings us to an important idea: in order deliberately to amuse another person, one must have some appreciation of that person's mental state and some knowledge of what might be found amusing. Being sensitive to the mind of another person may be an important requirement for effective communications of all kinds. For example, in order to decide what vocabulary to select when providing an explanation, one needs to know something of what one's conversational partner already understands. If you admit to an interest in psychology, you may be asked to elaborate. Your reply will be presented in the light of what you know of your questioner, be they a fellow student, a professional psychologist or a small child.

Dianne Horgan (1981) has reported a study of the development of joke-making in her own daughter Kelly. Playing with language demonstrates both developing language skills and the development of *metalinguistic ability*. Metalinguistic ability refers to the ability to think about and reflect on language itself. When you were invited to think about language at the beginning of this chapter, your metalinguistic ability was called into action. This ability to reflect on language is a more sophisticated ability than the ability to produce language. In addition, it is argued here that intentional joking requires that the joker has some idea of the mental state of the listener, since telling jokes often involves the manipulation of another person's mental state. The development and value of mental models in general will be considered more fully in Chapter 4.

Horgan describes Kelly's joking in terms of a four-stage progression. As each new stage appeared it was added to the preceding stage but did not replace it. The first stage involved the deliberate violation of semantic categories. For example, when Kelly was 16 months old and had a vocabulary of about 20 words, she added the word 'shoe' to her list.

> Several days later, she put her foot through the armhole of a nightgown, saying 'shoe', accompanied by shrieks of laughter.
>
> (Horgan, 1981, p. 218)

In Horgan's view semantic violation of this kind can be very useful in allowing a language learner to explore the boundaries of the concept represented by a word.

Horgan's second category of joking consists of games based on phonetic patterns. For example, at 20 months of age, Kelly said 'Cow go moo. Mommy go mamoo. Daddy go dadoo. Ha ha' (Horgan, 1981, p. 219).

In Horgan's view, the child must have begun to treat the sounds of a word as 'arbitrary symbols for the objects and not as essential properties of the objects' in order to be able to 'bend' the sounds to make a rhyme or fit into a regular pattern. You may recall two points made earlier in this chapter. The first is that in the early stages of development children seem to be developing a mastery of the ability to make sounds, which then allows them to make the sounds that are recognizable parts of their language. Secondly, there was some mention of the possibility that the 'arbitrary' nature of the symbols of language contributes to the possibility of novel and imaginative thinking, since the link between a symbol and the object it represents is rather tenuous.

The third kind of joke described by Horgan appeared in her daughter's speech early in the third year. Kelly produced a more sophisticated version of the earlier humour by introducing new words into established sequences. The new words were related in some way to the words that had been replaced. For example, Kelly produced 'Little Bo People had lost her steeple'. In this case the syntax is preserved and the introduced words are real words and make (a sort of) sense.

Rather later in the third year, Kelly began to produce jokes which had a regular form. This form was something like that of a riddle, although her parents reported that Kelly had never heard a riddle. For example:

> K: How do aspirins make?
> M: Huh?
> K: How do aspirins make?
> M: I dunno, how do aspirins make?
> K: They make you feel better.
>
> (Horgan, 1981, p. 220)

By the end of the third year, Kelly was able to make up jokes which still retained this form, although they were also used to set up a linguistically misleading context. For example:

> K: Mommy, do you love me?
> M: Yes.
> K: Do you love me to HIT you? Ha ha!
> and
> K: Do we kick Mary?
> M: No, we don't kick Mary!
> K: Do we kick Jennifer?
> M: No we don't kick Jennifer!
> K: Do we kick the swimming pool?
> M: No, we don't kick the swimming pool!
> K: We kick IN the swimming pool. Ha ha!

(Horgan, 1981, p. 221)

The purpose of describing these jokes is to illustrate the extent to which this particular child was able to manipulate what she knew about language in order to achieve surprise and amusement. In addition, the later jokes suggest that Kelly is able to make a joke by setting up her mother to expect one kind of outcome, while preparing the ground for another. This seems to be an attempt to manipulate the mental state of another person. In order to do this, the child needs to have some idea that alternative states exist and to have some idea about what they might be.

SUMMARY OF SECTION 6

- The way in which humans assemble and organize language can be described in a 'grammar'. As children's language develops it is possible to produce a sequence of such grammars or descriptions.
- The first stage of grammatical development can be defined by the absence of grammatical markers, such as the possessive 's' or the progressive '-ing' verb ending in English.
- The early language produced by children provides evidence that suggests they are not merely passive imitators of what they hear, but are able to abstract meaning.
- The creative use of language by children can also be seen as evidence of their active engagement with language learning.
- The development of the ability to make jokes indicates children's increasing ability to think about and reflect on language itself and on its effect on other people.

---

7 CONCLUSION

In the descriptions of language development described here there has been an attempt to ask, at each stage, about what value development has for the child. To close the chapter, it would now be helpful to ask what value the developments described here might have for our understanding of the nature of children in general, and for the theories which seek to account for language development in particular. You will have already come across the idea that children are born with considerable knowledge which appears at a suitable point in an individual's maturation. Alternatively, there have been those who take the view that children know what they know only because they have been taught it; these theoretical positions seem to regard children as passive with respect to the developmental process. A third view is that children are active agents in their own development. As you come across more and more information you should attempt to decide if it is consistent with what you might predict, given your knowledge of the history of ideas in developmental psychology.

7.1 Connectionism: a break with the past?

The three theoretical positions on the development of language outlined in this chapter are not the only ones available, even if they are the most prominent. A new challenger has now been identified, *connectionism*, an offspring of the disciplines of artificial intelligence and psycho-linguistics. Any discussion of connectionism can become very complex very quickly, so I shall confine myself to a brief outline before considering its potential as a model of language development. Connectionism is based on an understanding of the interconnected operation of the large numbers of neurons in human brains. Each neuron may be connected with large numbers of other neurons making up a complex network. Neurons produce electro-chemicals which can make other neurons 'fire' or 'stop firing'; in neurological terms, they can excite and inhibit. The main differences between the information processing and connectionist explanations concern the level and the process of information storage. Information processing models have information stored as 'symbols' (that is, meaningful units) in a 'long-term memory'. Connectionist models store information as a pattern of excited and inhibited neurons. So what happens when a person's sensory system is stimulated, perhaps by a particular sound, is that some neurons will fire and some will be prevented from firing. The pattern that this makes selectively strengthens the connections between the neurons involved. When the same sound is heard again, the pattern will be activated once again, further strengthening the connections. One other thing about these neural networks is that they can be activated as a whole if only a part of the stimulus sound is heard. One might think of them as a sort of memory which can recall on the basis of partial information (for example, a partially hidden face).

7.2 Connectionism and language

The main concern here is to consider connectionism as a candidate for an explanation of the process of language development. Connectionism has as its starting point a human neural system which has the ability to form and retain networks. Infants have such a system, although it continues to develop for some time after a child is born. In the connectionist view, neural systems will be constructed on the basis of what happens to the child's senses. As more information becomes available the system will be extended and modified to incorporate the new material.

One major advantage of this and all computer models of human cognition is that the model can be tested to see if it works in a similar way to humans. Let me take an example that has been widely explored, that of learning the English tense system. The usual explanation is that children have to learn a 'rule', that is, that to refer to the past, verbs must be given the '-ed' suffix. They must also learn that there are many irregular exceptions in English. So in this processing explanation, children have to learn and store the rule and its exceptions. As we know, children, in the early stages, over-use the rule, and add '-ed' to irregular verbs as well as to regular verbs. Rummelhart and McClelland (1986) made a connectionist model which was given information about verbs as its input and was required to produce past-tense verbs as its output. As the model began to work it produced the same pattern of verb usage that is found in the language of young children. The important point to note is that the model was able to produce this human-like behaviour *without* the necessity of learning a rule. So although language in general, and children's language in particular, *looks* as if it is 'rule-governed', perhaps there is no need for the complexity of rule knowledge at all.

At the time of writing, connectionist models of language and language development are an important area of research activity, with some very promising results. It is, however, unlikely that the insights and strengths of the earlier theorizing will be abandoned. It is more likely that, eventually, a new theoretical position incorporating all the available information will be produced. We are some way from this position but things are happening.

FURTHER READING

GALLAWAY, C. and RICHARDS, B. J. (eds) (1994) *Input and Interaction in Language Acquisition*, Cambridge, Cambridge University Press.

INGRAM, D. (1989) *First Language Acquisition: method, description and explanation*, Cambridge, Cambridge University Press.

McSHANE, J. (1991) *Cognitive Development: an information processing approach*, Oxford, Blackwell.

REFERENCES

BATES, E., CAMAIONI, L. and VOLTERRA, V. (1975) 'The acquisition of performatives prior to speech', *Merrill-Palmer Quarterly*, **21**, pp. 205–26.

BLOOM, L. (1973) *One Word at a Time*, The Hague, Mouton.

BRUNER, J. S. (1975) 'The ontogenesis of speech acts', *Journal of Child Language*, **2**, pp. 1–21.

BRUNER, J. S. (1976) 'Learning to do things with words' in BRUNER, J. S. and GARTON, A. (eds) *Human Growth and Development*, Oxford, Oxford University Press.

BUNZEL, R. (1959) 'Chichicastenango: a Guatemalan village', *Publications of the American Ethnological Society*, Vol. 12, Seattle, University of Washington.

DE LAGUNA, G. A. (1927) *Speech: its function and development*, New Haven, Yale University Press.

HORGAN, D. (1981) 'Learning to tell jokes: a case study of metalinguistic abilities', *Journal of Child Language,* **8**, pp. 217–24.

MARSHALL, J. C. (1970) 'The biology of communication in man and animals' in LYONS, J. (ed.) *New Horizons in Linguistics*, Middlesex, Penguin Books.

MCCARTHY, D. (1954) 'Language development in children' in CARMICHAEL, L. (ed.) *Manual of Child Psychology,* second edition, New York, Wiley.

NELSON, K. (1973) 'Structure and strategy in learning to talk', *Monographs of the Society for Research in Child Development,* **38** (serial no. 149).

OATES, J. (1994) 'First relationships' in OATES, J. (ed.) *The Foundations of Child Development*, Oxford, Blackwell/The Open University (Book 1 of ED209).

PYE, C. (1986) 'Quiché Mayan speech to children', *Journal of Child Language*, **13**, pp. 85–100.

RESCORLA, L. (1980) 'Overextension in early language development', *Journal of Child Language*, **7**, pp. 321–35.

RUMMELHART, D. E. and McCLELLAND, J. L. (1986) 'On learning the past tenses of English verbs' in McCLELLAND, J. L. and RUMMELHART, D. E. (eds) *Parallel Distributed Processing: explorations in the microstructure of cognition*, Vol. 2, *Psychological and Biological Models*, Cambridge, Mass., MIT Press.

SCOLLON, R. (1976) *Conversations With a One-Year-Old*, Honolulu, University of Hawaii Press.

SEARLE, J. (1969) *Speech Acts: an essay in the philosophy of language*, Cambridge, Cambridge University Press.

STARK, R. E. (1986) 'Prespeech segmental feature development' in FLETCHER, P. and GARMAN, M. (eds) *Language Acquisition*, second edition, Cambridge, Cambridge University Press.

VYGOTSKY, L. S. (1978) *The Role of Play in Development*, Cambridge, Mass., Harvard University Press.

 **READING**

Extracts from 'Some observations of error in context'

L. J. Ferrier

The present work is based on a series of observations of my one-year-old from the appearance of her first word. It contains four basic assumptions.

1. Mother and child are an interactional unit and it is pointless to look at a child's production without giving equal weight to the mother's contribution to the dialogue.

2. More interesting than the fact that the subject has acquired a particular lexical item are the changes in application of these items over time.

3. The child's early utterances are tied to particular routine contextual situations and therefore the analysis of language in the early stages must include a description of context.

4. It is a useful research method to pay attention to the child's 'mistakes' and a careful analysis of why the child is making them may reveal which strategies he is relying on in utilising maternal utterances to produce his own novel ones.

I made weekly notes of my daughter's vocabulary acquisitions with descriptions of the social and physical contexts in which they were first used and utterances of mine on which they appeared to be dependent. I noted subsequent uses of the same items and, in particular, any misuses.

I should like to begin by bringing to the attention of those who are not parents, a few facts vital to any study of early language development. Firstly, that in the first two years of life, a baby probably averages three nappy changes per day (conservative estimate) which means that he has over 2,000 nappies changed in that period. Similarly he probably averages about 2,000 meals and 2,000 snoozes.

The second point is that, contrary to Chomsky's view that language is new and creative, 'mothers' language to small children is repetitious, context-tied and ritualized' (Halliday, 1974). Observing my own behaviour when my daughter was about 15 months old, I discovered that whenever I took her out of her cot I said 'Hello my love. Where's my nice girl?' Whenever I sat her in her high chair I said 'Upsadaisy', and whenever she sneezed I said 'Atchoo'.

The combination of these facts means that the small baby finds himself with monotonous regularity in routine interactional contexts in which his mother produces a fairly limited and predictable set of utterances. It is both the regularity and the invariance of these routines which allows the baby to make his initial attempts at breaking the linguistic code. (My daughter's first word was 'Pretty' which had its roots in a bed-time ritual of admiring the geraniums on a window sill halfway up the stairs.) However, these interactions are idiosyncratic to particular mother–child pairs. (My daughter's earliest demand to be allowed to draw was 'Pussy' as I constantly drew cats for her. Such demands would have been incomprehensible to anyone outside the interaction.) They also evolve slowly from day to day, week to week, under the influence of either of the two parties but particularly subject to the developing capacities of the child. For example, when my daughter was just on the point of walking she virtually refused to lie down to have her nappies changed, so involved was she with her new skill. To accommodate the nappy-changing routine to this desire, I temporarily put her nappies on while she stood on the window sill, which distraction device brought into that routine new objects, i.e. the birds on the roof-top opposite. After a week the item 'birds' appeared in her vocabulary.

The child's early utterances are idiosyncratic for other reasons. Which items from his mother's productions a child selects for his own use will depend on the stratagems he is employing at the time. I would like to consider one stratagem hit upon by my daughter at about 16 months.

'Imitation' has had both its devotees and its detractors as a process in language development. That some children do it is well documented … why they do it, or whether it in fact advances the productive capacity of the child, is still in dispute. Imitation has generally been defined as the exact repetition of the whole or part of a preceding utterance produced by someone other than the child and following in fairly rapid temporal succession. This type of imitation is fairly readily picked up by the classical research method of running a tape-recorder for set periods of time and analyzing all the utterances within that text. I would like to suggest that there is a *second type of imitation* which I shall term 'dependency', not operating under those temporal constraints and not so readily picked up by the itinerant researcher, but available to the mother who can observe her child in the repeated and routine social contexts in which they interact. Examples of this are given below.

1   'Look': At the age of 16 months one typical and repeated demand made by my subject was for drawers and doors to be opened for her. Before this age her demands were transmitted by gesture (pulling at the drawer or door) accompanied by an item … from her protolanguage … At this point I observed that my typical reaction to such a demand was to check my interpretation of her utterance by asking 'Do you want to look?' She shortly afterwards produced 'look' in exactly those same physical contexts but as a demand form replacing her protolanguage term.

2   'Out': Shortly after the development of 'look', 'out' appeared in a similar manner. Until this time she communicated a desire to get out of her feeding chair by making efforts to get out accompanied by her protolanguage demand. I would once again check her message by saying 'Do you want to get out?' She subsequently used 'out' as her demand form. It was used appropriately in that specific physical context but when a week later she needed assistance to climb *into* a high chair, she generalized 'out' to that situation.

3   'This' and 'That': These were used in free variation as demands for objects out of reach and their acquisition had a similar history. The context of their first use was the bath, where there is a large basket of toys suspended from the shower for use at bath time. Her gestural demand was replaced by 'this' and later 'that', which were again lifted from my check utterances 'Do you want this/that?' 'This' and 'that' were subsequently extended to any situations in which she wanted an object out of reach and were used appropriately.

She shortly afterwards lifted 'up' from my check 'Do you want to get up?' which was then generalized to situations in which she wanted to get down. She also employed 'chair' from my check 'Do you want to get on the chair?' She then used it as a request for help to get onto tricycles, window sills and a rocking horse.

It appeared then, that many of her early utterances were tied to repeated family routines of the sort described, in which my language was notably repetitious. But the very invariance of those routines and of my language within them allowed my daughter to hit on the productive stratagem of utilizing the last word of my utterance by transforming its function to that of a demand for goods or services. The perceptual salience of sentence final position has been noted elsewhere ... (Two months after the period described she produced a beautiful example of this stratagem. I said 'Mummy would like one too', to which she responded 'Three, four, five'. Note that in each case, the word lifted from the source utterance carried the tonic which presumably added to its salience.) Almost immediately the term had been acquired in those social/physical contexts in which my source utterance was embedded, she generalized it to other similar situations, sometimes appropriately and sometimes not. This process of generalization has been noted by most diarist studies ... It is a capacity which is obviously of enormous importance to the child's cognitive and verbal progress. I am always awed by the children's unerring ability to generalize from real ducks to Walt Disney creations which bear little relation to the real thing. It is not therefore surprising that they sometimes stray across adult conceptual boundaries, as for example, when my daughter referred to the lawn mower as Daddy's vacuum cleaner.

However, a careful examination of those instances which were inappropriate suggests that the relationship between the social/physical situations and the language employed in them is not a simple one and that various categories of inappropriate usage can be analysed. To consider the ontogenesis of some other of my daughter's utterances:

4   'Oh, phew!' – an item which I systematically used for a while when I entered my daughter's bedroom each morning to be greeted by a rather offensive smell. My utterance was an exclamation and its 'application' ... was the smell. My daughter, after a couple of days, produced it in the same setting, i.e. her cot in the morning, but when in fact the smell was absent. For her it was a form of greeting and tied initially to that particular routine. Shortly afterwards I extended its use to nappy-changing situations in which for me the utterance had the same function and application – for her the function appeared simply 'ostension' and its application was her nappy. She subsequently used the term outside the nappy-changing situation to refer to nappies both clean and dirty, and finally to the nappy bucket which normally contained nappies but which was, on this particular occasion, empty.

The initial use of this term as a greeting suggests that –

(a) the recurring social situation of meeting her mother in the morning was for her the dominant feature of its use and

(b) that her own noxious odour did not have the perceptual salience for her it did for me!

The fact that the term then acquired an ostensive or perhaps naming function in the nappy-changing situation indicates –

(a) that which particular features of physical context an utterance is referring to is not always obvious to the language learner, and

(b) that while for me the application of my utterance was my reaction to a smell, the referent of her utterance was the object which was sometimes the cause of the smell, i.e. the nappy.

Finally, as mature speakers we tend to forget that even the humble exclamation is culture bound and has to be learned to have that particular function. (I have a notion that some of these early exclamations may in fact have an important function in delimiting the field of application later covered by specific verbs. So the accident markers 'Oh dear' and 'upsadaisy' are the precursors of such verbs as 'spill' and 'fall' which must obligatorily have attached the semantic feature 'non-purposive'.)

A further example of the confusion generated by the perceptual complexity of objects referred to, was my daughter's first acquaintance with aeroplanes. From about the time when she was one year and onwards, I frequently drew her attention to noises made by aeroplanes by use of 'Sh!' and an accompanying raised finger. She quickly learned to respond to aeroplane noises in the same way, but never in fact saw an actual aeroplane. The referent of 'Sh!' was a disembodied noise. At about this period, she developed an interest in books. I verbally labelled a picture of an aeroplane for her and she responded with 'Sh!' accompanied by the usual gesture, but of course inappropriately in the absence of any noise. When a few days later she saw her first aeroplane, she exclaimed 'Bird!' ...

Summary and conclusions

Mother and child in the first two years of life develop an exclusive and idiosyncratic relationship in the repeated and ritualized encounters of childcaring. Within these encounters the mother's language is limited and context-tied, thus allowing the child to make his first attempts at breaking the linguistic code. At least some children appear to lift items wholesale from their mother's productions and put them to their own uses. However, the fact that the relationship between language and the socio-physical world is both referentially and functionally complex, leads to the child's production of inappropriate utterances when he generalizes beyond the initial learning context.

Finally, the social functions of the child's early utterances appear to be developmentally dominant and only gradually do the semantic boundaries of the items in them approximate to those of adults.

Reference

HALLIDAY, M. A. K. (1974) in PARRETT, H. *Discussing Language: dialogues with W. L. Chafe, N. Chomsky, A. J. Greimas, M. A. K. Halliday et al.*, The Hague, Mouton.

SOURCE: FERRIER, L. J. (1974) 'Some observations of error in context', Language Development Project, University of Bristol.

Mark Coulson

CONTENTS

1   INTRODUCTION

The recollections of childhood have no order.

(Dylan Thomas, *Reminiscences of Childhood*)

What is your earliest memory? A birthday party, something that happened to you on holiday, the day your baby sister was born, perhaps? Our earliest memories are usually of single episodes, often divorced from other recollections, and frequently scenes or images as opposed to facts.

There is one sense in which this is inevitable. Our earliest experiences occur before we learn to speak, and are therefore more likely to be images and scenes as opposed to abstract facts which have to be given names. However, if we delve a little more deeply we find that although there may be a few remnants of extremely early memories (dating from the first year or two of life), our first five or so years are characterized by an almost total lack of well-structured memories. A typical research finding is summarized in Figure 1.

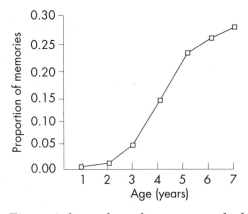

FIGURE 1 Proportion of childhood memories recalled for ages 1–7. (Adapted from Conway, 1990, p. 32.)

Figure 1 shows that when we are asked to recall childhood memories we recall most memories from around six and seven years, with this proportion decreasing sharply below these ages. Why is it that we are more or less unable to remember anything from the first few years of life (a phenomenon which has been termed *infantile amnesia*)? Notice that during this time children learn highly complex skills such as language and social interaction, which must be represented as some form of memory. Why then are we unable to remember the things that happened to us while we were learning these skills? Is it possible that the memories are there, but are just difficult to access?

ACTIVITY 1

Allow about 10 minutes on each of two separate days

ACCESSING REMOTE MEMORIES

This activity should give you an insight into how early memories are stored and retrieved.

Keep the results of this activity in a safe place. Come back to it in a couple of days and see how much further you can progress.

Think back to your school days, to when you were 7 or 8 years old (after the period of infantile amnesia). Try to picture one of the classrooms you occupied, preferably one that may hold some significance for you, and that was not the first classroom you ever studied in.

Can you remember the names of any of your classmates? Write down as many as you can.

Try returning to this activity in a couple of days' time. Do you manage to produce more names on this second occasion?

Comment

On the second attempt you may find that your performance increases, perhaps quite dramatically. You might like to extend the activity further. Once you have recalled some of the names in the class, can you go back further in time? Because the names of fellow students may not change all that much from year to year, try moving on to teachers' names. What was the teacher's name in the year you were trying to remember? What about the year previously?

You may find this activity quite difficult at first, being hard pressed to produce even a couple of names (if, that is, you are no longer in contact with the people you went to school with). Memories of long ago have been termed *remote memories*, and the way in which they are accessed has been used as evidence of how our memories are organized.

1.1 Organization in memory

Memory for personal events is not a list of unconnected events, it is highly organized. Furthermore, it appears that this organization is *chronological*. That is, facts and events are stored in a way which mimics the order in which they happened to the individual. Although at first it may be impossible to recall the name of your first teacher, by 'working back' through your memory you may be able to access that information via an indirect route. This is because memories which are originally impossible to retrieve are linked to other events in your life which either followed or preceded them, and these memories can act as *cues* for retrieval. Whitten and Leonard (1981) found that the teachers' names task was easier to perform (meaning that participants recalled more names) going from early years to later ones, implying that memory is organized in the order in which things occurred.

But is this the only way in which memory is stored? A simple reflection serves to inform us of the very different types of memory we possess. In addition to events concerning your own life, you also know facts about the world, about psychology, the rules of language and mathematics, your name, what your friends and family like to do, eat, wear. The list is endless. Does it make sense to assume that all information is organized in a chronological fashion?

ACTIVITY 2

Allow about 5 minutes

THE ORGANIZATION OF GENERAL KNOWLEDGE

This activity serves to demonstrate some of the ways in which general knowledge about the world is organized in memory.

Spend approximately two minutes trying to memorize the list of words below. As soon as the time is up, cover the words and write down as many as you can, in any order, on a piece of paper.

Car	Apple	Dog	Iron	Banana
Mouse	Zinc	Truck	Copper	Bicycle
Pear	Horse	Boat	Silver	Spider
Cherry	Grape	Fish	Gold	Plane

You may observe a certain *pattern* in the responses you have created. We are not really interested here in how many you recalled, although you might like to go back and check. Typically, adults reproduce word lists like these in *semantic categories* where the words share some aspect of their meaning with one another. In the above list the semantic categories are animals, metals, modes of transport and fruits. You will probably have found that you produced *clusters* of words from the different categories rather than reproducing them in the randomized order in which they were presented. This suggests that your memory for the words in the original list was being interpreted and making contact with a much larger store of information about what types of objects these words referred to.

Information seems to be organized in at least two different ways: the order in which we acquire it (chronologically), and by meaning (semantically). These methods of organization seem to apply to different types of memory. Chronological organization is used for information of a personal nature (things that have happened to you), whereas semantic organization is used for more general knowledge.

Endel Tulving (1972) has characterized these two different types of memory as *episodic* and *semantic* respectively, and argues that they are organized in the ways just described. Although it is not clear whether the two are truly separate, they provide a useful way of describing certain aspects of memory use and development. If the distinction is a real one, then it is possible that the systems develop in different ways.

1.2 Knowing about knowing

The last activity should have made it clear that, in addition to knowing a large amount of information, you are also good at organizing it. In fact, it can be argued that some of the changes we will observe in later sections on how memory improves throughout development are the result of an increasing ability to organize and reflect on memory processes rather than a simple increase in the available capacity.

In addition to our ability to organize our memories, we also seem to be extremely good at discriminating between what we know and don't know, an ability that has been termed *meta-memory*.

RESEARCH SUMMARY 1
META-MEMORY

Lachman *et al.* (1979) presented adult subjects with general knowledge questions. They were instructed to answer the questions only if they knew the answer, otherwise to respond 'don't know'. Later, they were given the questions they had responded 'don't know' to again, and asked to indicate which of the following they felt was true:

(i)   they could recognize the answer when shown it;

(ii) perhaps they knew the answer;

(iii) they definitely did not know the answer.

This was termed 'feeling of knowing'. Later still, subjects were again presented with the questions they had originally responded 'don't know' to, but this time they were given four possible answers, one of which was correct. They were asked to indicate which one they thought was correct, and also to say how confident they were that they were right. The results are shown in Figure 2.

(Lachman, Lachman and Thronesbery, 1979)

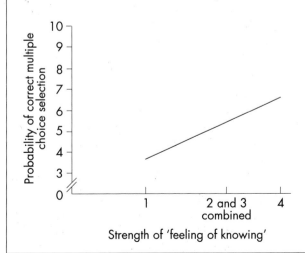

FIGURE 2 The relationship between knowing (probability of correct multiple choice selection) and confidence (strength of 'feeling of knowing'). (Adapted from Lachman, Lachman and Thronesbery, 1979.)

S G

The results show that the more confident you are about knowing something, the more likely you are to know it. This may seem obvious at first, but it tells us something interesting about memory – that we are good at knowing what we know and what we don't know.

1.3 How does memory develop?

What sorts of questions can we ask about how memory develops? It is clear that memory is not just a 'big box' into which goes everything we know. It consists of many different kinds of facts and experiences and includes complex organizational schemes. It has been said that the study of memory is just *applied cognition* because ultimately all psychological processes make use of memory. Talking about memory and how it develops, then, is a central issue in cognitive development.

Turning to questions about development, we might like to ask whether children's memories are inferior to those of adults. If so, are the differences observed between children and adults a function of adults' greater capacity, or their greater ability to make use of that capacity? If children's limitations are more due to how memory is used as opposed to its capacity, would it be possible to train children to use their memories more efficiently?

The development of memory obviously involves huge *quantitative* changes – the older we are, the more we know. This fact is really an issue about what and how we learn. In this chapter, we will explore whether there are *qualitative* changes in how memory works. Is the development of memory like the development of intellect, where the cognitive processes in children are sometimes radically different from those in adults? We know that the total amount of information in memory increases as we grow older, but need now to investigate whether the actual nature of memory – the way in which it is organized and used – also changes.

The next two sections are devoted to examining some of the major theoretical frameworks which have been put forward as explanations of memory. At all points we will be examining what the models say about how memory might develop, and how their predictions stand up to the experimental evidence. The models outlined in Section 2 all see memory as being an *information processing system*, that is a series of processes which handle information in various forms and organize it in different ways. Section 3 looks at an entirely different class of model, which you may have heard referred to as *neural networks*. Neural networks offer some fascinating insights into how brain-like structures may acquire knowledge and develop memory.

The activities in this opening section have exposed you to some important features of psychological research into memory. In Activity 1 you attempted to remember events from your own life experience – an investigation of your personal memories occurring naturally in an everyday context. In Activity 2, by contrast, you were presented with material to be remembered, and were then 'tested' on the effectiveness of your memory and recall (albeit in a fairly uncontrolled manner). Section 2 is concerned with this latter approach, and examines how well-controlled laboratory experiments on memory have led to the development of psychological models. Many psychologists, however, have adopted the first method, arguing that it is *ecologically valid*, making sense to the subject in an everyday context. Section 5 looks at models of 'everyday' memory and asks whether the more controlled scientific approach has unnaturally restricted the study of memory.

SUMMARY OF SECTION 1

- Memories of our earliest years are affected by infantile amnesia – a general lack of memory.
- Memory for individual events (episodic memory) seems to be organized in chronological order.
- Memory for facts (semantic memory), in contrast, seems to be organized by meaning.
- As well as knowing a great deal, we are also good at knowing what we know and what we don't know. Adult meta-memory is a highly developed skill.

2 INFORMATION PROCESSING AND MODELS OF MEMORY

Most of the work on human memory has taken place within the *information processing paradigm*. This approach classifies the mind as a set of processes which store and process information about the individual and the world he or she inhabits. The approach sees several important distinctions arising in memory.

- First, we need to describe *encoding*, the process of taking information about the world and converting it into a memory.
- Second, we need to look at *storage*, which is the way in which information is represented within the brain.
- Finally, we must take account of *retrieval*, which is how information in memory is made available to us.

A failure to remember can be due to a failure at any of these three stages; an encoding failure would mean the information was never placed into memory, a storage failure would mean it was not stored in a usable fashion, and a retrieval failure would mean the information, although 'in there', was not available. Even the simple notion of 'not knowing' or 'forgetting' is therefore more complex than it might at first appear.

2.1 The modal model of memory

In order to begin examining how memory is organized, we will look at a simple information processing model. An excellent example of this is the modal model of memory, which is shown in Figure 3. The model is really an amalgamation of several different models and ideas. It is an overly simple model, but one which captures certain important features of memory.

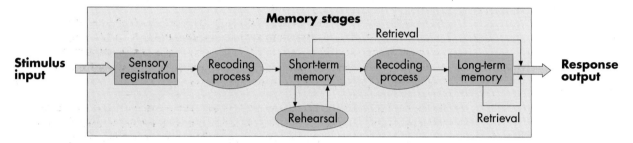

FIGURE 3 The modal model of memory. (Roth, 1990, p. 596, figure 12.10.)

The modal model sees the memory system in terms of three main processes, or stores, with intervening stages that alter the nature of the information passed between them.

The first stage, the sensory registration stage, holds information that has just entered the cognitive system. Examples are sounds and images. The information is in a 'raw' state – the only thing which has been done to it is to convert it from information in the environment (light or sounds, etc.) into electrical activity in the brain. In this form, the information is useless. For example, information from the eyes arrives in the brain in the form of 'blobs' and 'edges' of light and dark. These simple features of the visual environment are a far cry from the complex objects we eventually perceive. However, because the study of sensory registration is as much to do with physiology as psychology, we will not pursue it here.

2.2 The short-term store

The short-term store is the memory you use when you are remembering a telephone number, or calculating a shopping bill. It can typically hold around seven items of information (the 'magic number seven' – Miller, 1956), although this varies both with the individual and also with what you might call an 'item'. For example, for the author 21011966 is a single item of information because it is his date of birth; for you it may be a meaningless string of digits.

The lifespan of information in the short-term store is fairly variable. Usually, information will be forgotten within six to twelve seconds. However, this can be extended by using various strategies, the most important of which is *rehearsal*, which is simply repeating the contents of the short-term store either out loud or in your head. By using this strategy the duration of short-term memory can be extended indefinitely.

Do we know anything about how short-term memory develops? The capacity of adult short-term memory seems to be about seven items; is the same true of children?

 One way of measuring short-term memory is to use the *digit span test*. A series of digits (e.g. 729436) is read to a person, who has to repeat them back in the same order. The number of digits is gradually increased until errors are made. An adult will usually be able to remember from seven to nine digits presented in this way.

Research indicates that digit span increases with age. For example, 5 year olds can recall about four or five digits whereas 9 year olds manage about six (Dempster, 1981). There is a certain amount of variation in these numbers, but on average there is a definite trend for an increase in short-term memory capacity.

Does this mean that the capacity of short-term memory increases as we get older? Not necessarily – it is quite possible that young children have the same capacity as adults, but have not yet developed the ability to make effective use of it. In other words, the limitations may be because children have adult *capacity* but lack adult *strategies*.

Short-term memory is not a system divorced from the rest of memory. The fact that we can use strategies to improve our short-term memory suggests that information in long-term memory can have an effect on short-term memory. Where, after all, are the strategies stored if not in long-term memory? The modal model glosses over the relationship between long- and short-term memory, and also says nothing about the complexity of the short-term store. In addition to storing digits, we also memorize many other types of information for short periods of time, including sensory data such as visual and tactile information, the results of calculations, and maps of where we are in a town or building. In order to provide an adequate account of even the short-term store we have to give a more detailed account than the modal model offers us.

2.3 The development of strategy in short-term memory

If memory limitations are due to a lack of strategies rather than a lack of capacity, then we ought to be able to train children to improve their memories. Is there any evidence that this is possible? Taken that strategies such as rehearsal do eventually appear, a good place to start would be to identify when this happens. Does the strategy come into play suddenly, or does it develop slowly over a period of time? If it develops, what, if anything, can be done to speed it up?

Early research into the application of strategies indicated that spontaneous rehearsal first appears around the age of 7 (Flavell, Beach and Chinsky, 1966). Using a task where subjects had to reconstruct a model from pictures, Hashimoto (1991) found that children became aware of using a strategy around the age of 7, and that this awareness was clearly apparent around the age of 9. Once rehearsal starts to be used appropriately, it appears that the only difference between children and adults is in the *amount* of information they can rehearse. The rehearsal capacity of 10 year olds is only about 80 per cent of that of adults.

It is interesting to note that 10 year olds can also only *speak* about 80 per cent as quickly as adults. Furthermore, it appears that the capacity of short-term memory is linked to the speed of speech – the faster you speak, the more information you can rehearse. From these two observations, it appears as if the differences in rehearsal between adults and children are due to the speed of speech as opposed to the capacity of short-term memory. Recent work by Hulme and Tordoff (1989) has supported this position. Although the rehearsal capacity of their 4 to 10 year old subjects increased with age, this was matched by an increase in the rate of speech.

When a sample of children of different ages was given a list of pictures and told that they were only going to be tested on pictures drawn from the second half of the set, 15 to 18 year olds only rehearsed those in the second half. Eleven year olds, by contrast, did not make this distinction, choosing to rehearse *all* the information (Bray, Hersh and Turner, 1985). Therefore, while younger children can and do make use of rehearsal, it is only in adolescence that the strategy is modified to fit the task's demands. It is as if the younger children have realized that rehearsal is a useful strategy, but do not yet understand how best to apply it.

Taken that the development of rehearsal passes through at least two stages (the acquisition of the skill followed by the acquisition of the ability to use the skill selectively and flexibly), perhaps it is possible to teach young children both how to rehearse, and when rehearsal should be used.

In another experiment, Keeney, Cannizzo and Flavell (1967) trained 6 and 7 year olds who did not spontaneously rehearse to do so by telling them to whisper the words they were being asked to remember. They found that performance on short-term memory tasks was superior to that of a control group of children who had not received training. However, the children did not maintain their new-found skills and failed to rehearse outside the test situation. They had acquired the skill but could not see the point in applying it. Research Summary 2 gives another example of research in this area.

The position seems to be that, although children's short-term memories are in many senses comparable to those of adults, they do not possess the powerful strategies which allow adults to make fuller use of this capacity. One convincing example that children's short-term memories are limited by understanding rather than capacity comes from a study by Michelene Chi in 1978 (see Research Summary 3).

RESEARCH SUMMARY 2
THE DEVELOPMENT OF STRATEGY

Children aged 4, 7 and 11 years old were shown a series of pictures and either told or not told to try to remember them. The instructions had no effect on either behaviour or performance for the 4 year olds. For the 11 year olds, those told they should memorize the stimuli both engaged in more mnemonic-type activities such as rehearsal, and showed greater recall. The 7 year olds produced the most interesting results. Although the instructions had the effect of generating more rehearsal in those told to remember the pictures, this behaviour did not lead to improved recall. This is clear evidence that although children may be aware of the increased effort needed to recall information, and may have knowledge of the strategies by which this may be accomplished, their application of strategic processing may be inefficient and ineffectual.

(Appel *et al.*, 1972)

RESEARCH SUMMARY 3
WHEN CHILDREN OUTPERFORM ADULTS

Adults and 10-year-old children were tested on two separate tasks. The first was a digit span task which generated the usual results in finding that the adults recalled around eight items and the 10 year olds only about six.

The second task involved a series of chess pieces arranged on a chessboard. The adults and 10 year olds had to reproduce this pattern from memory on a blank board. In this case, the children scored on average over nine correct whereas the adults only managed six.

The significant feature of this experiment was that the children, but not the adults, were expert chess players. The knowledge of the rules of chess which the children possessed allowed them to spot patterns in the arrangement of the chess pieces which the adults could not see. It is notable that the effect disappears when the pieces are arranged at random.

(Chi, 1978)

The superior performance of the children in Chi's chess experiment demonstrates that differences in short-term memory between adults and children are almost certainly due to the application of strategies rather than rigid capacity limitations. This and the other findings allow us to put forward a sequence of how rehearsal develops. The strategy first appears around the age of 7 (although it should be emphasized that actual ages may differ vastly for individuals). It can be taught at earlier ages, but this does not enable children to apply their skill to new situations. Up until the age of about 10 or 11, this activity does not facilitate their performance to any appreciable degree. It is only after the age of 12 or so that the ability to rehearse and the understanding of how this ability should be applied come together and performance reaches adult levels.

2.4 The long-term store

We have already considered some of the complexities of the long-term memory system in Section 1. It was suggested that there are at least two kinds of organization in long-term memory. Personal (episodic) information is stored in a chronological fashion, with events being linked to when and where they occurred. Factual (semantic) information is stored in semantic categories, where concepts with similar or associated meanings are stored together.

The question of organization has prompted the greatest amount of research into long-term memory. The modal model (Figure 3) represents long-term memory as a single 'box'. Although there may actually be only one long-term store, this undoubtedly involves numerous types of representation, several types of organization, and many ways of extracting information. The contents of the 'box' are vast, and vastly complicated. Assuming that we never stop learning, they are also continually changing.

Although the capacity of long-term memory may be fixed, it never seems to run out. There seems to be plenty left over to ensure that, although it may seem to get more difficult as we grow older, we can still learn new facts and skills. During early development, and indeed throughout the entire lifespan, our long-term memories are continually being augmented. Even though we may leave formal education far behind, it is true to say that we never stop learning. Is the development of long-term memory merely the start of a process that will continue throughout life?

Models of long-term memory have tended to concentrate on organizational and representational aspects. They seek to provide answers to several related problems:

- how different types of information are held in memory;
- how they are linked to one another;
- how accessing one memory enables us to access others.

2.5 Schema theory

An important concept to grasp in the understanding of long-term memory is that of the *schema*. Memory schemas, which are similar but not identical to the sense in which Piaget used them, are discrete units of information which relate to a typical object or event in the world. The schema framework was first put forward by Frederick Bartlett (1932), who was interested in the ways in which memory was a *construction* rather than a *copy* of the information that is presented.

Schemas incorporate everything we know about a subject or object. For example, you should by now have a fairly well-defined schema about chapters in this book. Each contains a list of objectives, and sections containing text, research summaries and activities. On encountering each section you have a clear idea of what it is designed to communicate. Schemas come in all shapes and sizes, and are certainly not restricted to knowledge about the structure of textbook chapters. In addition to factual schemas, we also possess schemas about events such as picnics and going out to work, skills such as driving a car or playing the piano, and objects such as dogs and armadillos. Schemas are a way of representing all the different types of knowledge we possess.

As well as supplying a base of knowledge, schemas also provide a framework within which new information can be processed. Your knowledge of the structure of research summaries in this book enables you to process the information within them in a particular way – notably learning about a particular experiment or methodology.

In addition to being a storage mechanism, schemas can affect how information is processed and remembered. William James quotes an example of a man going upstairs to change for dinner (this was in the 19th century) and rather than getting into his dinner suit after taking his clothes off, climbing into bed instead (James, 1890). Other examples include going into the kitchen to fetch something and finding yourself washing up. Actions such as these indicate that a great deal of behaviour is under the control of schemas, and that sometimes schemas can cause us to act inappropriately. Research Summary 4 describes how such 'slips of action' have been investigated.

RESEARCH SUMMARY 4
SLIPS OF ACTION

Jim Reason studied what he terms 'action slips' – activities which 'go wrong' for various reasons, all to do with the psychology of the individual performing them. He used diary studies where he asked subjects to keep a daily account of events such as these. From a database of over 400 such occurrences he was able to identify several categories of error.

Many of the examples he has documented are all too familiar to most of us, such as intending to drive somewhere only to find you have mistakenly gone to work or somewhere else you travel to frequently.

(Reason, 1979)

One explanation of action slips is that we possess schemas for certain well-practised and familiar actions, such as driving to work. When a schema becomes activated in appropriate circumstances, it can sometimes 'take over' your actions. This is why you may find yourself driving along a familiar route rather than the one you intended – the 'driving to work' schema seizes control as soon as your attention is turned elsewhere.

Just as action schemas might take over your actions, so schema-like memories for events (called *scripts*) might influence how you remember events. A script for a restaurant might include information about waiters, who pays the bill, how long you might expect to wait to be served, and so on. Numerous experiments have demonstrated how information in scripts can influence what is remembered about an event. Bull and Barnes (1995) consider this in the context of children as witnesses. We will look at event memory in Section 5.

You may be asking what function schemas serve if they produce such maladaptive behaviour. The reason why schemas develop is that they normally serve a useful purpose. As with many areas of psychology, the ways in which behaviour is studied often concentrate on its failures as opposed to its successes. Nearly all behaviour is characterized by the sensible application of schemas which presumably make information more accessible and also free us from the repetitive demands of time-consuming activities. The 'automatic' nature of schematic actions also frees our memories to do other things, such as talking or listening to music while we are driving.

2.6 Semantic network models

The experience of action slips illustrates the interconnected nature of memory. Memory is not a compartmentalized system of discrete files, but is rather a massively interconnected web of information. For example your 'dog' schema might have information in it along the lines of 'refer to domestic pets', a schema which contains pertinent information.

FIGURE 4 The spreading activation model. (Roth, 1990, p. 610; adapted from Collins and Loftus, 1975, p. 412.)

A model which is concerned with the links between concepts rather than the concepts themselves was put forward by Collins and Loftus (1975). They produced what is termed a *semantic network*. An example of a fragment of a possible semantic network is given in Figure 4.

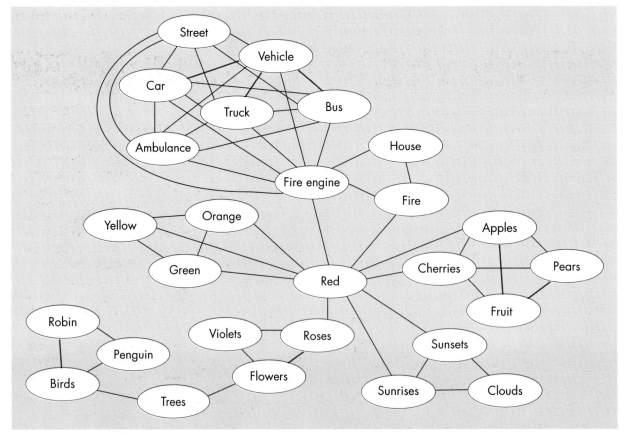

The connections between the concepts (or *nodes*) in the network specify the relationships between them. So, for instance, the link connecting the 'fire engine' node to the 'red' node would be a 'has colour' link. The link from 'cherry' to 'fruit' would be an 'is a' link, and so on.

Links also have strengths, in that concepts can be more or less strongly associated with one another. For example, fire engines are almost always red, so the link from fire engine to red would be very strong. Apples are only sometimes red, so the apple to red link would be somewhat weaker.

The semantic network captures the interconnectedness of memory. There is no such thing as a fact in isolation from all others. A great deal of memory is *associative* – one concept or fact is activated, and this in turn partially activates the concepts to which it is linked in a process known as *spreading activation*. Word associations and Activity 2 on semantic clustering in recall are examples of behaviour predicted by this model.

One way in which the emerging structure of semantic memory can be investigated is to look at how this organization is spontaneously used in rehearsal. In Activity 2 you probably found that you used your conceptual memory to aid your recall of the words. At what age does this ability manifest itself? As with normal rehearsal, it does not seem to appear until quite late in childhood, and interestingly is more often found in cultures where children are involved in formal education. The importance of interconnected semantic networks in remembering complex information over relatively long periods of time is illustrated in Research Summary 5.

RESEARCH SUMMARY 5
JURASSIC NETWORK

Chi and Koeske (1983) studied the memory of a 4½-year-old boy (the son of one of the researchers) who was interested in dinosaurs. This subject is useful because it involves a lot of structure in terms of different types of dinosaur (flesh eaters versus plant eaters, armoured dinosaurs, flying dinosaurs etc.), and information is likely to be represented as some form of semantic network.

The child's memory was tested for two sets of dinosaurs, one set well known and one less well known. This distinction was made by both asking his mother which dinosaurs he knew best and which were mentioned most frequently in his nine books on dinosaurs. There was a high agreement between both measurements of familiarity.

Two memory tests were used. In the first, the child had to recall a list of 20 dinosaur names (either well known or less well known) after hearing them. The second test took place a year later, and involved the child naming the dinosaurs from pictures.

It was assumed that all 40 dinosaurs which the child knew about were held in one network, but that the better known dinosaurs were more strongly and more extensively linked to one another than the less well known ones. This was supported by examining how the child responded in the first memory test. If two dinosaurs were mentioned in fairly rapid succession (less than ten seconds between naming) then it was assumed that the two were linked in some way. Based on this assumption, it was clear that the well known dinosaurs were more interlinked than the less well known ones.

During the second test phase, the child correctly named 11 out of 20 well known dinosaurs, but only 2 out of 20 less well known ones. The fact that he could originally name all 40 dinosaurs illustrated that the superior interlinking of the well known dinosaurs was leading to greater retention in memory, and that even at this young age he possessed a sophisticated network.

(Chi and Koeske, 1983)

Schema theory and network models produce similar accounts of infantile amnesia. Both assume that new information is interpreted with regard to that which is already held in memory. If there isn't much to go on (for example, few well-developed schemas, or a sketchy and incomplete semantic network), memories will not be well retained and we might expect a period of amnesia which would be terminated by the acquisition of sufficiently complex memory representations. As will be discussed in Section 5, one theory sees infantile amnesia as being the result of early memories forming the basis for general schemas, a process which 'strips' the memory of its detail. What is being retained in the early years, according to this theory, is a general conceptual structure for interpreting the world as opposed to specific memories about it. Episodic memories are 'sacrificed' by the developing memory system in order to produce semantic memory. The model outlined in the next section describes one way in which this might occur.

SUMMARY OF SECTION 2

- The information processing approach has provided a framework for theorizing about memory systems.
- Memory can be divided into short- and long-term memory. Changes in the apparent size of short-term memory as children grow older seem to be due to changes in strategy rather than a general capacity increase.
- Semantic memory can be thought of as an interconnected network of *schemas*, semi-independent packets of knowledge about specific objects or events.
- Schemas guide processing and may sometimes lead to slips of action when they take over responsibility for behaviour.
- Semantic networks model the interconnectedness of memory. They provide an account of the links between memories as opposed to the nature of the memories themselves.

3 THE CONNECTIONIST APPROACH

A recent approach to modelling memory marks a radical shift away from traditional 'box and arrow' models and offers a new way of thinking about memory. Although discussions about connectionism can become complicated, the approach has particular application to memory and development and an introduction is essential. In the text that follows, the technical side of connectionism is described in boxes while the surrounding text examines what it can tell us about the development of memory.

WHAT IS A CONNECTIONIST NETWORK?

A connectionist network consists of a set of very simple processing *units*. Units take in inputs from other units, calculate the sum of these, and then send this sum as outputs to more units. Units are linked to one another via *connections*.

All processing in a connectionist network consists of units sending signals to one another. Through this very simple mechanism, quite complex behaviour can emerge when sufficient numbers of units are linked together.

A connectionist network bears some similarities to the brain. The brain is a highly interconnected set of simple processing units (nerve cells) which connect to thousands of others by means of synapses. For this reason connectionist models are often referred to as *neural nets*.

One of the early connectionist networks was a model of conceptual memory. A description of this model serves to illustrate more fully both how connectionism works, and how very powerful ideas can emerge from simple premises.

3.1 McClelland and Rumelhart's distributed model of memory

McClelland and Rumelhart (1985) describe a simple computer model of conceptual memory which they believe provides a good account of how one aspect of human memory – the representation of object schemas or *prototypes* – can be modelled. Their model illustrates some of the important aspects of connectionism.

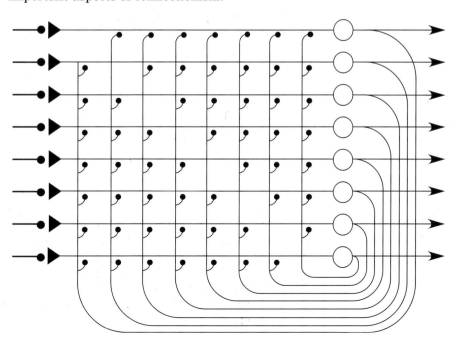

FIGURE 5
A connectionist network with eight units. (McClelland and Rumelhart, 1985, p. 162.)

HOW DOES A CONNECTIONIST NETWORK WORK?

The McClelland and Rumelhart network consists of 24 units, each of which is connected to all the others by a connection which has a strength, or *weight*. For the sake of simplicity, a smaller network consisting of only eight units is shown in Figure 5.

The model is designed to recognize stimuli. Because the model is quite simple, and does not have eyes or ears, these stimuli take the form of a series of numbers, one for each unit. When the network is 'shown' a stimulus, each unit becomes activated by the relevant amount. For example, the network might receive the input

$(+1 \ +1 \ -1 \ -1 \ +1 \ +1 \ -1 \ -1)$.

This means that the first two units each receive an input of +1, the third and fourth −1, and so on. We can think of this stimulus as a simple representation of an object.

Although technically incorrect, it might help to think about the value of each unit as indicating how confident the unit is that its aspect of the stimulus is present. So if a unit represented, say, the presence of brown eyes in a stimulus, then a value of +1 would mean that the network was certain that the stimulus had brown eyes, a value of +0.8 would mean it was pretty confident, and a value of 0 would mean it had no idea. A value of −1 might then represent complete confidence that the stimulus did *not* have brown eyes.

The model works on 'ticks' of a clock or timing cycle. On every tick the following events occur (each is described in more detail below). First, each unit calculates its activation level from all the inputs it is receiving. Second, it sends this activation to the units it is connected to. This process is repeated a number of times until the network reaches a stable state, at which point the connections between units are altered so as to make the network more accurate.

It is important to realize that the network is not 'seeing' or 'hearing' anything, but is instead being given information in a form which it can process. This is not such an artificial situation as you may think. Our eyes, for instance, convert information in the form of light into electrical activity in the brain. Information in the brain is therefore in a very different format from its 'natural' state. In a sense, numbers are very similar to the type of information the brain deals with.

The next two boxes tell you how the network processes the information it is presented with.

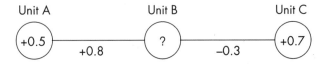

FIGURE 6   Three processing units linked together.

HOW DOES A UNIT CALCULATE ITS ACTIVATION LEVEL?

The numbers inside each unit in Figure 6 represent each unit's activation level. Unit B's is unknown. The numbers on the links between the units are the connection strengths.

Unit B receives activation from units A and C. (Normally it would also send activation back to them, but for clarity's sake these links have been omitted.) Unit A has an activation level of +0.5, and the strength of the connection from it to unit B is +0.8 (an *excitatory connection*). To find out how much activation unit B receives from unit A, we simply multiply these together.

+0.5 × +0.8 = +0.4

Unit B therefore receives +0.4 activation from unit A. If there were no other inputs to unit B, its activation level would be +0.4.

ACTIVITY 3

Allow about 10 minutes

CALCULATING ACTIVATION LEVELS

Now that you have seen how to calculate the signal from A to B, try calculating how much input unit B receives from unit C. Once you have done this, add up the inputs from units A and C to calculate the activation level of unit B.

Comment

Unit C has an activation level of +0.7, and the strength of the connection from it to unit B is –0.3 (an *inhibitory connection*). Unit B therefore receives +0.7 × –0.3 = –0.21 activation from unit C.

Adding the total inputs to unit B, +0.4 from unit A plus –0.21 from unit C gives a total of +0.19. This is the new activation level of unit B, which it will then send out to all the units it is connected to.

HOW DOES THE NETWORK PROCESS INFORMATION?

Once a unit has calculated its activation value, it sends this activation along all of the connections it has with other units. This can cause the other units to become more or less active depending on whether the connections have positive or negative weights. Positive weights cause excitation, negative weights cause inhibition.

After this cycle has been repeated about 50 times, the network will settle down to a stable pattern of activation across all the units. At this point, the state of the units will represent the *output* of the network.

Suppose that the network was presented with the stimulus

(+1 +1 –1 –1 +1 +1 –1 –1).

We will assume that activation levels can vary between –1 and +1. At first, the output of the network will be

(+0.5 +0.5 –0.5 –0.5 +0.5 +0.5 –0.5 –0.5),

as all the connections are the same. You do not need to understand why the network ends up like this – there is a certain amount of mathematics which governs its behaviour but which space precludes us from examining.

After a period of time during which units are continually sending signals to one another, the network will settle into a stable state, with the activation levels of all the units hardly changing at all. At this point, a comparison can be made between what the network has produced, and what it is supposed to have produced. This comparison enables us to see whether the network, with all its connections and weights, is able to reproduce the stimulus. Why this is such an important property of the network will become clear later.

The three diagrams in Figure 7 show the state of the network (a) when it is presented with a stimulus, (b) after processing but before any adjustment of connection strengths has taken place (see box below), and (c) after adjustment. (For the sake of clarity, all connections between the units have been omitted.)

(a) Network presented with stimulus

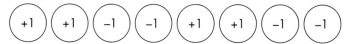

FIGURE 7 An illustration of the output state of an eight unit network, showing how it learns to recognize a stimulus. (a) Network presented with stimulus; (b) network after processing but before adjustment; (c) network after adjustment.

(b) Network after processing but before adjustment

(c) Network after adjustment

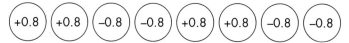

HOW DOES A CONNECTIONIST NETWORK LEARN?

After the network has settled into a stable state, the weights on the connections are altered slightly using a mathematical equation which makes the output more accurate. Although this may seem like 'fiddling the books', it is in fact based on neurophysiological theories of learning which state that a change in the strength of the connections between nerve cells is the basic process underpinning all memory. Changing the weights on the connections between units is analogous to this.

As can be seen from the initial sample output of the network (Figure 7(b)), all the outputs are in the right direction (positive when they should be positive, negative when they should be negative), but they are not particularly strong. In order to make them closer to the input, the weights can be increased or decreased, as necessary. This means that next time the network is presented with the same stimulus, its output will be closer to it than before.

For instance, units 1 and 2 should both have activation levels of +1. In order to make the network more accurate, the strength of the connection between them should be strengthened. Next time the network is presented with the stimulus, the units will activate each other more, and their output will be closer to +1. Likewise, the connection between units 2 and 3 should be made more negative, so that next time the output of unit 3 will be nearer −1.

3.2 Connectionism and child development

So far this discussion has concentrated on what the network learns and how it goes about learning, but what does all this have to do with child development? After repeated presentations of the stimulus, followed by small adjustments in the strengths of the connection between the units, the network makes successively closer approximations to the input stimulus. In state (c) from Figure 7, the network can be considered to have 'recognized' the stimulus. Because this ability has been acquired through time, we can say that the network has *learned* to recognize the stimulus.

A single network can learn several stimuli. Although it recognizes all the stimuli it has been presented with, it recognizes the average of these most strongly of all. Notice that it has never been presented with the average example, but has somehow learned it from the examples it has seen. This 'average example' corresponds closely to what is termed a *prototype* (see Chapter 4, p. 125, for details on prototypes). Without being told to, the model manages to extract a prototype from a series of examples.

Suggesting that conceptual representation is just a mathematical process seems to remove it from the realm of psychology. Is there any evidence to suggest that this 'averaging' process is similar to what goes on in human memory? Research Summary 5 suggests there might be.

RESEARCH SUMMARY 5
PROTOTYPES AS AVERAGES

Ten-month-old infants were shown fourteen faces each for five seconds, and then given pairs of faces which they could look at. Evidence from other research suggests that the more recognizable a face is to an infant, the less time it should be looked at for.

A face that was the average of all the fourteen others, but which the infants had never seen before, was more familiar (looked at for less time) than either:

(a) a completely novel face, or

(b) a face which was made up of non-averaged features from the fourteen test faces.

In other words, the infants' memory systems had extracted the prototypical face from this group, and recognized it more strongly than the others, even though they had never seen its features before, and the other faces had been constructed from features which they had seen before. The memory which the infants had developed for the faces therefore seemed to be based on averaging the features of all the examples they had seen.

(Strauss, 1979)

Using quite simple mathematical and statistical ideas, the connectionist network produces behaviour which seems quite close to aspects of human learning. Other networks have examined other types of learning; for instance, Rumelhart and McClelland (1986; the same two researchers who produced the model of conceptual memory described above) looked at learning the past tense of English verbs. Although their findings have been hotly contested, the model appeared to make some of the same mistakes that children make in learning to speak. (This work is discussed in more detail in Chapter 2, Section 5.)

The model of conceptual memory makes an important point about the relationship between semantic and episodic memory. Prototypes are an aspect of semantic memory. The model demonstrates a possible way in which episodic memories (individual examples) can produce a prototype (semantic memory). Semantic memory is an *emergent property* of episodic memory. Because of the way the network operates, similar examples are combined into a prototype. In other words, you get a semantic memory system 'for free'. It isn't a separate system at all, but a very useful by-product of the way our memory works.

If this is the case, and semantic memory is constructed from episodic memory, then children may have very complex stores of episodic information without necessarily having much semantic knowledge. If we wish to look at very early memory, we should concentrate on episodic information, perhaps in the form of memory for specific events, since this is more likely to be preserved in infants.

SUMMARY OF SECTION 3

- The connectionist account offers a different way of looking at memory in terms of large collections of very simple processing units affecting and being affected by each other.
- It suggests that semantic and episodic memory are aspects of the same underlying process, with the former emerging from the latter.
- Some developmental data suggest that the mathematical rules used in connectionist networks may approximate what happens to infants as they learn about their environment.

4 THE STATUS OF PSYCHOLOGICAL MODELS

Sections 2 and 3 have looked at a number of different psychological models of memory, all of which have strengths and weaknesses. We will now attempt to look at the overall picture of these models, and place them in the context of what they can and cannot be expected to achieve.

There is a great deal of philosophical debate about the relationship of models such as these to the actual workings of the brain. Models such as the modal model, the schema framework and semantic networks are all *functional* accounts, that is they attempt to describe what is happening in memory without saying precisely what goes on in the brain.

Connectionist models are more difficult to characterize. Some researchers believe they really are models of how the brain works whereas others see the neural analogy as at best loose, and at worst misleading.

One thing is clear: by looking at connectionist accounts we abandon the clear flow of information that is central to the more traditional models. It is hard to see a direction in which information flows in a connectionist network – it is just there, flowing around and through the entire system.

We are not yet at the stage of being able to say with any degree of certainty how memory operates in the brain. Although the neural representation of information is almost certainly held in the patterns and strengths of connections between nerve cells, this is as far as our knowledge of neuroscience has taken us. The point at which neuro-science and psychology can really begin to inform one another has yet to be reached. To quote Stephen Rose (Professor of Biology at The Open University):

> We know damn all about memories once they are made, and still less about the process of recalling or forgetting them.
>
> (*Guardian*, 27 May 1993)

Perhaps the greatest criticism of the approaches outlined in Sections 2 and 3 is that all these models and experiments tend to concentrate on the similarities between people rather than the differences. By looking at the structure and organization of the memory system rather than its contents, we are biased towards producing explanations which view all people in much the same way. The lack of *ecological validity* which characterizes much of the experimental work on memory clouds the fact that, to a great extent, differences between people are differences in their memories. The next section takes us away from the laboratory and, as far as possible, out into the real world.

SUMMARY OF SECTION 4

- The relationship between models of memory development and the way in which the brain itself develops is complex and controversial.

5 EVERYDAY MEMORY

An additional criticism of the models of memory dealt with in Sections 2 and 3 is that they are not concerned with the *purposes* of memory but dedicate themselves to its *processes*. Research in memory, although revealing some of the processes which operate when we remember and, to a lesser extent, forget, has tended to ignore the *contexts* under which memory normally operates. Experiments have focused on word lists and picture memory, tasks which don't have that much relevance to real life. Our memories have presumably evolved to be good at recalling certain events, but not necessarily others. For instance, we might expect that memory for meaningful or significant events is far superior to that for the meaningless types of word or digit lists which have occupied so much of psychologists' time.

In a seminal paper, Ulric Neisser (1978) made essentially this point, and urged psychologists to begin looking much more carefully at how memory operates in the real world. This plea prompted the blossoming of the study of *everyday* and *autobiographical* memory, and has special implications for the study of memory development. Although there are subtle differences between these two terms, we will use them in a general sense to refer to memories for naturally occurring events.

Martin Conway (1990) argues that the very act of remembering, and the sensation which accompanies this, only occurs for episodic memories. You are not aware of 'remembering' that Paris is the capital of France, but if you have ever been there you can probably remember what you did during your stay. This is a return to the episodic and semantic distinction. Episodic memories give rise to the feeling of remembering whereas semantic memory is just 'knowledge'. You *know* that J. F. Kennedy was assassinated on 22 November 1963 (well, you might) but you *remember* where you were at the time. Is this simply because episodic memory is tied to a time and place, and is therefore an altogether more detailed memory trace than a single fact divorced from context? Endel Tulving (1983) has argued that autobiographical memory and episodic memory are one and the same thing. If remembering really is all about episodic memory, then it would be fruitful to examine this rather than the semantic memory typically studied in laboratory experiments.

The most common technique for examining autobiographical memory has been to examine *event memory*. This is children's and adults' memories for events which they have witnessed or taken part in. By examining how memories for naturally occurring events are formed and represented, it is argued that we can move towards a greater understanding of how memory really works.

5.1 Studies of event memory

What can we learn from looking at young children's event memory? The overall picture that has emerged from the studies on memory conducted in the laboratory is that children's memory is no worse than adults', but the ways in which it is applied are relatively unsophisticated. Whether through limitations of understanding, practice, or speed of thought or speech, children perform consistently worse than adults for reasons which are not directly to do with memory.

The picture which emerges from studies on event memory is remarkably similar. It seems that memory is not a limiting factor at any stage of development, but rather that other developmental processes are responsible for the apparent gap between children and adults.

The complexity of early event memory also raises questions about why infantile amnesia exists. One explanation that has been put forward provides a useful starting point for the description of early event memory. As was first mentioned in Section 2, it has been argued that infantile amnesia results from early event memories being used to build general event schemas (Nelson, 1988). These are used to interpret subsequent events and form the basis for the developing semantic memory system. As the general schema is constructed, the distinctive aspects of the original event are 'stripped away', leaving just the core behind. The reason why we are able to recall so little from our early years is that the information we stored has lost its link to real events by being converted into a framework within which subsequent information is processed and stored. It is almost as if, in order to create the building blocks of knowledge which future memories will make use of, early memories are sacrificed by the developing system.

In contrast to this position, it has been found that children as young as 2.5 years show quite detailed memories of events which occurred up to six months previously (Fivush, Gray and Fromhoff, 1987). If Nelson is correct, then we would not expect superficial information to be retained for these lengths of time. The fact that it is suggests that infantile amnesia is not a result of schema formation.

One other possibility is that although memory for events is fairly good, there is no *thematic structure* to the memory traces laid down by young children. Early event memory may not be the highly organized, frequently hierarchical structure we observe in adults, but is rather a disjointed arrangement of images, facts and sensations. While the information is there, it is not readily accessible and does not form an integral part of a larger whole. Although accessible during the early years, these memories will not form part of the emerging semantic memory system and with time will become inaccessible. In terms of the three-stage model put forward earlier, infantile amnesia is characterized by a retrieval problem. The information is represented somewhere, but not in a form that can be accessed.

In order to investigate whether children preserve some form of thematic organization in event memory, it has proved necessary to adopt more controlled forms of experimentation. Research Summary 6 outlines one of the experiments carried out by Ratner, Smith and Padgett (1990).

RESEARCH SUMMARY 6
MAKING CLAY

Ratner and colleagues asked children from 3 to 5 years of age, and adults, to participate in a clay-making activity. The task was structured so that each of five main stages had to occur in a specified order:

- get ready;
- add dry ingredients;
- add wet ingredients;
- mix together;
- clean up.

The organization of the stages was hierarchical in that each main stage involved several sub-stages, for instance:

- *Mix together stage*
  - put clay on table;
  - knead clay;
  - roll clay into a ball.

Even after a single presentation of the clay-making event, the children demonstrated some evidence that they had formed a hierarchically structured representation of it. After a delay of two weeks, seven out of eleven children remembered aspects of the overall organization (the order of the five stages). Also, when prompted to start recalling from the last element in one stage (for instance, 'roll clay into ball' was the last element of the 'mix together' stage), they would start their recall from the next stage, implying that some temporal information had been stored.

(Ratner, Smith and Padgett, 1990)

Hierarchical organization is an important aspect of life, and therefore needs to be accurately represented in memory if we are to negotiate some of the complex social and technological obstacles which confront us. Any action which requires the co-ordination of sequences, or which involves dependencies between actions, must be represented in a suitable fashion. Information about driving a car, going to a restaurant, writing an essay, making a telephone call, and holding a conversation all involve the correct sequencing of component parts. Without some representation of this sequencing, normal activity would be severely disrupted.

One important finding in these studies is that, when asked about an activity, children tend to report more actions associated with *objects* (such as the tools used to mix the clay) whereas adults tend to focus on *goals* (the purpose of each activity). A possible explanation for some of the memory differences is therefore that adults possess a greater *understanding* of the event in terms of the underlying goals. It is this understanding which leads to greater recall. Once again, we return to the idea that the differences between adults and children are found in their level of intellectual understanding rather than their memory.

> It is not that individuals organise events differently because they are young or old; they organise events differently because they *understand* them or not.

(Ratner, Smith and Padgett, 1990, p. 80; emphasis added)

Ratner *et al.* also note that even adults did not always reproduce the events in the hierarchical order in which they had originally been presented. There is therefore no clear distinction between the way in which adults and young children remember information like this. It is not as simple as saying that adults perceive underlying causes and structures of events. The extent to which information is represented causally and hierarchically is a function of understanding. Although children tend to represent information in a more concrete fashion, this is only a tendency and can sometimes be reversed, as evidenced by the study on young chess experts reported in Section 2. At the same time as we are demonstrating the fallibility of children's memories, we should never forget that our own are far from perfect!

The role of understanding in memory has been demonstrated on a number of occasions. For example, Slackman, Hudson and Fivush (1986) showed how children are able to recall causally linked events at an earlier age than unlinked sequences. Notice that if linked sequences are remembered better than unlinked ones, children must have some understanding of the structure of the sequence. Huttenlocher and Lui (1979) found that 3 year olds were better at remembering lists of related information than unrelated items. Again, to produce this result the children must have been capable of applying their understanding of the links between items on the lists.

The extent to which children are applying knowledge and understanding to information can be extremely difficult to measure, and it is important to identify at what point understanding comes to play a part in memory. Even at the age of 2 years children are able to understand simple temporal links, such as the fact that you have to undress a teddy bear before giving it a bath (Bauer and Mandler, 1990). Future research may discover that even children less than 2 years old are using quite sophisticated methods of memorizing and learning. The more detailed and ingenious research into this area becomes, the more children's memories seem capable of. Although children's memories are in some ways different, they are in no real sense inferior to those of adults.

In summary, memory is affected by understanding, and understanding increases with age. When these factors are taken into consideration, the memory differences between adults and children disappear.

5.2 Explaining infantile amnesia

How far have we come towards a cognitive account of infantile amnesia? On the one hand we have very clear evidence that the phenomenon does exist, and yet on the other it is clear that even very young children have highly complex and partially structured representations of events. Is a cognitive account capable of explaining this paradox? Other theories have included such diverse factors as Freudian repression and the possible existence of separate systems in the brain which develop at different rates during childhood. Whichever theory proves to be correct, we are obviously still a long way from understanding exactly what causes infantile amnesia.

5.3 Methodological difficulties

Although the research described above has attempted to study memory in real-life situations, there are problems in interpreting the results generated. One of the advantages of the laboratory-based approach to memory is that the experimenter has a clear idea of the nature of the information to be remembered. To varying extents this disappears when we start to look at memory for naturally occurring events. There are several methodological problems in studying everyday memory, all of which will be examined in the light of an actual experience as reported below in Activity 4.

ACTIVITY 4

Allow about 15 minutes

MEASURING AUTOBIOGRAPHICAL MEMORY

This activity introduces you to some of the problems with measuring autobiographical memory. Read the account and try to list problems with verifying whether this is an accurate memory or not.

'When I was 4 years old I went for a walk to an abbey near Leeds with my parents. During the walk it began to rain and I quickly developed a fever. My father ran back to the car and drove me home where he made me drink hot milk and brandy. The doctor said I had bronchitis. I haven't been able to touch brandy or hot milk since.'

You might like to repeat this exercise with an event from your own past. Does this make the task easier or more difficult?

Comment

You probably produced a number of possible ways in which this account might not be an accurate reflection of what actually took place. In general terms, we can think of these problems as falling under three main headings:

• verifying the actual event;

• the adequacy of measurement;

• ensuring novelty.

Verifying the actual event

It is sometimes impossible to know the precise circumstances under which the initial memory was formed. Was it really raining, or have I imagined this in order to explain why I became ill? The difference between what could have been remembered and what was actually remembered may remain unknown. It might be possible to build up a consensus of what happened by asking a number of people all of whom experienced the same event, but if there are systematic biases operating (everyone has altered the facts in the same way), then these will cloud the true picture. With respect to studying infant memory, parents and carers can be consulted but this approach still suffers from the same problem. It is always possible that my memory is actually a memory of my father recounting the story to me and that *he* has got the facts wrong.

Although the aim of all autobiographical studies is to examine real-world memory, it has often proved a great deal easier, both from a practical and theoretical point of view, to provide subjects with an event rather than examine one which they have already experienced (see Research Summary 6). Although this makes the experiment slightly artificial, if sufficient care is taken the task can approximate closely to real-world experiences. This is perhaps even more true with children than with adults as the former are consistently in situations where they are being told what to do and are then closely observed while doing it. The ecological validity of developmental studies of event memory would therefore seem to be high.

The adequacy of measurement

A separate problem, and one which is perhaps a more general characteristic of studies into early learning, is how to measure the actual contents of young children's memories. As has already been discussed, children's linguistic abilities often lag behind their intellectual ones. Asking children to tell us what they remember will tend to result in an underestimation of both the amount and the complexity of information that is being stored.

Again, partial solutions have been developed and methods which do not rely solely on verbal recall as a measure of memory are frequently used. Whatever the procedure used to measure memory, we should always be aware of the possibility of having missed something. Generally, any measure of early memory runs the risk of underestimating the contents of memory.

Ensuring novelty

The novelty of an event (whether you have experienced anything like it before) is not just important for maintaining people's interest in an experiment. When we are examining early memory it is extremely important to ensure that what is being measured is memory for an actual event, not memory for similar events which may have occurred in the past. For instance, how much of a particular memory, such as eating in a restaurant, comes from a particular experience and how much comes from a general event schema? Studies of adult memory have demonstrated how memories for events can be 'filled in' by information stored in event schemas.

At the same time it is important to ensure that, although the task is novel, it is not so novel as to be confusing. Clearly, the impact of understanding on memory tasks cannot be overemphasized. The two factors pull in opposite directions – the task should not be contaminated by previous event knowledge, but sufficient understanding of the experimental situation must be present in order to allow the child to function as normally as possible. Research in early event memory calls for a great deal of methodological ingenuity.

SUMMARY OF SECTION 5

- The study of everyday and autobiographical memory is more concerned with what memory is *for* than what it *is*.
- Children's event memories have been shown to be quite sophisticated from a very early age.
- The difference between adult and child memory seems to rest more on the degree of understanding of the information or task than the state of the memory system. Memory limitations are more properly seen as intellectual limitations.
- The increasing sophistication of research into everyday memory is revealing just how complex children's memories are.

6 THE DEVELOPMENT OF MEMORY – CONCLUSIONS

The definition of memory can be expanded to include every piece of information we know and make use of. As such, it includes far too much to be discussed in one chapter, and what has been presented can and should be seen only as a selection of the current state of theories and experimental evidence.

The development of memory is inextricably tied up with the problem of learning in general. However, there are some interesting qualitative changes in the memory system which seem to emerge throughout development. For instance, young children do not seem able to spontaneously generalize strategies to new situations, and this type of limitation may underlie a lot of what we understand by the Piagetian term 'concrete operations'. It has been shown that when knowledge is appropriately organized, such as in the example of the young chess masters, children's memory can easily outstrip that of adults. Therefore the idea that memory limitations are generally due to strategy and organization rather than capacity seems to receive strong support. Memory is best seen as an interaction between the information under consideration, the context in which it is presented, and the understanding of the individual whose memory is being examined. The fact that understanding is confounded with age may have been responsible for a general underestimation of the complexity of children's memories.

From the point of view of a developmental sequence, children seem to learn simple mnemonics such as rehearsal at around the age of 7 but do not come to fully appreciate the application of these techniques until four or five years later. In tandem with this there is a general increase in cognitive speed which ends in the child performing at the same level as adults. At no time are the differences in performance between children and adults the direct result of memory limitations.

There is a tension between theories which grasp generalizations while losing the individual dimension and those which concentrate on the richness of individual memories at the expense of the ability to generalize. Undoubtedly, the greatest prospect lies in resolving these two parallel strands of research so that we can appreciate the ways in which the memory system operates at an individual level. The words of Don Norman, a prominent researcher in this field, are still as valid today as they were when written in 1980:

> Do not be impressed by all that is presumably known about the psychology of memory. Less is known than you might think.
>
> (Norman, 1980, p. 25)

SUMMARY OF SECTION 6

- Memory covers a huge range of psychological processes and as such is hard to define.
- Memory can be looked at both from the point of view of the similarities between people's memories, and the differences. Both are important.
- We are still a long way away from understanding exactly what memory is, and how it works.

FURTHER READING

General texts on memory

COHEN, G., KISS, G. and LEVOI, M. (1993; 2nd edn) *Memory: current issues*, Buckingham, Open University Press.

FIVUSH, R. and HUDSON, J. A. (eds) (1990) *Knowing and Remembering in Young Children*, Cambridge, Cambridge University Press.

SEARLEMAN, A. and HERRMAN, D. (1994) *Memory from a Broader Perspective*, New York, McGraw-Hill.

Connectionism

McCLELLAND, J. L. (1988) 'Connectionist models and psychological evidence', *Journal of Memory and Language*, **27**, pp. 107–23.

REFERENCES

APPEL, L. F., COOPER, R. G., McCARRELL, N., SIMS-KNIGHT, J., YUSSEN, S. R. and FLAVELL, J. H. (1972) 'The development of the distinction between perceiving and memorising', *Child Development*, **43**, pp. 1365–81.

BADDELEY, A. D. (1990) *Human Memory: theory and practice*, Hillsdale (N.J.), Lawrence Erlbaum Associates.

BADDELEY, A. D. and HITCH, G. (1974) 'Working memory' in BOWER, G. H. (ed.) *The Psychology of Learning and Motivation*, vol. 8, London, Academic Press.

BARTLETT, F. C. (1932) *Remembering*, Cambridge, Cambridge University Press.

BAUER, P. J. and MANDLER, J. M. (1990) 'Remembering what happened next: very young children's recall of event sequences' in FIVUSH, R. and HUDSON, J. A. (eds) *Knowing and Remembering in Young Children*, Cambridge, Cambridge University Press.

BRAY, N. W., HERSH, R. E. and TURNER, L. A. (1985) 'Selective remembering during adolescence', *Developmental Psychology*, **21**, pp. 290–4.

BULL, R. and BARNES, P. (1995) 'Children as witnesses' in BANCROFT, D. and CARR, R. (eds) *Influencing Children's Development*, Oxford, Blackwell/The Open University (Book 4 of ED209).

CHI, M. T. H. (1978) 'Knowledge structures and memory development' in SIEGLER, R. (ed.) *Children's Thinking: what develops?* Hillsdale (N.J.), Lawrence Erlbaum Associates.

CHI, M. T. H. and KOESKE, R. D. (1983) 'Network representation of a child's dinosaur knowledge', *Developmental Psychology*, **19**, pp. 29–39.

COHEN, G., KISS, G. and LEVOI, M. (1993; 2nd edn) *Memory: current issues*, Buckingham, Open University Press.

COLLINS, A. M. and LOFTUS, E. F. (1975) 'A spreading activation theory of semantic processing', *Psychological Review*, **82**, pp. 407–28.

CONWAY, M. A. (1990) *Autobiographical Memory: an introduction*, Buckingham, Open University Press.

DEMPSTER, F. N. (1981) 'Memory span: sources of individual and developmental differences', *Psychological Bulletin*, **89**, pp. 63–100.

FIVUSH, R., GRAY, J. T. and FROMHOFF, F. A. (1987) 'Two-year-olds talk about the past', *Cognitive Development*, **2**, pp. 393–409.

FLAVELL, J. H., BEACH, D. R. and CHINSKY, J. M. (1966) 'Spontaneous verbal rehearsal in a memory task as a function of age', *Child Development*, **37**, pp. 283–99.

HASHIMOTO, N. (1991) 'Memory development in early childhood: encoding process in a spatial task', *Journal of Genetic Psychology*, **152**, pp. 101–17.

HUTTENLOCHER, J. and LUI, F. (1979) 'The semantic organization of some simple nouns and verbs', *Journal of Verbal Learning and Verbal Behavior*, **18**, pp. 141–62.

HULME, C. and TORDOFF, V. (1989) 'Working memory development: the effects of speech rate, word length, and acoustic similarity on serial recall', *Journal of Experimental Child Psychology*, **47**, pp. 72–87.

JAMES, W. (1890) *Talks to Teachers on Psychology, and to Students on Some of Life's Ideals*, Holt.

KAIL, R. (1990; 3rd edn) *The Development of Memory in Children*, New York, W. H. Freeman.

KEENEY, T. J., CANNIZZO, S. R. and FLAVELL, J. J. (1967) 'Spontaneous and induced verbal rehearsal in a recall task', *Child Development*, **38**, pp. 953–66.

LACHMAN, J. L., LACHMAN, R. and THRONESBERY, C. (1979) 'Metamemory through the adult life span', *Developmental Psychology*, **15**, pp. 543–51.

MARKMAN, E. (1973) 'Factors affecting the young child's ability to monitor his memory', unpublished doctoral dissertation, University of Pennsylvania.

McCLELLAND, J. L. and RUMELHART, D. E. (1985) 'Distributed memory and the representation of general and specific information', *Journal of Experimental Psychology: General*, **114**, pp. 159–88.

MILLER, G. A. (1956) 'The magic number seven, plus or minus two: some limits on our capacity for processing information', *Psychological Review*, **63**, pp. 81–93.

NEISSER, U. (1978) 'Memory: what are the important questions?' *in* GRUNEBURG, M. M., MORRIS, P. E. and SYKES, R. N. (eds) *Practical Aspects of Memory*, London, Academic Press.

NELSON, K. (1988) 'Where do taxonomic categories come from?', *Human Development*, **31**, pp. 3–10.

NORMAN, D. (1980) 'Twelve issues for cognitive science', *Cognitive Science*, **4**, pp. 1–33.

RATNER, H. H., SMITH, B. S. and PADGETT, R. J. (1990) 'Children's organisation of events and event memories' *in* FIVUSH, R. and HUDSON, J. A. (eds) *Knowing and Remembering in Young Children*, Cambridge, Cambridge University Press.

REASON, J. T. (1979) 'Actions not as planned: the price of automatisation' *in* UNDERWOOD, G. and STEVENS, R. (eds) *Aspects of Consciousness*, vol. 1, London, Academic Press.

ROTH, I. (1990) *Introduction to Psychology*, vol. 2, Hove, Erlbaum.

RUMELHART, D. E, and McCLELLAND, J. L. (1986) 'On learning the past tense of English verbs' *in* McCLELLAND, J. L. and RUMELHART, D. E. (eds) *Parallel Distributed Processing: explorations in the microstructure of cognition*, vol. 2, Cambridge (Mass.), MIT Press.

SLACKMAN, E., HUDSON, J. and FIVUSH, R. (1986) 'Actions, actors, links, and goals: the structure of children's event representations' *in* NELSON, K. (ed.) *Event Knowledge: structure and function in development*, Hillsdale (N.J.), Erlbaum.

STRAUSS, M. S. (1979) 'Abstraction of prototypical information by adults and 10 month-old infants', *Journal of Experimental Psychology: Human Learning and Memory*, **5**, pp. 618–32.

TULVING, E. (1972) 'Episodic and semantic memory' *in* TULVING, E. and DONALDSON, W. (eds) (1972) *Organisation of Memory*, London, Academic Press.

TULVING, E. (1983) *Elements of Episodic Memory*, Oxford, Oxford University Press.

WHITTEN, W. B. and LEONARD, J. M. (1981) 'Directed search through autobiographical memory', *Memory and Cognition*, **9**, pp. 566–78.

Dennis Bancroft

CONTENTS

OBJECTIVES

When you have studied this chapter, you should be able to:

1 describe the process of categorization and recognize how this relates to and continues the discussion in previous chapters;

2 describe the classical view of the nature of concepts and the origins and character of more recent views;

3 outline three of the theoretical positions which have attempted to account for the relation between thought and language;

4 describe a research study concerning the relationship between language and concept formation;

5 recognize the process of making inferences as being involved in human reasoning and be able to illustrate this process in terms of reasoning about cause and time;

6 recognize the range of circumstances in which the term 'concept' is employed.

1 INTRODUCTION

> Without concepts, mental life would be chaotic. If we perceived each entity as unique, we would be overwhelmed by the sheer diversity of what we experience and unable to remember more than a minute fraction of what we encounter. And if each individual entity needed a distinct name, our language would be staggeringly complex and communication virtually impossible.
>
> (Smith and Medin, 1981, p. 1)

One way to simplify a complex world full of variation and individuality is to group objects and events together on the basis of some similarity between them. For example, chrysanthemums differ in terms of size, shape, petal organization, and so on. This individuality could merit the allocation of individual names, but, although they are different, we recognize the individual flowers as belonging to the group known as 'chrysanthemums'. As a more general level of organization we recognize chrysanthemums as being one of the range of objects we call 'flowers'. At a more general level still, flowers are part of that group of objects called 'plants'.

In other words, we humans organize our world – and make it less complex – by grouping together things which seem to us to share some common characteristics. The process of grouping together is termed categorization. The end-product of the process of categorization is often termed a concept, although the term has a much wider meaning than this restricted sense. For example, later in the chapter, the term

'concept' is used to refer to ideas like the 'concept of cause' and the 'concept of health and illness'. One other point to note before we leave the garden is that concepts at one level can be grouped themselves to form other concepts at a different level, e.g. chrysanthemums grouped with other flowers to form the concept of 'flowers', etc. The higher-level concepts are termed superordinate.

It should be clear that the human ability to impose organization on (and simplify) the world has considerable utility. For example, if we can recognize the similarity between a new experience and some previous experience we can use the knowledge we have already gained with the old to aid us in our dealings with the new. In other words the representation we have built on the basis of *experience* allows us to make predictions about similar happenings in the future.

Young children experience the world from the moment of birth and possibly before. Of course, 'experiences' of themselves are of little value to children unless they are able to make use of them. In order for a child to make use of experiences to become an effective and autonomous being, some basic skills need to be acquired or developed. For example, one needs to be able to *store* a memory of events and objects, one needs to be able to *organize* and *compare* stored information and to be able to *access* the results of comparison. With these skills a child can use experience gained in the past to deal with the problems of the present.

There has been a considerable volume of research directed at exploring the nature and development of concepts in children. Space precludes more than a selective introduction to the field and some of the debates within it. It is important to note that this chapter deals with a very active area of developmental research in which there is little certainty and much theorizing. One purpose of this chapter is to describe some aspects of conceptual development while another is to invite you to join in the discussion of these issues. For this reason, I have given space to the theoretical and philosophical background. This is illustrated by the work of developmental psychologists, which leads on to the more explicitly developmental material later in the chapter. In particular this chapter will address the following topics.

1.1 Representation

It seems clear that the products of the process of comparison and categorization must be stored in some form which captures characteristics and relations but which is not like a direct copy of nature (there are not many flowers inside a person's head). Just what form or structure human representations have is the subject of considerable debate. Candidates from the information-processing perspective have been lists or, alternatively, networks of symbols which can be used by the human thinker. Much of the evidence described in this chapter has been produced by psychologists working from within this very productive tradition. Since the early 1980s a persuasive alternative possibility has appeared. This 'connectionist' view of human representation, briefly introduced in the previous chapter, will be further developed later in this chapter.

1.2 Categorization

Having 'represented' some object or event, it is useful to be able to relate this to other similar experiences and to distinguish it from dissimilar experiences. In order to do this one must be able to *categorize* one's experiences. The process of categorization is a fundamental way in which representations are organized.

1.3 Concepts

Once experiences can be organized in terms of their similarity, children have the basic skills to develop *concepts*. The chapter will present some views from psychology of what concepts consist of and how they might be developed. One particular issue concerns the extent to which one person's concept can be said to 'overlap' with another's. One recent development considered here concerns boundaries that define and differentiate concepts and the possibility that these may be fuzzy rather than clearly defined.

1.4 The role of language

Investigating issues like those described above presents considerable difficulties if one is concerned with pre-verbal children. Once children begin to talk, psychologists are on rather firmer ground. Studying the language development of children has been used to investigate the nature of children's concepts: this practice will be discussed here, as will the issue of the role of language in the development of concepts themselves.

1.5 Reasoning

The last section of the chapter will describe some of the work which has investigated the ability of children to use and manipulate concepts in order to solve problems; in other words to *reason*. Three issues dealt with in turn are:

(a) children's ability to reason about a formal logical problem;

(b) their ability to reason about the concept of *cause*;

(c) their ability to reason about *time*.

SUMMARY OF SECTION 1

- Categorizing experience, involving the use of concepts, is an important way of simplifying the world.
- Quite what form concepts take, as mental representations, is a matter of theoretical dispute.
- Language is likely to be involved in conceptual development.

2 CATEGORIZATION

There have been many experiments that sought to establish what infants could perceive of their world. A common technique is to use that feature of infant behaviour called habituation. For example, if presented with some interesting sight or sound the infant will spend time attending to it. If the same experience is repeated the infant will attend but for a slightly shorter time and so on. If infants are then shown stimuli recognizably similar to the first experience, often they will not increase their attention. When a new experience is presented, the infant will attend as before. Notice how close this is to our earlier discussion of experience and how to make use of it. On the basis of this sort of experimentation we can see that infants have the ability to store experiences, to compare one experience with another and to recognize similarity and difference. Because newborn infants have these abilities it is sometimes argued that categorization is a 'fundamental ability' (McShane, 1991). However, John McShane continues with the following caution against inferring that some *concepts* are innate.

> Postulating an innate ability to categorize does not mean that an organism is born with preformed concepts; it means that an organism is born with the ability to form concepts – that is, the ability to detect similarity among instances along certain dimensions and also to detect dissimilarities between these and other groups of instances.
>
> (McShane, 1991, p. 133)

Categorization and conceptual development do not begin at toddler and infant-school age; rather, development at these age is founded in the intellectual achievements of infancy and based on the fundamental ability to categorize.

In 1976, Eleanor Rosch and her co-workers suggested that categorization could happen on several levels and that one level was more fundamental than the others. Three levels were described (although this simple formulation is a matter of some debate): *subordinate*, *basic* and *superordinate*. To take a commonplace example, if 'car' is a basic category, subordinate categories would be types of cars (VW or Rolls Royce), while cars are members of the superordinate category 'vehicles'. The 'basic' level of categorization was thought to be the most fundamental because it is the level at which there is most similarity in terms of the number of shared characteristics.

ACTIVITY 1

Allow about 5 minutes

CARS

Excluding the odd three-wheeler, list the features common to the basic category 'car'. Here is a starter:

1   Four wheels

2

3

4

5

6

A list of six features will not be enough to exhaust all the possibilities. However, your list might contain items like 'steering wheel' and 'seats' which are common to all cars. Another way to describe this is to say that the presence of steering wheels correlates very highly with the presence of four wheels, etc. We will make further use of this exercise a little later in the chapter.

It was argued by Rosch that if, as supposed, the basic level of categorization required less mental effort, then one would expect to find categorization at this level appearing earlier in development than those levels requiring more mental effort. Rosch *et al.* (1976) found that 3-year-old children were more accurate when sorting objects in terms of the basic category to which they belonged than they were in sorting objects by the superordinate category.

RESEARCH SUMMARY 1
DEVELOPMENTAL CHANGE IN LEVELS OF CATEGORIZATION

In Rosch's experiments children aged between 3 years and 10 years, with some adults, were divided into two groups. Both groups were shown sets of pictures. The pictures were of four categories of animals (cats, dogs, butterflies and fish) and four categories of vehicles (cars, trains, motorcycles and aeroplanes). The pictures were shown in threes. A 'basic-level' set could have two pictures of cats and one of a car. A 'superordinate-set' could have a car, a train plus an animal card. The two youngest groups of children (aged 3 and 4, with 20 in each group) were shown the cards in threes of the kind described and asked to put together the two that were alike.

	Basic level	Superordinate level
3 year olds	99% correct	55% correct
4 year olds	100% correct	96% correct

Rosch's summary was that children of this age were like adults in their ability to classify basic level categories while sorting superordinate level categories improves with age.

This finding implies that children of this age found the basic level task easier than the superordinate level task. Supporting evidence from language development is that words referring to basic categories, e.g. 'dog', are first to appear followed by words referring to superordinate categories ('animal') which in turn are followed by words referring to subordinate categories. The family dog can therefore expect to be called 'dog', 'animal' and 'golden retriever' in turn.

Carolyn Mervis and Maria Crisafi reported a series of studies in 1982 which sought to investigate this developmental sequence in more detail. They asked three age groups of children (aged respectively 2 years 6 months, 4 years and 5 years 6 months) to select from sets of three pictures examples of the 'same kind of thing'. The experimenters were concerned that the children taking part in the experiment might differ in the extent to which they were familiar with language and naming. Since linguistic and other knowledge might obscure the children's knowledge of categories as such, they decided to use 'nonsense' forms as the material presented to the children. These materials had something of the following form:

Superordinate	Angular shapes or curved shapes
Basic	Similar shapes, decoration
Subordinate	Detailed elaboration

SUP

BASIC

SUB

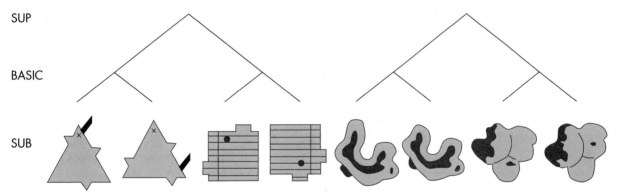

FIGURE 1 (Mervis and Crisafi, 1982, p. 260).

There were eight sets of cards for each of the three levels making 24 sets in all. If a child achieved a perfect score at a level, it would be 8. In the table of results below, we can see that the outcome was consistent with Rosch's original analysis of the difficulty of categorization at the three levels.

TABLE 1 Mean number of correct choices for each group.

	Category level		
Age	Basic	Superordinate	Subordinate
2–6	7.9	5.3	3.9
4–0	7.9	7.4	4.6
5–6	8.0	8.0	7.7

(Mervis and Crisafi, 1982, p. 262)

As you can see, the older children experienced no difficulty with the sorting problems set by Mervis and Crisafi. The 4-year-old children had difficulty only with the subordinate classification, while the younger children found each level progressively more difficult in just the way predicted by Eleanor Rosch.

> We have argued that the order of acquisition of the ability to categorize at various levels can be explained by the degree of differentiation of the categories at a given hierarchical level: the more differentiated categories at a given level are, the earlier categorization at that level will be acquired.
>
> (Mervis and Crisafi, 1982, p. 265)

A little caution needs to be exercised in accepting these findings. The experimenters contrived artificial categories in a way which was considered consistent with Rosch's analysis. Rosch *et al.* based their work on natural categories; it might be the case that Mervis and Crisafi's artificial stimuli are not organized and differentiated in just the same way as *naturally* occurring categories. Although their evidence is impressive, it needs to be supported by evidence about the relative difficulty of learning *naturally* occurring levels of categorization.

Before we leave our brief discussion of categorization we should note some recent work by Jean Mandler (1992) which questions the basis of much of the previous work in the field, including that described here. Mandler argues that there is confusion and difficulty in this area of research which derives from a failure to distinguish between 'perceptual' and 'conceptual' categories. Perceptual categories are based on perceptual similarities between objects and events, and derive from the workings of our perceptual systems.

They are not considered by Mandler to be easily describable since they are to do with how the sensory system operates, i.e. one knows *how* to do something without being able to account for it. This kind of knowledge is called *procedural knowledge*. The other kind of categorization, 'conceptual' categorization, involves categorization on the basis of knowledge of what things are like. This kind of knowledge is accessible to conscious thought and describable, and is called *declarative knowledge*.

Mandler's position is that perceptual and conceptual categorization are different processes, although both can be detected in early infancy. Mandler argues that the findings obtained by Rosch and others can be reinterpreted in the light of this distinction.

For our purposes in this introduction to the field it is enough to be aware of some of this discussion and debate and to be aware that these matters are far from settled.

SUMMARY OF SECTION 2

- In order to learn from experience humans need to be able to recognize similarity and difference. There is some evidence that infants have this ability.
- Objects can be grouped together at various levels of abstraction. Among those levels identified are the basic, superordinate and subordinate.
- It is hypothesized that these levels differ in the amount of cognitive difficulty needed to categorize at each level.
- There is some research evidence that the development of children's ability to categorize at the three levels coincides with the predicted difficulty.
- Research findings in this area are the subject of much debate as psychologists attempt to improve their understanding of conceptual development in children.

3 CONCEPTS: IS IT ALL GREEK?

If categorizing is the process, concepts are the product. In this section, we will consider something of the developmental psychology of concepts. In order to appreciate how far psychological speculation has reached, we need to spend a little time with the Greeks and the consequences of their theorizing.

Since the beginnings of psychology as a discipline, psychologists have been interested in the nature of conceptual organization and how it develops. Until the last third of the twentieth century, researchers had an understanding of the *kind* of thing they were studying which was based on the ideas of classical Greek philosophy. This theory is often described as the 'classical' theory of concepts (Smith and Medin, 1981). This theory was that all the examples of some concept shared a number of common properties or features. So if you were confronted by some strange animal and were asked what it was, you might run down a mental checklist of features and relate the animal before you to what you already knew. For example the list 'hairy, four legs, teeth at one end, tail at the other, has human attached by leather strap' coincides with the concept labelled 'dog'. In this scheme of things concepts are said to be monotheistic, i.e. all examples of the concept must share at least one common feature. It is important to this view that the set of features which describes a concept should not allow any non-member to be included or exclude any members. For this reason, our list for the concept of 'dog' must be incomplete since the list could describe 'cat' as well as a range of other animals.

Laboratory studies using specially constructed materials did show that human adults *could* derive concepts based on working out which of a set of features were *necessary* parts of the concept and *sufficient* to distinguish between that concept and any other. Of course, demonstrating that humans *can* think in some particular way is not the same as establishing that they habitually *do* think in that way. In any case, in the early 1950s the linguistic philosopher Ludwig Wittgenstein challenged the view that concepts consisted of necessary and sufficient features.

ACTIVITY 2

Allow no more than
10 minutes

WHAT'S IN A GAME?

This exercise is based on a famous example from Wittgenstein's own writing. The term 'game' is part of our vocabulary. We all know a 'game' when we see one so at some level we must have a concept of game that allows us to make this identification. The trouble is that games can take widely differing forms from solitaire through darts to croquet and football. Your task is to construct a list of features which are present in *all* games and which are not true of other concepts (so that rules out 'pleasure', I'm afraid).

P.S. The time limit and the short space allowed for the list is an indication of the difficulty of the task!

Common features of games

1

2

3

Comment

You should have found that, as your speculation moved from one sort of game to another, you noticed that some features might be common to card games and board games but not to ball games, some might be common to athletic games and ball games but not to computer games and so on. Some games have no winners and losers, some no competitive element. So whatever relationship exists between the various manifestations of the concept 'game' it is not captured by a list as in the classical tradition. In fact it turns out that the classical idea seems to work best for concepts like 'triangle' and 'square' and for those artificial concepts developed for laboratory work. The problem is that most concepts are *natural* rather than contrived and abstract. Natural concepts do not seem to obey Greek rules. In other words, they are not playing the game.

Wittgenstein used the term 'family resemblances' to describe the indefinite pattern of relationships between individual instances. In this view, the 'features' which compose some concept lose the 'necessary' and 'sufficient' aspects of Greek theory. Features are, nonetheless, related in a probabilistic way, i.e. the presence of tails is highly correlated with the presence of claws and fur in instances of the concept 'cat'.

Notice that 'highly correlated' does not mean inevitable, so when we come across a tail-less cat we are able to recognize it as a cat even if we are surprised at this violation of the usual state of catness. Highly dependable relationships between one characteristic and another allow us to reason about what we can't see on the basis of what we can. When discussing the principles of categorization, Eleanor Rosch (1978), on the basis of extensive research, has argued that much of the natural world seems to be organized in terms of highly probable relationships in much the way that the linguistic theoretician Wittgenstein suspected.

One important finding from the research work of Eleanor Rosch and Carolyn Mervis has been the notion of 'prototypicality'. The idea is that humans store a representative average example of a concept as a sort of yardstick against which to compare real-world examples. The research support for this idea comes from experiments which showed that people are able to assign values to objects in terms of 'how typical' they are (that is, in terms of how like the ideal or prototype they are). If we stay with the car example of Activity 1, we can see that while a three-wheeler and a family saloon are both cars, the saloon is somehow *more* car-like. One other relevant research finding is that people find it easier to recognize typical instances of a concept than they do to recognize unusual (but still legitimate) examples. A prototype will consist of that set of parts and relationships which experience shows have a high probability of occurring together.

Eleanor Rosch's ideas have important implications for our understanding of the development of concepts. One possibility is that the mental representation of a prototype is developed by abstracting from the various examples provided by experience. These examples will be more or less like the 'prototype' but not exactly like it. The abstraction of prototypes from examples occurs as a result of *activity on the part of the thinker*; prototypes are not directly provided by the world. There is research evidence which shows that adults are able to generate a prototype on the basis of specific examples which differ to varying degrees from the prototype. That is, humans can make these things (prototypes) without actually seeing them. It seems to follow that if concepts take the form of prototypes and are individually constructed, then one person's prototype may not be exactly like another's, although, of course, they will be quite similar. In other words it may be the case that our concepts are sufficiently similar for us to share meanings but since the overlap is not exact, we are able to argue about specific instances.

In contrast, then, to the classical position where one concept is seen as clearly distinct from the next, prototype theory allows that while prototypes are distinct from each other, the boundaries between concepts may be open to dispute, i.e. the boundaries may be *fuzzy*. It is widely reported that children may overextend and underextend the words they use to describe things (as described in Chapter 2). For example, the word 'horse' may be used with respect to horses *and* overextended to a range of other animals seen in fields. This has been thought to indicate that children have yet to progress to the conceptual clarity of adults. Bob Carrabine (1991) points out that this interpretation rests on an assumption that adults' concepts *are* clearly defined. As we have seen from the work of Wittgenstein and Rosch, this may be an unjustified assumption.

RESEARCH SUMMARY 2
'FUZZY' BOUNDARIES FOR THE CONCEPT 'DOG'

To test this possibility, Carrabine conducted a study in two parts. The first part was to identify the 'fuzzy' boundary that might exist in adults' use of the term 'dog'. For example, the adult participants were shown a large number of photographs of members of the dog family (dogs, wolves etc.) and of other animals with a greater or lesser similarity to dogs (hyenas to butterflies). The participants had first to sort them into dogs and non-dogs and then to rate them as being more or less dog-like. This process identified where complete agreement was to be found *and* where there was only relative agreement. The second part of the study was to use this information to investigate the extent to which adults' actual usage coincided with that of young children in their third year. Carrabine found there was a high degree of correspondence between the children and the adults in the range of objects to which they applied particular terms. It seems then that both adults and children have concepts with fuzzy boundaries. Children's boundaries may be 'fuzzier' but they are not different in kind.

Using the habituation technique to examine the perceptual development of infants and young children, researchers have identified infants' abilities to recognize similarity and difference. This ability is, arguably, the essential prerequisite for the development of a conceptual organization which links together individual instances on the basis of some perceived family resemblance. It seems then that infants and young children set about the business of developing concepts in a similar manner to that used by adults. Differences between adults and children could be a consequence of children having a less rich store of experiences and knowledge than adults. In other words the difference could be *quantitative* rather than *qualitative*. If we take this view we should recognize that this is something of a departure from the prevailing view up until the 1970s. Before this time it was thought, following the work of Lev Vygotsky among others, that children's concepts were different *sorts* of entity from the concepts possessed by adults. The basis for this belief was a considerable body of research which seemed to show a difference. As John McShane points out:

> ... this view was very much the product of the *type of research* on concepts that earlier studies conducted. The earlier research was influenced by the classical theory of concepts (Smith and Medin, 1981). The predominant paradigm of research was one in which the child had to discover the necessary and sufficient features that defined an arbitrary concept specified by the experimenter ...

(McShane, 1991, p. 137)

McShane is arguing that the outcomes of research can depend on the kind of research undertaken and the philosophical underpinning which determines what questions are to be asked. There are several strong proponents of *stage* theories of development. For example, much of Piaget's writing describes research which implies that children pass through distinct stages of increasing mental sophistication, each stage being a development of the previous one. Lev Vygotsky shared something of Piaget's view in that he also considered children's concepts to be fundamentally different from those of adults and to pass through three stages *en route* to the adult position. In his view, development proceeded from idiosyncratic concepts based on perceptual similarity leading, eventually, to abstract concepts characterized by a logical organization. One consequence of this position was that children in the earlier stages of development would have great difficulty with problems requiring abstract representation. Vygotsky considered that conceptual development and language development were closely interrelated and should be discussed together.

> [Vygotsky's] ideas on conceptual change were part of a larger theory about how language changes the nature of thought. For Vygotsky, only as one comes to internalize language does one have the ability to represent concepts in any other way than via concrete instances and the simple associative principles that operate over those instances. By his account, internalized language frees children from relying on memories of specific instances and enables them to use more abstract principled representations.
>
> (Kiel, 1989, p. 7)

We shall return to the issue of the relation between language development and the development of concepts in a later section. We have already seen something of the impact of the philosopher Wittgenstein on speculation and research into concept development. Wittgenstein's starting point was an analysis of language. Building on some of the claims of psychology, the work of the American philosopher Jerry Fodor has been very influential in both developmental and cognitive psychology. As you saw in Chapter 1, Fodor has raised several objections to some psychological speculation about concept formation. The first of Fodor's points is one we have already met. He points out that taking a concept to be a set of necessary and sufficient features seems to be the wrong starting point. Of course, we have also suggested that the 'classical' view of concepts seems to work for *some* human abstractions like 'triangles' for example, while this view does not seem to work for the 'natural' world. One could argue that the developmental history described by psychologists including Vygotsky, on the basis of formal experimentation, still has some substance but *only* for some formal and abstract concepts.

Fodor has two main reservations concerning the idea that children pass through distinct stages during development of concepts. First, if children's concepts are of a different kind from adult concepts, there would be a great deal of misunderstanding between children and adults. Indeed, perhaps communication would be impossible since a child's concept might have the same label as an adult's but would be composed quite differently. Fodor's second reservation concerns the means by which children move from one stage to another. If the stages that children pass through were quite different from each other, then children in the first stage could not learn anything of the second stage since it would involve a quite different level of thinking. This process needs explanation.

Fodor has argued that the 'stages of complexity' idea was unnecessarily complicated and that it was simpler to account for the developmental history of children by assuming they were rather *like* adults in terms of the intellectual system that they had but *different* from adults in terms of their ability to *use* the system.

One account which is apparently consistent with Fodor's argument comes from the literature describing recent developments in computer modelling of psychological processes, although it is not clear that Fodor himself would accept the link. Since the mid-1980s, researchers using connectionist networks have added to the literature of concept development. Connectionist models are constructed and tested using computer programs but protagonists claim that there are important similarities between them and human neurology. Human neurons are interconnected with numerous other neurons and, in a simple view, may be in a state of being on or off. Collections of neurons can be seen to be networks. As you may recall from the previous chapter, it is the nature of such networks that they become internally organized as a result of input from the human senses. The resulting organization can, in turn, be seen as a *model or representation* of that sensory input. It is possible to mimic this sort of structure or 'architecture' using a computer program. The computer program then stands as a working model of the proposed human process. If the computer is given bits of information and on the basis of this information generates prototypes of concepts similar to that observed in humans, then we can claim that our model works. Of course just because we can show one way to develop concepts does not mean that it is *the* way that humans do it, although this sort of evidence *is* strongly suggestive.

Kim Plunkett and Chris Sinha (1992) wish to argue that connectionist models of the type described in the previous chapter represent a considerable advance in theorizing about cognitive and language development in that these models avoid some of the assumptions and difficulties with the traditional information-processing model. One piece of evidence they describe to support their case comes from the work of Yves Chauvin (1988) in the United States. Chauvin's technique was to present his connectionist network with a series of inputs, *none of which* is the prototypical form. Once the series of 'experiences' had been presented to the network, there were several interesting outcomes. For example, it was possible to see whether the model had developed a prototype by testing its reaction to various new examples. The model is reporting as responding most accurately to a prototypical example even though it had not been presented with one in the training phase.

Plunkett and Sinha add:

> Interestingly, the network takes longer to discover the appropriate clusterings when labels are not included as input in the training régime. This finding indicates that the network exploits the predictive power of the label in identifying category membership ... In this respect, the findings ... [support] an interactional account ....
>
> (Plunkett and Sinha, 1992, p. 237)

The model described in detail by Plunkett and Sinha indicates that a connectionist account can produce an apparent development which is similar to that observed in children and adults. Psychologists prefer explanations which rest on fewest assumptions. The traditional information-processing explanation of cognition assumes the ability to develop and manipulate abstract symbols as units of meaning. One apparent advantage of the connectionist approach is that its starting point is a system which can be organized by its sensory input and which does not require complex processing by the 'owner of the system'.

At present, connectionist models are lively contenders in the race to account for human cognition. The next task for those wishing to advance a connectionist account is to produce evidence that *real children* operate in ways predicted by the connectionist model.

SUMMARY OF SECTION 3

- Until recently, psychologists investigating the development of concepts were using the venerable notion that a concept consisted of a sort of list of defining features. On the basis of this idea it was thought that children's concepts were of a different *kind* from those of adults.

- The philosopher Ludwig Wittgenstein demonstrated that the natural world could not be organized in terms of lists of necessary and sufficient features. The relationship between members of some conceptual grouping was more like the relationship of 'family resemblances'.

- The work of the psychologist Eleanor Rosch is consistent with that of Wittgenstein but develops in addition the idea that humans represent concepts as prototypes (or idealized versions) and use these to evaluate real-world instances.

- Also at issue is the early idea that children passed through stages of conceptual development, each of which was different from its neighbour and different from that of adults. The alternative is that children have the same conceptual system as adults but are in the process of acquiring experience and information. While this acquisition takes place children's conceptual systems *look* different to those of adults.

- Connectionist models seem to be a demonstration that this possibility is a feasible account of children's development.

4 LANGUAGE AND THOUGHT

Implied in Wittgenstein's work is the idea that there is some connection between the language we speak and the way we think of our world. As we shall see in this next section, there has been psychological speculation and experimentation concerned with investigating the relationship between thought and language.

Part of the importance of the quotation from Plunkett and Sinha's paper is that it points to a clear link between language and conceptual development, at least as far as the computer model is concerned. There is a considerable history of psychological interest in this relationship as far as humans are concerned.

> … language, and in particular the process of naming, carries with it an implicit conceptual mechanism. Providing a common label (e.g., 'animal') for multiple referents is in itself an act of classification. Likewise, providing different labels (e.g., 'dog', 'horse') reveals conceptual distinctions among referents
>
> (Waxman, 1990, pp. 123–4)

It seems possible, then, that some aspects of language like naming might contribute to the development of concepts by helping children with the process of categorization. A little later in this section we will consider a research study by Sandra Waxman which has investigated this particular issue. Psychological theorists have considered the wider relationship between language and thought and, as usual, several alternative views can be discerned. Some of the 'names' behind the theories will be familiar to you, but those of Edward Sapir and Benjamin Lee Whorf may be new. Sapir and Whorf gave their names to the Sapir-Whorf hypothesis which holds (in its strongest form) that language determines thought. This means that a person from a different language community may actually think about the world in a different manner from that of a speaker of English. As far as children are concerned, if language determines thought, as is claimed, then the particular language learnt by a child will determine what thoughts the child may have. As an example, it can be argued that women are often referred to in English in linguistic terms which are less positive than those used to describe men (Lakoff, 1975). According to the Sapir-Whorf hypothesis, children learning to speak English are at the same time learning something of these positive and negative images and of the way people *think* about men and women in English-speaking societies. There is a 'weaker' form of the Sapir-Whorf hypothesis in which language is supposed to *influence* rather than to *determine* thought, so that it is possible for the individual to escape from the constraints of the language.

ACTIVITY 3

Allow about 40 minutes

MS AND IDENTITY

In English there are terms which differentiate between women on the basis of their marital status, Mrs and Miss. The introduction of the alternative Ms was intended, in part, to remove what was seen as a largely irrelevant distinction. It was hoped that changing the terms Mrs and Miss to Ms would encourage a change in the way women were thought of. This hope assumes the Sapir-Whorf hypothesis is true. Did it work? Write Ms on several cards and get people to add a list of the things that the term makes them think of.

You may have found that the term 'Ms' generates quite a number of responses, some 'positive' and some 'negative', in addition to its primary aim of identifying a female without reference to marital status. Do you think that this example supports the Sapir-Whorf hypothesis? If not, can you think of other new terms in the language which might?

READING

The idea that language determines thought is not new or confined to linguists like Sapir and Whorf. Turn to Reading A, which is George Orwell's paragraph on the purpose of Newspeak, taken from *Nineteen Eighty-Four*. Do you think his apocalyptic vision is at all possible? Could it be that meanings, concepts or ideas are socially negotiated and not successfully imposed from without?

Discussion

Piaget assigned a less important role to language. He took the view that children needed to understand a concept *before* they could properly use the terms that refer to the concept. Put rather simply, one thinks before one can speak. Of course one can say words that one does not understand, but to *use* words appropriately one must have understanding. Piaget assigned a supporting role to language in the intellectual development of children rather than the determining role favoured by Sapir and Whorf.

One final view of the relation between language and thought comes from the work of Lev Vygotsky. He identified two separate roles for language, as a means of communication and as the basis of thought. In his view the two roles were initially separate. Infants were said to have non-language-based means of thought which co-existed with a form of language whose purpose was to regulate the infant's social world. Vygotsky took the view that language and thought came together at the end of the second year when children were able to use words as symbols for thoughts. After this time language and thought became closely interrelated and mutually supportive.

As far as the Sapir-Whorf hypothesis is concerned, current thinking accepts that the language one speaks does have some influence on the way in which one thinks of the world. However, we are obviously not completely constrained by our language since we can, with effort, identify the way the world appears to speakers of other languages. For example, when English speakers learn French they need to take note of aspects of life which are not linguistically marked in English, such as the kind of relationship which holds between speaker and listener ('*tu*' for family and intimate friends or '*vous*' for others). If language *determined* thought, as Sapir and Whorf proposed, then learning only English would prevent us from thinking like those who learn only French. Piaget and Vygotsky are often seen as offering contrasting views on the relationship between language and thought. It is fair to say that, since the 1970s, evidence and opinion has generally supported the Vygotskian position concerning the importance of language for the development of thought, although with some reservations. For example, both Piaget and Vygotsky took the view that conceptual organization was a considerable achievement of middle childhood, while subsequent research has sought to suggest that children have this ability much earlier in childhood. In the research study described below, we shall see one example of the way in which language can contribute to the process of categorization by drawing attention to particular relationships in the world.

In a study published in 1990, Sandra Waxman investigated the role that particular aspects of language might have in assisting children to develop concepts. Since the late 1950s evidence had emerged that indicated that young children were sensitive to the rather abstract information that is conveyed respectively by nouns and adjectives, etc. By way of example of this sensitivity, Waxman was interested in the possibility that it might contribute to the child's appreciation of hierarchies of concepts and allow distinctions like those between 'dog', 'mammal' and 'animal'. Waxman's way of distinguishing between levels of conceptual organization was similar to the way that Eleanor Rosch outlined, i.e. a basic level with subordinate and superordinate levels on either side, although Waxman introduced a new level, the 'intermediate'.

RESEARCH SUMMARY 3
LANGUAGE AND CONCEPTUAL DEVELOPMENT

The children in this study, aged between $3\frac{1}{2}$ and 5 years, were given picture cards of animals showing various levels of abstraction and asked to sort the cards into things which went together. Four levels of abstraction were used: a 'basic' level (a dog), a 'subordinate' level (a collie), an 'intermediate' level of mammals (cat, lamb, dog, goat) and a 'superordinate' level of animals (horse, elephant, duck, pig). For some of the children the cards were labelled while others had no labels. The children's performance on this task, and others, showed that using labels helped the youngest children classify objects at the superordinate level. This study demonstrated that the children, as a whole, were sensitive to the different roles played by parts of speech such as nouns and also adjectives, and could use this knowledge to distinguish between the various conceptual levels.

... preschool children are sensitive to powerful links between conceptual hierarchies and the language we use to describe them. They distinguish between the form classes 'noun' and 'adjective' and expect that each form class will have a unique referring function. In particular, they expect that nouns will refer to higher-order classes and that adjectival phrases will refer to lower-order classes. *These expectations or biases serve to guide the early formation of conceptual hierarchies* [my emphasis] ... Preschool children's sensitivity to these parallels ensures that in learning new words, they simultaneously learn about conceptual relations among objects and classes of objects.

(Waxman, 1990, pp. 142–5)

Here, then, is some research evidence which makes two contributions to our discussion. First, it gives information about one aspect of the relationship between language and thought in development. Secondly, it points to the impact that language can have on conceptual development in the earliest years.

SUMMARY OF SECTION 4

- There has been considerable interest in the relationship between language and thinking. The 'strong' form of the Sapir-Whorf hypothesis no longer has the influence it did and we are left with the 'weaker' form which holds that in learning a first language a child is learning the conceptual relations implied by that particular language.

- In Piaget's view, language made relatively little contribution to cognitive development. One important critique of Piagetian investigations concerns the linguistic demands they can make on children.

- Vygotsky's position contrasts with Piaget in that he assigned a crucial role to language as being the social instrument which complemented and facilitated the development of abstract thinking.

- Recent research has produced evidence to support the view that language learning can make a direct contribution to the formation of conceptual hierarchies and that this contribution is made at an earlier age than that previously supposed.

5 MAKING INFERENCES

The discussion up to this point has concentrated on the idea of the 'concept' as the product of a process of categorizing and organizing objects and groups of objects in the natural world. In this section we will consider something of the manipulation of concepts as part of the process of *reasoning*, as well as something of the developmental history of two 'concepts' of a rather different kind from those we have discussed up to now. The common thread which binds our former discussion and that which follows is that language is closely involved in both.

One of the things which becomes possible once one has developed a set of concepts and some understanding of the interrelationships between them is the ability to manipulate ideas and information in an organized and logical way. Also, given *some* information, it is possible to deduce *additional* information. This process of making inferences or deductions follows from the kinds of conceptual understanding described already in this chapter. For example if, when in France, a friend invites you to

come and see the hoopoe and tells you it is a sort of bird, you will be able to *infer* much about the creature even if this is to be your first encounter (has feathers, lives in trees, etc.). The novel experience coming your way may encourage you to modify your bird concept a little by adding something new that is particular to this sort of bird, but you should find that your experience of birds thus means that you will 'know' quite a lot about this new one already (e.g. has feathers, flies etc.). In this last section of the chapter we will review something of the considerable literature concerning *children's* ability to reason and make inferences, and something of the role that concepts play in these processes.

ACTIVITY 4

Allow about 5 minutes

MAKING SENSE OF TEXT

Here is a short story.

Once upon a time at a village fête people were waiting for the mayor to come and perform the opening ceremony. Since he was late, the priest occupied the crowd with tales of his experiences. He said that when he was first appointed he was horrified to hear his first penitent admit to a nasty murder. Eventually the mayor arrived and introduced himself by saying that he and the vicar were old friends and indeed that he had been the vicar's first penitent.

Who was the murderer?

(based on Boden, 1977)

Comment

Nowhere in the text does it actually say that the mayor committed the murder. So you must have inferred this fact from those presented to you in the story. Actually this is a rather common process, that of making inferences or deductions. It seems then that humans use logical processes a great deal. A child (or anyone else) who is unable to draw conclusions in this manner would have great difficulty understanding written material or even learning at all.

5.1 Making deductions

One kind of task that has been used to investigate children's ability to make deductions is the 'three-term series' problem. This sort of problem dates back to antiquity. It has the form of two statements that express some relationship and a question. The reasoner has to deduce the answer to the question on the basis of the information given. For example:

Relational information	*Question*
Anna is taller than Eleanor	Who is tallest?
Eleanor is taller than Alison	

The problem can be presented in different ways. For example, one can use negatives (Alison is not as tall as Eleanor, etc.) or use different adjectives which reverse the series (Anna is shorter than Eleanor, etc.).

The ability to make inferences is necessary to solve the three-term series problems and is, arguably, crucial to learning processes in general. Speakers and writers are seldom as precise and explicit as they mean to be, and much has to be deduced from what is said. An inability to make inferences also has implications for the learning of mathematics and science. Both of these disciplines rest on an ability to compare and to measure. A great deal of the basic research in this area comes from Piaget and those working with him in Geneva. The conclusion they reached in investigations of children's ability to solve syllogisms was that young children were unable to co-ordinate the information contained in the premises and so were unable to derive the conclusion implied by the premises. The ability of children to co-ordinate pieces of information was thought to be a rather late development, not appearing until after the seventh year. For our purposes, we should note that, if the above is true, Piaget has discovered a considerable limitation upon the kinds of thing a young child may be expected to do and limitations also on the kinds of material children are able to understand. This last point has obvious implications for the sort of teaching which would be appropriate at different ages.

In order to solve three-term series problems one has to hold some representation of the premises in memory and manipulate it such that it is possible to use the information to deduce the answer required. Experimentation has suggested that reasoning of this kind is problematic for children until late childhood. Indeed, as we have said, much of Piagetian work on reasoning takes this view, although there has been some research which shows that in some circumstances 4-year-old children may make the necessary inferences. Three-term series problems belong to the class of inferences known as *transitive inferences*. Since 1971, following the work of Peter Bryant and Tom Trabasso, it has been known that, in some circumstances, children as young as 4 years of age were able to make transitive inferences *if* they could remember the premises. These two psychologists took the view that the task for children really had several parts. Among these, children had to remember the two premises and store their contents. Without this memory they could not hope to solve the problem. Given that the material in the premises had been stored by the child there was a *separate process* which involved the manipulation of the material to derive the conclusion.

RESEARCH SUMMARY 4
DEVELOPMENT OF CHILDREN'S TRANSITIVE INFERENCE

Bryant and Trabasso went to considerable lengths to devise materials which would assist children to remember the essential information. They produced a set of wooden rods each of a different length and colour. Children were shown the rods, two at a time, protruding an equal amount from a box. Each pair was made up of a rod and the one next to it in size.

During the 'training' phase of the experiment the children were asked which of the two was the big one and which the little one. When they had made their choice, the rods were withdrawn from the box and shown to the child. The training continued until each child had achieved a good level of success. The testing phase of the experiment was similar except that the children were given no feedback once they had made their choice. In the test phase the children were asked about the sequential pairs they had seen during the training and several non-sequential new comparisons. To solve the new comparisons correctly they had to make transitive inferences.

Given this preparation of reducing the demands made upon a child's memory, the researchers were able to demonstrate that children as young as 4 years of age could make transitive inferences.

TABLE 2　Correct choices on tests for transitivity and retention (percentages).

Stimulus	B	C	D	E
4-yr-old children				
A	0.96	0.96	0.93	0.98
B	–	0.92	0.78	(0.83)* 0.92
C	–	–	0.90	0.94
D	–	–	–	0.91
5-yr-old children				
A	1.00	0.96	1.00	0.98
B	–	0.86	0.88	(0.80)* 1.00
C	–	–	0.92	1.00
D	–	–	–	1.00
6-yr-old children				
A	0.99	0.99	1.00	1.00
B	–	0.94	0.92	(0.92)* 0.99
C	–	–	0.98	1.00
D	–	–	–	1.00

* Predicted
(Bryant and Trabasso, 1971, p. 457.)

In this table, the first line under '4-yr-old children' shows that these children correctly identified rod A as being longer than rod B 96 per cent of the time. This is a direct comparison since A is next to B in the size series. Moving along the line we see that children of this age identified rod A as being bigger than rod C 96 per cent of the time. This success implies a transitive inference has been made since A was not directly paired with C during the training phase.

It is, however, true that making inferences of this kind can be problematic even for children who are much older than those studied by Bryant and Trabasso. Of course, most children do not have the advantage of the training opportunity given by these researchers. So if children's difficulty is with remembering the premises, in which part of the memory process does the problem lie? One, more recent, piece of experimental work sought to identify the factors which make inference difficult for children (Oakhill, 1984). As before, the possible reasons for difficulty included not understanding the premises, not being able to remember the information contained in the premises and not being able to manipulate this information in order to derive a suitable inference. Jane Oakhill asked 8 and 9 year olds a range of three-term series problems. These problems differed in terms of language and the order in which the information was presented. It is known that negatives (John is not as tall as Peter) take more mental effort to understand than positives (Peter is taller than John). It was reasoned that it would be harder to remember problems which were linguistically more complex. The children in this study were able to solve three-term series problems when they were presented using positive terms. From this outcome we can see that the children understood what they were being asked to do. The more linguistically complex negative presentation resulted in an increase in the mistakes made by the children. Oakhill's interpretation of this finding was that problems presented in this way exceeded the capacity of the children's working memory. In other words they were unable to remember the linguistically complex premises for long enough to work out a representation of what they meant. Clearly, then, the development of memory, which you read about in the previous chapter, is closely involved in inferential reasoning.

We have been discussing an aspect of children's ability to manipulate conceptual knowledge and deduce from it in a rather formal context. However, as we noted in the beginning of the chapter, much of our conceptual life is less formal, more pragmatic and located within culture. In the remainder of the chapter we will extend our discussion to include other domains of more obvious pertinence to daily life.

READING

Now read Reading B, in which Sara Meadows discusses children's concepts of health and illness. In addition to extending our discussion of concepts to include some relating to well-being, Meadows makes the point that how things are to be explained to children depends on our understanding of their concepts.

The ability to reason about objects and events in the natural world is an important basis of our understanding. Equally important for scientific thinking and schooling are the more abstract concepts of 'cause' and 'time'. It is to these that we now turn.

5.2 The concept of cause

To describe the notion of 'cause' as a *concept* is to extend the use of the term somewhat beyond that employed in the earlier part of this chapter. However, psychologists have been interested in the development of children's understanding of cause and their ability to make inferences about cause and effect. Children's understanding of 'cause' can be seen as another example of their ability to infer conclusions on the basis of the facts they know.

> Children's understanding of causal relations must depend to a large extent on their ability to make causal inferences. Such inferences usually concern changes over time, and they turn on differences between an initial and a later state
>
> (Das Gupta and Bryant, 1989, p. 1138)

In a chapter such as this, space precludes an exhaustive discussion of the psychological research on children's understanding of 'cause'. However, it is possible to describe two quite different studies which have contributed to our understanding of the area. The first of these comes from a social psycholinguistic tradition and the second from an experimental tradition. As with much of the content of this chapter, cognition and language are closely intertwined.

For the most part, the material in this chapter has been discussed with respect to what it is that children can be said to understand. The work of Vygotsky points to the social context as being implicated in all aspects of how it is that they obtain this understanding. Because language is a social construction, language-based investigations of children's understanding bring us to a point at which the social and cognitive worlds meet. Judy Dunn and Jane Brown have recently (1993) described a study of the development of children's participation in conversations about cause (see Research Summary 5 opposite). Dunn and Brown take the view that studies of natural language are particularly important since they often reveal children to be more competent than experimental investigations have discovered. This is a theme that will be picked up in the discussion of children's understanding of time concepts which follows later.

Does this mean that children of this age make inferences about cause? In the second study considered here, Das Gupta and Bryant (see Research Summary 6 opposite) have produced some evidence which suggests an important development in children's understanding of cause takes place sometime during the fourth year. They reasoned that to make *genuine* causal inferences, a child must make a comparison between an initial and a final state. In terms of our previous discussion these constitute the premises upon which the inference is to be based. A technique is to show children pictures which represent an initial and a final state (e.g., an intact window and a broken window) and then a set of possible causal objects (e.g., a plum, a stone and a brush). The children would then be invited to select the likely causal agent. The problem that Das Gupta and Bryant identify is that since children know a lot about the words and are given such a choice, they may choose a stone because of what they know about stones and windows rather than paying attention to the initial as well as the final state. The method chosen to explore this possibility and the basis of children's causal reasoning was to present the children with causal sequences which did not obey the normal rules, i.e. those which could not be easily solved by knowledge rather than inference and those in which a choice had to be made.

RESEARCH SUMMARY 5
CHILDREN'S 'CAUSAL TALK'

Dunn and Brown arranged for two recordings to be made of 50 children, first when they were 2 years 9 months old and then when they were 3 years and 4 months old. The children might be engaged in conversation with their mothers or with older siblings. Several measures were made of the language sample they obtained, including a measure of the number of occasions of talk involving causality for both mother and child and the variety of causal topics discussed. The first point to make is that the children in this study spent a fair amount of time talking about 'causes' of one kind or another at both ages. Next, the amount of talk about cause increased considerably over the seven months of the study and the content changed.

> There were marked increases in discourse about causality, and changes in content and in the social context in which children discussed cause, with an increase in causal talk about inner states and social practices. At 33 months children talked about cause chiefly in attempts to get their own needs met, at 40 months chiefly in reflective discussion.

(Dunn and Brown, 1993, p. 107)

It seems then, that in the third year of life children are able to talk about cause in some circumstances in a way which suggests a level of comprehension of the concept. Of course one should note that there may be some intellectual distance between talk of the kind investigated by Dunn and Brown and the inferential reasoning described earlier. One final point from this study was an observation that there was a positive relationship between the extent to which children at 33 months discussed cause in the context of a dispute and their later ability to appreciate the causes of emotions seven months later. Perhaps there is some (educational) point in arguing with children after all!

RESEARCH SUMMARY 6
CHILDREN'S CAUSAL INFERENCES

One example described by Das Gupta and Bryant was to show children, in order, a broken cup and then a wet broken cup. Alternatively they might begin with a wet cup and conclude with a wet and broken cup. The possible causal agents shown to the children included a hammer and water. If the children selected water for the first sequence and the hammer for the second, then one could conclude that they had paid attention to both the initial and final states and made an inference. If the children chose the hammer on both occasions then the basis for their choice was not likely to have been an inference but rather their previous knowledge of hammers.

Das Gupta and Bryant found that the 3 year olds were likely to choose the hammer in both circumstances while the 4 year olds were unlikely to make this error. The authors conclude,

> Our two experiments demonstrate that by the age of 4 years children do adopt ... the more sophisticated ... strategy. They can use the difference between an object's initial and final state to work out what happened to it in the meantime. In sharp contrast, the 3-year-old children have grave difficulties in using the difference between initial and final states when making a causal inference.
>
> (Das Gupta and Bryant, 1989, p. 1145)

Here we have some evidence of a development in reasoning strategy about cause occurring during a child's fourth year. The concept of cause and relation between cause and effect is a matter which receives considerable linguistic attention in the exchanges between parent and child, and it is likely that this plays a part in children's developing sophistication in this area.

5.3 The concept of time

One possible way of reconciling these two studies is to return to the point made earlier in the chapter when Jean Mandler argues for a distinction between procedural and declarative knowledge. In this case the children described by Dunn and Brown know about cause in this procedural sense but would not be able to reason about it in the way described by Das Gupta and Bryant.

It may be the case that we will find echoes of this story when we consider children's understanding of some of the concepts of time.

An understanding of the temporal concepts of 'order' and 'duration' is crucial to our ability to plan and organize as well as to our ability to understand things like stories and to solve problems where order is important. As is often the case in developmental psychology, we are indebted to Jean Piaget for original and influential theorizing about children's understanding of time. An understanding of 'time' in the sense used by Piaget involves understanding the notions of 'duration' and 'sequencing' rather than the ability to tell the time or to know the order of days and months. In Piaget's view, children would have difficulty understanding the concepts of time because they would be unable to co-ordinate the various parts of the problem. In other words, they could not retain and manipulate the premises. Research by Piaget and others seemed to show that children did indeed have difficulty with temporal problems until their ninth year. One common technique of investigation was to show children two trains moving along parallel tracks on a table. Experimenters can change this rather simple presentation in a number of ways. For example, one might vary the speeds of the trains so that one moved faster than the other, or their starting order, or both. Having been shown the trains performing, the children were asked to describe what had happened and to answer questions like 'which one finished first?' or 'which one took longest?' Children up to the age of about nine made many errors in a way consistent with Piaget's predictions. The trouble was that there are other possible explanations which can account for the children's difficulty, for example they may have had some problem with the language demands placed upon them or perhaps with their memory for the event that they had been shown.

As was the case in our discussion of the concepts of 'cause', useful information has come from language studies as well as from more experimental procedures. Languages vary considerably in the means they provide for speakers to talk about time. In English we can use different forms of verbs or add particular endings to them (*-ed*) to indicate that we are talking about the past. Unlike the French, we can't do something similar to talk about the future. Instead we have a selection of extra words like 'will' and 'might' which we use with present-tense verbs to talk about things which have yet to happen. These are just two of the several linguistic devices available to a speaker of English. A study of the development of the ability of English speaking children to talk about the time concepts of 'order' and 'duration' (Bancroft, 1985) has shown that children as young as 2 years of age have and use some of the available means. Children were recorded in interactions with their parents from the time they were 2 until they were 3.5 years of age. All references to the past were noted, with the following conclusion: the children's ability to talk about time developed in terms of the sophistication with which they used the available linguistic devices. In other words, there was some evidence that these children were talking about time concepts from the beginning of their third year. Being able to talk about time (and cause) is not necessarily the same as being able to *reason* about the concept, although to speak of anything in a consistent and clear way must involve some level of understanding. This psycholinguistic evidence can be seen as being at variance with some of Piaget's research findings which point to difficulties with the concept of time until a child's tenth year.

It may be the case then that some of the difficulty experienced by children in formal experimentation resides in the experimentation itself. In other words, what the children have been asked to do does not allow them to demonstrate their level of understanding. To investigate this possibility a more recent study (Bancroft and Slowen, 1993) has presented the Piagetian problem to children but this time using a scene involving the feeding of some ducks represented on a computer over which the children have some control. The children in the study, aged between 5 and 7 years, have to use the computer to help a duck get to the food first.

This task involves the manipulation of the time concepts of starting order and speed. When the problem of manipulating some of temporal concepts like order and duration was presented in this form, children in the study produced successful solutions. This is at variance with Piagetian predictions but is consistent with observations that young children's language contains appropriate reference to these temporal concepts. This suggests, as so often before, that great care is needed in devising tasks which attempt to identify what children understand.

Although there is evidence that children as young as 2 years have *some* understanding of the concepts of time, there are many pieces of research which suggest that time is a complex topic and that full understanding is a rather late achievement. A study by Danielle Maurice-Naville and Jacques Montanegro (1992) has explored something of this later development in a way which brings together understanding of time and cause by children up to their twelfth year. These researchers were interested in children's ability to locate an object of knowledge along a temporal perspective and to conceive of the past and future of that object. The object they had in mind was a diseased forest tree. The children were shown a World Wildlife Fund film on forest disease and later some photographs of a pine tree at various stages of decay. The researchers used the Piagetian clinical method which, in this case, involved the children being individually questioned about the progress of forest disease in the particular pine tree. On the basis of the children's replies, the psychologists identified three levels of understanding. In the first level (8–9 years) the children were unable to an give account of the continuous process involved, while at the second level (9–10 years) the children gave evidence of understanding the continuous progress of events. Finally, in the third stage (11–12 years) children have an understanding of the continuous process and the relationships that hold between one stage of decay and the next. An understanding of the links between past and future is a development that appears to have taken the child eleven years to achieve in respect of sick trees.

We have looked at some aspects of conceptual organization, but there can be others. Here is a conceptual organization of the animal kingdom which may give pause for thought.

> On those remote pages it is written that animals are divided into,
> (a) those that belong to the Emperor, (b) embalmed ones, (c) those that are trained, (d) suckling pigs, (e) mermaids, (f) fabulous ones, (g) stray dogs, (h) those that are included in this classification, (i) those that tremble as if they were mad, (j) innumerable ones, (k) those drawn with a very fine camel's hair brush, (l) others, (m) those that have just broken a flower vase, (n) those that resemble flies from a distance.
>
> (Borges, 1964, p. 103, describing the ancient Chinese encyclopaedia entitled *Celestial Emporium of Benevolent Knowledge*)

SUMMARY OF SECTION 5

- Human reasoning involves the process of drawing inferences from either speech, text or experiences.
- Psychologists have explored children's ability to manipulate concepts in laboratory studies and have explored their ability to understand concepts by evaluating the language they produce.
- Language (and the social context in which it is used) seems to be implicated in the development of children's understanding of concepts and their ability to reason about them.
- Although young children have been shown to have more understanding of concepts like 'cause' and 'time' than was formerly suspected, there is also evidence which suggests that a complete understanding is an achievement of late childhood.

FURTHER READING

McShane, J. (1991) *Cognitive Development: an information processing approach*, Oxford, Blackwell.

REFERENCES

Bancroft, D. (1985) *The Development of Temporal Reference: a study of children's language*, Nottingham, University of Nottingham (unpublished PhD thesis).

Bancroft, D. and Slowen, A. (1993) 'Some aspects of temporal reasoning by young children', *European Journal of Psychology of Education*, **8**(2), pp. 119–33.

Boden, M. (1977) *Artificial Intelligence and Natural Man*, Hemel Hempstead, Harvester Press.

Borges, J. L. (1964) *Other Inquisitions 1937–1952*, Austin, University of Texas Press.

Bryant, P. E. and Trabasso, T. (1971) 'Transitive inferences and memory in young children', *Nature*, **232**, pp. 456–8.

Carrabine, B. (1991) 'Fuzzy boundaries and the extension of object words', *Journal of Child Language*, **18**, pp. 355–72.

Chauvin, Y. (1988) *Symbol Acquisitions in Humans and Neural (PDP) Networks*, San Diego, University of California (unpublished PhD thesis).

DAS GUPTA, P. and BRYANT, P. E. (1989) 'Young children's causal inferences', *Child Development*, **60**, pp. 1138–46.

DUNN, J. and BROWN, J. R. (1993) 'Early conversations about causality: content, pragmatics and developmental change', *British Journal of Developmental Psychology*, **11**, pp. 107–23.

FODOR, J. A. (1972) 'Some reflections on L. S. Vygotsky's *Thought and Language*', *Cognition*, **1**, pp. 83–95.

KIEL, F. (1989) *Concepts, Kinds and Cognitive Development*, Cambridge (Mass.), MIT Press.

LAKOFF, R. (1975) *Language and Women's Place*, New York, Harper and Row.

McSHANE, J. (1991) *Cognitive Development: an information processing approach*, Oxford, Blackwell.

MANDLER, J (1992) 'How to build a baby II: conceptual primitives', *Psychological Review*, **99**, pp. 587–604.

MAURICE-NAVILLE, D. and MONTANEGRO, J. (1992) 'The development of diachronic thinking: 8–12 year-old children's understanding of the evolution of forest disease', *British Journal of Developmental Psychology*, **10**, pp. 365–83.

MERVIS, C. B. and CRISAFI, M. A. (1982) 'Order of acquisition of subordinate, basic and superordinate level categories', *Child Development*, **53**, pp. 258–66.

OAKHILL, J. (1984) 'Why children have difficulty reasoning with three-term series problems', *British Journal of Developmental Psychology*, **2**(3), pp. 223–30.

PLUNKETT, K. and SINHA, C. (1992) 'Connectionism and developmental theory', *British Journal of Developmental Psychology*, **10**, pp. 209–54.

ROSCH, E. (1978) 'Principles of categorization' in ROSCH, E. and LLOYD, B. B. (eds), *Cognition and categorization*, Hillsdale, NJ.

ROSCH, E., MERVIS, C. B., GRAY, W. D., JOHNSON, D. M. and BOYES-BRAEM, P. (1976) 'Basic objects in natural categories', *Cognitive Psychology*, **8**, pp. 382–439.

SMITH, E. E. and MEDIN, D. L. (1981) *Concepts and Categories*, Cambridge (Mass.), Harvard University Press.

VYGOTSKY, L. S. (1962) *Thought and Language*, Cambridge (Mass), MIT Press.

WAXMAN, S. (1990) 'Linguistic biases and the establishment of conceptual hierarchies: evidence from pre-school children', *Cognitive Development*, **5**, pp. 123–4.

WITTGENSTEIN, L. (trans. ANSCOMBE, E.) (1967) *Philosophical Investigations*, Oxford, Blackwell.

READINGS

Reading A   Newspeak

George Orwell

The purpose of Newspeak was not only to provide a medium of expression for the world-view and mental habits proper to the devotees of Ingsoc, but to make all other modes of thought impossible. It was intended that when Newspeak had been adopted once and for all and Oldspeak forgotten, a heretical thought – that is, a thought diverging from the principles of Ingsoc – should be literally unthinkable, at least so far as thought is dependent on words. Its vocabulary was so constructed as to give exact and often very subtle expression to every meaning that a Party member could properly wish to express, while excluding all other meanings and also the possibility of arriving at them by indirect methods. This was done partly by the invention of new words, but chiefly by eliminating undesirable words and by stripping such words as remained of unorthodox meanings, and so far as possible of all secondary meanings whatever. To give a single example. The word *free* still existed in Newspeak, but it could only be used in such statements as 'This dog is free from lice' or 'This field is free from weeds'. It could not be used in its old sense of 'politically free' or 'intellectually free', since political and intellectual freedom no longer existed even as concepts, and were therefore of necessity nameless. Quite apart from the suppression of definitely heretical words, reduction of vocabulary was regarded as an end in itself, and no word that could be dispensed with was allowed to survive. Newspeak was designed not to extend but to *diminish* the range of thought, and this purpose was indirectly assisted by cutting the choice of words down to a minimum.

Source: Orwell, G. (1949) Nineteen Eighty-Four, *London, Secker and Warburg, pp. 241–2.*

Reading B   Children's concepts of health and illness

Sara Meadows

Eiser (1985: 15) claims that 'there is beginning to be considerable evidence that children's beliefs about these issues [the causes and prevention of illness, and their definitions of health and behaviours they think important in maintaining health] develop in a systematic predictable sequence'. She bases this claim very largely on the work of Bibace and Walsh (1981), who describe neo-Piagetian stages in children's concepts of health and illness. They interviewed 24 children at each of the three age levels of 4, 7 and 11, using questions such as 'what does it mean to be healthy?', 'were you ever sick?', 'how did you get sick?', 'how did you get better?', 'what makes colds go away?', 'what is a heart attack?', 'why do people get heart attacks?', 'what are germs?', 'what do they look like?', 'can you draw germs?', 'where do they come from?'.

In the 'prelogical' stage of the youngest children, the main cause of illness was contagion, though God and certain other external causes were cited ('How do people get colds?' 'From trees'). In the 'concrete-logical' stage (7–10) illness arose through contamination by physical contact with the illness, more elaborately by swallowing or inhaling it. In the 'formal-logical' stage illness was seen as caused by specific malfunctioning or non-functioning of an internal organ or process, with psychological and physiological functions ultimately interacting.

Similarly Brewster (1982) found that young children believed that illness was the result of human action and children from 7 to 10 that it was caused by 'germs', while only children over 11 acknowledged that illnesses were the result of interaction between several factors, different for each specific illness. Kister and Patterson (1980) also found lack of differentiation between different illnesses: young children judged that a cold, toothache and a scraped knee could all be explained by contagion (or even immanent justice). Eiser, Patterson and Eiser (1983) describe children's ideas about health. Being energetic, taking exercise and eating good food were increasingly frequently mentioned between 6 and 11 years of age, and were the main components of descriptions of 'health' throughout this age range.

It is not entirely clear that these findings represent children's concepts of health and illness completely fairly (see Harbeck and Peterson 1992, Siegal 1988, 1991). The work stemming from a neo-Piagetian 'cognitive developmental' approach focuses very much on cognition without examining social or cultural influences; it seems very likely that phenomena like the young child's tendency to say that illness is caused by wrong-doing owes something to parental invocations of illness as a consequence of not doing what you're told – 'if you don't eat up your dinner/wrap up warm/wear your boots, you'll get ill'. Neo-Piagetian analyses of such data, focusing on cognitive structures characteristic of discrete stages, will run into the same problems that have brought Piaget's own stage model under question (see Gelman and Baillargeon 1983, Mandler 1983, Meadows 1983). In particular they will fail to account for transition from one stage to another and to acknowledge the existence of individual differences which may be associated with different experiences and cultures. Further, the interview technique used may be insensitive to the understanding of young children, so underestimating their competence. Siegal (1988, 1991) for example, investigated children's understanding of contamination and contagion by asking children to judge other people's (a puppet's or another child's) account of why they got a cold or toothache or a scraped knee. Even 4-year-olds showed a good substantial knowledge of contagion and contamination: they knew that contagion was a good explanation for a cold and a poor one for a scraped knee, and believed that milk into which a foreign body such as a cockroach or a dirty comb had fallen was no longer really safe to drink. Further research using more ingenious techniques such as these, or examining children's scripts (Eiser 1988, Eiser and Eiser 1987) may uncover more understanding in young children and more variation at a particular age than Bibace and Walsh (1981) found.

In particular, it is essential that alternative theories of why cognition develops about health and illness should be considered, both for the improvement of accounts of cognitive development and for the improvement of the care of chronically sick children who need explanations of their illness to allay their fears and increase their co-operation with treatment (Eiser and Eiser 1987).

References

BIBACE, R. and WALSH, M. E. (eds) (1981) 'Children's conceptions of illness', *New Directions for Child Development*, vol 14, San Francisco, Jossey Bass.

BREWSTER, A. B. (1982) 'Chronically ill hospitalised children's concepts of their illness', *Pediatrics*, 69, pp. 355–62.

EISER, C. (1985) *The Psychology of Childhood Illness*, New York, Springer-Verlag.

EISER, C. (1988) 'Explaining illness to children', *Communications and Cognition*, **20**, pp. 277–90.

EISER, C. and EISER, J. R. (1987) 'Explaining illness to children', *Communications and Cognition*, **20**(2/3), pp. 277–90.

EISER, C., PATTERSON, D. and EISER, J. R. (1983) 'Children's Knowledge of Health and Illness: implications for health education', *Child Care, Health and Development*, **9**, pp. 285–92.

GELMAN, R. and BAILLARGEON, R. (1983) 'A review of some Piagetian concepts' in FLAVELL, J. H. and MARKMAN, E. (eds) *Handbook of Child Psychology*, vol 3 *Child Development*, series ed. MUSSEN, P.H., New York, Wiley.

HARBECK, C. and PETERSON, L. (1992) 'Elephants Dancing in my Head: a developmental approach to children's concepts of specific pains', *Child Development*, **63**, pp. 138–49.

KISTER, M. C. and PATTERSON, C. J. (1980) 'Children's Conceptions of the Causes of Illness: understanding of contagion and use of immanent justice', *Child Development*, **51**, pp. 839–46.

MANDLER, J. (1983) 'Representation' in MUSSEN, P. H. (ed.) *Handbook of Child Psychology*, vol 3 *Child Development*, New York, Wiley.

MEADOWS, S. (ed.) (1983) *Developing Thinking: approaches to children's cognitive development*, London, Methuen.

SIEGAL, M. (1988) 'Children's knowledge of contamination and contagion as causes of illness', *Child Development*, **59**, pp. 1353–9.

SIEGAL, M. (1991) *Knowing Children: experiments in conversation and cognition*, Hove, Erlbaum.

SOURCE: MEADOWS, S. (1993) The Child as Thinker: the development and acquisition of cognition in childhood, London, Routledge, pp. 122–3.

Ken Richardson

CONTENTS

1 INTRODUCTION

1.1 Intelligence in a word

To indicate the range of issues raised in this chapter try the short questionnaire in Activity 1. Let me explain straightaway that the questions presented there are but a few from a much more extensive research project carried out by Mugny and Carugati (1989). (If some of the wording seems a little strange, that may be due to translation from the original Italian.) We will be returning to these questions in the last section of this chapter.

ACTIVITY 1

Allow about 15 minutes

QUESTIONNAIRE

Indicate your level of agreement with the following statements using a scale from 1 (disagree absolutely) to 7 (agree absolutely). If you would like to qualify your response in any way, or make any further comments, do so on a separate sheet of paper.

Q1 Intelligence above all is a question of character

Q2 Intelligence is gauged by the capacity for abstract thought

Q3 The brain is the birthplace of intelligence

Q4 The development of intelligence is the gradual learning of the rules of social life

Q5 The development of intelligence occurs in stages, each of which results in the reorganization of previous capacities

Q6 The development of intelligence progresses according to a biological programme fixed at birth

Q7 Everyone is intelligent in their own way

Q8   Some people are born with more intelligence, others with less

Q9   The child develops intelligence by his or her own activity

Q10 Have a group of children working together; they will develop their intelligence better than if they each work for themselves

Q11 Children who do not like school will not develop their intelligence

Q12 Children are capable of understanding logic because they understand the rules of social life

(selected from Mugny and Carugati, 1989, pp. 165–72)

This exercise should have demonstrated one thing already: that intelligence is, to most people, a meaningful aspect of children's development. Indeed, intelligence is one of the most-used words both in everyday communication and in psychological discourse. Probably most people would agree that it is our intelligence which chiefly distinguishes humans from other animals. Nearly all societies, past and present, in many different parts of the world, have used something like a concept of intelligence. It is applied in a wide variety of situations and at all ages. This suggests that the concept has a very important social role. In our own society, it is embraced by the vast majority of people and attributed to others with remarkable confidence. Newson *et al*. (1977, cited by Goodnow, 1984) have shown that parents feel quite sure about their judgements of their children's intelligence from an early age, often in the first few days of an infant's life. Goodnow (1984) for example, cites one study showing such judgements in the first 48 hours of life! And, as we shall see later, teachers' abilities to judge, impressionistically, their pupils' intelligence, is used as a basis for constructing intelligence tests.

1.2 Commonsense and scientific views of intelligence

Intelligence is a very common idea in everyday discourse; but what have scholars and scientists had to say about it? Intelligence has actually been the subject of study for a very long time. Two conceptions of intelligence appear to have emerged in Greece at least two thousand years ago. The philosopher Plato, living around 340 BC, spoke of men of Gold (the leaders or Guardians), of Silver (their administrators) and of Brass (industrial and agricultural workers), distinguished by differences in general intellectual strength. Because he thought the degree of intellectual strength was innate, Plato deduced that it could be improved in the population, generally, by planned breeding (eugenics). Thus he advocated a system of marriage and reproduction confined to the Guardians (the Rulers) whose (superior) offspring would thus increasingly upgrade the intelligence of future generations.

Plato was not too concerned to describe or characterize this intellectual strength further. Rather, he saw it as a useful social label and a basis for social policy. His student, Aristotle, adopted a different approach, and wanted to describe all natural phenomena in as much detail as possible. He attempted to characterize the properties, functions and development of intelligence, just as he dissected cadavers, studied plants closely, and observed the development of embryos in hens' eggs. Thus Aristotle observed intelligence as a common property of citizens (i.e., excluding slaves) but one peculiar to humans: 'that whereby the mind thinks and reasons'. And he argued that 'intellectual virtue in the main owes its birth and its growth to teaching (for which reason it requires experience and time)'.

The fact that Plato was writing for an authoritarian regime, and Aristotle for a much more liberal one, has been thought to be more than incidental to these rival approaches to the understanding of intelligence (Robinson, 1981). These approaches have been bequeathed to successive generations of scholars right up to modern times. One approach has suggested intelligence as a general mental strength or power, determining social ability and status, but without clear form and content. The other has sought to describe that form and content in as clear detail as possible. In the twentieth century, the first approach became dominated by attempts to actually measure the supposed 'mental strength or power', and came to be known as the *psychometric approach*. The second approach, seeking to understand intelligence in terms of actual knowledge and reasoning processes, is probably best described as the *cognitive approach*.

What follows is a brief review of the emergence and diversification of these approaches in modern times, and what each of them has to say about development. We examine the 'psychometric' and 'cognitive' approaches in turn, and then, in the final section, introduce an alternative approach to the understanding of intelligence that has been emerging recently.

SUMMARY OF SECTION 1

- The concept of intelligence is used frequently both in everyday discourse and as part of scientific studies.
- Most scientific study has taken one or other of two approaches, with rival purposes and outcomes, and this duality of approach persists today.
- One of these has treated intelligence as an all-round intellectual power and forms the modern 'psychometric' approach. The other seeks to describe underlying processes of knowledge and reasoning and forms the modern 'cognitive' approach

2 THE PSYCHOMETRIC APPROACH

2.1 Galton

The modern psychometric approach undoubtedly begins with Sir Francis Galton in the late nineteenth century. The Platonic nature of Galton's view is shown in his belief that the marked social grades in Britain were the inevitable expressions of different biological endowments, and he repeatedly condemned 'pretensions of natural equality' (Galton, 1869, p. 14, quoted by Evans and Waites, 1981, p. 38). This belief led Galton, like Plato, to favour a eugenic breeding programme for the improvement of society, and he wanted scientific measurement of intelligence to further that end. Such measures would serve, he argued, 'for the indications of superior strains or races, and in so favouring them that their progeny shall outnumber and gradually replace that of the old one' (Galton, 1883, quoted by Evans and Waites, 1981, p. 41).

ACTIVITY 2

Allow about 10 minutes

NATURAL INEQUALITY OF INTELLIGENCE

The psychometric approach has its roots in this notion of 'natural inequality' of intelligence. To what extent would you say that such natural inequality exists among children in the characteristics listed below? Mark with 1 for quite a lot; 2 for a moderate extent; 3 for not very much:

(a) Language ability

(b) Motor skills (as in sports or gymnastics)

(c) Social reasoning skills

(d) Motor skills (as in cultural tools like using eating implements)

(e) Musical ability

(NB You have already done this for intelligence in Activity 1, Q8).

Comment

Of course, I cannot be certain, but my guess is that you were able to provide 'estimates' without too much difficulty. That is the point of the activity. Most people feel able to form impressions of this sort, often with remarkable confidence, just as Galton did with intelligence, largely on the basis of subjective experience, or hearsay evidence. We must be wary about relying on what appears to be 'obvious' to superficial impression. For one thing, only a little detachment allows us to see that such impressions are culturally situated, and have changed from time to time. For example, among Japanese, intelligence is not considered to vary significantly among individual children; with few exceptions everyone has 'enough', and effort and motivation are considered to be far more important to culturally-valued development (Fallows, 1989; cf. Hanson, 1993). We will be returning to such culturally variant views later on.

So how was Galton to measure this intelligence in real individuals? Because he viewed intelligence as an overall mental strength or power –

what he called 'natural ability' – he reasoned that it must be manifest in all individual activities, even quite simple sensorimotor tasks. Thus we could measure this intellectual power by assessing individuals' performance on quite simple sensory and motor tasks. Galton and his associates, such as J. McKeen Cattell, devised a number of such tasks. Here is a set devised by Cattell in 1890:

1   *Dynamotor Pressure.* How tightly can the hand squeeze?

2   *Rate of Movement.* How quickly can the hand move through a distance of 50 cm?

3   *Sensation-areas.* How far apart must two points be on the skin to be recognized as two rather than one?

4   *Pressure Causing Pain.* How much pressure on the forehead is necessary to cause pain?

5   *Least Noticeable Difference in Weight.* How large must the difference be between two weights before it is reliably detected?

6   *Reaction-time for Sound.* How quickly can the hand be moved at the onset of an auditory signal?

7   *Time for Naming Colours.* How long does it take to name a strip of ten coloured papers?

8   *Bisection of a 10 cm Line.* How accurately can one point to the centre of an ebony rule?

9   *Judgement of 10 seconds of Time.* How accurately can an interval of 10 seconds be judged?

10 *Number of Letters Remembered on Once Hearing.* How many letters, ordered at random, can be repeated exactly after one presentation?

(Cattell, 1890, quoted in Miller, 1962, pp. 310–1)

Immediately, we encounter a problem that has dogged the psychometric approach throughout its history. Most measures devised by humans can be shown to correspond with something existing in real life, either because we can sense it directly (e.g. length or weight) or through some intermediate measure that itself has a proven correspondence with that 'something' (e.g. the concentrations of certain gases in a breathalyser test and the amount of alcohol in the bloodstream). In the case of Galton's and Cattell's tests, how are we to know that people's performance on these sensory and motor tasks is actually measuring the 'something' he claimed to be measuring?

Galton's solution was to become the hallmark of the 'intelligence' test: the performance of individuals simply needs to be compared 'with an independent estimate of the man's powers … ' (quoted by Evans and Waites, 1981, p. 37). Galton's 'independent estimate' was much the same as Plato's. A person's position on the social ladder could itself be a 'measure' of intelligence. If individuals' performances on the tests corresponds with such status then the tests are measuring intelligence. Or, as Hunt put it: 'We are presumed to know who is intelligent and to accept a test as a measure of intelligence if it identifies such persons' (1983, p. 141) .

You should note how this strategy bypasses any connection with the actual entity to be measured. A similar pragmatic strategy would calibrate the gaseous output of a breathalyser test against some other 'independent estimate' – such as walking down a white line – instead of real blood-alcohol levels. Consequently, many people have pointed to the flaw in Galton's reasoning. Far from being an 'independent estimate' of intelligence, it is possible that people obtain their high social status from other means – from inheritance of wealth and privilege, or effort, for example.

In the event the tests did not 'work' as Galton and Cattell had hoped. Differences were found among individuals on such measures. But, when the measures were compared with social status, it was found that there was little or no relationship. In other words, because the measured differences did not parallel differences assumed to be the 'real' expression of intelligence, the tests were disappointing. In spite of this failure, however, the general strategy devised signals the origins of the intelligence-testing movement. The development of the strategy into a successful test simply awaited the invention of different kinds of tasks.

2.2 Binet

READING

The French psychologist, Alfred Binet, continued the development of measures of intelligence. Reading A is an account of his contribution. As you read it, note:

- the sorts of tasks which Binet devised;
- the criteria he used for accepting some items as suitable and others as unsuitable;
- any theoretical grounds he used as the basis of such criteria;
- the origins of the IQ.

Miller refers to the myriad different items which Binet incorporated in his first test. Here are some of the types of items he used:

Imitating gestures and following simple commands

Naming objects in pictures

Repeating spoken digits

Defining common words

Drawing designs from memory

Telling how objects are alike ('similarities')

Comparing two lines of unequal length

Putting three nouns or three verbs into a sentence

'Abstract' (comprehension) questions (e.g. 'When a person has offended you, and comes to offer his apologies, what should you do?')

Defining abstract words (by describing the difference between such words as 'boredom' and 'weariness', 'esteem' and 'friendship')

(quoted from Wolf, 1973, pp. 179–83).

ACTIVITY 3

Allow about 10 minutes

BINET AND SIMON: COMPARISON OF TEST ITEMS WITH INDEPENDENT ESTIMATES OF INTELLIGENCE

Like Galton, Binet and Simon used the indirect approach of using other indices of intelligence as the criteria for selecting their test items. What were the independent estimates of intelligence against which Binet and Simon gauged the success of their test items? Write them down; then think about them for a moment. Do you think they are reasonable?

Comment

'If a test did not distinguish the brighter from the duller, or the older from the younger, it was abandoned.' The criteria of item acceptability were thus: (i) age – more of the older children should be able to do them than the younger children; (ii) more of the 'brighter' children should be able to do them than the 'duller' children, which in effect meant that test results should agree with the impressions of teachers and others in the school situation. The first of these seems uncontentious (although it assumes that intelligence develops gradually with age). There may be doubts about the second one, though; it equates intelligence with school achievement – or at least views them as expressions of the same thing. Is this a reasonable assumption? Bear this point in mind – we will be returning to it later.

Binet's approach was similar to that of Galton, then; but it was different in significant details. First he used 'brightness' in school as the 'independent estimate' of intelligence. And his tasks were ones which teachers would set or expect pupils to be able to do in the classroom (thus virtually guaranteeing some association). He largely disregarded the whole question of a model or theory of the 'intelligence' being measured. The test was successful because it 'worked' in identifying the children it was intended to identify.

Note, also, that Binet's purpose was quite different from that of Galton: he wanted a diagnostic tool, not the instrument of sweeping social policy that Galton had failed to produce. However, Binet's test was found to 'work' in that other sense too: scores on Binet's test (for whatever reason) tended to correlate to some extent with social status, in a way which would have delighted Galton. Others soon came to use the test in ways other than Binet had intended, and he was later to protest about the interpretations which they made of test scores (Wolf, 1973).

2.3 The growth of intelligence testing

Within a matter of years, Binet's test was in use in many other parts of the world. The most rapid developments took place in the US, when Henry H. Goddard translated Binet's test into English in 1910. Soon other, similar, tests were being constructed. The use to which they were put, however, was frequently unpleasant, giving rise to allegations of racism and social injustice.

ACTIVITY 4

Allow about 10 minutes

BINET'S TEST ITEMS: INVALID CONCLUSIONS

Look again at Binet's (translated) items(p. 155). In the US, over a period of many years, they were administered to adults and children from widely differing social backgrounds, and even to newly-arrived immigrants as they disembarked at sea ports. Can you say why the resulting scores may give rise to invalid conclusions about people's intelligence?

Comment

The promoters of these tests strongly tended to adopt Galton's view on natural inequality and to ignore important factors like background knowledge, language and cultural experience. The 'results' of these surveys led to the conclusion that Blacks, Jews, Irish, and so on, had little native intelligence, whilst Anglo-Saxons had most. These conclusions fuelled eugenic and anti-immigration bills in the US and created debates about cultural bias in IQ tests which reverberate to this day.

2.4 The Stanford-Binet scale and the Wechsler scales

In 1916 Lewis Terman at Stanford University published a revision of the Binet-Simon Intelligence Scale. Like the Binet test, it was based on a variety of items selected according to their ability to discriminate among children of different ages who, 'on other grounds' were known to be bright or dull (Terman, 1916, p. 47). But there were many more items (ninety in all). It very quickly became the standard IQ test on both sides of the Atlantic. This test was revised in 1937 and in 1960 to include a wider variety and greater number of items. Here are examples of items which an average 10 year old would be expected to pass.

1   *Vocabulary*. Showing they know the meaning of words such as 'orange', 'envelope', 'straw', 'puddle', 'scorch', 'brunette'.

FIGURE 1
Block counting.

2   *Block counting*. Correctly counting the blocks in eight out of fourteen three-dimensional pictures where some of the blocks are obscured.

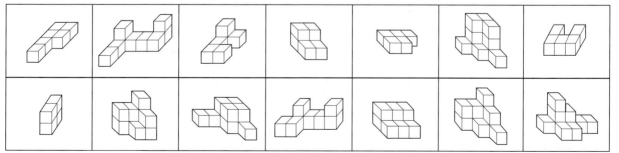

3   *Abstract words*. Defining two of the following:
    (a) pity   (b) curiosity   (c) grief   (d) surprise

4   *Finding reasons*.
    (a) Giving two reasons why children should not be too noisy in school.

5   *Word naming*. Producing as many words as possible in one minute. (Credit given for twenty eight words.)

6   *Repeating digits*. Repeating in order at least one of the following sequences:

   (a)   4–7–3–8–5–9

   (b)   5–2–9–7–4–6

   (c)   7–2–8–3–9–4

For each of these items detailed scoring instructions are given, and a list of acceptable and unacceptable answers is provided.

The American psychologist David Wechsler, believing that the Stanford-Binet was not very satisfactory in form or content for assessing adults, devised a new test in the 1930s, the Wechsler Adult Intelligence Scale. In 1949 it was augmented by the Wechsler Intelligence Scale for Children (the WISC), revised in 1974 and 1992; and by the Wechsler Pre-school and Primary Scale of Intelligence. In these scales, IQ was not derived from the ratio of mental age to chronological age, but as 'deviation IQ's', or the relative degree to which any child differs from the mean of the age group.

Like the Stanford-Binet, the Wechsler scales include a variety of items but separate them more definitely into Verbal sub-tests (which include vocabulary, arithmetic, similarities, general information and comprehension) and Performance sub-tests (which include picture completion, mazes, geometric design, and block design). Such division was provided 'not because the author believes they represent different kinds of intelligence' but to suggest how 'a subject's assets and liabilities may influence his overall functioning...' (Wechsler, 1967, p. 2).

The Stanford-Binet and the WISC have been the most widely used tests on both sides of the Atlantic, and probably still are. For example, in a small survey in the UK, Quicke (1982) found that the WISC and the Stanford-Binet were regularly used by 82 per cent and 42 per cent, respectively, of educational psychologists. They have been augmented in recent years with the British Ability Scales which were constructed in order to provide a scale of general mental capacity or 'educability' adapted to British children and standardized on a British population (Elliott, 1983). They provide twenty-three subscales from 'speed of information processing' to 'social reasoning' (reasoning about and solving a fictitious moral dilemma).

2.5 Group tests

Although Binet-type tests rapidly became popular among psychologists, the fact that they were administered by one tester to one testee at a time soon proved a major drawback. Psychologists often wanted to test large numbers of people at a time, as with children in school, or recruits in the armed forces. The result was the devising of paper-and-pencil tests which could be given to large numbers of people simultaneously.

As with the earlier tests, their construction consisted of devising batteries of items which had an intuitive correspondence with what the constructor saw as intelligence, and then selecting those which trials showed would make up a test with the required overall properties.

Soon such tests became very widely used. In Britain group tests were available from the early 1920s and were included in the 11+ school examinations after World War 2. Today many such tests are employed for personnel selection in, for instance, the civil service, the armed forces, and in industry and commerce. From the 1940s they were extensively used in educational selection. There is scarcely a person, in fact, who has not been given such a test at one time or another.

The types of items used in group tests include a range of general information, verbal and arithmetic problems, classifications, sequences, opposites, and so on. A very common item is some type of analogy, having the general form A is to B as C is to ? (select D from a range of alternatives); for example:

> Teacher is to pupil as Doctor is to
>
> (hospital, nurse, patient, medicine, child)

Matrix items are also very common in group tests (see the example in Figure 2). Perhaps the best-known of all group tests is Raven's Progressive Matrices, made up entirely of such items. These tests are usually timed.

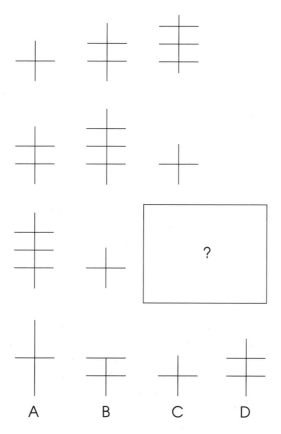

FIGURE 2 Example of a simple matrix item.

READING

Now turn to Reading B (from Berger and Yule, 1985). The section
you have just read offers a very brief description of the composition
of the most widely used tests, and the criteria that are used in their
composition. Many psychologists have a very favourable view of the
tests. This reading offers a favourable account of the range of uses of
IQ tests. As you read it pay particular attention to the following
points:

- the main justifications for them as useful instruments;

- the range of purposes to which they may be put;

- any indications of the nature of the intelligence they are said to
  measure.

In the next section we look at some of the criticisms that have projected
a less favourable view of the psychometric approach to understanding
intelligence.

2.6 Some evaluation

There are very many psychologists who believe that IQ tests are
misleading, even phoney, and have raised many questions about them.
What is actually being measured? What are differences in scores really
differences in? Can multiples of performance on very simple tasks really
tell us about levels of fundamental cognitive functions? Or are such
performances simply a reflection of more elusive personality or cultural
variables? Can they legitimately be called 'intelligence' tests or should
they more accurately be called tests of educational prediction? Why do
we not have a clearer theoretical connection between IQ scores and the
entity being measured? Perhaps the main concerns are as follows.

Atheoretic composition of tests

Each task which children are asked to tackle, or question which they are
required to answer, is called an item. You should remember that Binet
selected from a 'pool' of items only those which 'bright' children (as
judged by teachers' impressions) did better at than 'dull' children. This
procedure has been followed, directly or indirectly, ever since. But,
because the criteria provide no direct purchase on intelligence
(impressions of 'brightness' and 'dullness' arise from a number of
causes) many people feel uneasy (as did Binet himself) about inferring
differences in scores as fixed 'differences in intelligence'.

Do IQ tests predict anything else?

IQ scores do indeed predict school achievement. Correlations of IQ with
school grades vary a great deal, but most fall within the range 0.4 to 0.6
(Block and Dworkin, 1976; Brody, 1985). There should be no mystery
about this: 'From the very way in which the tests were assembled it

could hardly be otherwise' (Thorndike and Hagen, 1969, p. 325). But do IQ scores predict performance in the outside world? IQ inevitably correlates with job status because school achievement is used as a criterion of access to different job levels. But as Jensen (1970, p. 63) concludes, there are 'surprisingly low correlations between a wide variety of intelligence tests and actual proficiency on the job'. In more recent analyses Ceci (1990) has put this correlation at virtually zero. So, again, the simple equating of IQ, school achievement and 'intelligence' may be too simple.

The intuitive bases of test structure

Terman reckoned intelligence to be an all-round, 'general' power, rather like Galton had. Wechsler, too, characterized intelligence as an 'aggregate or global capacity' (Wechsler, 1958). So, in these tests, items were only selected if, in addition to agreeing with school achievement, performance on any one of them also tended to agree with performance on every other item (conversely, if a child's score on a particular item was wildly different from average performance on most other items, then that item would be rejected). This inevitably leads to a convergence of scores from the different parts of the test, 'as if' it was assessing a single, general, power.

Other test constructors have assumed, not a single global ability, but a number of separate constituent abilities, and constructed their tests to exhibit a set of 'special abilities', scores on any one of which may not correlate with scores on any other. (The British Ability Scales are based on this assumption). Again, you should be able to see how these rival patterns of test scores emerge from assumptions used in test construction rather than insights about intelligence as such.

Assumptions about group differences in intelligence

It might be clear by now that judicious item selection produces the required pattern of scores and that it is possible to increase, decrease, or even invert differences between children's scores depending on prior expectations. Thus the first version of the Stanford-Binet exhibited substantial sex differences in favour of males. Later versions adjusted the test composition so that such an overall difference was abolished. The nature of the existence of other group differences such as those between social classes and ethnic groups has produced constant debate about whether they are 'real' differences or artefacts of test construction.

Negative characterizations of children's abilities

A child's failure to complete certain items is often taken to suggest cognitive deficits in a way that might starkly contrast with that child's behaviour in the real world. Consider, for example, a 'spatial reasoning' item like block counting (Figure 1). A child who fails such an item may be perfectly adept at working out the whereabouts of her sock in the bottom left hand drawer of the far chest, in the second room on the left, on the third floor of the house next door, and propelling herself in the appropriate directions to get it – yet be assessed as having little spatial reasoning. So what is it that makes this everyday activity 'unintelligent'? This is a major issue that remains unresolved.

A useful index of a child's cognitive functioning, or simply a numerical surrogate for impressionistic ratings? We cannot continue these debates any further, here. You will often find reference to IQ as an index of cognitive development in tacitly favourable terms. You should bear in mind at least some of the criticisms mentioned here, and make up your own mind about how meaningful such references are.

2.7 Development in IQ

So far we have scarcely mentioned development of intelligence at all. In the psychometric approach this has never been much of an issue, and the reasons for that are fairly clear. If intelligence is some underlying, all-round strength or power, or even a set of sub-powers, then it simply increases with age in a maturational sense, rather than involving a complex sequence of changes over time, in a developmental sense. As Anderson (1992) put it, 'although there are massive changes in intellectual competence through childhood ... there is virtually no developmental story to psychometric intelligence ... This sad state of affairs is a necessary consequence of the essentially atheoretical development of psychometry ...' (Anderson, 1992, p. 29).

Development within the psychometric approach has been described by the kind of graphic representation of IQ shown in Figure 3 – i.e. 'growth curves' showing how individuals' scores increase with age. The main problem is that we don't really know to what extent such 'growth curves' reflect something actually happening in children, or whether they are artefacts of test construction. For example, the 'development' of IQ tails off after the age of fifteen years or so – in spite of the fact that most people would agree that our knowledge and our reasoning capabilities continue to increase.

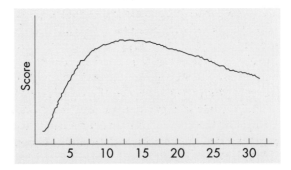

FIGURE 3 The development of intelligence according to the psychometric view – typical changes in test score with age (horizontal axis).

ACTIVITY 5

Allow about 5 minutes

IQ TESTS

From what you know so far about methods of IQ test construction, write down how you would make a test that would show the development of intelligence continuing after the school-leaving age.

Comment

If we devise items that seem to us to indicate post-school achievement and combine them with items used in the school-age tests, our test will produce an IQ that continues to grow well beyond the school years.

You should know by now that an adequate account of development requires not only a description of 'what develops' but also of the sequence of changes that takes place over time, together with the various factors that influence, or 'cause' such changes, including the way that they result in individual differences. This is, of course, a tall order, involving a number of logical and empirical difficulties.

Although there have been determined efforts to understand intelligence in this way (see the sections which follow) researchers working in the psychometric tradition have tended to reduce this complex question to simpler ones like the question of whether individuals' intelligence relative to peers remains stable or changes with age.

For example, a number of researchers have measured 'attention' as an index of intelligence in young infants and then administered an IQ test to the same individuals at some later age. These measures correlate around 0.3 with IQ twelve years later (Sigman *et al.*, 1991) thus supporting the conclusion that 'intelligence' advantages or disadvantages that are evident in infancy are still present when children are 12 years old.

But is this conclusion valid? We need to stress, first, that such correlations are very small and that a correlation is not necessarily a cause. But the main problem is that we cannot be clear about what is being measured at either end of the sequence. As Sigman *et al.* (1991) note, the bases of sustained attention in infancy are still unclear and individual differences may be based on a number of possibilities unrelated to intelligence. The problem of interpretation of IQ scores has already been discussed. As Slater (1990) warns, such observations 'refer to [the] consistency in the relative standing, or ordinal position, of individuals in a group over time: they should not be taken as implying that the cognitive or mental abilities which underlie performance at the different ages are the same, for they surely are not' (Slater, 1990, p. 113).

SUMMARY OF SECTION 2

- Galton aimed to measure intelligence as an instrument of social policy, especially eugenic reproduction.
- His strategy for measuring intelligence was the indirect one of devising simple sensorimotor tasks calibrated against an 'independent estimate', namely social status.
- The calibration he had hoped for failed, so the tests were disappointing.
- Binet used a similar indirect strategy, but devised items whose form was closer to the independent estimate of intelligence ('brightness' in school) he used for their eventual selection.
- These fulfilled Binet's purposes, but were also found to meet the wider purposes which Galton and his followers had had in mind.
- Binet was subsequently to protest against this wider usage and interpretation.
- Binet's test was translated and his strategy used to construct more elaborate tests.
- The main individual tests have been the Stanford-Binet and the WISC (both American) and the British Ability Scales.
- Group tests have also been devised, the main one being Raven's Progressive Matrices.
- Opinions as to the validity and utility of the tests vary widely.
- Development of intelligence tends to have been neglected in the psychometric approach, which has stressed, instead, simple increments of IQ with age.
- Studies of the continuity of 'intelligence' with age are empirically interesting, but are difficult to evaluate or interpret without being clearer about the status of the measures used, and whether the correlations reported are causal ones.

3 THE COGNITIVE APPROACH

Many psychologists have been concerned about the uncertainties in the psychometric approach and argued that 'No serviceable definition can possibly be found for general intelligence until the entire psychology of cognition is established' (Spearman, 1923, p. 5). This has led to increasing demands recently for more 'process-focused' theories; in other words for 'attempts to define the abilities of intelligence in terms of basic, essential capacities, rather in the way a physical scientist describes matter in terms of atoms ...' (Horn, 1986, p. 43).

In this section we will consider a few expressions of this approach. The first one, however, may be considered to be a half-way-house since, as we shall see, it attempts to identify such processes in terms of IQ.

3.1 Intelligence as speed of information processing

Is it possible that different individuals can process information at different speeds and that this is the basis of intelligence? As mentioned earlier, Galton saw mental speed as one of the best indicators of intelligence, and included reaction times (RTs) as one of his measures, though with disappointing results. We will now look at a few studies which have attempted to pursue this idea further.

Most of the recent work on speed of information processing has used the kind of reaction time (RT) apparatus shown in Figure 4. The subject keeps a 'home' button depressed until a light appears nearby. The subject has then to 'hit' the nearest button as quickly as possible.

FIGURE 4 Apparatus for RT experiments (from Anderson, 1992).

Although some association has been found between RT and IQ (Detterman, 1987) there have been many problems of interpretation. A closer look at RT has shown that it is not as simple a process as it at first seems. Far from being a pure, simple measure, it involves a number of complex cognitive, non-cognitive and social factors. The possible factors cited by Detterman as contributing to performance (and thus to individual differences) include understanding instructions; familiarity with the equipment; motivation in the task; sensory acuity; different strategies in various aspects of response selection and construction; and a number of others. Carlson and Widaman (1987) cite studies indicating that level of arousal and attention strongly affect RT. This is one reason why investigators have turned to a slightly different measure.

Imagine that you are presented with two lines, close together on a TV screen, for very brief, but slowly increasing, periods (measured in fractions of a second). You are asked to judge whether they are of the same or different lengths. The duration of presentation required (or 'inspection time') before you are able to make a judgement is considered by some psychologists to be a measure of your 'processing speed' (Nettlebeck, 1987).

Several studies have reported moderate correlations between inspection time (IT) and IQ in both adults and children (Nettlebeck, 1987; Nettlebeck and Young, 1989). Although these results have been questioned on a variety of methodological grounds (e.g. Mackintosh, 1986; Howe, 1988) a correlation in the range -0.3 to -0.5 seems reliable.

M H

Does this mean that development of intelligence (or IQ) is a reflection of maturation of processes like inspection time? There are some doubts about this. For example, there is doubt whether IT itself decreases with age (Anderson, 1986). Anderson concluded that IT derives from the speed of a central information-processing mechanism which does not change significantly with age. Instead, individuals have a genetically-determined speed at which that mechanism operates, and the individual level is important to the development of intelligence (as measured by IQ) because it 'constrains thought' and thereby leads to more rapid knowledge acquisition (Anderson, 1992).

Although this idea sounds reasonable, it has been questioned by Nettlebeck and Vita who found remarkable improvement in IT with practice in most subjects. They found that if children were given just a little practice, the correlations between IT and IQ 'diminished steadily, eventually to negligible proportions' (Nettlebeck and Vita, 1992, p. 189). This, again, suggests that a seemingly 'pure' measure of processing speed is grounded in other factors such as attention, confidence, motivation, and so on (Nettlebeck and Vita, 1992).

Finally, note, again, the problem of interpretation of correlations wherever they are presented as developmental data. Correlations alone cannot indicate that relationships are causally connected (e.g. that differences in IT 'cause' differences in IQ).

RT and IT studies are illustrative of those that have, as it were, taken IQ as a starting point and attempted to discover a cognitive basis for IQ (in effect, thus explaining 'what IQ is') and for its development. There are many other cognitive theories, however, that have started from quite different positions. The remaining parts of this section will look at some of these.

3.2 The development of cognitive processes underlying intelligence

Instead of viewing intelligence simply as a basic unitary power, a broader information-processing approach has attempted to characterize it in terms of specific cognitive processes or components. The developmental problem is then one of describing those that change with age, and how they do so. Sternberg (1988) considers several possible candidates:

- the development of control strategies such as monitoring, chunking of information, and selectivity of responses in problem solving;
- increase in the sheer amount of information that can be processed by the individual at any one time;
- ability to analyse increasingly complex, or 'higher order' relations (as in analogies between analogies);
- increase in flexibility of thinking.

Pascual-Leone (1970) has suggested that general cognitive ability develops through increase in size of a 'central computing space'. Other authors have noted that as children get older they tend to use more complex rules or strategies of reasoning or knowledge management. For example, they use more efficient and more productive computational strategies in simple arithmetic (Kail and Pellegrino, 1985). They are capable of using more complex rules in problem solving (Siegler, 1976). And they may be said to construct more complex 'mental models', and better procedures for constructing and testing them with age (Oakhill, 1988). We will now look at two relatively well worked out theories of this kind.

3.3 Cognitive components and intelligence

Sternberg (1984) has suggested that development in intelligence consists of increases in the efficiency of quite discrete mental operations which he calls 'components'. A 'component is an elementary information process that operates on internal representations of objects or symbols' (Sternberg, 1984, p. 281).

A good illustration of the approach is that of research into 'analogical reasoning', using IQ test items referred to earlier ('A is to B as C is to ?').

The research has entailed breaking subjects' responses down, impressionistically, into various steps (the putative components) and comparing individuals' performance on them. Such steps or 'components' have included:

- *encoding*, or the representation of the salient information in memory;
- *inference* – e.g. of the changes in A necessary to produce B;
- *mapping* – e.g. the correspondence between A and C;
- *applying* – the changes inferred in (ii), to C, to produce the 'best' D;
- *evaluation/justification* of the selection;
- *response*.

Sternberg's results have suggested that individuals who perform well on tasks like analogies tend to spend most time in the *encoding* component, but less in most other components. Development is considered to consist of improvements in efficiency in the operation of components like this.

Thus, children (or less accurate adults) who fail such items tend to perform the inference and application components less readily, and tend to be more easily distracted.

In most of the research, though, it has to be said that the relationships described have tended to be weak ones. The componential approach has also been criticized because it reduces intelligence to sequences of quasi-mechanical operations: i.e. it is excessively mechanistic. Although such operations may have been identified on the surface, how they actually work in the cognitive system underneath, remains unclear.

3.4 Multiple intelligences

Another theory that looks for cognitive grounding of intelligence – although eschewing the mechanistic nature of componential theories – is Gardner's (1984) theory of 'multiple intelligence'. The basic suggestion, here, is the existence within the cognitive/neurobiological system of discrete information-processing operations which deal with the specific, but different, kinds of information which humans encounter in the course of their regular activities. These have evolved by natural selection and their development is genetically determined. 'One might go so far as to define a human intelligence as a neural mechanism or computational system which is genetically programmed to be activated or 'triggered' by certain kinds of internally or externally presented information. Examples would include sensitivity to pitch relations as one core of musical intelligence, or the ability to imitate movement by others as one core of bodily intelligence' (Gardner, 1984, p. 64).

Among these different 'modules' Gardner includes linguistic intelligence, musical intelligence, logico-mathematical intelligence, spatial intelligence, bodily kinaesthetic intelligence, and personal intelligence (access to personal feelings and relationships with others). Although development of their respective processes is conceived to be essentially genetically pre-programmed, they may be subject to some developmental plasticity (and thus amenable to cultural specialization and to educational assistance). Individuals differ in the 'strength' of these intelligences, and thus possess personal 'profiles of intelligences' (Gardner, 1993).

Gardner has spelled out some far reaching implications of his theory for education, arguing that children already enter school with distinctive 'profiles of intelligences'; that these need to be cultivated through suitable activity-centred curricula in order that they will shape to adult social roles; using 'assessment procedures that can provide reliable information about ... a student's profile of capacities at a given moment in his development' (Gardner, 1993, p. 210).

There are a number of possible criticisms of such a theory, though, and Gardner (1984) acknowledges and discusses some of these himself. Perhaps the most serious is that the theory is rather vague (though no more so than many others) in that the way that intelligence develops from 'dumb', innate, computational processes is barely specified.

ACTIVITY 6

Allow about 5 minutes

GARDNER'S THEORY

Would you describe Gardner's theory as rationalist ('innatist'; 'nativist'; 'maturationist'), associationist or constructivist? Why?

Comment

Because it specifies genetically determined mental operations, the development of which is genetically programmed (but dependent upon suitable exercise for manifestation) it is clearly rationalist. However, Gardner allows his intelligences some accommodation to actual experience in development (i.e. some developmental plasticity) and claims that the nature of this accommodation is a responsive, creative one. There is thus also a (secondary) constructivist element in his theory.

3.5 Piaget and intelligence

Piaget's theory has already been described in some detail in Chapter 1, so here we shall only consider its implications for intelligence.

According to Piaget, intelligence arises neither from the 'inside' nor from the 'outside' alone, but from the action of the individual on external objects. The most basic constituents of intelligence are the 'co-ordinations' that are revealed in such actions, and which become represented in mental structures. Take, for example, a ball of clay rolled out into successive shapes:

According to Piaget, the actions of the subject on the object reveal many co-ordinations. First, the length and the thickness are not independent dimensions. There is a necessary connection between them – as one changes so does the other; that is, they vary together, or co-vary. In other words they are co-ordinated. But this co-ordination is itself only part of a wider system of co-ordinations which even a simple action like this reveals – co-ordinations between the visual appearance and the motion of the ball, for example, and between these and other sensations in muscles and joints.

But the really exciting prospect is that, when these co-ordinations have been represented in the sensorimotor system, a set of new powers becomes available which vastly increases our predictive abilities (our intelligence) about the world. For example, there is *compensation* between the variables. We can predict that reducing the length will increase the thickness proportionately, and vice versa:

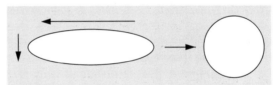

This also illustrates *reversibility*. Given a transformed shape, we can predict what effort would be required to return it to its original shape. There is a 'logical' relation involved.

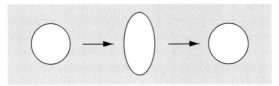

In everyday thoughts and actions like digging, riding bikes, lifting objects, and so on, we take these powers for granted; but they would not be available without representations of co-ordinations being constructed. This is why co-ordination over and above 'raw' experience is such an important idea in Piaget's theory: '... intelligence ... depends as much on progressive internal co-ordinations as on information acquired through experience ...' (Piaget, 1988, p. 3).

Most people think of 'Piaget's theory' as the famous stages through which development passes. But these are only the outer symptoms of the inner developmental processes. Let us remind you of these, very briefly.

3.6 Sensorimotor intelligence

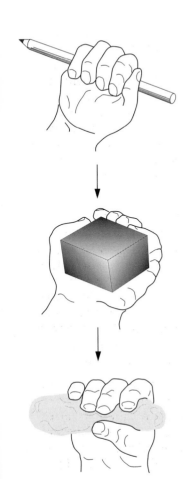

Infants enter the world with a set of innate, but relatively simple, co-ordinations which we call reflexes, and which Piaget called 'innate schemes'. Apart from these, the infant has no 'knowledge' of the world, and is incapable of making any 'cognitions' about it. No distinction can be made, even, between stimuli arising from the inside world and from the outside world. The individual does not yet form a 'subject' with an identity separable from the outside world.

But the innate schemes ensure action on the world – actions which encounter frequent disturbances. Take the scheme (or palmar reflex) of 'grasping' – the tendency to grasp anything placed in the palm of the hand. Studies in infancy show how the original tight grasping pattern slowly accommodates to the range of shapes of objects which, at first, disturb it.

In this way new co-ordinations are constructed from those present at birth by sequences of 're-equilibrations'. Similar sequences apply to all the innate schemes – including seeing, hearing etc. – starting from the first moments of birth (see Figure 5).

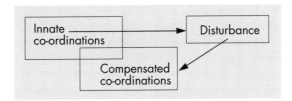

FIGURE 5

The separate sets of co-ordination in developing schemes, (e.g. looking and grasping) then become *inter*-co-ordinated. Important new powers emerge, including the concept of object permanence. One object no longer simply 'replaces' another when covering or screening it; the infant now appreciates that what is seen or not seen is a consequence of relations between objects in a co-ordinated system, rather than one set of fleeting stimuli replacing another. Similarly, the infant can now conceive of him or her self as an 'object' distinct from, but co-ordinated with, those in the outside world, a momentous development which Piaget called a 'Copernican revolution'.

Piaget called these co-ordinations sensorimotor knowledge. As with rolling out a ball of clay or with our knowledge of many physical actions, such as cycling, it is, so to speak, 'in the muscles'. It involves no conscious reflection.

After the first year, however, a slow process of 're-presentation' of these co-ordinations begins at a conscious, reflective level. But for a long time they have the same inadequacies as those which first appeared at the sensorimotor level. The co-ordinations are incompletely represented. Thus there is incomplete reversibility, and, instead, 'centration' on particular variables; and the poor representation of co-ordinations between objects (including people) means that there is a conspicuous 'egocentrism'. Fully compensated operational structures which emerged at the sensorimotor level do not yet have counterparts at the conscious level. Thus, this stage, lasting to about seven years, is called pre-operational intelligence.

Co-ordination among variables in thought becomes evident around seven or eight years. The emergence of these co-ordinations at the operational level appears as 'logical' understanding in the child: e.g. the height and width of liquids in the conservation task (see Chapter 1). But up to about 10 to 11 years, thinking is still concerned with concrete stimuli and concrete actions. Eventually, however, the co-ordinations tied to particular objects and events themselves become co-ordinated under a more general system of representation, detached from concrete objects in the way that mathematics and scientific logic are. These allow thought which is abstract and mathematical; logical and circumspect.

In this developmental process, then, co-ordinations themselves become co-ordinated into progressively more complex 'operational structures' until 'the final operational structures are enclosed within themselves' (Piaget, 1975, p. 65). By 'closure' Piaget meant that the co-ordinations constituting a cognitive structure are so comprehensive as to allow us to make inferences and predictions about the world that are 'logically necessary' – i.e. we can 'think through' and invent solutions to problems detached from concrete experience, as in mathematical and scientific reasoning. Cognitive development – and our intelligence – is then complete.

ACTIVITY 7

Allow about 10 minutes

PIAGET AND STAGES IN INTELLIGENCE

Even very young children can co-ordinate their balance in riding a bike, 'know' that they will go slower uphill, and faster downhill, but cannot tell you why. Some years later they should be able to answer this question. Explain how Piaget might have described the differences in intelligence between these two stages.

Comment

At the earlier age the co-ordinations are 'known' only at a sensorimotor level. Later they are represented mentally, appearing as logical relations, and as predictions and explanations communicable to other people.

Piaget's theory has been much criticized in recent years; these criticisms have consisted, by and large, of:

- demonstration of 'logical' abilities in children well before Piaget predicts;
- dependence of these on particular, especially social, contexts;
- serious doubts about the course of development leading inexorably to general logical structures.

We will now turn to some of the research on which these doubts have been based. But it is worth remembering that Piaget's account remains far and away the most comprehensive theory of the development of intelligence – of 'the whole system of cognition' that Spearman wanted to see described – that has yet been produced.

3.7 Intelligence in context

The psychometric approach tends to have viewed intelligence as consisting of the strength or power of some quasi-mechanical (albeit unspecified) *processes*, as distinct from the knowledge which people have (although operating on it). A number of recent theories – some based on Piaget's theory – have pointed to the inseparability of reasoning from the knowledge of which it is part and parcel. In such theories the structure of knowledge representation determines the structure of reasoning in much the same way that the structure of the cells and tissues of the body organs, such as the kidneys, determines their functions.

Note the drift of the argument, here. If intelligence is 'in' the knowledge-reasoning representation, then an assessment of intelligence divorced from the child's personal experiential history becomes extremely difficult, if not impossible. It is possible, for example, that some children perform better on IQ test items, such as matrix items, because of subtle knowledge requirements built into them.

To test these ideas, Richardson (1991b) sought to devise 'socio-cognitively meaningful' items that paralleled the reasoning required to solve matrix items. Richardson's items told stories based on everyday contexts that were considered to be meaningful to the vast majority of school-age children, and thus to be less discriminating in terms of subtle knowledge prerequisites. An illustration of a matrix item like one from Raven's Matrices is shown in Figure 6 (R items). A socio-cognitive (SC) item parallel to this is shown in Figure 7. All children performed much better on the SC items than on the R items (Figure 8). More surprisingly, there was little association between subjects' performance on one kind of item and their performance on the other, the correlation being 0.183.

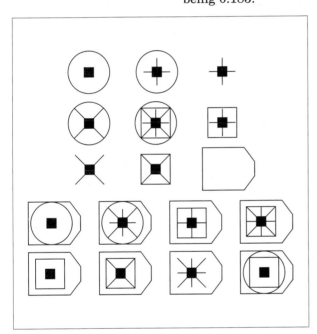

FIGURE 6   Example of Raven's type item.

FIGURE 7   A socio-cognitive item parallel to the Raven's item of Figure 6.

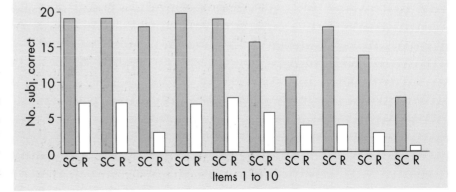

FIGURE 8   Numbers of subjects (out of 20) correct on Raven's (R) compared with socio-cognitively meaningful (SC) items (from Richardson, 1991b).

S G

A large number of similar studies in recent years have confirmed Donaldson's (1978) view that reasoning is tapped much more effectively when the problem makes 'human sense' (Cheng and Holyoak, 1985; Light, 1988). This has led to a much more 'ecologically' oriented view of intelligence, which is critical of accounts positing context-free cognitive mechanisms (as in the psychometric approach) or 'logical operations' (as in Piaget's approach) (Light and Butterworth, 1992). Put in *social* context, this view is similar to that of Vygotsky, described in Chapter 1.

SUMMARY OF SECTION 3

- Enquiry over the last decade or so has attempted to identify basic cognitive processes or operations underlying intelligence and its development.

- Correlations have been found between RT/IT and IQ, but their interpretation is debatable.

- A wide range of possibilities has emerged, from increases in the capacity of processing space to increases in more complex strategies and processes, but most of these have not been worked out in more detail.

- Two more detailed theories are Sternberg's 'componential' theory and Gardner's theory of 'multiple intelligences'.

- In Piaget's theory intelligence is based on the construction of schemes or representations of the co-ordinations in experience.

- These are revealed by the individual's actions on the world.

- The 'motor' of development is the recurrent 're-equilibrations' to these schemes which new 'disturbances' in experience frequently necessitate.

- The systems of co-ordination which make up the schemes, themselves become *inter*-co-ordinated, first at the sensorimotor level, then at the representational level, until final 'closure' (the attainment of detached mathematical and scientific thinking) is possible.

- Piaget's theory has been subjected to a number of criticisms.

- Some of these have stressed the importance of context for cognitive development.

4 INTELLIGENCE AS A SOCIAL CONSTRUCT

We have so far considered a wide range of views about intelligence. And this is only a sample of the diversity that actually exists. The lack of theoretical coherence has been pointed out many times. For example, Detterman and Sternberg (1986) repeated a study first carried out in 1921. They wrote to a couple of dozen theorists, asking them to define intelligence, just as the experts did in 1921. Sternberg and Berg (1986) analysed the responses for frequencies of mentioned attributes. Twenty-five attributes were mentioned: but only three of these were mentioned by 25 per cent or more of respondents.

The fact that 'intelligence' seems to mean different things even to different psychologists has led to recent suggestions that it is better understood not as a fixed natural phenomenon (something pre-existing *within* people) but one created through social activities, and represented *between* people as a 'social construct'. This idea harks back to the social psychological ideas of theorists like G. H. Mead. The development of gender can also be considered as a social construct in this sense.

As with identity and gender, these views have led to the suggestion that the locus of intelligence is not the individual as such, but the social body in which the individual is an 'actor'. It follows from such a perspective that the proper study of intelligence is not its individual 'machinations' but its social representations.

READING

A recent study by Mugny and Carugati (1989) firmly advocates this approach. The passages from the preface of their report (appended as Reading C) offer a strong assertion of this position. Do not be too concerned about the technical language (the term polysemous, for example, simply means 'many meanings'). The point is to get an impression of the premises and implications of the approach.

As Mugny and Carugati explain, the function of social representations is to help people make sense of and conserve a complex social world. Intelligence arises as a social representation because we live in a hierarchically-ordered social world. This gives rise to certain 'signals' of superiority/inferiority which we conceptualize as part of intelligence. These signals have been shown to include quite superficial aspects of personal appearance, social-class dialect, and self-presentation. We then attribute 'intelligence' differentially to different people according to how much they display the accepted signals. The idea is shown diagramatically in Figure 9 (overleaf). (If you have any difficulties with this diagram substitute the term 'gender' for the term 'intelligence'.) What the diagram suggests is that intelligence, like gender, is a social construct. Such a construct defines a particular 'developmental target' for children. Intelligence, in turn, becomes attributed according to the degree to which individual children display the signals that are seen as exemplifications of that target.

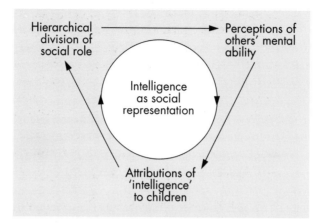

FIGURE 9 Intelligence as social representation.

The task of a scientific study of intelligence in this view, then, is to demonstrate how such representations are related to particular social contexts, and then show how they bear on children's development. This approach has been expressed in different ways in different studies. We will briefly mention three of these.

4.1 Representations of intelligence in different cultures

Notions of what counts as intelligence may be different at different times and places. We mentioned above how the representations of Western psychologists have changed between 1921 and 1986.

READING

Now turn to Reading D from Dasen (1984). The reading is mostly self-explanatory, but again note how what is seen as 'intelligence', and which children are likely to be attributed with intelligence, is at variance with the definitions of Western psychologists.

4.2 What counts as intelligence at different ages

In a study in Canada, Fry (1984) asked teachers to rate attributes of intelligent behaviour in children of different ages for their perceived importance. Responses tended to fall into three categories, as follows:

(a) 'cognitive attributes' (e.g. 'reasons well'; 'is quick in decision-making'; 'is organized and efficient');

(b) 'verbal attributes' (e.g. 'speaks clearly'; 'studies hard');

(c) 'social attributes' (e.g. 'is fair in dealing with others'; 'is very popular').

Wide differences in the views held by these (Canadian) teachers became evident. None the less, it was clear that elementary school teachers tended to stress the social attributes; secondary teachers tended to stress verbal attributes; tertiary teachers tended to stress cognitive attributes. In other words, intelligence tends to be defined in terms of specific developmental targets, the content of which varies with age rather than reflecting a single, permanent, entity.

4.3 Representations of intelligence vary with different social experiences

Mugny and Carugati (1989) using methods similar to those of Fry, found that parents' representations and attributions of intelligence changed as their experience of parenthood increased. The arrival of more offspring in a family tended to amplify views of a 'natural inequality' in intelligence, beliefs in 'giftedness' in children, and a maturationist and biological view of development.

A similar shift was found among teachers who subsequently became parents (and who thus found themselves potentially the targets of blame for school failure from both sides of the parent–school divide). Mugny and Carugati suggest that such a shift – which puts the credit or the blame for development on individual biology – may be a defence mechanism against personal responsibility for the school failure of their own and others' children: in effect parents/teachers saying 'it's not my fault'!

SUMMARY OF SECTION 4

- The 'social representation' approach sees intelligence as a set of shared ideas within a culture for explaining and discussing apparent differences in competence among individuals.
- The proper study of intelligence, in this view, is the origin of such representations, and their relationship to particular situations, rather than hypothetical individual mental processes.
- The approach has been exemplified in the different conceptions of intelligence at different ages, between different cultures, and as a result of personal experiences.

5 CONCLUSION

Clearly this is an ongoing debate. We do not aim to resolve it here. Instead, all that we have attempted is to help you find your way around this theoretical forest, and to understand the different assumptions on which the different approaches to understanding intelligence are based. To help you pick up further signposts for enquiry, both in this book and elsewhere, we return to Activity 1. You should look again at the responses you gave to that activity.

COMMENT ON ACTIVITY 1

The questions (or statements) you responded to are taken from those used by Mugny and Carugati. We offer below the mean responses given by their subjects, which consisted of about three hundred parents in Bologna and Geneva (the study was much more extensive than this, so these data are selective for reasons of space). After the question number, the figure in brackets gives the mean rating the parents gave each statement. The comment which follows picks up the issue concerned.

Q1 (2.41) The moderate rating for this item (out of 7, remember) indicates that intelligence is considered to be a cognitive rather than an affective or 'moral' characteristic (with some hedging perhaps).

Q2 (4.14) Perhaps a surprisingly low rating in view of the emphasis given to abstract thought by some theorists and test designers (e.g. Raven).

Q3 (5.06) Very much located in the cerebrum for these respondents, then. Compare with the next item.

Q4 (3.62) Moderate agreement. Consider the view of Dunn (1988) that adapting to a social life is far more cognitively challenging than adapting directly to the physical world. The need to do so in the course of human evolution may account for our bigger brains.

Q5 (5.87) This is the classical Piagetian view (see Chapter 1, and Section 3 above). In contrast remember Vygotsky's view (also Section 3).

Q6 (3.22) Some support for this statement, but some hedging, too. By comparing this rating with that of the previous item we can note how contradictory views may be embraced by the same people at the same time (an important strand in the 'social representations' view).

Q7 (5.00) See the theory of multiple intelligences in Section 3.4.

Q8 (4.97) Considerable support – but note, again, a contradiction with the previous statement.

Q9 (4.82) Considerable support for this view which is consistent also with a Piagetian constructivist view. Compare and contrast with 'social constructivist' views such as those of Vygotsky.

Q10 (5.26) This view is illustrated in studies on 'peer collaboration'. Note, again, that it apparently contradicts the large measure of agreement with the previous statement.

Q11 (2.66) This appears to contradict the Anglo-American notion of school as the 'arena' in which intelligence is both developed and assessed (see above on school achievement as the main criterion in IQ test construction).

Q12 (3.55) Moderate agreement. Note how this notion reflects Vygotsky's theory, but is alluded to in many descriptions of social development.

FURTHER READING

GARDNER, H. (1993) *Multiple Intelligences: the theory in practice*, New York, Wiley.

STERNBERG, R. J. and WAGNER, R. K. (1994) *Mind in Context: interactionist perspectives on human intelligence*, Cambridge, Cambridge University Press.

STERNBERG, R. J. and RUZGIS, P. (1994) *Personality and Intelligence*, Cambridge, Cambridge University Press.

REFERENCES

ANDERSON, M. (1986) 'Inspection time, information processing and the development of intelligence', *British Journal of Developmental Psychology*, **6**, pp. 43–57.

ANDERSON, M. (1992) *Intelligence and Development*, Oxford, Blackwell.

BANCROFT, D. (1994) 'The genesis of thought' in OATES, J. (ed.) *The Foundations of Child Development*, Oxford, Blackwell/The Open University (Book 1 of ED209).

BANCROFT, D. and CARR, R. (eds) (1995) *Influencing Children's Development*, Oxford, Blackwell/The Open University (Book 4 of ED209).

BLOCK, N. and DWORKIN, G. (eds) (1976) *The IQ Controversy*, New York, Pantheon.

BRODY, N. (1985) 'The validity of tests of intelligence' in WOLMAN, B. B. (ed.) *Handbook of Intelligence*, New York, Wiley.

CARLSON, J. S. and WIDAMAN, K. F. (1987) 'Elementary cognitive correlates of *g*: progress and prospects' in VERNON, P. A. (ed.) *Speed of Information Processing and Intelligence*, New York, Ablex.

CECI, S. J. (1990) *On Intelligence, More or Less*, Englewood Cliffs (New Jersey), Prentice Hall.

CHENG, P. W. and HOLYOAK, K. J. (1985) 'Pragmatic reasoning schemes', *Cognitive Psychology*, **17**, pp. 391–416.

DASEN, P. (1984) 'The cross-cultural study of intelligence – Piaget and the Baoulé' in FRY, P. S. (ed.) *Changing Conceptions of Intelligence and Intellectual Functioning*, Amsterdam, North-Holland.

DETTERMAN, D. K. (1987) 'What does reaction time tell us about intelligence' in VERNON, P. A. (ed.) *Speed of Information Processing and Intelligence*, New York, Ablex.

DETTERMAN, D. K. and STERNBERG, R. J. (1986) *What is intelligence? Contemporary viewpoints on its nature and definition*, New York, Ablex.

DONALDSON, M. (1978) *Children's Minds,* London, Fontana.

DUNN, J. (1988) *The Beginnings of Social Understanding*, Oxford, Blackwell.

ELLIOTT, C. D. (1983) *British Ability Scales*, Manual 2, Windsor, NFER–Nelson.

EVANS, B. and WAITES, B. (1981) *IQ and Mental Testing: an unnatural science and its social history*, London, Macmillan.

FALLOWS, J. (1989) *More Like Us*, Boston, Houghton-Mifflin.

FRY, P. S. (1984) 'Teachers' conceptions of students' intelligence and intelligent functioning: a cross-sectional study of elementary, secondary and tertiary level teachers' in FRY, P. S. (ed.) *Changing Conceptions of Intelligence and Intellectual Functioning*, Amsterdam, North-Holland.

GALTON, F, (1869) *Hereditary Genius: an inquiry into its laws and consequences*, London, Macmillan.

GALTON, F, (1883) *Inquiries into Human Faculty and its Development*, London, Macmillan.

GARDNER, H. (1984) *Frames of Mind: the theory of multiple intelligences*, London, Heinemann.

GARDNER, H. (1993) *The Unschooled Mind*, London, Fontana.

GOODNOW, J. J. (1984) 'On being judged "intelligent"' in FRY, P. S. (ed.) *Changing Conceptions of Intelligence and Intellectual Functioning,* Amsterdam, North-Holland.

HANSON, F. H. (1993) *Testing, Testing: social consequences of the examined life*, Berkeley, University of California Press.

HORN, J. (1986) 'Intellectual ability concepts' in STERNBERG, R. J. (ed.) *Advances in the Psychology of Human Intelligence*, vol. 3, Hillsdale, New Jersey, Lawrence Erlbaum.

HOWE, M. (1988) 'Explaining away intelligence', *British Journal of Psychology,* **80**, pp. 121–7.

HUNT, E. (1983) 'On the nature of intelligence', *Science,* **219**, pp. 141–3.

JENSEN, A. R. (1970) 'Another look at culture-fair testing' in HELLMUTH, J. (ed.) *The Disadvantaged Child*, New York, Brunner-Mazel.

KAIL, R. and PELLEGRINO, J. W. (1985) *Human Intelligence: perspectives and prospects*, New York, Freeman.

LIGHT, P. (1988) 'Context, conservation and conversation' in RICHARDSON, K. and SHELDON, S. (eds), *Cognitive Development to Adolescence*, Hove, Erlbaum/The Open University.

LIGHT, P. and BUTTERWORTH, G. (eds) (1992) *Cognition in Context*, Brighton, Harvester.

MACKINTOSH, N. J. (1986). 'The biology of intelligence?' *British Journal of Intelligence*, **77**, pp. 1–18.

MILLER, G. A. (1962) *Psychology: the science of mental life*, Harmondsworth, Penguin.

MUGNY, G. and CARUGATI, F. (1989) *Social Representations of Intelligence*, Cambridge, Cambridge University Press.

NETTLEBECK, T. (1987) 'Inspection time and intelligence' in VERNON, P. A. (ed.) *Speed of Information Processing and Intelligence*, New York, Ablex.

NETTLEBECK, T. and VITA, P. (1992) 'Inspection time in two childhood age cohorts: a constraint or a developmental function?', *British Journal of Developmental Psychology,* **10**, pp. 180–97.

NETTLEBECK, T. and YOUNG, R. (1989) 'Inspection time and intelligence in 6-year-old children', *Personality and Individual Differences*, **10**, pp. 605–14.

OAKHILL, J. (1988) 'The development of children's reasoning ability: information processing approaches' in RICHARDSON, K. and SHELDON, S. (eds) *Cognitive Development to Adolescence,* Hove, Erlbaum/The Open University.

PASCUAL-LEONE, J. (1970) 'A mathematical model for the transition rule in Piaget's developmental stages', *Acta Psychologica,* **32**, pp. 301–45.

PIAGET, J. (1975) *The Development of Thought: equilibration of cognitive structures*, Oxford, Blackwell.

PIAGET, J. (1988) 'Extracts from Piaget's theory' in RICHARDSON, K. and SHELDON, S. (eds) *Cognitive Development to Adolescence*, Hove, Erlbaum/ The Open University.

QUICKE, J. C. (1982) *The Cautious Expert*, Milton Keynes, Open University Press.

RICHARDSON, K. (1991a) *Understanding Intelligence*, Milton Keynes, Open University Press.

RICHARDSON, K. (1991b) 'Reasoning with Raven: in and out of context', *British Journal of Educational Psychology*, **61**, pp. 129–38.

ROBINSON, D. N. (1981) *An Intellectual History of Psychology*, New York, Macmillan.

SIEGLER, R. (1976) 'Three aspects of cognitive development', *Cognitive Psychology, 8*, pp. 481–520.

SIGMAN, M., COHEN, S. E., BECKWITH, L., ARSANOW, R. and PARMALEE, A. (1991) 'Continuity in cognitive abilities from infancy to 12 years of age', *Developmental Psychology*, **27**, pp. 47–57.

SLATER, A. (1990) 'Infant development: the origins of competence', *The Psychologist*, **3**, pp. 109–13.

SPEARMAN, C. (1923) *The Nature of 'Intelligence' and the Principles of Cognition*, London, Macmillan.

STERNBERG, R. J. (1984) 'Toward a triarchic theory of human intelligence', *Behavioural and Brain Sciences,* **7**, pp. 269–315.

STERNBERG, R. J. (1988) 'Intellectual development: psychometric and information-processing approaches' in BORNSTEIN, M. H. and LAMB, M. E. (eds) *Developmental Psychology: an advanced textbook*, Hillsdale (New Jersey), Erlbaum.

STERNBERG, R, J. and BERG, C. A. (1986) 'Quantitative integration; definitions of intelligence: a comparison of the 1921 and 1986 symposia' in DETTERMAN, D. K. and STERNBERG, R. J. (eds) *What is Intelligence? Contemporary viewpoints on its nature and definition,* New York, Ablex.

TERMAN, L. M. (1916) *The Measurement of Intelligence*, Boston, Houghton-Mifflin.

TERMAN, L. M. (1942) 'The revision procedures' in MCNEMAR, Q. (ed.) *The Revision of the Stanford-Binet Scale*, Boston, Houghton-Mifflin.

TERMAN, L. M. and MERRILL, M. A. (1960) *Stanford-Binet Intelligence Scale, Manual for the Third Revision*, Boston, Houghton, Mifflin.

THORNDIKE, R. L. and HAGEN, E. P. (1969) *Measurement and Evaluation in Psychology and Education,* New York, Wiley.

VYGOTSKY, L. S. (1988) 'The genesis of higher mental functions' in RICHARDSON, K. and SHELDON, S. (eds) *Cognitive Development to Adolescence,* Hove, Erlbaum/The Open University.

WECHSLER, D. (1958) *The Measurement and Appraisal of Adult Intelligence,* Baltimore, Williams and Wilkins.

WECHSLER, D. (1967) *Wechsler Preschool and Primary Scale of Intelligence: manual*, New York, The Psychological Corporation.

WOLF, T. H. (1973) *Alfred Binet*, Chicago, University of Chicago Press.

READINGS

Reading A Binet

G. A. Miller

In a series of articles in *L'Année psychologique* from 1894 to 1898 Binet and his assistant Victor Henri described their attempts to measure higher mental processes in children and adults. They were quite clear that sensory and motor measurements were easier to make and less variable when repeated, but, for all their virtues, such tests did not seem to distinguish sufficiently among different people. Binet wanted to measure mental functions that different people performed in different ways, with different degrees of skill. Since memory is an important component of intelligence, everyone agreed that it should be included. But Binet thought it might be possible to make similar measurements on many other psychological functions. For example, why not measure the vividness of imagery, or the kind of imagery that a person has? Why not test his comprehension, both its scope and its duration? Why not test comprehension of sentences, or synonyms, or ask the person to find logical errors in a text? Many tests of suggestibility were available from the studies of hypnosis; could suggestibility be related to intelligence? Even aesthetic judgements could be obtained and scored against the aesthetic judgements of experts. Why not ask people to make moral judgements, or judge emotions from pictures of facial expression? Why not study their will by asking them to withstand pain or fatigue? Why not measure the speed with which they could acquire a motor skill?

Why not, indeed? Who could say that all those higher mental functions were not involved in intelligence? No one had ever measured those functions in a large number of different people in order to relate the results to intelligence … .

In 1904 the Minister of Public Instruction in Paris assembled a commission to consider the problem of subnormal children in the public schools. If the children who were likely to fail could be placed in special schools, they might be helped; Binet, whose studies of child psychology were well known, was a member of the commission. As early as 1894 he had begun to try his tests on school children; in 1903 he had reported an intensive study of the intellectual development of his own two daughters.

Binet quickly became disturbed because the discussions of the commission were so vague that everything they tried to do seemed confused and pointless. He took it upon himself, therefore, to provide clear definitions for the terms that were being used to describe subnormal children. He devoted his research thereafter to the problem of finding a scientific basis for a medical classification that would be more useful to educators. His principal collaborator in this attempt was Dr Simon, a young physician in an asylum for backward children. From 1905 until Binet's death in 1911 at least twenty-eight articles and one book were written by Binet and Simon together.

In 1905, primarily to facilitate the work of the commission, Binet and Simon published their first results. They used a large battery of different mental tests, some hard, some easy. Binet collected tests from everywhere, and his own mind bubbled over with ideas for others. To discover which tests were useful, he and Simon spent endless hours in the schools with the children, watching, asking, testing, recording. Each proposed test had to be given to a large number of children. If a test did not distinguish the brighter from the duller, or the older from the younger, it was abandoned. Tests that worked were retained, even though they often failed to conform with the theoretical principles Binet and Henri had announced ten years earlier. The memory tests worked. And the tests of comprehension worked – comprehension of words, of statements, of concepts, of pictures. Binet did not retain the tests on the basis of a theory; he watched the children and let their behaviour decide which tests were good and which were irrelevant. The 1905 version of the 'Metrical Scale of Intelligence' simply arranged all the tests that Binet had selected in an order of increasing difficulty. Each child passed as many tests as he could until they became too difficult for him. How far the child got down the list of tests could then be compared with how far other children of the same age usually got.

In 1908 a revised version was published. The tests were grouped according to the age at which fifty to seventy-five per cent of a large sample of children passed them, from age three up to age thirteen. In 1911, the year of Binet's death, there was still another revision that extended the age up to fifteen years.

According to the 1911 scale an average three-year-old French child should pass half these tests: he should be able to point to his nose, eyes, and mouth; repeat two digits; enumerate objects in a picture; give his family name; and repeat a sentence of six syllables. By age seven the child should pass half of these tests: be able to show his right hand and left ear; describe a picture; execute three commands given simultaneously; count the value of six sous [sous are small french coins], three of which are double; and name four cardinal colours. By fifteen the youngster should be able to repeat seven digits; find three rhymes for a given word in one minute; repeat a sentence of twenty-six syllables; interpret pictures; and even interpret given facts.

These should give the flavour of Binet's tests to anyone who (though it is hard to imagine how) might have been sheltered from them heretofore. The age group of tests that a child could pass half the time defined his mental age, regardless of what his chronological age might be.

Binet used as the measure of retardation simply the difference between the child's mental age and chronological age. Thus a child who was six years old but passed only the items on the four-year age group would have a mental age of four, and so would be retarded two years in mental development. Binet regarded two years as a serious deficiency. Other psychologists decided later that it was better to use the ratio, rather than the difference between the two ages. Mental age divided by chronological age gives a mental quotient. If the two ages are the same, then the child is average for his age and the quotient is unity. If the child is retarded, the mental is less than the chronological age, and the quotient is less than unity. If he is advanced, the quotient will be greater than unity. When this quotient is multiplied by 100, the result is usually referred to as the intelligence quotient, or IQ. The various confusing arguments about whether the IQ. is constant throughout life, or whether it can be raised or lowered with special circumstances, came later and cannot be blamed on Binet. His contribution was a simple, reliable method for determining a child's mental age.

Source: Miller, G. A. (1962) 'Alfred Binet: psychologist' in Miller, G. A. (ed.) Psychology: the science of mental life, Harmondsworth, Penguin, pp. 311–4.

Reading B IQ tests and assessment

M. Berger and W. Yule

Clinical utility

1   Such tests provide an index of cognitive functioning that has concurrent and prognostic implications.

2   They sample areas of functioning that are easily accessible by other means and, properly used and interpreted, do so in a reliable manner.

3   They enable a discrimination between general and circumscribed strengths and weaknesses, pointing to differential abilities in the individual. Given the high incidence of language disorders in children with mental retardation ... this property of IQ tests is of particular value in assessment.

4   Not uncommonly, in our experience, these tests provide the first indication that a person's abilities are being misconstrued. For instance, the child in a mainstream school, referred because of difficult behaviour, who turns out to be less able, or on occasion very much more able, than believed; or the noncommunicating or autistic child who turns out to have good nonverbal skills.

5   Test results, depending on their magnitude, can reduce or increase the number of alternative 'hypotheses' or explanations the clinician needs to involve in attempting to understand presenting problems.

6   Tests provide a systematic baseline for monitoring aspects of progress, or the lack of it.

7   IQ data facilitate the interpretation of other forms of information, derived from other tests or other sources.

8   The process of testing, particularly for the experienced examiner, provides an opportunity for structured observation that can be useful in providing hypotheses about stylistic aspects of the person's functioning that may be clinically or otherwise relevant (e.g. impulsivity, poor error checking, motor slowness, mild or gross incoordination). Even when the individual produces wrong solutions, the astute examiner may on occasion spot that these are rule-governed rather than random.

SOURCE: BERGER, M. and YULE, W (1985) 'IQ tests and assessment' in CLARKE, A. M., CLARKE, A. D. B., and BERG, M. J. (eds) Mental Deficiency: the changing outlook, London, Methuen, pp. 88–9.

Reading C Social representations of intelligence

G. Mugny and F. Carugati

Intelligence, if such a thing exists, is the historical creation of a particular culture, analogous to the notion of childhood ... The old idea that it is a singular entity is no longer tenable: we have to recognise the plurality of the concept ... The acknowledgement that intelligence is polysemous, and obviously social in origin, leads naturally on to studying the social representations of intelligence. In fact, as Goodnow (1984) has emphasised, a change in our perspective today is essential: we need to stop thinking and recognise it for what it actually is: a value-judgement, a label, slapped on everybody who happens to have (or not to have) the characteristics regarded as typical of an intelligent person. A semantic change of this sort opens up a new perspective, in which intelligence, instead of being regarded as a quality *per se*, can be seen as an attribute, admittedly socially necessary, which is culturally and historically determined, and therefore as liable to vary between the sub-groups of a single society as from one latitude to another. In short, intelligence needs to be defined socially (Doise and Mugny, 1984) so as to account for the origin of the social issues involved in its measurement, those 'natural' divisions ... which persist even into socialist societies with their claims of classlessness. The 'epistemic subject' of the work of Piaget and the Piagetians appears, perhaps now more than ever, to be a chimera.

How are we to escape from this impasse? Rather than looking for the answer in the development of scientific conceptions of intelligence or of the workings of the intellect (see Sternberg, 1982 ...), we have deliberately chosen to investigate the social representations of intelligence, or in other words ordinary, everyday attitudes to intelligence, which are often less naive than they appear. This approach is fully justified, given a recognition that conceptions of intelligence are actually social constructions, with a multiplicity of significances which, as we shall hope to show, are related to different social integrations. In the end, we should at least be in a better position to distinguish between myth and reality in the notion of intelligence ...

Doise, W. and Mugny, G. (1984) *The Social Development of the Intellect*, Oxford. Pergamon.

Goodnow, J. (1984) 'On being judged "intelligent"', *International Journal of Psychology*, 19, pp. 391–406.

Sternberg, R.J. (1982) *Handbook of Human Intelligence*, Cambridge, Cambridge University Press.

Source: Mugny, G. and Carugati, F. (1989) Social Representations of Intelligence, Cambridge, Cambridge University Press.

Reading D Piaget and the Baoulé

P. R. Dasen

N'glouèlê: the integration of cognitive and social skills

Indeed, the Baoulé have the term *n'glouèlê* that translates as intelligence. If they apply it to children, they always use it in the future tense '*ô yo n'glouèlê fouè*': who will own intelligence. They are reluctant to assess the child in the present, because a child can always change, either spontaneously or through educational interventions; on the other hand they are willing to take some aspects of the child's behaviour as a predictor of future intelligence. The generic term *n'glouèlê* includes a number of component attributes, outlined in table 5.

The most often quoted attribute, illustrated by many practical examples, is *ô ti kpa*, the readiness to carry out tasks in the service of the family and the community. Of course the child has to be obedient in answering any request immediately, but it is also important to do the task well, and to take on responsibilities; what is particularly valued is the initiative in carrying out a needed task without being asked. The second most important attribute is *agnyhiè*, respect of elders, politeness and compliance. Speaking well in public, knowing how to use proverbs (*o si hidjo*), and wisdom (*angundan*) are also part of intelligence, but they cannot really be expected of children; applied to children, these terms mean to retell a story with precision, respectively to act like an adult.

We can distinguish between these attributes that are clearly social, and those that are more technological: skills of observation, attention and fast learning (*I gni ti klè klè*), manual dexterity (*I sa si n'glouèlê*) and especially memory skills, that are either mentioned specifically (*I ti ti kpa*) or in relation to the other attributes. *O si floua* relates to literacy, to school intelligence, and is seen as part of *n'glouèlê* by most informants, although a few make an explicit distinction between a traditional intelligence and a school intelligence: 'One may know how to read and write, but be quite dumb'; 'You may know much of the Baoulé intelligence without knowing much on paper' some informants said. The general feeling, however, is that the more technological skills have to be integrated with the social skills. The child's abilities are useless unless they are applied for the good and well-being of the social group. It is in this integration of social and cognitive attributes that the Baoulé definition of intelligence is most at variance with the Western and psychometric definitions we have discussed at the beginning of this paper.

TABLE 5 Outline of the components of *n'glouèlê*, and their meanings.

–O yo *n'glouèlê* fouè	Who will have *intelligence*
–O ti kpa	– Serviceableness, responsibility, initiative, know how, obedience, honesty.
–Agnyhiè	– Politeness, obedience, respect.
–O si hidjo	– To retell a story (or an event) with precision; verbal memory. To speak in a socially appropriate way. Adults: To speak well in public; to know how to use proverbs.
–Angundan	– To act like an adult. Reflection, responsibility, memory. Adults: wisdom.
–I gni ti klè klè	– Observation, attention, fast learning, memory.
–O si floua	– Literacy, school intelligence.
–I ti ti kpa	– Memory (especially for school). To be lucky, to bring luck.
–I sa si n'glouèlê	– Manual dexterity. At school: writing and drawing.

SOURCE: DASEN, P. (1984) 'The cross-cultural study of intelligence – Piaget and the Baoulé' in FRY, P. S. (ed.) Changing Conceptions of Intelligence and Intellectual Functioning: current theory and research, Amsterdam, North-Holland.

6 MATHEMATICAL AND SCIENTIFIC THINKING

Terezinha Nunes

CONTENTS

OBJECTIVES

When you have studied this chapter, you should be able to:

1 understand the difference between *generative* and *reproductive* knowledge;

2 reflect on ways of analysing children's thinking in mathematics and science;

3 understand the importance of situations, and not just computations, in problem solving in mathematics;

4 reflect on the impact of cultural settings on mathematical and scientific thinking;

5 think about possible connections between the development of intelligence and learning science and mathematics;

6 consider different theories about how children progress in their mathematical and scientific thinking and the implications of this analysis for education.

1 INTRODUCTION

1.1 What is the nature of mathematical and scientific knowledge?

In this chapter I will introduce the idea that mathematical and scientific knowledge is not simply a 'collection of facts' but a 'way of thinking'. I will also provide an overview of some of the research that illustrates this perspective of mathematical and scientific knowledge.

Often the way we think about how children learn mathematics and science creates the impression that what is involved is the acquisition of facts and procedures. For example, in mathematics young children learn to count, to write numbers, to do additions and subtractions, the multiplication table, to do long division, etc. All these are either procedures (*how to ...*) or facts (for example, the number names or $6 \times 7 = 42$). Similarly, in science children learn facts (for example, the world is round) and procedures (such as how to solve problems in physics, chemistry or genetics). According to this way of thinking, we expect that children will know what they were taught and will not know what they were not taught. Is this view of mathematical and scientific learning justified? Try Activity 1 now.

ACTIVITY 1

Allow about 5 minutes

LEARNING TO COUNT IN JAPANESE

Study the numbers below which are in Japanese but written in our alphabet.

1	*ichi*	10	ju	20	ni ju
2	*ni*	11	ju *ichi*	21	ni ju *ichi*
3	*san*	12	ju *ni*	22	ni ju *ni*
4	*shi*	13	ju *san*		
5	go	14	ju *shi*		
6	roku				
7	sichi				
8	hachi				
9	ku				

How do you say 15 in Japanese? How do you say 43? How do you say 67? Do you think you could count to 99? How did you get your answers?

Your performance in Activity 1 can show you that you know more facts about Japanese numbers than you were taught. Learning mathematics means understanding a system that goes beyond the examples you learn from. For this reason, we say that mathematics learning is *generative,* i.e., learning the system allows you to generate new facts that you were never taught about. If mathematical and scientific knowledge were simply *reproductive* (i.e., the repetition of what the person was taught), you could not have answered the questions in Activity 1.

In this respect, children learn in a way that is similar to the way adults learn. However, a learner, whether a child or an adult, does not always grasp the system in the way the system was created. Children form their own ideas about what they are taught in mathematics and science. Sometimes they are able to repeat some of the facts they were taught without integrating them in a way of thinking. Can you try to figure out the systems used by the four children whose writing of numbers is part of Activity 2?

ACTIVITY 2

Allow about 5 minutes

GENERATING NUMBERS

Look at Figure 1. It contains numbers written by four children, 5 and 6 years of age. They had not been taught how to write multi-digit numbers in school. However, they see numbers around them and do their own analysis of how numbers should be written. Can you figure out how each one generates the writing of numbers? Which children seem to think similarly about writing numbers? What similarities and differences are there?

hi ิ P (9)

5 (5)

5ƅ (25)

4ร (45)

loo (100)

L U ʀe.

looɕƐ (123)

loo P (109)

lOOO (1000)

2 OOO (2000)

2 OOO P (2009)

lOOO5 OOOOPƐ (1598)

Susane

9 (9)

5 (5)

25 (25)

4o (40)

loo (100)

looƐ (103)

loo q (109)

looo (1000)

loo oɪ (1002)

looo q (1009)

l looo 5 loo 6ɛ (2568)

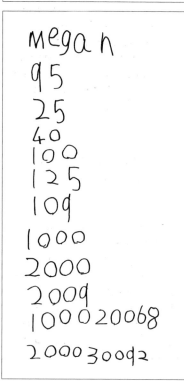

megan

95

25

40

100

125

109

1000

2000

2009

10002006ƀ

2000300q2

Alice

eight   8

five   5

twenty-five   15

forty   4

|ſ   one hundred

|ſ   two hundred

|ſ P   one hundred and nine

| e   one thousand

| e ſ   one thousand and five

| e ∟ ɛ   two thousand and fifty-three

FIGURE 1 Four children's written productions of numbers. Can you figure out their systems?

In order to understand children's learning of mathematics, we have to analyse their productions – the way they count, write numbers, solve problems, etc. – and try to figure out how they think. It is not enough to try to find out what number facts they know or do not know.

It may seem that this notion of generative knowledge applies more readily to mathematical than scientific knowledge. One could argue that there are many 'scientific facts' about the world that we can teach children in school and they will learn them without difficulty – and this is to some extent true. However, we often think of scientific information we transmit in school as 'mere facts' when this information is not only that. Often what we call a scientific fact is important because it reflects a way of thinking. Try Activity 3 now and think about facts and ways of thinking in science.

ACTIVITY 3

Allow about 10 minutes

FACTS AND IDEAS

We have known now for a long time that the world is round and not flat, as it was thought in the past. This is a fact. But is this a 'mere fact' or is it a way of thinking? This is what Nussbaum, Novack and his colleagues at the University of Cornell decided to figure out (Nussbaum, 1985; Nussbaum and Novack, 1976).

Look at the picture of the world in Figure 2. It illustrates the idea that there are two girls, one who lives in the North Pole and one who lives in the South Pole. They have two bottles each, one with a cork in and one that is open. Their bottles are half filled with juice. Can you draw in the juice in their bottles?

FIGURE 2 What will happen to the juice in the bottles?

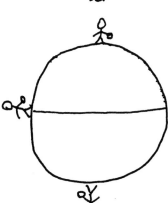

Look at the second picture of the world in Figure 3. It shows three boys, one living in the North Pole, one living on the Equator, and one living in the South Pole. They each have a ball in their hand. What will happen to the ball if they drop it? Can you draw in the path the ball will follow?

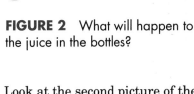

FIGURE 3 What will happen to the ball if it is dropped?

As with mathematical knowledge, scientific knowledge is not the accumulation of facts but is defined by 'ways of thinking'. Most children in primary school will *know* and tell you (if asked) that the world is round. Yet, their *thinking* may be governed by the idea that the world is flat, with the sky above and the ground below. This is what their drawings of people on earth and rain clouds suggest (see Figure 4). Their answers to the questions in Activity 3 also indicate a way of thinking that is consistent with a flat world conception.

Lucas (6 years) and Frances (8 years) were asked (following Nussbaum and colleagues) to imagine that they were astronauts and were looking at the world from a distance. What would the world look like? The answer to this question typically is 'round' or 'like a ball' or something of the sort – and both Lucas and Frances answered in this way. They were then asked to draw the world as it would be seen from the space-craft. After this was accomplished, they were asked to put in some people, some clouds and some rain in the picture. I also asked the children to show me the North and the South Pole as a preparation for the next activity.

Both drew a round world and both decided to put in some countries. Lucas put in a rather good outline of South America and England plus what he thought was not a good outline of Australia, but he wanted to have it in anyway. Frances put in some countries but was not sure what they were supposed to look like. As you can see, apart from these similarities, their drawings of people on earth, clouds and rain differ in significant ways. For Lucas, each country had its own cloud 'on top' and its rain falling from top to bottom. His round world contains people all standing in one direction with clouds above and not all around. Even though 6-year-old children have been told that the world is round and draw it round when asked to, they place people, clouds and rain in a way that is more fitting with a belief in a flat world. They have learned the fact but not the way of thinking that goes with it. For Frances, the conception of the round world prevails in this drawing; she also put in some countries, each one with a rain cloud but the clouds are positioned all around the world. She said it was funny to draw the rain as she did for the South Pole but had no doubts about what it should look like.

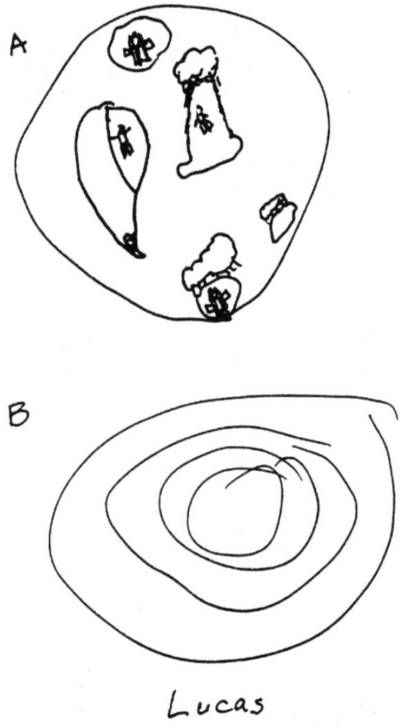

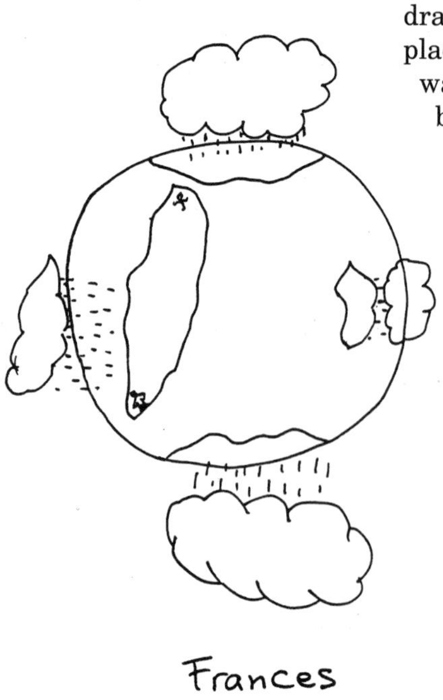

FIGURE 4 Children's drawings of earth and rain clouds.

Lucas

Frances

INTERVIEWER TO LUCAS: ... Can you draw it for me?

LUCAS: I learned this in school. There are all these circles around the world.

(Lucas draws the circles in (B)).

INTERVIEWER: What are these circles? Do you know?

LUCAS: I don't remember.

INTERVIEWER: Are they other planets?

LUCAS: No they are circles around the world.

INTERVIEWER: What were these circles made of?

LUCAS: I don't know.

(Then he draws the world and puts in the countries.)

INTERVIEWER TO FRANCES: ... Can you draw this for me?

FRANCES: Yes. *(Later, as she draws the South Pole)* ... I used to think that people would fall off the earth. I didn't know why they wouldn't fall off when they were here.

INTERVIEWER: Do they fall off?

FRANCES: No *(laughing)*.

INTERVIEW: Why not?

FRANCES: My father told me. It's because of gravity. *(She draws the rain falling on the South Pole and remarks that isn't it funny to think of rain falling this way).*

The drawings by the children are coherent with the solutions they give to the problems posed in Activity 3 – presented in Figure 5. Lucas's solution is typical of the children of his age. The drink in the uncorked bottles owned by the little boys at the South Pole and at the Equator falls out of the bottles. When they drop their balls, they fall the same way as the liquid. Frances thought that the liquid would stay in the bottles but was quite doubtful when giving her answer about the little girl's liquid at the South Pole. When asked about the ball, she commented it would go 'right down into space'. Frances seemed to hesitate between a round and a flat world way of thinking.

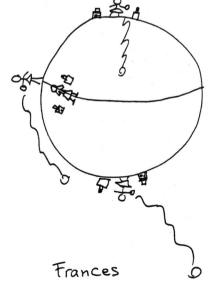

FIGURE 5 Drawings by children in response to the questions in Activity 3.

> INTERVIEWER TO LUCAS: ... I asked another boy to draw for me a boy in the North Pole and this is how he did it. *(Interviewer draws a circle and the boy in the North Pole).* Is this the right way to do it?
> LUCAS: Yes.
> INTERVIEWER: Then I asked him to do another boy in the South Pole. This is how he did it. Did he do it right?
> LUCAS: *(Looks and frowns).* No, I don't think so. No, it's not right.

The interviewer then asks whether Lucas knows about the Equator, draws a line to represent it, asks whether it is right to draw the boy on the Equator that way (see Figure 5). Lucas thinks it is the wrong way to put the boy in. Then the bottles are added and the questions are asked about the juice in the uncorked bottles and what happens to the ball when the boy drops it.

Frances thought that the drawings of girls in the North and South Pole were right but decided to do a second girl for the Equator.

SUMMARY OF SECTION 1

- We looked at the distinction between *generative* and *reproductive* knowledge. Mathematics learning is *generative*, it enables you to use a system that will allow you to generate new facts that you were not taught.
- Sometimes children evolve their own systems of adapting knowledge, or they merely repeat certain facts without being able to integrate them into a system.
- Scientific knowledge, similar to mathematical knowledge, is defined by 'ways of thinking', not just learning facts.

---

2 THE DEVELOPMENT OF MATHEMATICAL CONCEPTS

We will now turn to the study of children's knowledge of mathematical and scientific concepts. We will examine these two topics in succession and then will consider the relationship between the development of intelligence and the acquisition of mathematical and scientific knowledge.

2.1 The Piagetian contribution

The study of mathematics learning is as old as the study of learning in psychology. E. L. Thorndike, in 1922, was already interested in how people learn mathematics. His view of mathematical knowledge was, however, reproductive, and he was strongly criticized by gestalt psychologists, most notably Wertheimer, whose work on mathematical knowledge concentrated on productive thinking in problem solving. Wertheimer (1966; first edn 1945) analysed children's solutions to the problem of calculating the area of a parallelogram. The children had been instructed on how to find the area of a parallelogram, drawn as in Figure 6(a). Wertheimer showed the children a parallelogram drawn as Figure 6(b). Few children could solve this formally identical problem. He interpreted their inability as an indication that problem solving is not a matter of reproductive thinking but rather a matter of insight. However, his ideas were not developed enough to suggest what made 'insight' come about.

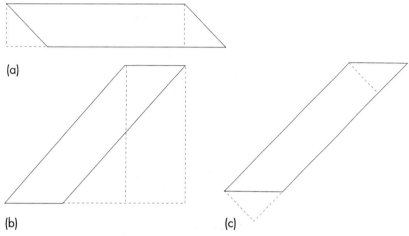

FIGURE 6 Three views of a parallelogram.

Wertheimer observed a class of children who had been taught to find the area of the parallelogram by drawing perpendiculars to the corners, as drawn in Figure 6(a), and then multiplying the value of the perpendicular by that of the base. He wanted to impress on the teacher the notion that children should not just learn to reproduce procedures but should come to understand problems. In the first case, they would just have reproductive knowledge; in the second case, their knowledge would be productive, generating solutions to new problems.

Wertheimer then presented the children with a parallelogram oriented as in Figure 6(b) above (without the dotted lines, of course). Some children protested against solving this problem, they had not yet learned this one. Others carried out the drawing routine obtaining the figure in (b) above. This second group of children was then divided. Some did not believe that their drawing could lead them to the solution. Others did not think enough to doubt their production and carried on with the multiplication. A small number of children demonstrated they had an insight: after some thinking, they showed a positive reaction, and produced a drawing like that presented in Figure 6(c).

Wertheimer's point in this observation was to demonstrate that, although this was considered a good class, teaching them a procedure to solve mathematical problems without understanding was not a fruitful method of instruction. A slightly different problem could baffle the children. The teacher's reaction was: 'You certainly gave them a queer figure. Naturally they are unable to deal with it.'

Piaget's studies on the development of intelligence (Piaget, 1950) represent an attempt to go beyond both learning theory and gestalt psychology. He criticized the learning theorists for their reproductive view of knowledge and the gestalt psychologists for their lack of explanation for the origin of knowledge. His theory was an attempt to develop a view in which knowledge would be structured and generative and the origin of knowledge structures would also be accounted for. For this reason, his theory was called a constructivist theory of knowledge.

Piaget suggested that the origin of the structures of knowledge was in the internalization of actions. For example, children's understanding of number, according to Piaget, did not result from learning the number labels but from the realization that the number of objects in a set was invariant unless objects were added or taken away. Adding and taking away are actions that modify quantities. Even young children (4 or 5 years of age) realize that adding increases and subtracting decreases the number of bricks in a box, for example. But, Piaget argued, young children also believe that spreading the objects out means that there are now more of them and putting them closer together means that there are now fewer (Piaget and Szeminska, 1952). This is what he concluded from his studies of children's understanding of conservation. Children were shown two rows of coins with, for example, eight coins in each and established that there were as many coins in one row as in the other. They would then see the experimenter performing a transformation on one of the rows – for example, spreading the coins in one row farther apart, so that one row was now longer than the other. Even children who could count, and therefore ascertain that there were still eight coins in each row, might still say that there was more money in the row where the coins had been spread apart. According to Piaget, these young children did not understand fully the results of their actions and did not realize that only addition of more coins would have increased the quantity. Through their own interactions with objects, by changing displays in several ways and checking the results of such changes, they would later on come to understand the *invariance of number*.

The discovery of the invariance of number in spite of spatial displacements that make sets look larger or smaller (around the age of 6) was considered by Piaget so important that it was taken as a mark of a new stage in children's intellectual development: the stage of concrete operations, a stage in which children become capable of carrying out logical deductions that previously eluded them.

This was not the end point of development, though, for at this stage children's mathematical understanding was, according to Piaget, restricted to one-variable problems for which addition and subtraction are sufficient. If 7-year-old children have to solve a problem that requires establishing a proportional relationship between two different variables, they are not able to cope. For example, in a study by Inhelder and Piaget (1958), children were told that eels have to be fed amounts of food that vary with their size. They were asked to look at some values in both variables, length of the eel and amount of food it needs and then say how much food an eel of a certain length should receive. Children at age 7 will normally suggest higher values for longer eels but will not derive these values systematically. In contrast, older children (about 11–13 years of age) will try to establish a relationship between the two variables and use this relationship to deduce how much food the longer eel will need.

Similarly, if 7-year-old children are asked to balance weights on a balance beam, they can come to understand that identical weights affect the equilibrium of the balance differently if they are placed at different distances from the fulcrum: the farther away from the fulcrum you place the weight, the more the arm of the scale will go down. However, 7-year-old children will not establish a systematic relationship between how far they move the weight and the way the equilibrium is affected. It is only later that youngsters will realize that a weight that is half of another will balance with it perfectly if placed twice as far from the centre.

Piaget and his colleagues (Piaget *et al.*, 1968; Inhelder and Piaget, 1958) considered the achievement of *proportional* reasoning as another mark in the development of intelligence. Proportional reasoning involves the recognition that the *relationship between two variables remains invariant although the values in both variables are changed.* It requires establishing an invariant relation among relations – a higher order operation, according to Piaget, that indicates the achievement of a new level of thinking, that of formal operations.

2.2 Recent developments

Although Piaget's contribution to the current approaches to the study of children's mathematical and scientific thinking is broadly recognized, some aspects of his work have been subjected to criticism in the last two decades. The most serious criticisms have been directed at his idea that our intellectual structures determine the way we think above and beyond any other influences. Much of the recent research on mathematical reasoning seems to suggest that both children and adults may show different levels of success when solving problems that involve the same intellectual structures but differ in other respects, such as the *content* of the problem, the particular *mathematical representation* they are using, or the *social situation* in which they are engaged. With respect to the *content* of the problem, for example, it is easy to imagine that someone may grasp that the relationship between quantity purchased and amount of money that has to be paid is proportional. In other words, the more sweets you buy, the more you pay, and the amounts vary in a fixed ratio – for example, 5p per sweet. Yet, this same person may not realize that, if you enlarge a rectangle, the ratio between length and width must be kept constant for the figure to look similar – if the length is twice the width in the small rectangle, it must also be twice the width in the larger one, otherwise the figures look different. With respect to the type of *mathematical representation*, for example, Nunes (1993) has shown that pupils (of approximately 12–13 years) who were able to solve problems with negative numbers if they did so orally made significantly more errors if they were asked to write the information down before solving the problem. Although the content of the problem and the social situation were the same, the written representation had characteristics that confused the pupils when they were solving the problems. Finally, Lave (1988) showed that adults in California performed very differently when solving the same type of proportion problems across *social situations*. They were much more successful in the supermarket than in a written test. Thus it now seems clear that intellectual structures may influence performance in problem solving but they do not directly determine what a subject will actually do. Other aspects of the problem situation need consideration.

Gérard Vergnaud, a French developmental psychologist, has suggested that, in order to analyse mathematical concepts, we must look not only at the invariant properties of the concept, as Piaget proposed, but we must also consider the situations that give meaning to the concept and the symbols used in its representation (Vergnaud, 1985). He proposes that in mathematics we should think not of concepts, but of conceptual fields that include several related concepts and their interrelations. As in the case, for example, of addition and subtraction. There are situations in which addition can be understood without reference to other concepts – for example, when two sets are put together or when a transformation is carried out on one set by increasing the number of its elements. However, a careful analysis of other 'addition problems' (that is, problems that can be solved by an addition operation) shows that some of these problems can only be understood in relation to subtraction. Similarly, there are 'subtraction problems' that relate directly to actions that result in decreasing quantities, like giving away or losing objects from a set, whereas other subtraction problems can only be understood in relation to addition. These different situations are all part of the addition and subtraction concepts but are not all understood at the same time. Can you make predictions about their difficulty? Try Activity 4 now.

ACTIVITY 4

Allow about 5 minutes

HOW DIFFICULT ARE THESE ARITHMETIC PROBLEMS?

Read the arithmetic problems presented below. They have different levels of difficulty for young children. Try to figure out which one is easier, which is more difficult and why. Then look at Figure 7 and verify whether your predictions are correct.

Problem 1
John had some marbles. He played with a friend and won 4 marbles. Now he has 9. How many did he have before the game?

Problem 2
Mary had 9 sweets. She gave 4 to her sister. How many does she have now?

Problem 3
Paul had 9 buttons in his pocket. His pocket had a hole and some fell out. Now he has 4 buttons. How many buttons did he lose?

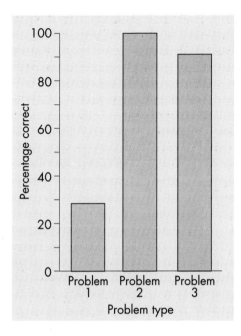

FIGURE 7 Proportion of first graders who solved the problems correctly. (Data from Riley, Greeno and Heller, 1983.)

Different addition and subtraction situations

Much research has been carried out comparing the difficulty that children face in solving addition and subtraction problems (see, for example, Riley, Greeno and Heller, 1983; Carpenter and Moser, 1982). This research shows that children may know how to solve a particular numerical computation – that is, they may know, for example, that 9–4 = 5 – but may still not be able to solve problems that require just that computation. The understanding of addition and subtraction does not depend only on knowledge of number facts but also on the children's ability to analyse the situations. Brown (1981) and Vergnaud (1982), who studied more complex addition problems, found that there were some problems which were difficult even for 11 year olds, although the easiest ones could be solved by 4 year olds.

The simplest addition/subtraction situations are related to questions about the *results of transformations* in which elements are added to/taken away from original sets. A related and similarly easy type of problem has to do with *joining / separating* two sets and asking about the results of this union/separation – for example, 'in a family there are 3 girls and 2 boys, how many children altogether?' Rather more difficult are problems that involve the *comparison* of two sets, like 'Mary has 5 books; Tom has 3 books; how many more books does Mary have than Tom?'

The analysis of the situation described in the problem is not sufficient to characterize the level of difficulty of a problem. Which piece of information is not known is also important. For example, a transformation problem is very easy when the information to be calculated is the result of the transformation (see Problem 2 in Activity 4). In this case, the action in the story and the operation to solve the problem are directly related: a transformation that increases the number will be solved by addition and one that decreases the number will be solved by subtraction. On the other hand, when the initial situation is unknown and must be calculated on the basis of information about the transformation and the end result (see Problem 1 in Activity 4), the relationship between the action and the operation is inverse: if the action in the problem increases the quantity, the operation needed to solve it is a subtraction. Inverse problems are significantly more difficult than direct problems.

Different addition and subtraction strategies

When young children solve transformation story problems, they often *model* the relationships in the problem with concrete objects, like their own fingers. For example, they may solve the problem 'Mary had 4 sweets; she got 3 more from her Granny; how many does she have now?' by lifting up 4 fingers, then lifting up 3 fingers, and then *counting them all*. This procedure, although correct, is inefficient. The children could simply lift up 3 fingers and *count on* from 5 (that is, from the first number after 4). Groen and Resnick (1977) have shown that children do not have to be taught how to count on in order to improve their efficiency. They can discover this improvement by themselves in the course of solving a large number of addition problems. Groen and Resnick worked with five pre-school children (average age 4 years and 10 months) and started out by teaching them to solve addition problems by representing each *addend* with a set of blocks and then counting all the blocks together. The children were then asked to solve a large number of problems and their procedures were observed. Children not only invented the new procedure of counting on, instead of counting all, but also invented a more efficient procedure, which the researchers termed *'counting on from the larger'*. In this latter case, if the first addend happened to be smaller than the second, instead of representing the second addend and counting on from the first, children represented the first and counted on from the second, changing the problem (for example, 2 + 6 was solved as if it read 6 + 2).

As they used this more efficient solution, they implicitly relied on the property of *commutativity* of addition, that states that the order of the addends does not alter the sum. This does not mean that the children could necessarily explain the property of commutativity but they simply relied on it for their reasoning. Vergnaud (1982) has termed such use of mathematical properties 'theorems in action'. The analysis of children's theorems in action as they solve problems can clearly enrich our understanding of their mathematical knowledge.

Different arithmetic practices

The research reviewed above concentrated on the situations and the strategies used in solving addition and subtraction problems. In this section, the symbolic systems used as a resource for computation will be considered.

When manipulatives (such as blocks, strokes on paper, or fingers) are used as a support during computation, the operation is 'off-loaded' onto the manipulation (Hatano, in press). The use of manipulatives to solve computation problems is not a part of Western cultural practices (but note that it is part of culturally-transmitted calculation procedures wherever the abacus is used). Counting on fingers still survives as a personal means of obtaining answers and is observed quite often among children. Western cultures tend to transmit two other arithmetic practices, oral and written arithmetic, with different degrees of emphasis on the transmission of oral arithmetic.

Oral arithmetic is often observed in connection with the manipulation of money. When we count money, we are actually carrying out additions that correspond to the values of the notes and coins. Often in shops change is checked by counting up from the value spent as the coins/ notes are placed in front of the buyer. That is a way of subtracting the amount spent from the total amount of money paid in by the buyer.

Nunes, Schliemann, and Carraher (1993) studied the uses of oral and written arithmetic practices in Brazil. Oral arithmetic is more frequent in everyday settings, outside school, where people are unlikely to turn to paper and pencil or even calculators. For people engaged in the informal economy in settings like street markets, oral arithmetic is the rule rather than the exception. Written arithmetic, in contrast, is the preferred form of problem solving and calculation for school purposes. It is preferred because it offers a formal representation of the problem and because it leaves a trace so that the teacher can see later on how the problem was solved.

These two *cultural practices*, oral and written arithmetic, may be more or less known by anyone. They have, however, been described in countries as diverse as the United States and the Ivory Coast (Ginsburg *et al.,* 1981), Liberia (Reed and Lave, 1981), and Brazil (Nunes, Schliemann and Carraher, 1993).

Research Summary 1 presents three protocols of oral addition and subtraction obtained when interviewing young street vendors in Brazil (Carraher, Carraher and Schliemann, 1985). These protocols exemplify the procedure known as *decomposition* that is used in the solution of addition and subtraction problems. This procedure involves breaking a number into parts that usually coincide with its analysis into orders in the numeration system (hundreds, tens and ones) and working out the calculations on the parts sequentially. Decomposition uses the *property of associativity* of addition as a theorem in action.

Research Summary 2 presents examples or protocols of oral multiplication and division obtained in the same study. The procedure used in these operations is known as *repeated addition (for multiplication) or subtraction (for division)*. It consists of keeping in mind the correspondence between the two variables in the problem – in the example of multiplication, number of coconuts and corresponding price – and increasing these values proportionally. This procedure relies on the *property of distributivity* as a theorem in action (see Nunes, Schliemann and Carraher, 1993).

RESEARCH SUMMARY 1
EXAMPLES OF PROTOCOLS OF ORAL ADDITION AND SUBTRACTION

1.   Subject: L. Condition: Word problem. Computation: 200 – 35.

L: If it were thirty, then the result would be seventy. But it is thirty-five. So it's sixty-five; one hundred sixty-five. *(The 35 was decomposed into 30 and 5, a procedure that allows the child to operate initially with only hundreds and tens; the units were taken into account afterwards. The 200 was likewise decomposed into 100 and 100; one 100 was stored and the other was used in the computation procedure.)*

2.   Subject: E. Condition: Store. Computation: 243 – 75.

E: You just give me the two hundred [he meant 100]. I'll give you twenty-five back. Plus the forty-three that you have, the hundred and forty-three, that's one hundred and sixty-eight. *(Instead of operating on the 243, the child operated on 100, subtracted 75 and added the result to 143, which had been set aside.)*

3.   Subject: Ev. Condition: Computation exercise. Computation: 252 – 57.

Ev: Take fifty-two, that's two hundred, and five to take away, that's one hundred and ninety-five. *(The child decomposed 252 into 200 and 52; 57 was decomposed into 52 + 5; removing both 52s, there remained another 5 to take away from 200.)*

(from Nunes, Schliemann and Carraher, 1993, p. 41)

RESEARCH SUMMARY 2
EXAMPLE OF PROTOCOLS OF ORAL MULTIPLICATION AND DIVISION

1.   Subject: JG. Condition: Store. Computation: 15 x 50.

JG: Fifty, one hundred, one fifty, two hundred, two fifty. *(Pause)* Two fifty. Five hundred, five fifty, six hundred, six fifty, seven hundred, seven fifty. *(The child was monitoring the number of 50s on one hand. When he reached five 50s, he doubled that number, obtaining ten 50s, and then went on counting in single 50s.)*

2.   Subject: F. Condition: Word problem. Computation: 75 ÷ 5.

F: If you give ten marbles to each (child), that's fifty. There are twenty-five left over. To distribute to five boys, twenty-five, that's hard. *(Experimenter: That's a hard one.)* That's five more for each. Fifteen each. *(The problem was solved by successively subtracting the convenient groups distributed while keeping track of the increasing share that each child received; 10 marbles each were given to 5 children, which accounted for 50 marbles, and the remaining 25 were distributed among the 5 children – 5 to each, totalling 15 for each child.)*

3.   Subject: Ev. Condition: Computation exercise. Computation: 100 ÷ 4.

(After attempting unsuccessfully to solve the exercise on paper, Ev. claimed that it was impossible. She first attempted to divide 1 by 4, which was not possible, then to divide 0 by 4, and finally gave up. The examiner asked for a justification.)

Ev: See, in my head I can do it. One hundred divided by four is twenty-five. Divide by two, that's fifty. Then divide again by two, that's twenty-five. *(She proceeded here by factoring; two successive divisions by 2 replace the given division by 4.)*

(from Nunes, Schliemann and Carraher, 1993, p. 43)

The five youngsters who participated in this study were interviewed in two situations: (1) in the streets, where they worked as street vendors, and (2) in a school-like situation, where they answered questions about story problems and arithmetic computations. In the streets they relied exclusively on oral arithmetic. They were very successful and answered correctly 98 per cent of the problems. In the school-like situation they relied mostly on written procedures and proved much less efficient: their rate of correct responses was 74 per cent to word problems and 37 per cent to computation exercises.

The comparison between their successful performance in the streets and their rather high rate of failure when solving computation exercises suggests that symbolic systems are not accessories to people's reasoning. They *mediate* complex reasoning functions, as suggested by Luria (1979), and thus have an impact on how the function is carried out. Nunes, Schliemann and Carraher (1993) analysed in a later study the influence of symbolic systems not only on the rates of correct and incorrect responses but also on the size of the errors made by children when using either oral or written arithmetic. Three different error bands were defined for this comparison: errors that fell within 10 per cent of the value of the correct answer (for example, between 18 and 22 if the correct response to the problem was 20); errors that were larger than 10 per cent but did not differ by more than 20 per cent from the correct answer; and errors that differed from the correct answer by more than 20 per cent. The frequencies of correct responses and errors in each error band for oral and written addition and subtraction are presented in Figure 8. The figure clearly shows that written arithmetic led to larger errors, a tendency that was supported by a statistical analysis of the association between type of strategy used in solving the problem (oral vs. written) and error band.

The qualitative analyses of oral and written arithmetic also indicated another important difference between these two cultural practices. In oral arithmetic, subjects seemed to keep the meaning of the problem in mind. For example, in the division problem presented in Research Summary 2, the subject clearly keeps in mind the fact that he is trying to figure out how many marbles each of the five children will get. The references to marbles and children are clear throughout the problem solving procedure. In contrast, in written arithmetic, references to the problem and even to the relative values of digits are set aside. For example, when solving in written arithmetic the same computation, 75 divided by 5, we will speak about the *digit* '7' as 'seven', not seventy, which would take into account its relative value. This loss of meaning in written arithmetic is probably one of the reasons for children's acceptance of responses to computations that would seem, under other circumstances, unacceptable, such as a result in a subtraction that is equal to or larger than the starting point.

In a later study, Nunes (1993) analysed young people's performance in solving problems with negative numbers. Arithmetic as such played a very minor role in this study where the numbers were always relatively

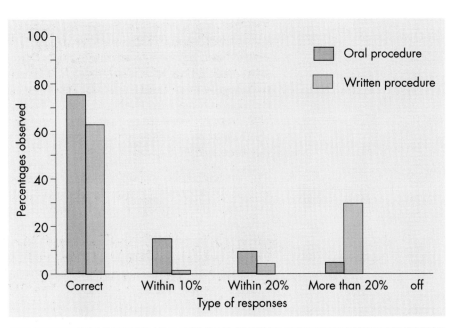

FIGURE 8 The frequencies of correct responses and errors for oral and written addition and subtraction. (Data from Nunes, Schliemann and Carraher, 1993, p. 47.) (a) Percentage of correct responses and of errors within each error band in addition problems.

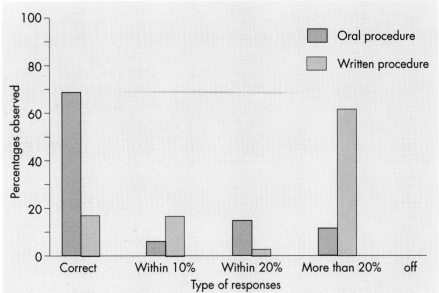

(b) Percentage of correct responses and of errors within each error band in subtraction problems.

small and included only tens (no units and no hundreds). The study aimed at looking at the influence of the mode of representation used, either oral or written, on the rate of correct responses. The problems were about a farmer's profits and losses with his crops during a season. Four pieces of information were involved: (a) his situation at the beginning of the season, when he could either have some savings or be in debt; (b) the results of his dealings in each of two crops, which could also be profit or debt; and (c) his situation at the end of the season. The subject was always told about the profits or losses in the crops and was asked either about the farmer's situation at the beginning of the season or at the end. The participants in the study were distributed randomly to either an oral or a written condition of solution. As in the preceding studies, oral practices resulted in significantly higher percentages of correct responses. Especially informative was the performance of some subjects who had been assigned to the written condition. They often made mistakes when solving the problem but then, when attempting to explain their answer orally, realized their mistake and clearly demonstrated their competence in understanding the cancellation of profits and debts. One such example is presented in Research Summary 3. It seems that the subject was in a sense trapped by a poorly learned written practice but, given the opportunity to think without having to manipulate the written symbols, he could well make the appropriate inferences about directed numbers (that is, positive and negative numbers).

RESEARCH SUMMARY 3
SOLVING PROBLEMS WITH DIRECTED NUMBERS IN THE WRITTEN AND ORAL MODE

Problem (from group 3): Seu Pedro (the farmer's name) started the season with a debt of 10 cruzados (Brazilian currency). He planted manioc and beans. He gained 10 on the manioc and 20 on the beans. What was his situation at the end of the season?

JC: (19 years old, sixth-grader, assigned to the written condition) wrote line 1 without indicating whether the number was positive or negative, and line 3 without a sign. Added all the numbers, obtaining 40, which was written on line 4.

Interviewer (I):   Was that a profit or a debt?

JC: Profit. No, it's not that. I can't do it on paper.

I: Why?

JC: He had a profit of 10, paid the 10 he owed. Then he still has his profit from the beans, he has 20.

(adapted from Nunes, 1993, p. 69)

SUMMARY OF SECTION 2

- Mathematical knowledge is organized and generative. However, it is not sufficient to describe the organization or structure of knowledge in order to understand it fully.

- It is also necessary to consider the situations in which it is used, which define the boundaries of the concept, and the symbolic systems that mediate the subject's reasoning process.

- All three aspects of mathematical knowledge need to be considered in the analysis of children's learning of mathematics.

3 THE DEVELOPMENT OF SCIENTIFIC REASONING AND CONCEPTS

3.1 Living in the physical world and learning about physics

Our actions in everyday life require that we take into account the nature of the physical world. In order to balance on a bicycle or to throw a dart at a particular spot we must in some sense 'conquer' the physical forces. However, how much do we accomplish without understanding? Try Activity 5.

ACTIVITY 5

Allow about 5 minutes

ONE'S ASSUMPTIONS ABOUT THE PHYSICAL WORLD

Throw a ball across the floor and observe how it moves until it stops. Why does it move? Why does it stop?

Now imagine you are *running across a room* and want to drop (not throw) a ball into a box as you run. Where should you be when you drop the ball? Look at Figure 9 and put an x where you should be when you drop the ball so that you make sure it will go into the box.

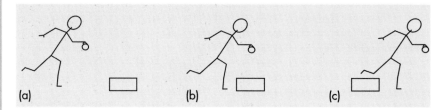

(a)　　　(b)　　　(c)

FIGURE 9　Where should you drop the ball if you want it to fall into the box?

Gunstone and Watts (1985) reviewed students' views of force and motion and contrasted their views with Newtonian physics, which forms the basis of what is taught in school about force and motion. The two simple questions included in Activity 5 show that it is possible to be successful in carrying out actions without understanding the physical forces one has to contend with.

The first question tends to bring up the notion that if there is movement, then it is because a force was applied to the object. Something must have started movement. When the object stops, the force must have been used up. Further, if an object is not moving, then there is no force acting on it.

This view of the world contrasts strongly with the physicist's view. Gunstone and Watts summarized this contrast by pointing out that, in essence, the first law of mechanics states exactly the opposite of what students assume about the world: that unless a force is acting on a body then it will move with a constant velocity. However, students will not spontaneously see the world in the same way. They live in a world where friction is present and do not conceive of friction as a force. Thus they do not see anything acting on the ball to stop it as it rolls across the floor. If an object is at rest – for example, on a table – students either see no forces acting in the situation or, at most, conceive of gravity as a force acting on the object. They do not think of the table as exerting a force that stops the object from falling. From the students' perspective, what needs explanation is movement, and force is called upon to explain it. From the physicist's perspective, what needs explanation is change in motion or acceleration. Thus students have different conceptions of the world, termed alternative conceptions in the science education literature, which affect both the choice of events requiring explanation and how they are to be explained.

The second question illustrates another difference between an everyday perspective and a physicist's perspective of an event. This task was studied by McClosky, Carmazza and Green (1980), who asked college students in physics and in other subjects to say where they should drop the ball from if they were running across a room and wanted to make sure that they let the ball drop right into the box. The students were asked to answer by choosing the correct one from a set of three pictures: (a) one in which the man seemed to be dropping the ball before reaching the target, (b) one in which the man dropped the ball directly over the target, and (c) one in which the ball was dropped after reaching the target. Physics students were significantly more accurate in answering this question although, as McClosky and his colleagues suggested, they were unlikely to be more successful in actually dropping the ball into the basket. Whereas 73 per cent of the physics students chose the picture where the man dropped the ball before reaching the target, only 13 per cent of the non-physics students made this correct choice. Among the physics students, the answers were divided between the correct choice and the picture where the ball was dropped directly above the box (27 per cent of the physics students chose this alternative). In contrast, 80 per cent of the non-physics students chose the picture of the man dropping the ball directly over the target and there were also choices in which the ball was dropped after the man had already run past the box (7 per cent). These results seem to indicate that physics students were thinking about the action differently from the non-physics students with respect to force and motion. The physics students took into account the fact that the ball was already in motion when carried across the room by the running man and thought of its path as it was dropped as the result of this initial force and direction plus the effect of gravity, whereas the non-physics students disregarded the motion of the ball while it was in the man's hand, and thought only about gravity.

3.2 Learning science in the classroom and developing new ways of thinking about the world

The college students majoring in physics interviewed in the study by McClosky *et al.*were remarkably successful compared to the majority of students from the secondary level that have received physics instruction. Gunstone and Watts (1985) suggest who had after students have been taught Newtonian physics and have learned the formula *F=ma,* a formula that indicates that force is proportional to *mass* and *acceleration*, they continue to think about force as proportional to motion, and not to acceleration. Similarly to the 5 year olds who know that the world is round but reason about it as if it were flat, students seem to learn the formula *F=ma* as a fact, but do not easily change their way of thinking about forces. Instruction designers are exhorted by Gunstone and Watts to consider this issue carefully.

There are many difficulties involved in learning scientific concepts and making them into ways of thinking about the world. One of the difficulties in learning science is making distinctions that we would not ordinarily make in everyday life, such as the distinction between temperature and heat. Although the temperature of two ice cubes is the same, even if one ice cube is twice the size of the other, the effect they have in cooling a drink is different. Many students think that the larger ice cube is actually colder, has a lower temperature than the smaller one, perhaps as a consequence of the fact that they have different effects in cooling a drink (for a review of students' ideas about heat and temperature, see Erickson and Tiberghien, 1985). Similarly, the temperature of boiling water is the same regardless of the amount of water but different amounts of water will transfer different amounts of heat to the surroundings, and will cool at different rates. Perhaps as a result of this experience, pupils tend to think that if there is more boiling water, the temperature of the water will be higher. Thus they do not distinguish between heat and temperature, a distinction that is important in physics.

Another difficulty in turning scientific concepts into a way of thinking is caused by the fact that many scientific concepts represent *intensive*, rather than *extensive* quantities, and must thus be treated differently from extensive quantities. Extensive quantities are measured through the simple application of a unit of measurement that is repeated until the number of units (plus, if necessary, some fraction of the unit) completely describes the quantity. For example, when we measure length in centimetres, the value we obtain by this measurement is equivalent to the number of times we can fit one centimetre – that is the unit – on the object measured. Intensive quantities, in contrast, are not measured directly, through the repeated application of a unit to the dimension that is being measured, but through a ratio between two other measures (for a discussion of extensive and intensive quantities, see Schwartz, 1988). Density, for example, is measured by a ratio of mass to volume. Similarly, speed involves a relationship between distance and time, and force involves a relationship between mass and acceleration. As Schwartz (1988) pointed out, we encounter intensive quantities in everyday life and even in everyday life it is more difficult to reason with intensive than extensive quantities. For example, it is possible to buy two kinds of coffee beans (say Brazilian and continental roast) of different prices (perhaps we pay £1.20 for the Brazilian coffee and 75p for the continental roast) and have them ground together into a blend that suits our particular preference (for example, $\frac{1}{3}$ continental roast and $\frac{2}{3}$ Brazilian). In this situation, there are two extensive quantities: (1) the total amount of coffee purchased, which is the *sum* of the amount of Brazilian coffee and the amount of continental roast; and (2) the total price paid, which is the *sum* of the cost of the Brazilian coffee and the continental roast. There is also one intensive quantity involved in this situation, the price per pound of this mixture, which is *not the sum* of the two prices per pound but the *weighted average* between them. Whereas the total price will vary with the quantity purchased, the price per pound will be constant for any quantity we buy. The difficulty of dealing with intensive quantities is clearly exemplified in this rather simple situation. Intensive quantities in science are often more complex because, as pointed out above, they require distinctions that we may not ordinarily make in everyday life. It is likely that science teaching involving intensive quantities could profit from the use of analogies with simpler intensive quantities used in everyday life, in the same way that mathematics teaching seems to profit from the use of everyday situations as models for teaching about mathematical concepts and operations. However reasonable this hypothesis may seem, we still need research on its validity before we can accept it.

A third source of difficulty may be the fact that scientific concepts often require reasoning about non-perceptible aspects of the physical world. This difficulty is most easily exemplified by the studies on pupils' ideas about the particulate nature of matter. We deal in everyday life with a world that is continuous, in which objects are solid and undivided. Yet, to understand many of the changes that we observe in the world, we need to develop a way of thinking about the world that describes our solid objects as bundles of 'particles', 'molecules', or 'atoms' – that is, discontinuous elements that are kept together somehow. Piaget and his colleagues (Piaget and Inhelder, 1974) were pioneers in the investigation of children's understanding of the particulate nature of matter. They set out a pattern of investigation by pointing out that it is when children have to understand change that they come to 'invent' an atomic theory about the world. They asked children to explain what happened to sugar when it was put into water and then stirred. Whereas the younger children seemed to believe that the sugar somehow disappeared, those at the ages of 11–13 were aware of the fact that if the taste of sugar remained in the water, then the sugar itself must still be present in some form. This permanence of a property of sugar – its taste – contradicted the apparent disappearance of sugar from the viewpoint of the older children. In order to eliminate the contradiction between the disappearance of sugar and the preservation of its taste, the older children 'invented' an atomic theory about physical quantities.

Many studies have refined Piaget's original ideas about children's understanding of the particulate nature of matter. Driver *et al.* (1985) and Hesse and Anderson (1992), for example, studied other chemical transformations such as combustion (what happens when wood is burned?) and oxidation (rusting and cleaning bits of iron) and also investigated pupils' conceptions when they observed other changes of state, such as evaporation and sublimation. An example of responses observed by Driver *et al.* (1985) is presented in Figure 10.

Finally, a major source of difficulty may be that students have already developed some knowledge about the world and this knowledge differs from that which teachers are aiming to teach in the classroom, both with respect to the different conceptions students have and the formal characteristics of the concepts used. In the previous section we raised the issue of alternative conceptions, which affects which events need explanation and how they are explained. Here we wish to add that everyday concepts developed about the world and scientific concepts have different formal characteristics. Whereas scientists strive to explain the largest number of phenomena with the smallest possible set of assumptions, a principle known as parsimony, in everyday life we do not strive to achieve this principle. In everyday life it does not matter that we have one set of explanations for the fact that the same volume of two different materials has two different weights and another for the fact that one of them may float and the other one may sink when placed in water. In science both observations will be reduced to the same concept, that of density.

A second formal difference is that scientists strive for great consistency and are (or should be) willing to reject their theories if they are inconsistent. In everyday life we may not be so ready to use consistency as a criterion for validating our knowledge. For example, Hatano (1993) has observed that young children can respond correctly to some questions about heat, whereas they give other answers to other problems that are utterly inconsistent with the first ones. If asked what they would do in order to cool the water in a bath, even young children will say that they would add cold water to it and thereby treat the resulting temperature in the bath as being somewhere between that of the hot and the cold water. However, when asked what is the temperature of the water in a container into which one litre of water at the temperature of 60 degrees and one litre of water at the temperature of 20 degrees were poured, the most frequent answer by young pupils is '80 degrees'. Whereas in the first problem about the temperature of the water in the bath the resulting temperature is intermediate between hot and cold, in the science classroom problem the resulting temperature is viewed as the sum of the temperature in the two volumes of water.

Vygotsky (1978) has described this difference between everyday and scientific concepts by suggesting that we learn scientific concepts from the general to the particular, but we learn everyday concepts from the particular to the general. Saxe (1982) has cast these ideas in information processing terminology by indicating that scientific concepts are formed from the top down and everyday concepts are formed from the bottom up.

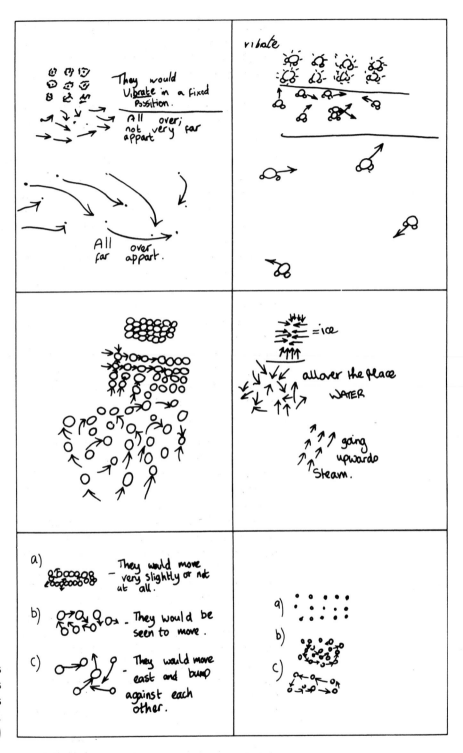

FIGURE 10 Drawings of 11 to 12 year olds representing the three states of matter. (Driver *et al.* 1985, p. 145.)

These different ways of comparing everyday and scientific concepts have one common feature: they emphasize that scientific concepts require consistency because particular cases should be deduced from general rules, whereas this does not apply to everyday concepts.

3.3 Solving problems in science: experts and novices

The difficulty of teaching scientific concepts to secondary school pupils has been stressed so often in the literature that it would seem that little is accomplished through teaching. It would seem that pupils need to think it all out themselves and that it is only their intellectual development that matters when it comes to learning mathematical and scientific concepts. Eleanor Duckworth, a developmental psychologist and educator, expressed this somewhat bleak view of education in a paper entitled 'Either we're too early and they can't learn it or we're too late and they know it already' (1979).

However, there is a growing body of research that suggests that knowledge, and not only reasoning skills, plays a part in problem solving in science. One hint in this direction was already given in the study by McClosky and colleagues, where physics students performed significantly better than non-physics students in the task of indicating where a ball should be dropped by a running man if he wants it to fall inside a box. The difference between being an expert in physics and being an expert in some other domain of knowledge mattered indeed.

The idea of comparing the way experts and novices think about the same problem is not new. It was tried out decades ago by de Groot (1965), who compared experts and novices in another domain, that of playing chess. He observed that experts organized their memory of a chess-board differently from novices because they could recognize thousands of game patterns on the board, instead of having to remember the location of individual pieces. Later, Chi, Feltovich and Glaser (1981) and Larkin, Heller and Greeno (1980) were able to show that experts in physics (graduate students) classified physics problems into groups by using criteria that differed from those used by novices. Experts grouped problems according to the concepts that had to be used in reasoning about the problems (such as conservation of energy) whereas novices sorted the problems in terms of physical similarities (for example, problems with pulleys, problems with inclined planes, etc.)

More recently, Smith and Good (1984) conducted a novice–expert study of solutions to genetics problems. Their novices were science and non-science major college students and their experts were genetics graduate students. All of the college students had recently completed an undergraduate course in genetics and thus had been exposed to the information needed to solve the problems. Among the differences between experts and novices described by Smith and Good were:

(a) a tendency among experts to treat problems as tasks of analysis and reasoning rather than trying to remember *algorithms* that would lead to solution (observed among novices);

(b) a tendency among experts to use a knowledge development approach (termed by Larkin *et al.*, 1980, a 'forward-working' strategy), that required structuring the information obtained and testing possible conclusions against new information; and

RESEARCH SUMMARY 4
DO EXPERTS AND NOVICES APPROACH PROBLEMS DIFFERENTLY?

The problem in this study required students to figure out the parental genotypes and mechanism of inheritance given the parental phenotypes and the frequency of different phenotypes in the offspring.

The expert forms a hypothesis about the parental genotype and the mechanism of inheritance and works through the problem, calculating the expected frequencies for different phenotypes if the hypothesis were correct. The selection of a hypothesis already takes into account information from the observed frequencies but may not be the correct one. The subject says: 'That looks like all the F1 [offspring, first generation] are gonna be heterozygous at two different loci, and the way I've got it set up with this assumption, there's no way that can come about [the subject seems to have compared the observed frequencies with those expected from the hypothesis]. So I'm just gonna work through other problems and get some other, other information about the genotype' (from Smith and Good, 1984, p. 904).

The novice looks at the problem and does not try to raise a hypothesis about the genotype, following it through to the offspring phenotypes and their frequencies, but rather tries to reproduce knowledge obtained in the course: 'I was thinking about the flowers. If, ahm, if one flower is white, or say if two flowers are pink, pink is usually recessive, whereas the white, OK, the right-white is recessive, and the red's, uh, the dominant genes. So if you put 'em together, $3/4$ will be ... OK, one will be white. Only this, least recessive one ...

I: Uh hum.

S: Will be white and then $3/4$ will be either, what is it, pink, yeah, pink. OK, two will be pink and one will be red.'

Throughout this section the subject has been closing her eyes and pointing in the air, apparently to some remembered visual pattern (from Smith and Good, 1984, p. 903).

The protocols illustrate that knowledge plays a part for both subjects but it is used rather differently. The problem also illustrates the role of knowledge in a different way: there is a whole way of thinking which is illustrated in the vocabulary (genotype, phenotype, dominant, recessive) and in the way hypotheses are tested (looking at expected and observed frequencies for the offspring). The totally uninitiated in genetics cannot take part in such conversations.

(c) a tendency among experts to have and use accurate knowledge of genetics.

These are certainly not independent trends since structuring the information in this case required knowledge of the system of representation used in genetics and the relationship between genotype and phenotype expressed in the notation system. Similarly, testing hypotheses cannot be considered as independent from the knowledge of which kinds of offspring could not be produced by parents with particular genotypes. Thus experts appeared to have a clear edge over the novices even if the novices have been exposed recently to a course that contained the basic information needed to solve the problems. However, being an 'expert' (as defined in their selection of subjects) was not a necessary condition for showing expert-like strategies. Smith and Good observed that, although the graduate students were more likely to deploy problem-solving strategies that were characteristic of 'experts', approximately 30 per cent of their novices used similar strategies and were also successful, in spite of a disadvantage in their level of knowledge. An excerpt of a protocol by one of their experts and a contrasting novice protocol are presented in Research Summary 4.

SUMMARY OF SECTION 3

- There are differences between the physicist's conception of the world and that of pupils. Pupils' *alternative conceptions* involve different questions about the world (what requires explanation) and also different answers (how it is explained).

- Some of the difficulties involved in applying learned scientific concepts to our ways of thinking about the world result from having to make distinctions that we would not ordinarily need to make.

- Many scientific concepts represent *intensive*, rather than *extensive*, quantities. Intensive quantities are measured through a ratio between two other measures, whereas extensive quantities are measured directly, through the repeated application of a unit to the dimension that is being measured.

- Scientific concepts often require reasoning about non-perceptible aspects of the physical world.

- Students may experience difficulty in learning about scientific concepts because the knowledge and conceptions they already have conflict with the formal concepts being introduced by the teacher.

- Scientists operate on the principle of *parsimony*, i.e., explaining the largest number of phenomena with the smallest set of assumptions.

- Scientists strive for *consistency* in their theories where particular cases can be deduced from general rules. This is not necessary in everyday life.

- Finally, experts and novices have different approaches to problems. This indicates that knowledge of a particular field significantly influences and helps experts when they are solving problems.

4 INTELLECTUAL DEVELOPMENT AND THE DEVELOPMENT OF MATHEMATICAL AND SCIENTIFIC CONCEPTS

Much of the recent research on the growth of children's scientific knowledge has focused on the pupils' understanding of particular concepts in science. For this reason, it is worthy of mention that science is not simply made up of concepts but involves a commitment to an approach to knowledge, a scientific approach, that contrasts with philosophy and art, for example. Inhelder and Piaget (1958), once again, were the pioneers in the investigation of children's ability to reason in a scientific way, and suggested that the understanding of scientific methods only develops in adolescence. In this section we will consider the issue of the relationship between cognitive development and the acquisition of mathematical and scientific concepts.

There are two different questions that can be posed with respect to the relationship between the development of scientific reasoning in adolescence and the acquisition of scientific concepts. One is whether it is necessary or, perhaps less strongly, advantageous to understand scientific reasoning in order to master the scientific and mathematical concepts taught in school. The second is whether, once scientific reasoning has developed, young people will be able to tackle easily the task of understanding scientific concepts taught in school.

Piaget and his colleagues seem to have taken a strong position in this respect. There are two parts to their assumptions. First, they did not believe that secondary school students would actually master scientific concepts (such as density) or mathematical concepts (such as combinatorial analysis) without having developed the appropriate cognitive structures for the *assimilation* of their teaching (see Inhelder and Piaget, 1958). Second, they also postulated an harmonious development of intelligence according to which, once the appropriate cognitive structures had developed, youngsters could actually discover the concepts on their own. In a sense, they expected the 'power of reasoning' to generalize to all contents, once it had developed.

There is relatively little research that can help test these hypotheses but the limited evidence available so far seems to support the first part of their assumptions but not the second. A recent study by Piburn (1990) correlated students' success in their science courses with their performance in a test of *propositional reasoning* (that is, a test of their ability to reason about if-then propositions). A significant correlation ($r = .57$) was found between students' performance in the task of propositional reasoning and their grade in science. An item analysis indicated that this correlation relied on those items which relate to reasoning that Inhelder and Piaget expect to develop only at the level of formal operations, whereas those that can be solved at the concrete operational level were not predictive of success in science. Although this study is not sufficient to clarify why the relationship between propositional reasoning and learning science is observed, it is an initial indication that it may be advantageous to achieve propositional reasoning in order to learn science. In order to put this hypothesis to a stronger test, however, it is necessary to obtain at least longitudinal evidence, in which the science learners are tested for their propositional reasoning *before* the science course. Unfortunately, no such studies seem to have been carried out so far.

The second prediction of Piaget's theory relates to the generalization of formal operational reasoning across contents. The stage of formal operations was conceived by Piaget (see Piaget and Garcia, 1971) as a stage in which the operations of thought (such as propositional reasoning, for example) become abstract and independent of their content. Whereas at the concrete operational level the operations of thought are connected to objects, at the level of formal operations the operations of thought are applied to other operations of thought. This means, according to Piaget, that thinking can now function in a formal way and allows for progress in the understanding of any scientific domain without the development of new operations of reasoning. This prediction about the generalization of the structures of thought has met a growing degree of scepticism in the last two decades. Specifically with respect to the schema of propositional reasoning, much work has been carried out that indicates its susceptibility to influences of the content of the proposition. Luria (1976), Scribner (1975) and Johnson-Laird, Legrenzi and Legrenzi (1972) pioneered this work by showing that propositions about contents familiar to the subjects were more likely to result in correct responses than either those that were about unfamiliar contents or those in which the proposition went against the subjects' everyday experiences. More recently, Cheng and Holyoak (1985) and Girotto, Light, and Colbourn (1988) have expanded on this work by looking at young people's reasoning about several types of *if-then propositions*. They have suggested that we reason about these propositions not in a formal, content-free way, as originally suggested by Piaget and his colleagues, but rather we rely on pragmatic schemas that involve both formal and content specific elements. When the if-then proposition is a prohibition we are likely to make inferences that differ from those we make when the proposition is a promise. Thus the content of a proposition has a clear influence on the inferences we are willing to make even if the propositions have the same form. Activity 6 presents an example of the contrast between prohibitions and promises.

ACTIVITY 6
Allow about 3 minutes

DOES THE CONTENT OF A PROPOSITION AFFECT REASONING?

Here are two types of if-then propositions: promises and prohibition/permission.

1 If you mow the lawn, I will give you £5.

   You didn't mow the lawn. Do I give you £5?

2 If you drive a truck, you must not drive through the city centre.

   You drive a car. Can you drive through the city centre?

In (1), the if-condition is denied; what do you conclude?
In (2), the if-condition is denied; what do you conclude?
Are there differences? Why?

SUMMARY OF SECTION 4

- There is some support (although better designed research is still lacking) for the idea that, as children's reasoning becomes more sophisticated, they become better learners in science.
- There is little support, however, for the idea that young people reach a stage of formal operations where sophisticated forms of reasoning, such as propositional reasoning, are easily applied to any content. Inference-making, it seems, is not the same when inferences are made about meaningful contents or irrelevant ones, for example.
- Moreover, the situation in which problems are solved and the type of representation used during problem solving also affect problem solving in a significant way.

5 HOW DO YOUNG PEOPLE CHANGE THEIR WAY OF THINKING IN SCIENCE AND MATHEMATICS?

A major point of the preceding discussion is that learning mathematics and science is not so much learning facts as learning ways of thinking. Conceptual definitions often sound like 'statements of facts' but they remain meaningless if the concepts do not become part of our way of thinking. It has also been emphasized that in order to learn science we must often change the way we think in everyday life. For example, in order to understand even simple concepts such as heat and temperature, we must abandon our way of thinking of temperature as a measure of heat and learn to distinguish between the two. These changes in ways of thinking are referred to as *conceptual changes*. But how do conceptual changes happen? How do young people change their ways of thinking as they develop and as they learn in school?

Traditional instruction based on telling students how modern scientists think does not seem to be very successful. Students may learn the definitions, the formulae, the terminology, and still maintain their previous conceptions (or alternative conceptions, as they are often called). This difficulty has been illustrated many times, for example, when instructed students are interviewed about heat and temperature or forces, as discussed earlier. It is often identified by teachers as a difficulty in applying the concepts learned in the classroom; students may be able to repeat a formula but fail to use the concept represented by the formula when they explain observed events.

Piaget suggested an interesting hypothesis for the process of cognitive change. Cognitive change was expected to result from the pupils' own intellectual activity. When confronted with a result that challenges their thinking – i.e., when faced with conflict – pupils realize that they need to think again about their own ways of solving problems, regardless of whether the problem is one in mathematics or in science. Conflict was hypothesized to bring about disequilibrium and would result in the setting off of *equilibration* processes, that would ultimately produce cognitive change. For this reason, according to Piaget and his colleagues, in order for pupils to progress in their thinking they need to be actively engaged in solving problems that will challenge their current mode of reasoning.

However, Piaget also pointed out that young children do not always discard their ideas in the face of contradictory evidence. They may actually discard the evidence and keep their theory. Activity 7 describes a science class where children aged about 6 were asked to observe whether objects floated or sank in water and later in the afternoon were interviewed about what they had learned in their science lesson.

ACTIVITY 7

Allow about 10 minutes

DO HEAVY THINGS SINK AND LIGHT ONES FLOAT?

Read the transcript of the interactions below and think about what they mean for the development of scientific concepts.

The first of the interactions was recorded during a science lesson in which children were asked to make predictions about whether some things would float or sink when put in a basin full of water. The second is an excerpt of an interview carried out with one of the pupils after the lesson.

TEACHER: You have to tell us what you've chosen (to place in the water).

BILLY: I've got a milk.

T: You've chosen a carton of a milk.

B: And it's a bit heavy ...

T: Yeah!

B: And you can drink out of it and eh ...

T: What's it made from?

LOUISA: It's a carton.

T: It's a carton. What's a carton made from? ... Do you know what cartons are made from? Louisa?

(*Teacher addressing question to group before asking Louisa.*)

L: Cardboard.

(...)

T: What's going to happen to your milk?

B: Sinks.

(*Billy puts the carton in the water.*)

T: Oh! What's happened to it?

B: It floats.

T: It's bobbing about on the water. Isn't it? And … Louisa … You didn't guess just …

Interview with Billy after lesson one.

INTERVIEWER: What can you remember about what you have just done? Can you tell me a little about what you have been doing?

BILLY: These are all the things that floated and these are all the things that sunk (*referring to chart composed during the lesson*).

I: Tell me a bit about them.

B: The carton floated.

I: Why did it float?

B: It was a bit light … it's light … because it's little and light.

Now think about these interactions.

What do you think of Billy's conclusion after the lesson. Did he discard his explanation for why some things float and others sink? What does this say about children's reaction to conflicting evidence?

Piaget's hypothesis about how cognitive change progresses was later translated into a teaching approach now termed 'discovery learning'.

Discovery learning initially took the route of what is now considered the 'lone learner' route. The teacher played the role of the selector of situations that challenged the pupils' reasoning; the pupils' peers had no role in this process at all. In the last three decades, however, it became clear that interpersonal conflict, especially with peers, may play an important role in promoting cognitive change. This hypothesis, originally advanced by Perret-Clermont (1980) and Doise and Mugny (1984), has been investigated in many recent studies of science teaching and learning.

Howe and her colleagues, for example, have compared children's progress in understanding several types of science concepts when they are given the opportunity to observe relevant events either on their own or with peers. In one study (Howe, Tolmie and Rodgers, 1992) they compared 8- to 12-year-old children's progress in understanding what influences motion down an incline. In order to ascertain the role of conflict in group work, they created two kinds of groups of children: one in which the children had dissimilar views according to a pre-test (the conflict group) and a second type of group in which the children had similar views. They found support for the idea that children in the groups with dissimilar views progressed more after their training sessions than those who had been placed in groups with similar views. However, they found no evidence to support the idea that the children worked out their new conceptions during their group discussions, because progress was not actually observed immediately after the sessions of group work but rather in a delayed post-test (that is, a new evaluation of how the children understood motion down an incline given around four weeks after the group work).

In another study, Howe and her colleagues (Howe, Tolmie and Anderson, 1991) set out to investigate whether the progress obtained through group work could be a function of the exchange of ideas during the group sessions. They investigated in this study the progress made by 12- to 15-year-old pupils in understanding the path of falling objects, a topic that clearly involves conceptual difficulties, as we saw earlier. In order to create groups with varying levels of dissimilarity in their initial conceptions, the pupils' predictions and explanations of the path of falling objects were assessed before they were engaged in group work. The group work sessions involved solving computer-presented problems, again about predicting and explaining the paths of falling objects. A post-test, given individually, assessed the progress made by pupils in their conceptions of what influenced the path of falling objects. It was expected that pairs of pupils who had more dissimilar conceptions would engage in more discussion, refer more to their explanations during their discussions, and subsequently show greater progress. In this study Howe and her colleagues were also interested in analysing whether gender would affect significantly the pattern and results of group work, because they believed that there is evidence that indicates adolescent boys to be more likely to exchange ideas during discussion than girls. Thus they wondered whether the pattern of greater cognitive change through group work in solving science problems would be stronger among boys than girls. Their results supported the idea that intellectual conflict and discussion play a role in cognitive change. Significant correlations were found between the level of dissimilarity between the children in the pair before the collaborative work and the number of references to explanatory factors during discussion, and also between the level of initial dissimilarity and later progress in explanations. No evidence was found to support the existence of differences in the number of references to explanatory factors made by male, female or mixed pairs. There were also no differences between the amount of progress in explanations by male, female or mixed pairs. In short, the results support the hypothesis that conflict and discussion with peers can promote progress in understanding concepts in science and do not indicate gender differences in the validity of this hypothesis.

Although the work on peer collaboration can be seen as initially stemming from the Piagetian ideas about the processes of conflict and equilibration, much of the interest that currently surrounds peer collaboration in problem solving is motivated by other views of conceptual development. Within this other perspective, motivated by researchers such as Vygotsky, Luria and Bruner, conceptual changes are viewed as resulting not solely from the child's own activity but also from the child's interactions in a social world. A new concept was developed by Vygotsky in order to address the social nature of cognitive change: the concept of the *zone of proximal development*. The zone of proximal development is the difference between what a child can accomplish in solving a problem working independently and what can be accomplished by the same child with adult help.

> More generally, the concept refers to an interactive system within which people work on a problem which at least one of them could not, alone, work on effectively. Cognitive change takes place within this zone, where the zone is considered *both in terms of an individual's developmental history and in terms of the support structure created by the other people and cultural tools in the setting*.
>
> (Newman, Griffin and Cole, 1989, p. 61, my italics).

The concept of zone of proximal development originates within a theory that assumes that all higher psychological functions have socio-cultural origins – a theory that is different from Piaget's. Piaget's concept of assimilation, with its biological connotations, is replaced by the concept of *appropriation*, which takes into account the idea that many objects in the child's world are not so clearly defined by their physical properties as by their social history – such as language, that has acoustic properties but is only understood in terms of socially constructed meanings, or objects such as hammers and computers, the physical properties of which tell us little about their use. Socially constructed *systems of knowledge* are also part of the environment children interact with and it is through interaction that pupils can start to use the socially constructed systems of knowledge. They do not need to understand the systems fully in order to start using them but their understanding is expected to develop as they act and use the system. For interactions to be productive in the zone of proximal development, teachers have to be able to devise ways in which they and the children can function within two different understandings of the task, their own and the children's.

Newman, Griffin and Cole (1989) describe, as an example of such interactions, a lesson they devised with a teacher about different types of chemicals. The teacher initially told the pupils how certain types of chemicals turn different colours when mixed with an acid or a base. Children were then paired up to do the work and each pair received two chemicals and two indicators (acid or base). They were asked to mix the chemicals and the indicators and to record the four chemical reactions on a worksheet. However, young children have difficulty in being systematic about mixing chemicals and might have mixed the same ones twice, thereby losing important information. In order to prevent this, the teacher gave each child in a pair only one chemical to mix with the two indicators. Thus, although the children worked in pairs and recorded the four results, each child was only responsible for two mixtures.

The teacher and the children had different views of the lesson. The children had no knowledge of the sequence of lessons: they became involved and interested in the chemical reactions. The teacher had a particular goal within the sequence of her teaching, and the recording of the chemical reactions to be carried out by the children was an important goal of the work for her. She thus structured the activity so that the children could mix the chemicals, compare results, and discuss what they had seen without being unduly pressured by the planning of the mixing of chemicals. The planning of the experiment was 'off-loaded' by the teacher's assignment of chemicals (one to each child) so that they could (as a pair) effectively generate a full table of mixes and use the results to come to conclusions. This example illustrates how pupils were allowed to use effectively some aspects of a system of knowledge without its full appreciation. Due to their difficulty in organizing the mixture of chemicals systematically, they might have not come up with a full table. Thus although the design of the experiment may have been beyond their level of cognitive development, they were still able to participate in a research activity, recording observations, comparing results, and trying to come to conclusions that would be relevant to the learning of chemical mixtures.

ACTIVITY 8

Allow about 7 minutes

HOW DO CHILDREN FIGURE OUT WHAT SCIENCE IS?

Children can be genuine participants in science lessons in school without a full understanding of what science is. From the teacher's viewpoint, a science lesson has certain characteristics. From the pupils' viewpoint, it may have others. Working in the zone of proximal development means developing some common ground for understanding science as children gain experience under the teacher's guidance. The transcript below is an illustration of just how difficult it is for children to gain an understanding of what science is. They participate in concrete activities which are not direct illustrations of what science is. Read the transcript below and consider the difference between the teacher's and the pupils' views.

Setting: The class teacher is explaining to the children, who are about 6 years old, the various science tasks that she wants them to do. She is then interrupted by a question.

CAIN: What's science?

TEACHER: Oh, go on … you said 'what's science?'

CAIN: What's science?

TEACHER: What's science? Does anybody have any ideas what science is? … Marcia.

MARCIA: It's when … you sit down and do your work.

TEACHER: Yeah! What sort of work is science? Daniel.

DANIEL: When you stay in your place.

TEACHER: When you stay in your place. Sarah.

SARAH: Number work.

TEACHER: Number work, is it? Something to do with numbers? Billy.

BILLY: Like when you work with the sand.

TEACHER: Like when you work with the sand. What sort of … What sort of sand work is science work, because sometimes I get you to work with the sand for number, don't I?

BILLY: Em ...

TEACHER: What sort of things do I ask you to do of ... say ... if it was science and I asked you to go and work with the sand? What sort of things would you be doing?

CAIN: Measuring work.

TEACHER: Em ...

CAIN: I know.

TEACHER: Sh ... we have hands, don't we? (*Shushing Cain, who started the whole thing.*) Paul.

PAUL: Measuring how much sand.

TEACHER: That's more a number job, isn't it? Excuse me, Sarah. ... Jodie.

JODIE: Like when you put heavy things.

TEACHER: Em. Tara.

TARA: Adds up.

TEACHER: Adds up. Richard.

RICHARD: If you could see whether a thing was sinking or floating in the water.

TEACHER: Em, that's science, isn't it?

CAIN: Being quiet.

TEACHER: Tara

TARA: Pushing the chairs in.

TEACHER: Science is sort of what we call investigating. When we're seeing what's happening ... you were going to say that were you, I thought you might be about to say that. When you think ... I wonder if such and such happens? I wonder what will happen if? Those are the sorts of science questions. I wonder ...

What is the teacher's view of science? What is the children's view of science? How can the teacher engage the children in *her* science?

SUMMARY OF SECTION 5

- The search for what promotes cognitive changes in the development of mathematical and scientific concepts has generated at least three main hypotheses that are alternatives to the traditional way of teaching: *discovery learning*, in which children are active but work mostly on their own; *collaborative learning*, in which peers work together to solve problems; and the model of *learning as appropriation*, in which a cultural object – a system of knowledge – is progressively mastered as the learner uses it effectively, although initially without a full appreciation of what the system does for him or her.

6 CONCLUSION

Mathematical and scientific conceptual development does not seem to be simply a question of learning facts or procedures. Both involve the achievement of new ways of thinking and reasoning in generative ways. But it is not enough to analyse the structures of reasoning, as Piaget originally proposed, in order to understand children's progress in mathematics and science. Children do not interact only with the physical environment and do not discover only by themselves the properties of actions and of objects. Our societies have developed systems of representation and knowledge to which children are exposed both in school and out of school. Through their participation in social situations, where people use these knowledge systems, the children come to use this knowledge, even if they do not at least initially grasp it in the same way that adults in the society do. Whilst exploring their ideas with peers or participating with adults in situations (such as experiments) which they themselves could not create, children become engaged in mathematical and scientific thinking. They can thus restructure their ways of reasoning and make progress.

FURTHER READING

DRIVER, R. (1983) *The Pupil as Scientist?*, Milton Keynes, Open University Press.

NUNES, T., SCHLIEMANN, A. D. and CARRAHER, D. W. (1993) *Street Mathematics and School Mathematics*, Cambridge, Cambridge University Press.

REFERENCES

BROWN, M. (1981) 'Number operations' in HART, K. M. (ed.) *Children's Understanding of Mathematics: 11–16*, Oxford, John Murray.

CARPENTER, T. P. and MOSER, J. M. (1982) 'The development of addition and subtraction problem-solving skills' in CARPENTER, T. P., MOSER, J. M. and ROMBERG, T. A. (eds), *Addition and subtraction: a cognitive perspective,* Hillsdale (N.J.), Lawrence Erlbaum Associates.

CARRAHER, T. N., CARRAHER, D. W. and SCHLIEMANN, A. D. (1985) 'Mathematics in the streets and in schools', *British Journal of Developmental Psychology*, **3**, pp. 21–9.

CHENG, P. W. and HOLYOAK, K. J. (1985) 'Pragmatic reasoning schemas', *Cognitive Psychology*, **18**, pp. 293–328.

CHI, M. T., FELTOVICH, P. J. and GLASER, R. (1981) 'Categorization and representation of physics problems by experts and novices', *Cognitive Science*, **5**, pp. 121–52.

de GROOT, A. D. (1965) *Thought and Choice in Chess*, The Hague, Mouton.

DOISE, W. and MUGNY, G. (1984) *The Social Development of the Intellect*, Oxford, Pergamon.

DRIVER, R., GUESNE, E. and TIBERGHIEN, A. (1985) 'Children's ideas and the learning of science' in DRIVER, R., GUESNE E. and TIBERGHIEN, A. (eds), *Children's Ideas in Science* , Milton Keynes, Open University Press.

DUCKWORTH, E. (1979) 'Either we're too early and they can't learn it or we're too late and they know it already: the dilemma of "applying Piaget"', *Harvard Educational Review*, **49**, pp. 297–312.

ERICKSON, G. and TIBERGHIEN, A. (1985) 'Heat and temperature' in DRIVER, R., GUESNE, E. and TIBERGHIEN, A. (eds), *Children's Ideas in Science*, Milton Keynes, Open University Press.

GINSBURG, H. P., POSNER, J. K. and RUSSEL, R. L. (1981) 'The development of mental addition as a function of schooling and culture', *Journal of Cross-cultural Psychology*, **12**, pp. 163–79.

GIROTTO, V., LIGHT, P. H. and COLBOURN, C. J. (1988) 'Pragmatic schemas and conditional reasoning in children', *Quarterly Journal of Experimental Psychology*, **40**, pp. 469–82.

GROEN, G. J. and RESNICK, L. B. (1977) 'Can pre-school children invent addition algorithms?', *Journal of Educational Psychology*, **69**, pp. 645–52.

GUNSTONE, R. and WATTS, M. (1985) 'Force and motion' in DRIVER, R., GUESNE, E. and TIBERGHIEN, A. (eds), *Children's Ideas in Science,* Milton Keynes, Open University Press.

HATANO, G. (1993) Discussion in the symposium 'Children's concepts of heat and temperature', paper presented at SRCD Biennial meeting, New Orleans.

HATANO, G. (in press) 'Learning arithmetic with an abacus' in NUNES T. and BRYANT P. (eds), *How do Children Learn Mathematics?* , Hove, Erlbaum.

HESSE, J. J. and ANDERSON, C. W. (1992) 'Students' conceptions of chemical change', *Journal of Research in Science Teaching*, **29**, pp. 277–99.

HOWE, C., TOLMIE, A. and ANDERSON, A. (1991) 'Information technology and group work in physics', *Journal of Computer Assisted Learning*, **7**, 133–43.

HOWE, C., TOLMIE, A. and RODGERS, C. (1992) 'The acquisition of conceptual knowledge in science by primary school children: group interaction and the understanding of motion down an incline', *British Journal of Developmental Psychology*, **10**, pp. 113–30.

INHELDER, B. and PIAGET, J. (1958) *The Growth of Logical Thinking from Childhood to Adolescence,* London, Routledge.

JOHNSON-LAIRD, P. N., LEGRENZI, P. and LEGRENZI, M. (1972) 'Reasoning and sense of reality', *British Journal of Psychology*, **63**, pp. 389–400.

LARKIN, J. H., HELLER, J. I. and GREENO, J. G. (1980) 'Instructional implications of research on problem solving', *New Directions for T eaching and Learning*, **2,** pp. 51–65.

LARKIN, J. H., McDERMOTT, J., SIMON, D. P. and SIMON, H. A. (1980) 'Models of competence in solving physics problems', *Cognitive Science,* **4**, pp. 317–45.

LAVE, J. (1988) 'Cognition in practice', *Mind, Mathematics and Culture in Everyday Life*, Cambridge, Cambridge University Press.

LURIA, A. (1979) *Curso de Psicologia Geral*, Rio de Janeiro, Civilizacao Brasileira.

LURIA, A. (1976) *Cognitive Development: its cultural and social foundations*, Cambridge (Mass.), Harvard University Press.

McCLOSKY, M., CARMAZZA, A. and GREEN, B. (1980) 'Curvilinear motion in the absence of external forces: naive beliefs about motion of objects', *Science*, **210**, pp. 1139–41.

NEWMAN, D., GRIFFIN, P. and COLE, M. (1989) *The Construction Zone: working for cognitive change in school*, Cambridge, Cambridge University Press.

NUNES, T. (1993) 'Learning mathematics: perspectives from everyday life' in DAVIS, R. B. and MAHER, C. A. (eds), *Schools, Mathematics, and the World of Reality* , Needham Heights (Mass.), Allyn and Bacon, pp. 61–78.

NUNES, T., SCHLIEMANN, A. D., and CARRAHER, D. W. (1993) *Street Mathematics and School Mathematics*, New York, Cambridge University Press.

NUSSBAUM, J. (1985) 'The earth as a cosmic body' in DRIVER, R., GUESNE, E. and TIBERGHIEN, A. (eds), *Children's Ideas in Science,* Milton Keynes, Open University Press.

NUSSBAUM, J. and NOVAK, J. D. (1976) 'An assessment of children's concepts of the earth utilizing structured interviews', *Science Education*, **60**, pp. 535–50.

PERRET-CLERMONT, A. N. (1980) *Social Interaction and Cognitive Development*, London, Academic Press.

PIAGET, J. (1950) *The Psychology of Intelligence*, London, Routledge and Kegan Paul.

PIAGET, J. and GARCIA, R. (1971) *Les Explications Causales,* Paris, Presses Universitaires de France.

PIAGET, J., GRIZE, J. B., SZEMINSKA, A., and BANG, V. (1968) *Epistemologie et Psychologie de la Fonction,* Paris, Presses Universitaries de France.

PIAGET, J. and INHELDER, B. (1974) *The Child's Construction of Quantities*, London, Routledge and Kegan Paul.

PIAGET, J. and SZEMINSKA, A. (1952) *The Child's Conception of Number*, London, Routledge and Kegan Paul.

PIBURN, M. D. (1990) 'Reasoning about logical propositions and success in science', *Journal of Research in Science Teaching*, **27**, pp. 887–900.

REED, J. J. and LAVE, J. (1981) 'Arithmetic as a tool for investigating relations between culture and cognition' in CASSON, R. W. (ed.), *Language, Culture, and Cognition: anthropological perspectives*, New York, Macmillan.

RILEY, M. S., GREENO, J. G. and HELLER, J. I. (1983) 'Development of children's problem-solving ability in arithmetic' in GINSBURG, H. P. (ed.), *The Development of Mathematical Thinking*, New York, Academic Press.

SAXE, G. B. (1982) 'Developing forms of arithmetical thought among the Oksapmin of Papua New Guinea', *Developmental Psychology*, **18**, pp. 583–94.

SCHWARTZ, J. L. (1988) 'Intensive quantity and referent transforming arithmetic operations' in HIEBERT, J. and BEHR, M. (eds), *Number Concepts and Operations in the Middle Grades*, Hillsdale (N.J.), Lawrence Erlbaum Associates.

SCRIBNER, S. (1975) 'Models of thinking and ways of speaking' in JOHNSON-LAIRD, P. N. and WASON, P. C. (eds), *Thinking*, New York, Cambridge University Press.

SÉRÉ, M. G. (1985) 'The gaseous state' in DRIVER, R., GUESNE, E. and TIBERGHIEN, A. (eds), *Children's Ideas in Science*, Milton Keynes, Open University Press.

SMITH, M. U. and GOOD, R. (1984) 'Problem solving and classical genetics: successful versus unsuccessful performance', *Journal of Research in Science Teaching*, **21**, pp. 895–912.

STAVY, R. (1990) 'Children's conception of changes in the state of matter: from liquid (or solid) to gas', *Journal of Research in Science Teaching*, **27**, pp. 247–66.

THORNDIKE, E. L. (1922) *Psychology of Arithmetic*, New York, Macmillan.

VERGNAUD, G. (1982) 'A classification of cognitive tasks and operations of thought involved in addition and subtraction problems' in CARPENTER, T. P., MOSER, J. M. and TOMBERG, T. A. (eds), *Addition and Subtraction: a cognitive perspective*, Hillsdale (N.J.), Lawrence Erlbaum Associates.

VERGNAUD, G. (1985) 'Concepts et schèmes dans une théorie opératoire de la représentation', *Psychologie Française*, **30**, pp. 245–52.

VYGOTSKY, L. S. (1978) *Mind in Society: the development of higher psychological processes*, New York, Cambridge University Press.

WERTHEIMER, M. (1966) *Productive Thinking*, London, Associated Book Publishers (first edn 1945).

Paul Light and Peter Barnes

CONTENTS

OBJECTIVES

When you have read this chapter, you should be able to:

1 recognize some of the main themes of developmental psychology in the research literature on children's drawings;

2 understand how the common focus of drawings has been used to explore both the cognitive/perceptual and the affective/expressive aspects of development;

3 indentify ways in which cultural variations in drawing styles and conventions inform the debate about the influence of culture on development.

1 INTRODUCTION

Why are children's drawings interesting to the psychologist? It is plain that they are, because children's drawings have been collected and studied, argued over and written about since the very dawn of the discipline, a century ago. The reasons, as we shall see, are various, but central to many of them is the idea that children's drawings offer a 'window on the mind', a window through which the development of perception, thought and emotion can all be observed.

In this chapter we will briefly trace some of the early psychological interest in the development of children's drawings, and then go on to examine its significance within the context of Piagetian theory. Then, we will examine more recent experimental research on how children manage to represent three-dimensional objects and scenes in two-dimensional pictures. After briefly considering the relevance of cross-cultural studies of drawing development, we will shift the focus from the cognitive to the emotional and expressive aspects of drawing. Our aim is not to provide a comprehensive account of children's drawings and their development. Rather, it is to give some insights into developmental psychology by examining some of the ways in which psychologists have studied this feature of children's lives.

ACTIVITY 1

Allow about 10 minutes

WINDOWS ON THE MIND?

If children's drawings are, indeed, 'windows' through which to study development, what might we hope to see through them?

Consider what aspects of drawing development might make it particularly useful as a means of studying child development more generally. Note down the various points that occur to you. Include practical as well as theoretical considerations. Think about any implicit assumptions you might be making in each case.

Comment

Among the practical considerations, you may well have included the relative ease with which drawings can be collected. Especially before sound and video recorders came on the scene, the fact that children's drawings were permanent records on paper made them a particularly attractive form of data. Drawings could be collected from individual children at intervals during their development, or from whole classrooms of children all at the same time, without the psychologist necessarily even being present.

This advantage does, however, embody an assumption that what is psychologically interesting about children's drawing is contained in the *product*, the completed drawing itself. Research on drawing has characteristically focused much more on this product than on the *process* of drawing or the *context* within which the drawing activity was undertaken.

On a more theoretical level, part of the attractiveness of studying drawing is that it is seen as a natural and *spontaneous* form of expression. Whereas reading, writing and arithmetic are so plainly the products of teaching and learning, drawing can be regarded as a direct, untutored expression of the child's own conception of the world. Thus, age-related changes in the way children draw may be seen as indicators of much more general shifts in the way they perceive or understand the world around them.

This view fits well with theories which see development as a regular stage-by-stage progression of the child's capabilities. However, it embodies a number of questionable assumptions. For instance, it assumes that the form children's drawings take offers a direct reflection of their conceptual development rather than being affected by the demands and constraints of the medium (pencil and paper, or whatever). It also assumes that children's drawings are largely individual in origin, being essentially unaffected by teaching, by the reactions of adults, by the drawings of other children, or by exposure to pictorial input from books, posters, television and so on. This is obviously a very large assumption to make, and also a very difficult one to test.

These various considerations and assumptions have played a large part in the shaping of research in this field. Look for them as you work your way through the chapter.

2 DRAWING ON THE PAST

The pioneers of developmental psychology who founded the 'Child Study Movement' at the end of the nineteenth century attempted to keep systematic records of many aspects of children's development. The starting point of a growing interest in drawings, in particular, is often attributed to Corrado Ricci who published an account of the drawings of some Italian children – *The Art of Little Children* – in 1887. It was not until the early twentieth century, however, that full, developmental records of individual children's drawing development were collected and made available. In 1910 Clara and William Stern, in Germany, published an extensive collection of the drawings made by a boy between the ages of 4 and 7 years. And in France, Georges-Henri Luquet (1913) published a catalogue of all the 1500 or so drawings that his daughter made between 3 and 8 years of age.

M H

The Sterns and Luquet adopted a *longitudinal* approach, each collecting drawings from the same child over a period of time. Others chose a *cross-sectional* approach, taking samples of drawings from a number of children at a series of age levels, in many respects an easier and less time-consuming way of gathering data. This was often part of a wider plan to relate drawing to other aspects of development. For example, in the early 1900s Claparède investigated whether there was a relationship between aptitude in drawing and children's general intellectual ability as indicated by their school work. One of his co-workers, Ivanoff, devised a way of scoring the drawings which included such features as a sense of proportion and 'imaginative conception'. There was a positive correlation between these scores and children's measured general ability (see Harris, 1963).

If drawings are to be scored in some way as a means of making comparisons from age to age or looking for relationships with other aspects of development, then there is a need for some common base for what is being scored. If children are free to draw what they like, how can, say, a house, a tree, a person or a dog be treated in an equivalent way? In 1895 Louise Maitland was one of the first to record that, given a choice, children under the age of ten draw the human figure for preference. This finding has been confirmed by many studies since and over a wider age range. It's not surprising, then, that the human figure has played a major part in investigations both of the development of drawing ability itself and also of what representation in drawing might tell us about other facets of psychological development.

In 1901 Schuyten, in Holland, began to develop a way of scoring children's pictures of a man drawn from memory. This involved minute measurements of the separate parts of the body and a comparison of these with classic standards. Although the procedure itself proved to be unproductive, it can be seen as the beginning of attempts to devise an objective measuring scale and to relate it to age standards (Harris, 1963).

Attempts to chart normal development through human figure drawings were complemented by studies with children who were referred to at that time as 'imbeciles', but who are now described as having severe learning disabilities. These children produced markedly less mature figure drawings than other children of the same age. Taken with the evidence of correlations between drawing ability more generally and scholastic abilities, this set the scene for the development of a standardized test of general intelligence based on human figure drawing.

2.1 Drawings as a measure of intelligence

In America in 1926, Florence Goodenough published the first workable test of this kind. She constructed a point-by-point scoring system for drawings of the human figure and provided a set of standardization tables based on large samples of children. From these it was possible to compare the performance of a given child with the average or 'normative' performances of children of different age levels. The individual child could then be assigned a 'mental age', i.e. that age at which children *normally* performed as well as the individual child had done.

The appearance and adoption of Goodenough's Draw-a-Man test fitted into a broader scene, namely the great enthusiasm for mental testing (psychometrics) which gripped the US, Britain and Japan right up to the 1960s (see Chapter 5). The test was relatively quick and easy to administer and became widely used. In the 1960s, it underwent major revision at the hands of Dale Harris, who re-standardized it with more up-to-date and accurate norms (Harris, 1963).

How does the test work? Children are asked to draw three pictures: a man, a woman, and themselves. The instructions include the direction to 'make the very best picture that you can; take your time and work very carefully'. The drawings are then scored in terms of the details they contain and in accordance with a checklist of seventy or so features provided in the test manual; a selection of these is provided in Example 1.

EXAMPLE 1
SCORING ITEMS FROM THE REVISED GOODENOUGH DRAW-A-MAN TEST

Head present

Eyes present

Eye detail: brow or lashes shown

Eye detail: pupil clearly indicated

Eye detail: proportion – horizontal greater than vertical dimension

Eye detail: obvious glancing

Fingers present

Correct number of fingers shown

Detail of fingers correct

Opposition of thumb shown

(from Harris, 1963, pp. 248–53).

Note, in Example 1, that items range from the presence or absence of significant body parts (head, eyes, fingers) to quite precise detail over the depiction of those parts. So, for example, for the detail of the fingers to be counted as correct, 'length of individual fingers must be distinctly greater than width' (Harris, 1963, p. 253). The manual provides examples of what is required in a picture for credit to be given. A child's raw score is the sum of the individual credits awarded for features correctly included and this is then converted into a standard score (which resembles an IQ, having a mean of 100) according to the child's chronological age, using the tables provided. Figure 1 shows two examples of drawings, with the scores they obtained on this test.

FIGURE 1 (a) Drawing of a man by a girl aged 5 years 0 months. This achieves a raw score of 19 and a standard score of 105, i.e. slightly above average for her age. (b) Drawing of a man by a girl aged 9 years 6 months. This achieves a raw score of 34 and a standard score of 104, i.e. slightly above average for her age. (both from Harris, 1963, p. 264)

(a)

(b)

ACTIVITY 2

Allow about 10 minutes

SCORING DRAWINGS

This activity aims to give you further insights into the Draw-a-Man test and the issues that arise from its use.

(a) Look at the detail of the two drawings in Figure 1 and identify which of the features given in Example 1 are present and would add to the score. Make a note of any uncertainties.

(Answers can be found on p. 265).

(b) Now that you have some idea of what is involved in using children's drawings of human figures to derive a measure of intelligence, what questions are prompted by their use and how might these be answered? You may find it helpful to refer back to Chapter 5.

Comment

In your response to the second part of the activity, you might have questioned the assumptions involved in using a figure-drawing task as a test of general mental development. What criteria would such a test have to meet in order to prove itself? How can we evaluate it, to see how well it is doing what it claims? Harris set out his key assumptions as follows:

> The child's drawing of any object will reveal the discriminations he has made about that object ... as a *concept*. In particular, it is hypothesized that his concept of a frequently experienced object, such as a human being, becomes a useful index to the growing complexity of his concepts generally.

(Harris, 1963, p. 7)

This argument has two parts: first, drawings of the human figure provide measures of the development of concepts of the human figure; secondly, concepts of the human figure provide indices of conceptual development more generally. What evidence is there that these assumptions hold true? To start with, is the test *reliable*? *Test-retest reliability* is a matter of whether the same child, given the same test on different occasions, will obtain essentially the same score. *Inter-tester reliability* is a matter of whether two different examiners scoring the same drawing will arrive at the same score. On both counts, the Draw-a-Man procedures come out well (Harris, 1963).

More importantly, though, is the test *valid*? Validity is a matter of whether the test measures what it sets out to measure. Does it really provide a good measure of general mental abilities? One way to approach this is to examine how well the results of the Draw-a-Man test tally with those of much fuller and more comprehensive individual intelligence tests, such as the Stanford-Binet scale or the Wechsler Intelligence Scale for Children (WISC) (see Chapter 5). Here the evidence is much less convincing: correlations are typically positive but quite low, much too low to allow the Draw-a-Man test to be safely used as a 'shorthand' intelligence test. Nor, apparently, does the test tap any discernible subset of intellectual skills. The WISC, for example, gives separate scores for verbal skills and performance skills. It might be expected that the Draw-a-Man test would be highly correlated with the latter rather than the former, but in practice it does not turn out to be highly correlated with either.

Attempting to validate one test of intelligence by comparing it with another has its limitations! But as tests like the WISC, which accesses a range of different abilities, gradually established themselves as 'gold standards' in intelligence testing, the use of the Draw-a-Man test as a measure of intelligence declined. Then, as you saw in Chapter 5, the enterprise of intelligence testing itself came increasingly into question. So this avenue in the study of children's drawings was eventually closed. Others which had been opening up at the same time, in the 1920s, were to prove more fruitful.

2.2 Identifying stages in drawing development

The psychometric tradition of Goodenough and Harris involved the careful counting and measuring of features of drawings which changed regularly with age. However, it did not lend itself well to the characterization of broader qualitative *stages* of development in drawings. This task was initially taken up mainly by researchers interested in educational matters.

Across Europe the pioneers of developmental psychology gathered large numbers of examples of drawings completed by children of different ages. For example, Kerschensteiner (1905; cited in Harris, 1963) collected and studied 100,000 drawings produced by children in southern Germany. And, as we have already noted, Luquet's activities in France were also considerable and destined to be influential.

These early researchers described what they saw as the major stages through which children's drawing developed, and their accounts had a great deal in common. Drawing begins with scribbling, before there is any evidence of an intention to represent an object (see Plates 8 and 9 – note that when you are referred to 'Plates' in this chapter, you should look at the eight pages of full-colour pictures which have been included as near as possible to this text). Luquet regarded the child's activities at this stage as consisting of 'trace-making activities for their own sake' (Luquet, 1927, p. 112). The child may scribble in imitation of adults' or other children's activities with pencils, or may simply be engaging in what Luquet called 'spontaneous perceptuo-motor activity'.

The earliest 'representations' may occur by chance, the children seeing a resemblance between the marks they have made and some object. Luquet called this *fortuitous realism*. It is through such interpretation of accidental forms that children come to understand that their graphic productions can represent real objects (Luquet, 1927). Gradually, they begin to establish what it is they are intending to represent earlier in the drawing process. They may have difficulty in sustaining these intentions, though, and change them several times as a particular drawing progresses. Even when children do manage to establish an 'intention' at the outset and sustain it throughout the course of producing a drawing, they may still fail to achieve something that is recognizable to others as that object. Luquet called this *failed realism*.

Beyond this, the earliest phase of deliberate representation is marked by drawings which are schematic or symbolic – certain elements 'stand for' objects without necessarily looking very much like them. Children at 5 or 6, asked to draw their own house, may use a standard format (Figure 2) even if they live in a bungalow or a block of flats.

FIGURE 2   House drawn by boy aged 5 years 6 months.

This is an example of what Luquet termed *intellectual realism*: children at this stage draw what they know and not what they are able to see from a particular viewpoint. It is as if they need to include what they consider to be characteristic and defining features of the object to be drawn.

This particular feature of children's drawings was well documented, even in the nineteenth century. Sully (1896), for example, wrote about the way in which intelligence 'corrupted' children's perceptions. The implication is that children's drawings are a kind of 'print out' of their internal mental model of the object concerned.

Visual realism – another of Luquet's terms – arises later, round about the ages of 8 or 9. It is marked by a shift towards drawings which represent objects or scenes viewed from particular station points. In seeking to achieve visual realism, the child artist has to grapple with many problems associated with how best to represent a three-dimensional world on a two-dimensional surface – a sheet of paper. How to show that some objects are further away than others? How to represent the fact that a nearer object is obscuring part of the object behind it? Kerschensteiner (1905; cited in Harris, 1963), in his analysis of his own vast collection of drawings, saw the successful representation of three-dimensional space as the highest level of achievement. The attainment of full visual realism is marked by:

- showing an object in the foreground partially masking one behind (partial occlusion);
- making more distant objects smaller (size–distance scaling);
- some form of linear perspective.

Though distant in time, these early accounts of children's drawings provide a valuable starting point for issues that concern current students. The age-and-stage accounts of drawing development came to play quite an important role in the history of developmental psychology. Luquet's work, in particular, informed Piaget's thinking, and, as we shall see in the next section, became integrated into Piaget's more general account of the course of children's mental development.

SUMMARY OF SECTION 2

- Large scale *longitudinal* and *cross-sectional* studies of children's drawing development were undertaken in the early years of the twentieth century.
- These provided the foundations for *psychometric tests*, in which individual children's drawing development was assessed against norms derived from large groups of children at various age levels.
- The Draw-a-Man test is the best known of these tests. It is easy to use and *reliable*. However, attempts to assess the *validity* of drawing tests as measures of intelligence have given disappointing results, and the use of such tests has declined.
- Attention gradually shifted from using drawings in order to compare the relative performance of children to using drawing development as a way of studying development more generally.

3 PIAGET'S ACCOUNT

In his theory, Piaget sought to tie all aspects of the child's development into a single coherent sequence. One of the key concepts which he used to achieve this was childhood *egocentrism* – a state in which children lack the flexibility and relativity of thinking to recognize and accommodate a variety of possible points of view. Piaget was interested in children's drawings as their attempts to represent the world as they saw it; their drawings, therefore, provided access to changing developments in mental representation.

For Piaget, infants at birth don't recognize the existence of anything except their immediate perceptual experience. With the achievement of object permanence, the continuity of existence of objects in the external world comes to be recognized. The transition from the sensorimotor to the preoperational period of development at about 2 years of age is marked by the appearance of symbolic thought – the child can begin to understand and use symbolic representations such as those involved in language, imaginary play or drawing. But throughout the pre-operational period the child remains highly egocentric; indeed, overcoming this egocentrism constitutes the major hurdle in the way of achieving concrete operational thinking in the early school years.

Whether Piaget was justified in his claims about egocentrism is questionable (see, for example, Cox, 1980; 1991). However, his account fitted in rather well with Luquet's stages of drawing development. The shift which Luquet had described from an early intellectual realism to a later visual realism can be interpreted in terms of a transition from egocentric to non-egocentric ways of thinking. Young children who draw houses like that in Figure 2 regardless of the house they are asked to draw, are in effect saying, 'A house is a house – and this is how I draw houses'.

Luquet's stages of drawing development can also be mapped on to the stages of spatial development which Piaget and Inhelder described in their classic book *The Child's Conception of Space* (1956). They asked children to draw a number of simple objects in differing orientations. For example, a thin metal disc was presented tipped back away from the child so that, from the child's point of view, its visual appearance ranged from a full circle (Figure 3, A) to a straight line (Figure 3, E). At 4 and 5 years old, however, children always drew it as a full circle: 'The object is in fact imagined and shown by and for itself, independent of the angle at which the observer actually views it' (Piaget and Inhelder, 1956, p. 173).

FIGURE 3 Successive presentations of a disc, seen in perspective (Piaget and Inhelder, 1956, p. 173).

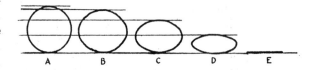

Invariably, 5 and 6 year olds choose a viewpoint which shows the essential features of the object in a recognizable fashion. So, a road may be drawn as in Figure 4, and a tree as in Figure 5. What, then, does the child do when asked to draw a row of trees each side of the road? At this age, the likely response is as shown in Figure 6: an 'impossible' view, but one which combines conveying *what* the objects are and *where* they are in relation to one another.

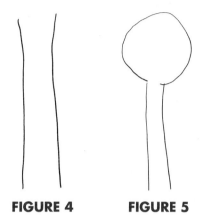

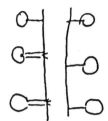

FIGURE 6   Children draw the trees perpendicular to the edges of the road if the edges of the road itself do not appear to converge (Piaget and Inhelder,1956, p. 174).

FIGURE 4   **FIGURE 5**

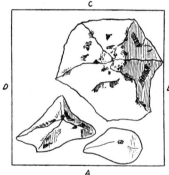

FIGURE 7   The three mountains. Each of the three model mountains has a distinctive feature at the summit – snow, a house or a cross. The child sits in one position (B) and a doll is placed at another (C). The child is asked to identify what the doll can see from its position. Under certain conditions, children below the age of about 7 years are most likely to select the picture which represents the view from their *own* positon (Piaget and Inhelder, 1956, p. 211).

Piaget saw children of 7 or 8 years (entering the period of *concrete operational thinking*) as starting to distinguish between viewpoints in their drawings, and consequently moving away from 'ready made' symbolic forms. The actual appearance of objects in a picture, and their relationship to one another, is determined by the position of the viewer. Thus, visual appearance is relative, not absolute. This flexibility, and their recognition of the relativity of points of view is, for Piaget, one of the clearest indications of the overcoming of childish egocentrism and the achievement of operational thought.

There are a number of problems and ambiguities in Piaget's account of drawing and its development. For example, it seems that the pre-operational child doesn't take any account of the particular viewpoint from which something is seen – they 'draw what they know', so that a disc is drawn as a circle regardless of its orientation. But, in Piaget and Inhelder's classic 'three mountains' task, children at the same sort of age apparently showed a marked tendency to draw the scene (or select a particular picture of it) showing how they see it from where they are sitting. Piaget and Inhelder say the child at this age 'seems to regard his own point of view as the only one possible' (Piaget and Inhelder, 1956, p. 213).

However, they are not suggesting that the choice of 'own view' is a conscious one. Rather, any view that shows all three of the mountains clearly will suffice. Actually the choice of 'own' view in the three mountains task may arise as an artefact. It was shown only with some methods of response – e.g. using cardboard cutouts to show the view. Also, the youngest children always started at position A (Figure 7) from which they had the 'best' view, with the biggest mountain in the background. A study by Paul Light and Carolyn Nix (see Research Summary 1) highlights the significance of this point.

RESEARCH SUMMARY 1
IT DEPENDS ON YOUR POINT OF VIEW

A large jar of coffee and a bottle of orange squash were placed side by side on a table. One at a time, 40 five year olds were asked to sit at the position shown as N (north) in Figure 8. A small doll was placed at E and each child was asked to select one photograph from four, (showing the view from each of the four compass point positions) to indicate what the doll could see. This was presented as a game.

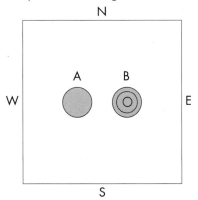

FIGURE 8   Positioning of the coffee jar and squash bottle relative to children's/doll's points of view.

In Figure 8, A is the coffee jar, B the squash bottle; the distance between them is 10 cms. Children sitting at N see both objects, side by side. The view from E shows the one partially occluding the another.

Later, the same children repeated the procedure, except that they sat at E and the doll was placed at N.

Table 1 shows the numbers of each photograph selected under the two conditions.

TABLE 1   Photograph selections depending on child's point of view.

	North photo	East photo	South photo	West photo
Child sitting at N (good view)	20	10	6	4
Child sitting at E (poor view)	15	5	15	5

Source: Light and Nix, 1983, p. 482.

ACTIVITY 3

Allow about 10 minutes

INTERPRETING THE DATA

Study the data in Table 1. What do they suggest about the way these children chose photographs to represent what the doll could see in relation to what they could see themselves?

Comment

When children are sitting at E, they have a 'poor view' because the objects are behind one another. There is no real evidence that they choose a picture which resembles their own point of view; only 5 out of 40 do so. On the contrary, they typically choose a picture which shows the two objects well (either the N or S photos). There is some evidence, though, that when the child has a good view (i.e. from N), they do select that view (20 out of 40) rather than the other equally 'good' one (i.e. from S: 6 out of 40).

So it seems that two selection principles are operating:

- 'Choose a picture that shows the array of objects well.'
- 'If there are several that show the array equally well and your own view is among them, choose that.'

Nawratil and Cox (Cox, 1991) replicated this study, and obtained similar results. However, when the jar and the bottle were far enough apart so that there was no occlusion of the further object by the nearer one, the tendency to substitute a side-by-side picture disappeared. So it seems to be a distaste for occlusion rather than a preference for side-by-side representations that influences their picture selections.

Studies like this which have pursued some of Piaget's leads have revealed that there are plenty of loose ends in his account, and he never developed his work on drawings to anything like the degree to which he pursued research on mathematical and scientific thinking. But Piaget's work has served two important purposes:

(a) To integrate the study of drawings into a broad theory of development: his claim is that drawing development goes through stage changes that reflect the major stages in the development of thinking generally. Thus 'intellectual realism' is part and parcel of pre-operational egocentrism.

(b) To help to establish an *experimental* approach to drawing development, in that he asked children of different ages to draw the same thing under controlled conditions to try to pinpoint the nature of the changes which occur. As we have seen, Piaget was not the first to adopt this approach, but the widespread influence of his work, especially in British psychology from the early 1970s, greatly stimulated the experimental work on spatial organization in drawings, which we will turn to in the next section.

SUMMARY OF SECTION 3

- Piaget and Inhelder (1956) provided an account of children's drawing development which attempted to show that the stages through which it passed reflected the general progression of their cognitive development.

- A shift from *intellectual realism* to *visual realism* in children's drawing was seen to correspond to a shift from the egocentric thinking of the child in the pre-operational period towards the decentred thinking of the child in the concrete operational period.

- Piaget and Inhelder's work helped to establish a tradition of experimental research on the spatial organization of children's drawing which has continued to the present day.

4 SPATIAL ORGANIZATION

We saw in Section 1 that much of the early work on children's drawing looked at it in relation to cognition. Similarly, Piaget described how the characteristics of children's drawings accorded with their general cognitive development. Since the early eighties, British developmental psychologists have extended this by conducting a wide range of studies of how young children's drawings are organized, and why they look like they do. In this section we will consider some examples of this work. To begin with, we will return to children's early drawings of the human figure, and especially to that endearing form of representation which students of drawing refer to as the 'tadpole'.

4.1 Tadpoles

'Tadpole' drawings of the human figure have no differentiated head and body. They often consist only of a circle (with facial features) and some legs. Arms, if present, may be attached to the circle (head?) or to the 'legs'. This type of drawing of the human figure may not be universal but is very common. Cox and Parkin (1986) conclude from an examination of cross-sectional and longitudinal data that most children go through a tadpole stage, but that for some it lasts as little as a few days, while for others it may last many months. These figures appear between the ages of 3 and 6 and are commonest at about 4 years (Cox, 1992). The tadpole in Plate 10 was drawn by a girl aged 3 years 9 months.

Does the circular part of the tadpole figure represent just the head, or the head and body combined? Maureen Cox (1992) reports a series of studies in which she asked children (aged between 3 and 4 years) who had drawn tadpole figures to add a tummy button to their drawing. Nearly all did so, but half put it in the 'head' (Figure 9a) and half put it between the 'legs' (Figure 9b).

FIGURE 9 Two types of response to a request to add a tummy button to a 'tadpole' figure. (a) indicates that the 'head' may also stand for the body; (b) is a 'transitional' form (Cox, 1992, p. 34).

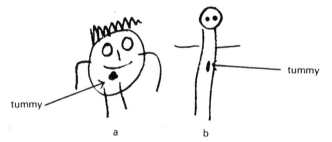

Most of the cases where the tummy button was in the 'head' had a large 'head' relative to the 'legs' (as in Figure 9a), so it seems probable that the circle in these cases represents both head and trunk. Where the tummy button was between the legs, these were typically longer, making it likely that the 'legs' represent both legs and trunk. Cox and Parkin suggest that this second type of tadpole (in which the 'arms' are also typically attached to the 'legs') comes later, and is transitional between the tadpole form and the conventional form of the human figure. However, here again it is far from clear that *all* children follow this or any other fixed developmental sequence of figure drawings. Different representational forms (e.g. tadpoles and 'conventional' figures) may co-exist in the child's repertoire for considerable periods of time.

ACTIVITY 4

Allow about 1 hour

CATCHING TADPOLES

If you have the opportunity to do so, ask some children between the ages of about 3 and 5 years to draw a person. See if you get any tadpole figures. If you do, ask them to add features they may have missed out (arms, tummy button, hair, etc.) and see how they do so. Ask the tadpole drawers to produce drawings of different people (mummy, friend, baby, etc.) and see how consistent they are in what they produce.

Why do children so regularly produce these tadpole drawings? A variety of explanations has been suggested. For example, is it dependent on what body parts they can name, or that they consider important? Probably not, because they can often name the tummy and other parts that they miss out. Indeed, given a set of cut-out felt or cardboard body parts to assemble, many tadpole drawers produce a 'conventional' figure. And, if features are added to the cut-out pieces, all tadpole drawers can assemble them in the appropriate way (Cox, 1992).

It has been suggested by Rhoda Kellogg (1970) that the tadpole form emerges as a natural development of earlier scribble forms. From a large collection of children's very early drawings she identified some frequent patterns involving circular scribbles with radiating lines, and suggested that these go on to form the basis of tadpoles, and also of the radiating 'suns' which frequently adorn children's pictures. However, Claire Golomb (1981) failed to find much evidence to support this view; on her evidence it seemed that many children don't pass through the sequence Kellogg predicted.

Another interpretation of tadpoles is in terms of problems that children encounter when *planning* their drawings. Norman Freeman (1980) has pointed to some of the demands that confront the young child when drawing a person. Among these are the need to know which parts of the body are conventionally included in drawings, to be able to recall all of these parts while drawing, and to fit all of them on the page. Freeman suggests that the cognitive overload this creates encourages the tadpole form; the 'end' elements – the head and the legs – are better produced than the middle elements because of what are known as 'linear order effects'. Just as when people are asked to remember lists of objects or names they tend to remember the first and the last items best and to forget those in the middle, so the child may begin by putting down on paper the first and last items on the body checklist (head and legs), and then have nowhere to put the body, even if it is remembered subsequently.

If this is the correct explanation, then we might expect to find that children who produce tadpoles 'by mistake' in this way *prefer* to produce conventional figures. Do they see conventional figures as 'better'? Maureen Cox (1992) showed the three pictures in Figure 10 to 25 children whose own drawings most resembled (a) and asked them which they thought was the best. Twenty-one chose the tadpole form (a). When asked which was the 'silliest', 15 chose (c) and the other 10 chose (b). Thus, tadpole drawers tend to select the tadpole form as best.

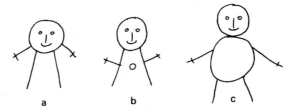

a   b   c

FIGURE 10   When asked to select from (a) a tadpole (b) a transitional and (c) a conventional figure which is the best drawing of a person, tadpole drawers choose their own style (Cox, 1992, p. 43).

So, even if the tadpole figure does arise as a kind of planning short-circuit, the result is clearly judged quite satisfactory by most of the children concerned. It may not look much like a person, but it works; it conveys the essence of 'personhood' rather well. In truth, the 'conventional' version in Figure 10 – (c) – doesn't look much like a person either, though we, as adults, tend to see it as a step on the way towards more realistic drawing. But if the job is to project a neat and economical representation that clearly 'stands for' a person, the tadpole drawing does the trick.

In rather the same way, the 'birds' in the top righthand corner of Plate 5 do not look very much like birds, but they do the job of signifying 'birds' quite economically and effectively. Children, clearly, pick up devices like this from one another. Many an exasperated teacher has had to abandon attempts to get children to draw birds realistically in the face of an invasion of these 'seagulls'. Young children's enthusiasm for such highly reduced and schematic forms in their drawing seems to owe at least as much to what they are *using drawing for* as it does to any technical or cognitive deficiencies. Their drawing of a man or a bird is a *symbol* more than a *representation*. It conveys man or bird in almost the same way that, a little later on, the written words 'man' or 'bird' will do. The development of drawing beyond this stage, then, may reflect not just improvements in what children are capable of, but changes in their understanding of the function of drawing, as they move towards visual realism.

4.2 Canonical representation

Young children's drawings of the human figure, whether tadpole or conventional, are nearly always 'full face' rather than in profile.

Similarly, houses are typically drawn as seen from the front (Figure 2), while cars, horses or fishes are shown in side view. Even when objects to be drawn are placed before them in differing orientations, children persist in representing them in what is known as their *canonical* orientation, as if to make them more easily recognizable for what they are.

A number of experimental investigations of canonical representation have centred on the familiar tea cup. When children up to the age of about 7 years are asked to draw a cup that has been put in front of them with the handle facing away so that it is concealed, most include the handle in their drawing, nevertheless.

Freeman and Janikoun (1972) explored this phenomenon further. A cup was placed with the handle turned away from the child, and so out of sight. On the side of the cup facing the child was a flower decoration. They were asked to draw what they could see. The 8 to 9 year olds included the flower and omitted the handle (i.e. they represented what they could see), but 5 to 7 year olds typically did the reverse, omitting the flower (a non-defining feature of a cup) and including the handle (a defining feature).

The tendency to produce such canonical representations is not absolute, however. Alyson Davis (1983), for example, showed that when *two* cups are placed in front of children, one with the handle visible and the other not, and the children are asked to draw the latter, 5 and 6 year olds will leave out the handle. It seems that the motivation to *differentiate* the two cups one from another is enough to overcome the tendency to include the handle as a defining feature. By contrast, getting the children to *name* a cup as a cup before drawing it, actually increases the tendency to include a non-visible handle (Bremner and Moore, 1984). It is as if, having identified the object verbally, the children feel a need to include its defining features in their drawing to make it identifiable.

Children up to the early school years, then, give priority in a number of ways to showing what objects are and how they are related to one another. They apparently have a lot less interest in showing how things look from their particular viewing position, even if specifically asked to draw what they see from where they are sitting. At the same time, the way in which the task is presented can have a critical effect and this makes any simple account of drawing in terms of 'stages of development' very difficult to sustain.

4.3 Occlusion

We have already noted that one of the major problems generated by the act of drawing is how to represent a three-dimensional world in two dimensions on paper. If you look around you now, you are aware that the room you are in contains a number of objects. If you try to draw accurately what you can see, you will need to find a way of showing that, say, only the top of the chair is visible from behind the table or

FIGURE 11 The rider's farther leg can be seen through the body of the horse (Cox, 1992, p. 109).

that the vase on the sideboard obscures part of the picture that it is standing in front of. Typically, as adults, we deal with this by drawing those parts of the further object which are visible, with their contours emerging from behind those of the nearer object – what is known as *partial occlusion*. Children very rarely use this device in their drawings.

Sometimes they produce 'transparencies', in which the complete outline of the further object can be seen 'through' the nearer object. In Figure 11, the horse and its rider are in contact in such a way that part of the rider is obscured by the horse. In simpler situations where one object is merely *behind* another, young children will typically contrive their drawings so as to separate the various elements from one another.

ACTIVITY 5

Allow no more than
30 minutes

DRAWING ONE OBJECT BEHIND ANOTHER

If you have access to children aged from 4 to 9, try this simple task when you have an opportunity. If not, think about ways in which children in this age range might respond.

You need two spheres of the same size and contrasting colours (e.g. apples or snooker balls), some paper and two pens or crayons of the same colours as the objects. Sit the child down at a table and place the spheres on it, one after the other, so that they are touching and with one behind and slightly to one side of the other, as seen by the child. So, what the child can actually see is, say, a red ball with part of a green ball visible behind it (see Plate 1). Then ask her to draw what she can see.

Children up to the age of about 5 typically draw the two objects separately side-by-side (Figure 12a). Slightly older children (up to about 7) tend to draw them one above the other, usually with the more distant object towards the top of the sheet (Figure 12b). From about 8 years they begin to use partial occlusion (Figure 12c) (see Cox, 1981).

FIGURE 12 One object behind the other. (a) 5 year old's drawing: the balls are side-by-side. (b) 7 year old's drawing: the farther ball is drawn vertically above the nearer one. (c) 8 year old represents occlusion by showing only part of the farther ball.

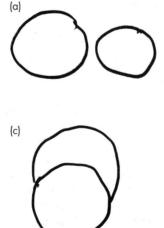

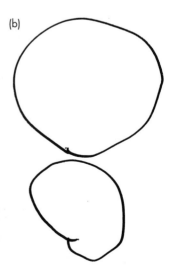

It isn't that the younger children don't understand partial occlusion in drawings. They are well able to interpret pictures correctly which use this device to signify one object behind another. It has been suggested (e.g. Freeman, 1980) that their reluctance to use partial occlusion stems from the difficulty they have with 'hidden line elimination' (i.e. leaving out the hidden bits of the further object) or with managing the 'join' between the drawings of the further and the nearer object.

This is probably only part of the story. In a study by Light and MacIntosh (1980) a small toy house was placed either *inside* or *behind* a transparent beaker (see Plate 2) and 6- and 7-year-old children were asked to draw what they could see. In practice what they could see was virtually the same in both cases, and is drawn pretty faithfully in Figure 13(a). This was a drawing made when the house was actually inside the beaker – and in fact *all* of the children drew it this way, with the house contained within the outline of the beaker. Figure 13(b) shows what the same child drew when presented with the house *behind* the beaker. About half of the children separated the images of the beaker and the house when drawing the house behind the beaker, despite the fact that they clearly *could* draw it 'as they saw it'.

FIGURE 13 Typical drawings of (a) a toy house placed inside a glass beaker and (b) behind a glass beaker (Light and MacIntosh, 1980, p. 83).

(a)

(b)

In this case, it seems that the children were deliberately avoiding drawing what they actually saw because if they drew the house 'inside' the outline of the beaker it would look like a picture of a house *in* a beaker. Avoiding ambiguity may be an important consideration for young children in their choice of how to organize a drawing.

However, sometimes showing that something *can't* be seen is critically important, and even quite young children can apparently use some form of occlusion successfully to achieve this. Cox (1981) told children aged 4 to 10 years a story in which a robber, being chased by a policeman, ran to hide behind a wall. The policeman knew where the robber was because he could see the top of his head poking out above the top of the wall. The story was acted out with model characters; the model policeman was placed on the table near to the child's own position, and the robber's head protruded above the wall (Plate 3). The children were asked to draw what they, and the policeman, could see. Most of the children from 6 upwards, and even about half of the 4 and 5 year olds, drew only part of the robber showing above the wall.

Figure 14 shows some of the ways they did it. The junctions between the outlines of the nearer and further objects are not usually fully mastered until about 8, but the younger children nonetheless succeed rather well in encoding the spatial relation of 'behindness'.

(a)   (b)   (c)   (d)

FIGURE 14   Children's drawings of a robber partially hidden behind a wall. Half of the 4 year olds (a) drew only that part of that they could see; some younger children drew the whole robber above the wall (b). (c) is another representation, with a semicircle for the head floating above the wall. It isn't until about 8 years that children attached the semi-circle to the contour of the wall (d) (Cox, 1992, pp. 118–9).

How is the task of drawing a robber behind a wall different from drawing a green ball behind a red one? Most obviously, perhaps, because the robber behind the wall is part of a story that the children understand, and that makes it important that all but the top of his head is hidden. The situation makes *human sense*, in Margaret Donaldson's memorable phrase (1978).

However, there may be other factors involved. For example, children are more likely to use partial occlusion in their drawings when the objects concerned differ in shape, perhaps because the differences between the nearer and the further object force the child to look back at the objects themselves while drawing. Where the objects are the same – as with the two balls – the child may simply take them in at a glance as 'two balls', and run off a drawing showing the two separately. We can say that how children organize their drawings reflects the relationships that they take to be *important*. If it is important to show that the house is *not* in the beaker, or that the man is *not* completely hidden behind the wall, children can generally find a way of showing that. But when something is just behind something else by what seems to be chance (to the child), children up to about 8 years of age are likely to simply sidestep the problem by disregarding their own point of view and rearranging the scene so as to show the objects fully.

4.4 Drawing in perspective

Solving the problem of how to represent one object behind another is only one part of the challenge of representing three dimensions in two.

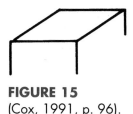

FIGURE 15
(Cox, 1991, p. 96).

The individual objects are also typically three-dimensional. Young children's drawings, as we can see from the examples so far, tend to show just one plane or face of an object. But around 7 or 8 years, drawings begin to appear, such as those in Figure 15, which show *more than one face* of an object, and which use oblique lines to show how the faces are related to one another. This use of parallel oblique lines is an effective way of getting a 3D effect for objects with rectangular surfaces, and examples can be found quite widely in the adult world.

ACTIVITY 6

Allow about 15 minutes

ADDING A NEW DIMENSION

Look for examples of parallel oblique perspective, for example in books or magazines with technical illustrations or diagrams. If possible, look in books available for children to see how the 3D representation of rectangular objects is handled.

FIGURE 16
(Cox, 1991, p. 93).

In practice, what we think of as true perspective involves not *parallel* oblique lines but *converging* oblique lines. Figure 16 shows a table as viewed from directly in front. The top is foreshortened (i.e. the front and back edges appear much closer than they are), and the receding edges *converge* strongly.

Perhaps the most striking example of perspective convergence is where parallel lines recede toward the horizon, as with railway tracks or a road going off into the distance. Karen Littleton (1991) asked 6 and 7 year olds, adolescents and adults to draw a road 'going into the distance' while they were standing on a bridge viewing the road beneath and in front of them. The adolescents and the adults drew converging lines, but all of the children represented the road by parallel lines (Figure 17).

FIGURE 17 Roads, as drawn by 6 and 7 year olds; note that the sides of the road are drawn in parallel (Littleton, 1991, p. 156).

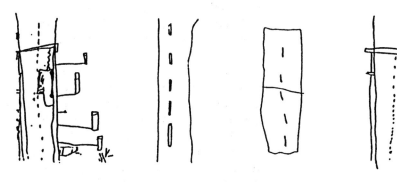

John Willats (1977) tried to establish stages in the development of what he called 'projection systems'. He presented children aged from 4 to 16 with a table on which were some familiar objects, and asked them to draw what they saw. Figure 18 (overleaf) shows examples which reflect the six main stages he identified in the child's progress towards 'perspective projection'. The last two stages involve convergence of receding lines, which began to make its appearance only at about the age of 14.

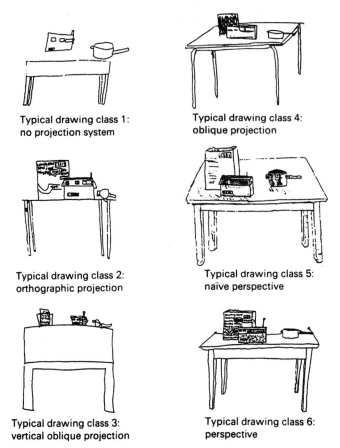

Typical drawing class 1:
no projection system

Typical drawing class 4:
oblique projection

Typical drawing class 2:
orthographic projection

Typical drawing class 5:
naïve perspective

Typical drawing class 3:
vertical oblique projection

Typical drawing class 6:
perspective

FIGURE 18   Willats's six-fold classification of drawings of
objects on a table completed by children aged 5–16 years
(Cox, 1992, p. 150).

Willats argued that these 'drawing systems' developed largely
independently of formal schooling, but this is difficult to establish in a
society where all children go to school. Gustav Jahoda (1981) tried to
put this proposition to the test by using the same task with schooled and
unschooled adults in Ghana. Almost all the drawings he obtained could
be assigned to one or other of Willats's six classes of projection system.
More interestingly, there was no significant difference between the
projection systems used by unschooled and schooled subjects.

This result may tell us more about the neglect of drawing in Ghanaian
schools than anything else. The large majority of the drawings fell into
the first three of the classes illustrated in Figure 18, and only one
(schooled) subject showed any perspective convergence. He was a
mechanic who had seemingly received some technical instruction. So,
Jahoda's study testifies to the robustness of Willats's classification
system, but doesn't do much to clarify the extent to which the
development of children's drawings beyond the early stages depends
upon teaching.

All these various approaches to indexing the forms of representations in and spatial organization of children's drawings (canonicality, occlusion, perspective projection etc.) have tended to assume some kind of stage-by-stage development of children's competencies, much in the style of Piaget. But the research reported here has tended to point in a different direction, emphasizing that children at any given age may do quite different things in different circumstances, and that it is what they are using drawings *for* that appears to change with age. In the early stages, drawing seems to take the form of a 'graphic vocabulary' rather than a set of skills for precisely replicating an object or a scene. Development from this point – and, indeed, the graphic vocabulary itself – may be highly dependent on the culture the child is growing up in and what uses of drawing are valued within that particular setting. In the next section we will take a broader look at cross-cultural studies, and what they can tell us about the development of drawing.

SUMMARY OF SECTION 4

- Children's human figure drawings frequently go through a 'tadpole' phase. Attempts to explain this have suggested that the tadpole (i) is an adaptation of children's earlier scribbles, (ii) may arise as the result of planning errors on the part of the children, (iii) is actually a highly economical and effective means of communicating the idea of a person, and (iv) is a 'conventional' way of drawing among children of a certain age that they learned from each other. These explanations may all be partly true and none of them seems entirely satisfactory on its own.

- Young children's drawings tend to represent objects in particular *canonical* orientations which show them to best advantage. However, this tendency can be influenced by the way the particular task is presented, and even 5 and 6 year olds can be induced to represent things in non-canonical ways.

- Young children's drawings are marked by an absence of *occlusion*. Objects are sometimes treated as if transparent or are separated so that each 'has its own space' in the picture. This shows an apparent disregard for the actual appearance of the scene from the viewer's standpoint. However, there are circumstances in which children as young as 4 *will* represent occlusion in their drawings.

- Young children typically depict only one plane or face of an object. By around 7 or 8 years, they begin to use oblique lines to show how the various faces of an object are related to each other. Convergence of receding oblique lines makes its appearance at about 14.

5 CROSS-CULTURAL COMPARISONS

So far in this chapter we have referred to examples of drawing development which mainly come from Western European sources. Is this development the same the world over, or are there differences from one culture to another? If so, do these differences relate to such things as children's access to and experience of drawing materials or to the artistic conventions of the society as a whole? One reason for taking an interest in these matters is that they might offer a way of deciding between those theories which see drawing developing according to an invariant succession of stages (depending on general cognitive development) and those theories which see it in terms of learned skills or acquired cultural conventions. If drawings offer a direct reflection of general cognitive development, then the essential pattern of drawing development should be universal, and adults who have no drawing experience should still draw like adults who do. If more specific *graphic skills* play an important role, then inexperienced adults might be expected to go through some of the same stages as children do. If, on the other hand, there is a great deal of *variation* in how children's drawings develop from place to place and from time to time, then it is very likely that drawing development depends heavily upon cultural conventions.

In the culture in which we are writing, the large majority of children are surrounded by pictorial material from an early age: in books, papers, and comics; in advertising; and on television. Paper, pencils and other drawing materials are very much a part of most children's lives at home, at play group and at school. Although this culture is rapidly pervading all corners of the globe, there are still places where children grow up with little or no access to drawing materials, and where pictorial images are largely absent from daily life. There are also parts of the world where children grow up surrounded by quite *different* sorts of pictorial images from those which are familiar to the Western child. How are these variations in experience reflected in the ways children draw?

The Draw-a-Man test (Section 2) was seen as an attractive way to measure children's cognitive level partly because it was quick and easy to administer, but also because it was said to be 'culture-free'. It was argued that, regardless of ethnic group or cultural background, children would be on even terms because the test did not rely on language or on knowledge acquired in school. However, this claim ran into problems from an early stage. For example, Havinghurst *et al.* (1946) reported that American Indian children scored significantly higher than their white counterparts on the test, and Dennis (1957) found that Egyptian and Lebanese children's IQ scores from the test showed an apparent consistent *decline* with increasing age, except for those in Western-oriented schools. Dennis (1960), in a later study, found that unschooled Bedouin children scored as severely intellectually retarded. On this evidence it would appear that the development of human figure drawings is affected by cultural context.

PLATE 1 How do children draw two objects when one is partly hidden by the other?

PLATE 2 How to distinguish in a drawing between a model house inside a clear beaker and another behind one?

PLATE 3 How is partial occlusion handled when the object is a robber hiding from a policeman behind a wall?

PLATE 4 Drawing of a family group by a young Warlpiri girl from Yuendumu, Northern Territory, Australia.

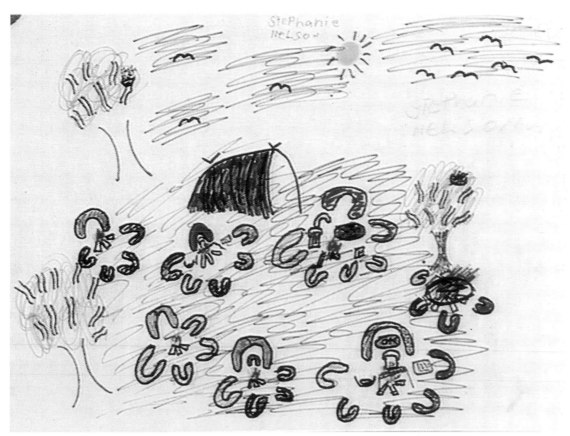

PLATE 5 Family groups round camp fires, by a young Warlpiri girl from Yuendumu.

PLATE 6 Detail from Plate 5. Note the combination of the traditional semicircular representation of the mother and the stick figure of the child.

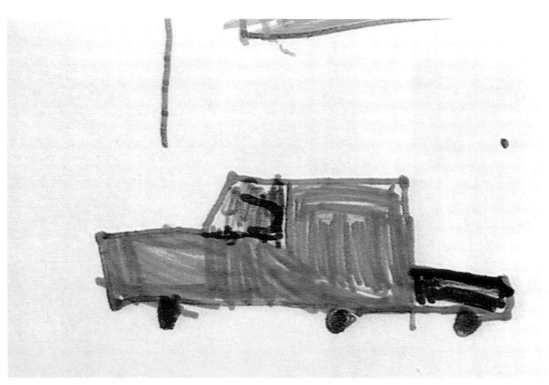

PLATE 7 A 6-year-old Warlpiri girl's picture of a van, with the driver shown as a semicircle.

PLATE 8 The first stage in graphic production: little control of stroke direction, strokes derive mainly from lower arm movement. Jenny, aged 16 months.

PLATE 9 The beginnings of control of strokes: arcs and loops, plus 'dotting'. Jenny, aged 2 years.

PLATE 10 The classic 'tadpole' person; this drawing is of a person on a bike. Jenny, aged 3 and three quarters.

PLATE 11 Development of the 'tadpole' to include some rudimentary indications of a body; the small figure represents a baby. Lucy, aged 4 years.

PLATE 12 The next stage after 'tadpoles': firm indication of body and appropriately attached limbs. Jenny, aged 5 and a half years.

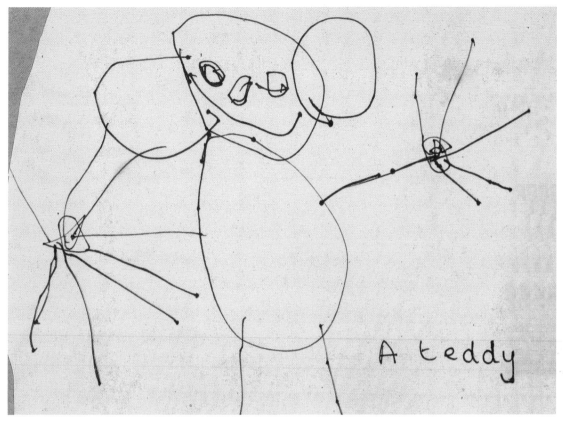

A teddy

PLATE 13 Details such as fingers begin to appear. Anna, aged 3 years.

PLATE 14 The limbs acquire solidity and fingers, toes and clothes appear. Charlotte, aged 3 and a half years.

PLATE 15 Further development of figure drawing; arm and leg attachment more advanced. Joe, aged 6 and a half years.

(a)   (b)

PLATE 16 More mature drawings: details of clothing, facial features and so on approximate more closely to Western artistic conventions.
(a) Victoria, aged 8 years.   (b) Luke, aged 10 years.

On the other hand, drawings of the human figure collected from children from different cultures do show signs of considerable consistency. For example, Paget (1932) noted that the human figure drawings of 4 and 5 year olds fall into two broad groups. If they use 'outlines' to the figure, they characteristically produce tadpoles. Otherwise, they typically produce stick figures. Both of these forms were found to be very widespread in the non-western world, but with local variations. Thus 'pin-headed' stick figures with very long bodies were exclusive to Africa. Another 'local convention' Paget found was the use of a single continuous line resembling the letter 'W' to depict a nose and eyebrows. This was exclusive to black children, but occurred from West Africa through the Caribbean to British Guyana. It seems plausible that this is a convention, quite possibly passed from child to child and maintained in the culture from generation to generation, much in the same way as a skipping chant or a childhood game are handed on.

Claire Golomb, whose review of cross-cultural work informs much of this section (Golomb, 1992), points out another example of the way cultural context and everyday experience are reflected in early figure drawing. African children's drawings, at least in early surveys like Paget's, almost always include genitals, both male and female, while Western children's drawings almost never do. Whether this is a function of greater exposure, or of lesser inhibition, or even of the greater significance of male–female differentiation, is hard to know. Nevertheless, Golomb concludes that while such cultural conventions and specific experiences have a role to play, the basic organization of the figure has more consistency than can be accounted for by the idea of local conventions. Stick figures, for example, occur in ancient rock carvings, and anthropologists have described how such drawings are produced by both children and adults in the course of their very first exposure to drawing materials.

Moreover, even where children use radically different ways to represent the human figure, there is evidence that they also have access to these more universal forms. For example, when a group of 5 and 6-year-old Bedouin children were introduced to drawing materials for the first time in their lives, they quickly produced the same kind of outline figure with an oval trunk that would be familiar with children of the same age in the UK (Haas, 1978, cited in Golomb, 1992). But these children then went on to represent female figures quite differently, using an overall triangular shape, filled in except for a slit in the top part for the eyes. This representation seems to depict the traditional dress of Moslem women. It appears that a specific cultural consideration is 'overlayed' upon a more general representational form. As Kellogg and O'Dell neatly put it, 'the art of young children everywhere is identical. Not until the weight of culture lays a burden upon the child can the art of one country be told from that of another' (Kellogg and O'Dell, 1967, p. 105).

In other words, whether the more universal forms really come first, developmentally, seems still to be an open question. But it is striking that, from an early age, children's drawings may contain quite different forms of representation of the human figure alongside one another. Plate 4, for example, shows a drawing by a young Aboriginal (Warlpiri) girl from Central Australia. The semicircles in blue in the top lefthand corner are people, sitting around a fire. The semicircles with a smaller semicircle inside (at two o'clock and seven o'clock) apparently represent a mother and child, viewed from a kind of aerial perspective. These forms can also be found in the symbolic repertoire of the adult Warlpiri culture and they are passed on by older members of the community. But in the same picture there are stick and outline figures which much more closely resemble those drawn by Western children. Roger Wales (1990), who collected this picture, speculates that the latter depict white people in the community. There is no direct evidence of this, but it is clear, nonetheless, that this artist has two distinct ways of representing people. (This same mixture can also be seen in Plate 6.) The car in Plate 7 was drawn by another 6-year-old Warlpiri girl, in side view, very much as a Western child might draw it, but the driver is depicted using the traditional semicircle. Here, again, we see the intermingling of distinct graphic repertoires, one fairly universal and the other very culture-specific.

5.1 Creative flourish or learned skill?

The differences of graphic/artistic conventions between cultures are often profound and extend well beyond the issue of how particular objects are represented. Chinese art, for example, makes quite different use of space and represents depth in quite different ways from Western art. In China, children paint more than they draw, and they do so in two quite distinct styles (Winner, 1989). One involves the use of water colours to produce 'Western-style' pictures, often with lots of human figures, each with a big round head, two big black dots for eyes and a smiling mouth. Alternatively, they use ink to produce pictures in the Chinese style, depicting traditional subjects such as a branch with a flower, amidst a sea of blank space.

Winner attributes the great skill which many Chinese children show in both these styles to their willingness to comply and their ability to concentrate. From a very early age children are taught by direct instruction and demonstration how to paint particular subjects in the traditional style; 'Western-style' painting and drawing are taught in the same way. Winner describes a teacher instructing a primary school class in how to draw penguins, using a precise, step-by-step method which was replicated exactly in the children's textbooks. In this way, children are taught specific formulae for representing a variety of subjects in two dimensions. How far they are able to generalize these formulae to other subjects is not clear. Neatness and uniformity are of the utmost importance. Creativity may be present in some degree, but, for the most part, for these Chinese children the act of painting is rather like performing a piece of music written by someone else, as distinct from composing the work themselves.

Cultural contrasts, then, may be as much a matter of the *significance* attached to graphic representation in different societies as of the particular symbolic 'vocabularies' they make available to the child. In the UK and the US, we tend to regard handwriting as something which has to be carefully and deliberately taught, but drawing as something in which the teacher should not 'interfere'. Drawing is regarded as 'natural' – an expression of development and an opportunity for creativity, whereas writing is a skill to be learned. In China, it seems, this distinction hardly exists, and drawing is taught in very much the same way that writing is.

5.2 Changing conventions over time

Before we leave the issue of cultural variability in drawing, we should take a brief look at one instance of variability over time within a single culture. Brent and Marjorie Wilson (Wilson and Wilson, 1982) report on the mysterious case of 'the disappearing two-eyed profile'. The two-eyed profile is one in which the face is shown in profile, but both eyes are depicted. This looks like some kind of transition between the frontal view of a face which young children produce and the fully-fledged profile view which older children can produce when required. The mystery is that while many examples of this two-eyed profile are to be found in early twentieth-century studies of American and European children's drawings, it seems to have almost entirely disappeared from drawings collected more recently. The Wilsons suggest that the two-eyed profile was actually not some kind of natural (even inevitable) transitional phenomenon, but rather, that it was a local convention, part of the stock-in-trade of generations of children, and probably passed on from child to child. They speculate that it may have been transmitted as much through graffiti as through drawings on paper. Of itself, this account does not explain the profile's disappearance, but just as words fall out of use or change over time – as in the case of the slang that children use – so might their graphic 'vocabulary'. Golomb (1992) resists this interpretation, and offers a number of others. One is that nowadays children are allowed more freedom in their drawings and can stay longer with the full-face view. Thus, when they do eventually move to the profile view, they do so more successfully, eclipsing transitional forms such as the two-eyed profile.

These examples illustrate how difficult it is to use the evidence of cross-cultural and cross-generational studies to reach unambiguous conclusions about the processes involved in drawing. The degree of variability that they reflect argues against any strong form of the 'universal stages of development' view. Indeed, we have seen a number of examples in which characteristic features of children's drawing and painting can be directly related to specific features of their cultural environment. But it is still possible to argue that the degree of similarity in the ways children draw, across a wide range of times and places, shows that drawing development is not entirely an arbitrary and conventional process. Certain rather basic graphic forms are extremely widespread, if not universal. Local cultural considerations may interact with these basic forms, or may displace them, or may sit alongside them as an alternative 'code'.

In this section we have only dipped into the available literature on cultural variability in drawing. We have concentrated largely upon human-figure drawing, which has been the subject of most research. However, this may itself reflect an ethnocentric perspective (i.e. one centred in our own culture). The human figure may be pre-eminent as a topic in US and Western European children's drawings, but it is not universally so. Elspeth Court (1989), for example, found that rural Kenyan children were much more likely to draw boats, cows and horses than people, and devoted much more detailed attention to the former, even when people did occur in their drawings.

The interpretation of such differences in the chosen subject matter of drawings, or of the way different subjects within the drawing are handled, opens up a dimension of cross-cultural work which we cannot embark on here. But these issues of interpretation will be addressed, albeit in a rather different way, in the next section, where we go on to examine drawings as indicators of children's personality and emotional state.

SUMMARY OF SECTION 5

- Early experience with the use of the Draw-a-Man test in different cultural contexts showed that culture and schooling make a considerable difference to drawing development.

- Local variations may in some cases represent conventions passed on from child to child, and in other cases may reflect the impact of the artistic conventions of the adult culture. Children's figure drawings thus show both universal and more culturally specific features. Sometimes the more universal forms seem to appear first, to be displaced later by more culturally specific forms. Sometimes several quite different ways of representing the human figure exist in the child's repertoire at the same time.

- In some cultures children are very deliberately and carefully *taught* how to draw in one or more styles. In others, drawing is treated much more as a natural, spontaneous means of expression.

- Differences in the way children draw occur over time as well as place. Taken together, these differences are such that we cannot characterize drawing development in terms of universal ages and stages. Rather, we have to explore the ways in which certain general tendencies in children's drawing development interact with the cultural and historical circumstances in which any given child is growing up.

6 A WINDOW ON PERSONALITY

We have already seen in Section 2 that children's drawings have been regarded by psychologists as a source of information about stages of cognitive development. In a similar fashion, another tradition within psychology has looked to them for insights into children's personality and emotional state. This approach owes much to the psychoanalytic ideas of Freud and his followers. Drawings, like dreams, are seen as *projections* of the child's personality characteristics and inner conflicts. While speech may be guarded and censored, drawings might allow a more direct access to the inner world of the emotions.

Just as Goodenough's Draw-a-Man test aimed to provide a standardized measure of intelligence, so Karen Machover's Draw-a-Person test (Machover, 1949) was designed to elicit expressions of enduring aspects of children's personality. Children are asked to draw a person and, when that is complete, to draw another figure of the opposite sex. The tester notes the order in which the parts of the body are drawn and any comments that the artist makes while drawing. Machover claimed that certain features of drawings have clinical significance: the size of the figure, where it is placed on the page, whether certain features are included or not, and so on. So, for example, the gender attributed to the figure with the larger head is the one that is accorded more intellectual and social authority in other respects. And, in line with Freud's ideas about sexual symbolism and the pervasive influence of sexuality in human motivation, the nose is regarded as a symbol of the penis and its omission from a drawing is seen as an indication of castration anxiety.

ACTIVITY 7

Allow about 5 minutes

EVALUATING THE DRAW-A-PERSON TEST

Look back to the questions we raised about how to assess the usefulness of Goodenough's Draw-a-Man test (p. 237) and identify what sort of questions might be asked about the Draw-a-Person test.

Comment

There are questions to be asked about *reliability* and *validity*. Reliability can be considered in two respects. Do children consistently produce similar drawings? If they don't, what can be deduced from any single test is hit and miss. And are the *interpretations* reliable – do any two psychologists diagnose the same personality features from the same drawing? For the test to be valid, the predictions or 'diagnoses' that arise from it need to be supported by other independent evidence of the existence of these personality characteristics. In practice, there seems to be very little evidence that individual features of children's drawings can be meaningfully interpreted in this way (Anastasi, 1982). Children are reasonably consistent in the way that they draw, but different testers often differ dramatically in their interpretation of a given drawing, and there is little independent evidence of validity.

One problem with Machover's approach was that it paid insufficient attention to the changes in children's drawings of the human figure that occur as part of the process of normal development. Elizabeth Koppitz (1968) attempted to take this into account when devising her own Draw-a-Person test by distinguishing between features that might be expected in the drawings of children of a given age and those which she regarded as indicative of emotional disturbance. Among the thirty emotional indicators listed by Koppitz are poor integration of parts of the body, a tiny head, and gross asymmetry of the limbs. She produced evidence that the indicators on this list were more prevalent in a sample of children attending a child-guidance clinic than in a sample from ordinary schools who were judged by their teachers to be well adjusted. However, as with Machover's test, there are grounds for extreme caution. In practice, only eight of the thirty items were found significantly more frequently in the sample of emotionally disturbed children, and a quarter of the 'well adjusted' children used one or two of the supposed emotional indicators in their drawings (Golomb, 1992).

Do criticisms of this sort indicate that drawings have no place in a scientifically defensible identification of emotional difficulties? Golomb is fairly damning about these approaches to the 'projective' analysis of human figure drawing: 'Psychodynamic jargon is not a substitute for formulating a set of propositions derived from a theoretical framework and leading to testable statements' (Golomb, 1992, p. 277). Rather, she argues, instead of looking for 'signs' of deviant personality or maladjustment, a more holistic approach is needed:

> For an adequate assessment, a set of thematically different drawings ought to be analyzed in terms of their formal characteristics as well as their content. Attention to the formal characteristics of a drawing calls for an examination of compositional strategies, drawing systems, figural and size differentiation, the use of pictorial space, and the role of color. Content variables call for an analysis of themes and their elaboration and for the child's personal associations to his own drawing.
>
> (Golomb, 1992, p. 278)

Golomb has conducted an investigation in this vein. She studied a sample of 138 severely disturbed children aged between 7 and 15 and a sample of 72 normal children (aged 7–12). The children were all asked to complete five drawings on the subjects: 'Your family', 'Children playing', 'A birthday party', 'A garden with trees, flowers and a pond', and 'Your house and street'. When the drawings from the two samples were compared in terms of the ways in which the major figures and objects were organized into 'pictorially meaningful statements' i.e. *composition*, they were quite similar. Likewise, when scales were devised to measure the degree of *figural differentiation* – e.g. from 'tadpole' people at one end, to fully detailed figures drawn with a continuous outline and some indications of three dimensions; or trees that ranged from ones with an undifferentiated trunk to ones where branches were detailed in two dimensions, thinning out as they stretched away from the trunk – the two samples were broadly comparable. However, there were significant differences between the groups in two respects. The children in the 'disturbed' sample tended to draw smaller pictures and there was some evidence that the human figures were smaller. More clearcut was the finding that these same children preferred to use single colours and ignored the range of coloured pencils available to them. They were also less concerned to achieve realism through colour, by making, for example, the grass green and the sky blue. Golomb offers two hypotheses to explain these differences: the preponderance of single colours and the lack of concern for realism may be indicative of depression, and the lower incidence of local true colour perhaps reflects 'the child's lack of concern with the social reality and its demands, indicating both his opposition to the surrounding world and his withdrawal from it' (Golomb, 1992, p. 305).

Golomb's conclusion from this study was that, of themselves, the drawings from these 'normal' and 'disturbed' children did not provide a useful way of identifying the two groups. However, she does acknowledge that what the children actually *talked about* while they were completing the drawings was revealing and in this respect the process of drawing may have a valuable part to play in therapeutic work:

> For some youngsters, drawing is a substitute for verbal communication, for others it is an additional avenue for discovering and communicating important feelings the child harbors about herself and others … Drawing in the presence of the therapist encourages the child to understand his own message. This may enable him to become more active on his own behalf, to pursue an attainable goal, to gain greater self–respect, and ultimately, to feel better about himself … However, a drawing does not provide solutions magically, and in most therapeutic situations drawings are seen as aids in the working through of the child's emotional problems.
>
> (Golomb, 1992, p. 306)

6.1 Sizing up the evidence

Golomb's study has re-emphasized the importance of controlled and systematic comparisons. And even though she acknowledges that her two samples were not adequately matched for such important variables as IQ and socio-economic level, her approach argues for the rigour that such carefully designed research offers. One illustration of this approach is provided in Research Summary 2, which you should read now. It illustrates some of the complexities of investigating this area but, like Golomb, offers an optimistic prospect that the questions raised can be investigated through careful experimentation.

RESEARCH SUMMARY 2
CHRISTMAS IS COMING ...

Is there a relationship between the significance of people or objects to the artist and the size in which they are depicted in their drawings? One series of experiments has attempted to shed light on this by measuring whether North American children's drawings of Santa Claus become larger with the approach of the personally highly significant event of Christmas, and smaller again as it becomes an event of the past.

Some of these studies have indicated that this does indeed happen, but does it follow that it's the personal and emotional significance of Christmas as an event that is responsible? Other, rather different, explanations have been suggested. For example, as 25 December draws near, children are increasingly exposed to depictions of Santa Claus in shops, on television etc. Might they, as a result, become aware of more details in his appearance which they then want to include in their drawings, thus requiring a larger outline to accommodate them? There is evidence, more generally, of this correlation between size and detail (e.g. Freeman, 1980).

Glyn Thomas, Elizabeth Chaigne and Tania Fox set out to control for this problem of detail and other possible confounding factors in a study which had a more all-the-year-round appeal. First, they asked 4 to 5-year-old children to draw an outline of a person (along the lines of a silhouette shape in front of them) without any identifying description; the size of this figure served as a baseline for subsequent comparisons. Then they were asked to draw the outline of a 'very nice' and a 'very nasty' person (the order in which they drew these varied from one group to another). When the height of these drawings was compared with that of the baseline drawing it was found that the 'nasty' ones were significantly smaller; the 'nice' drawings were larger, but the difference was not statistically significant. (Another group of children drew a second 'neutral' figure and there was no identifiable difference in its size when compared with the baseline.) Thomas *et al.* interpreted this as evidence that drawings of threatening topics may be smaller than drawings of similar sized but non-threatening ones.

However, although the children in this study were asked not to include details of body parts in their drawings, some could not resist the temptation and so interpretation of the findings remained open to the sorts of criticisms previously made by Freeman. In a second experiment Thomas *et al.* repeated the procedure, but using the simpler shape of a 'nice' or 'nasty' apple. In this case, the drawings of the nice apple were significantly bigger than the baseline but the nasty apples, unlike the nasty people, were not drawn significantly smaller.

Taken together, these two studies indicate that there appears to be a relationship between the size of children's drawings and some emotional associations. The difference, here, between the outcomes for the person and the apple suggests that this relationship is not a straightforward one, though it has the potential to be further studied through carefully designed experiments.

Thomas *et al.* (1989)

SUMMARY OF SECTION 6

- Drawings have sometimes been held to be expressions of children's personality and inner feelings. Various characteristics of drawings have been interpreted as symbolic indicators of particular emotional preoccupations or conflicts. However, there is little evidence to support the validity of such interpretations.

- Attempts to use drawings of set themes to differentiate emotionally disturbed children have met with only very limited success. Drawing abilities seem relatively unaffected by even severe degrees of emotional disturbance. However, giving children the opportunity to draw what they like and eliciting comments and associations with the drawings may still represent a useful clinical approach.

- There are ways of investigating, systematically, the extent to which children's drawings are an index of their emotional and inner states. These have shown some relationships, but the overall picture is complex.

7 CONCLUSIONS

In this chapter we have been discussing the development of children's drawings with little or no reference to other forms of artistic expression (e.g., painting or clay moulding) or to other kinds of 'marks on paper' (e.g., writing, or making maps or diagrams). The child may be learning to use several of these forms of representation over the same developmental period and the relationship between them is complex.

Writing, for example, can be distinguished from drawing on the grounds that the elements of writing (letters, words, numbers etc.) have their meaning only by *convention* – they do not directly resemble the things they represent. But certain writing forms (e.g., hieroglyphics and pictograms) do resemble the things they represent, albeit in a formalized way. And musical notation is also to some degree a 'picture' of the sound patterns it encodes.

Similarly, we tend to think of drawing as a matter of creating direct resemblances between the marks on the paper and the real form of the objects depicted. But, as we have seen, children's drawings may actually be highly conventionalized at times. They may depict a person or a house or a bird, using very standardized graphic forms which have little direct resemblance to the particular person or house or bird they are looking at or thinking of. And good maps and diagrams need not show much literal resemblance to the objects depicted, provided they convey certain information about them in an effective way.

So the dividing lines between different types of 'representational activity' are fuzzy, even for us as adult observers. It may be even fuzzier for the children concerned! Interesting work has been done on young children's responses when asked to 'draw movement', or to 'draw music' (Catan, 1989) or to 'draw number' (Hughes, 1986). Earliest attempts at writing words have much in common with drawing, while young children's attempts to understand maps also provide interesting insights into their grasp of conventional symbolism (Goodnow, 1977).

In all these areas we can see children engaged in a creative search for meaning. In this search they express a good deal of themselves – their understanding of the world around them and their sense of their relationship to it. But they are also constrained by the medium they are using: paper and pencil, for example, require that they find ways of getting three dimensions into two, while clay modelling does not. And they are constrained by the available graphic repertoires and representational conventions of the culture that surrounds them.

As we have seen in this chapter, the study of children's drawings goes back a long way, and in its various developments may be seen a clear reflection of many of the strands which go to make up developmental psychology. For example, we can see the influence of the psychometric tradition clearly represented in the attempt to use drawings as standardized tests of children's level of intellectual development. We can see the psychodynamic tradition reflected in attempts to use drawings to uncover hidden emotional conflicts. And we can see cognitive-developmental stage theories of development clearly reflected in the attempt to identify regular and highly general stages in the drawing development of the child. These approaches are not necessarily incompatible with one another, and each has its value and its limitations.

In recent years a good deal of research has been directed towards analyzing how children master the representation of the third dimension in their drawings. Here, the constraints of the medium are very clear, requiring children to use graphic devices like occlusion and perspective convergence. But even then, development is not simply a matter of development of graphic skill. Children's responses to drawing tasks vary a great deal depending upon the context and upon precisely what information it seems to them most important to convey in a particular situation.

Drawing development has often been regarded as a progression towards increasing visual realism. However, consideration of the way we, as adults, use drawings should sound a cautionary note, since there are lots of situations (e.g., making maps, sketches and plans of various sorts) where 'photographic' visual realism is not the aim. Also, of course, there are plenty of artistic traditions in Western as well as non-Western societies, where visual realism is not the aim at all. In particular, linear perspective is often held out as the zenith of drawing development in childhood, but it is actually extremely rarely used in this or any other society by adults, whether in artistic or other contexts.

However, visual realism does become an important criterion for children in criticizing their own drawings. In our society we all too frequently see the spontaneous enthusiasm which young children have for drawing being lost by adolescence. The drawings can become laboured and fussy, and the artists less and less satisfied with them. We know of no evidence on the point, but our guess would be that if asked whether they can draw, most preschool children would say 'yes' and most adults would say 'no'!

This decline presumably says something about the relatively low valuation of drawing within the adult culture. It might be argued that drawing skills atrophy because we don't *teach* children how to achieve the visual realism they seek, and that we don't teach them because we don't think drawing is important. Our own feeling is that the first part of this proposition is probably true but the second part is false. We typically don't teach children to draw, but this may be precisely because what we value about young children's drawing is its naturalness and spontaneity.

To pursue this argument further would be well beyond the scope of this chapter, but we hope that raising the issue will highlight another respect in which drawing development is intimately connected with the social (and in this case the educational) context in which the child is growing up. If children's drawings offer us a window, it is as much a window on the culture as a window on the child's mind.

ANSWERS TO ACTIVITY 2

In Figure 1(a) credit would be given for: head present; eyes present; eye detail; pupil; fingers present; correct number of fingers shown; opposition of thumb shown. You may question this last feature; the Manual notes 'there are clearly five digits on each hand, one of which is oriented quite differently from the others, in each case' (Harris, 1963, p. 265).

In Figure 1(b) credit would be given for: head present; eyes present; fingers present. Although this man scores less than the one in Figure 1(a) in terms of the features listed in the box, the higher total results from credit given for correct body proportion and items of clothing.

FURTHER READING

Cox, M. V. (1992) *Children's Drawings*, Harmondsworth, Penguin Books.

Cox, M. V. (1993) *Children's Drawings of the Human Figure*, Hove, Lawrence Erlbaum.

Thomas, G. V. and Silk, A. M. J. (1990) *An Introduction to the Psychology of Children's Drawings*, London, Harvester Wheatsheaf.

REFERENCES

Anastasi, A. (1982, 5th edn) *Psychological Testing*, New York, Macmillan.

Bremner, G. and Moore, S. (1984) 'Prior visual inspection and object naming: two factors that enhance hidden feature inclusion in young children's drawings', *British Journal of Developmental Psychology*, **2**, pp. 371–6.

Catan, L. (1989) 'Musical literacy and the development of rhythm representation' in Gellatly, A., Rogers, D. and Sloboda, J. (eds) *Cognition and Social Worlds*, Oxford, Clarendon Press.

Court, E. (1989) 'Drawing on culture: the influence of culture on children's drawing performance in rural Kenya', *Journal of Art and Design Education*, **8**, pp. 65–88.

Cox, M. V. (1980) 'Visual perspective taking in children' in Cox, M. V. (ed.) *Are Young Children Egocentric?*, London, Batsford Academic.

Cox, M. V. (1981) 'One thing behind another: problems of representation in children's drawings', *Educational Psychology*, **1**, pp. 275–87.

Cox, M. V. (1991, 2nd edn) *The Child's Point of View*, New York, Harvester Wheatsheaf.

Cox, M. V. (1992) *Children's Drawings*, Harmondsworth, Penguin Books.

Cox, M. V. and Parkin, C. E. (1986) 'Young children's human figure drawing: cross-sectional and longitudinal studies', *Educational Psychology*, **6**, pp. 353–68.

Davis, A. (1983) 'Contextual sensitivity in young children's drawings', *Journal of Experimental Child Psychology*, **35**, pp. 478–86.

Dennis, W. (1957) 'Performance of Near-Eastern children on the Draw-a-Man test', *Child Development*, **28**, pp. 427–30.

Dennis, W. (1960) 'The human figure drawings of Bedouins', *Journal of Social Psychology*, **52**, pp. 209–19.

Donaldson, M. (1978) *Children's Minds*, London, Fontana/Collins.

FREEMAN, N. (1980) *Strategies of Representation in Young Children,* London, Academic Press.

FREEMAN, N. and JANIKOUN, R. (1972) 'Intellectual realism in children's drawings of a familiar object with distinctive features', *Child Development,* **43**, pp. 1116–21.

GOLOMB, C. (1981) 'Representation and reality: the origins and determinants of young children's drawings', *Review of Research in Visual Art Education,* **14**, pp. 36–48.

GOLOMB, C. (1992) *The Child's Creation of a Pictorial World,* Berkeley, University of California Press.

GOODENOUGH, F. L. (1926) *Measurement of Intelligence by Drawings,* New York, World Book Co.

GOODNOW, J. (1977) *Children's Drawings,* London, Fontana/Open Books.

HARRIS, D. (1963) *Children's Drawings as Measures of Intellectual Maturity,* New York, Harcourt Brace and Co.

HAVINGHURST, R. J., GUNTHER, M. K. and PRATT, L. E. (1946) 'Environment and the Draw-a-Man test: the performance of Indian children', *Journal of Abnormal and Social Psychology,* **41**, pp. 40–63.

HUGHES, M. (1986) *Children and Number,* Oxford, Blackwell.

JAHODA, G. (1981) 'Drawing styles of schooled and unschooled adults: a study in Ghana', *Quarterly Journal of Experimental Psychology,* **33**, pp. 133–43.

KELLOGG, R. (1970) *Analysing Children's Art,* Palo Alto (Calif.), Mayfield.

KELLOGG, R. and O'DELL, S. (1967) *The Psychology of Children's Art,* Del Mar (Calif.), Random House.

KERSCHENSTEINER, D.G. (1905) *Die Entwickelung der zeichnerischen Begabung,* Munich, Gerber.

KOPPITZ, E. (1968) *Psychological Evaluation of Children's Human Figure Drawings,* London, Grune and Stratton.

LIGHT, P. H. and MACINTOSH, E. (1980) 'Depth relationships in young children's drawings', *Journal of Experimental Child Psychology,* **30**, pp. 79–87.

LIGHT, P. and NIX, C. (1983) ' "Own view" versus "good view" in a perspective-taking task', *Child Development,* **54**, pp. 480–3.

LITTLETON, K. S. (1991) *The Representation of Depth in Children's Drawings,* unpublished DPhil thesis, University of York.

LUQUET, G. H. (1913) *Les Dessins d'un enfant,* Paris, Alcan.

LUQUET, G. H. (1927) *Le Dessin enfantin,* Paris, Alcan.

MACHOVER, K. (1949) *Personality Projection in the Drawings of the Human Figure,* Springfield (Illinois), C.C. Thomas.

PAGET, G. W. (1932) 'Some drawings of men and women made by children of certain non-European races', *Journal of the Royal Anthropological Institute*, **62**, pp. 127–44.

PIAGET, J. and INHELDER, B. (trans. LANGDON, F. J. and LUNZER, J. L.) (1956) *The Child's Conception of Space*, London, Routledge and Kegan Paul (first published in France in 1948).

RICCI, C. (1887) *The Art of Little Children*, Bologna, N. Zanichelli.

SULLY, J. (1896) *Children's Ways*, New York, D. Appleton and Co.

THOMAS, G.V., CHAIGNE, E. and FOX, T. J. (1989) 'Children's drawings of topics differing in significance: effects of size on drawing', *British Journal of Developmental Psychology*, **7**, pp. 321–31.

WALES, R. (1990) 'Children's pictures' in GRIEVE, R. and HUGHES, M. (eds) *Understanding Children*, Oxford, Blackwell.

WILLATS, J. (1977) 'How children learn to draw realistic pictures', *Quarterly Journal of Experimental Psychology*, **29**, pp. 367–82.

WILSON, B. and WILSON, M. (1982) 'The case of the disappearing two-eyed profile; or how little children influence the drawings of little children', *Review of Research in Visual Arts Education*, **15**, pp. 19–32.

WINNER, E. (1989) 'How can Chinese children draw so well?', *Journal of Aesthetic Education*, **23**, pp. 41–63.

CHAPTER 8 DEVELOPMENT IN READING

Jane Oakhill

CONTENTS

> **OBJECTIVES**
>
> 1 Identify the stages normal children go through in learning to read.
> 2 Understand the possible relation between other skills and reading development.
> 3 Describe different methods of teaching reading and their advantages and disadvantages.
> 4 Assess the role of contextual cues in reading.
> 5 Understand the factors that contribute to effective text comprehension.

1 INTRODUCTION

ACTIVITY 1

Allow 5–10 minutes

PRECONCEPTIONS ABOUT READING

Before you start reading, it may be useful to consider some of your own preconceptions about what is involved in reading and learning to read.

Imagine a 5 year old who is just beginning to learn to read. Write down the skills that the child will need to acquire in the next few years, on the road to becoming a skilled reader.

When people think about children acquiring reading skills, they usually think of learning to read words – 'cracking the code' – and perhaps this is the aspect of reading that you emphasized in your response to Activity 1. However, the ultimate purpose of reading is getting the (or a) meaning from the text, and I intend to give some coverage also to this aspect of reading – comprehension.

Reading seems to have captured the attention of psychologists perhaps precisely because it encompasses such a wide range of cognitive skills: from perception to language comprehension. Indeed, as long ago as 1908, Huey commented that 'to completely analyse what we do when we read would almost be the acme of a psychologist's achievements, for it would be to describe very many of the most intricate workings of the human mind …'. As we shall see as this chapter unfolds, this analysis is still by no means complete. Reading has also been an important topic of research because, despite the best efforts of teachers and researchers, some children still fail to learn to read. There has been a very large amount of research into how children learn to read and the best method of teaching them, and this chapter will, necessarily, be selective, concentrating on some recent developments in the areas which have a relation to developmental psychology. Almost all the research has concentrated on how children read words, and the balance of the chapter reflects this bias.

The first section considers the child's task in learning to read and how the development of reading skills has been captured in stage models. The second section outlines a variety of reading-related skills that children acquire in their pre-school and early school years, and considers how these skills might be related to beginning reading. In this section, I also survey some current methods of teaching children to read. In the third section, I give an account of some important aspects of the development of reading skills – in particular, the relevance of phonological recoding, and the use of context in reading. In the fourth section, comprehension will be considered: both its normal development, and the underlying causes of comprehension difficulties.

2 MODELS OF READING DEVELOPMENT

2.1 The alphabetic principle

Alphabetic writing systems, such as that used for English, capitalize on the fact that speech is already associated with meaning. Alphabetic systems use the principle of (roughly) using letters to represent phonemes (the small units of spoken language, of which spoken words are comprised). The alphabetic principle is the key to a productive writing system; an infinite number of words can be produced from a small, reusable set of letters. Once children have understood this principle, they will have the capacity to become independent readers, since they will be able to decipher words for themselves. These rules, which relate letters or groups of letters to sounds, are called grapheme phoneme correspondence rules (GPC rules) because they state the relation between small units of written language (graphemes) and small units of spoken language (phonemes). For example, the word 'that' has three graphemes because it is comprised of three phonemes, the sounds corresponding to 'th' 'a' and 't'.

However, although alphabetic systems result in economies in the amount to be learned, they can also be very problematic for beginning readers. In English, in particular, the mapping is not straightforward: for a start, we have only 26 letters and over 40 phonemes in English. Vowels, in particular, may be difficult: for instance in 'cat', 'car' and 'cake', the vowel represented by the 'a' is different in each case. In addition, some words do not follow the rules at all (e.g. 'yacht', 'colonel'), perhaps because many are 'loan' words from other languages. However, there is more regularity than we might suppose, especially if we take account of higher-order pronunciation rules (e.g. c before i, e and y is pronounced /s/, before a, o and u it is pronounced /k/).

A second major problem with alphabetic systems is that children may find it very difficult to conceptualize and to identify phonemes at the age at which they typically begin to read, for reasons we will discuss later. Because of these difficulties in analysing words into phonemes, most children begin to read words as visual patterns – they may recognize individual letters, but do not use the letter-sound mappings to help them. They rely on salient features of the words – the beginning and end letters and length in particular. However, such strategies soon become unreliable as the number of words they try to learn increases. Trying to learn every word as a separate visual pattern (as the Japanese learn the logographic system, Kanji) would make enormous demands on memory, and would be a very inefficient and time-consuming process. Indeed, it takes Japanese readers many years to acquire a reasonable working knowledge of their logographic system.

2.2 Stage models of reading development

The progression from recognizing words as visual patterns to a more analytic approach has been captured in *stage models* of reading. It is proposed by many theorists that children go through a number of stages as they learn to read. These stages will vary somewhat according to how children are taught, and the precise details of the developmental models vary, but they have the same overall approach. It is important to consider such models and the research that supports them, because they can have important implications for how children should be taught to read. Uta Frith's (1985) stage model is representative and will be outlined here. Frith has proposed three stages of development, each of which builds upon the previous one.

(a) In the *logographic* stage, the child treats words as logographs, recognizing them by looking for salient features. Thus, if they recognize the word 'daddy' they might think that any word beginning with 'd' also says 'daddy'. At this stage, the child has no way of deciphering new words, except guessing if the word is in context.

(b) In the *alphabetic* stage, the child begins to learn letter-to-sound mappings, and acquires the ability to decode unfamiliar words, and pronounceable non-words.

(c) In the *orthographic* stage, the child learns the conventions of English orthography, and can identify words by making use of larger orthographic units and analogies between such units, without the need for grapheme-to-phoneme conversion. For example, they might learn to use larger spelling patterns, such as: *ight, ing*. This is the stage at which the skilled adult reader operates, although skilled readers can, of course, fall back on earlier strategies if need be (e.g. using GPC rules to decode words that are in their spoken vocabulary, but which they have not seen before in print). Frith has linked these stages in reading development with spelling development. She argues that normal development of reading and writing proceeds out of synchrony, with either reading or writing skill acting as a catalyst to the development of the other skill. For instance, the alphabetic spelling principle is likely to appear in children's writing first, and then feed back into their reading development. Conversely, reading at the orthographic level is likely to occur while spelling is still in the alphabetic phase, and may trigger a change in spelling strategies.

The existence of such stages in reading development has been supported by evidence from research. Initially, children confuse words they know with other words beginning with the same letter, or which are similar in length or some other distinguishing feature. By around 7 or 8 years, there is evidence that children are capable of using GPC rules. They are more accurate at reading words with regular grapheme-to-phoneme mappings than irregular ones (e.g. 'cave' is easier than 'have'). A visual, or salient feature, method of identification would predict no such difference. At this stage, children also produce nonword errors, and tend to regularize irregular words (e.g. pronouncing 'pint' as though it rhymes with 'mint'). By about 9 to 10 years, children tend to be more flexible. They are equally accurate at reading regular and irregular words, which indicates a decrease in reliance on spelling-to-sound rules, and they make extensive use of orthographic cues and analogies, as well as graphemic information. In one study, Marsh, Desberg and Cooper (1977) asked children to say nonsense words such as 'tepherd' and 'faugh'.

ACTIVITY 2

Allow 5 minutes

PRONUNCIATION BY RULE OR ANALOGY?

Before you read about their results, think about how you might pronounce the non-words 'tepherd' and 'faugh'. Write down your initial responses.

Now, think about how you might pronounce them if you were applying GPC rules, and then see if you can find a real word analogy that might help you pronounce them. Are the pronunciations you come up with by the two routes the same or different?

Marsh, Desberg and Cooper claim that GPC rules indicate that the ph should be pronounced /f/, but that the analogy with 'shepherd' suggests a syllable boundary between the two separate phonemes, /p/ and /h/. Similarly, you would pronounce 'faugh' as 'farf' if you were making an analogy with 'laugh', but 'faw' if you were not.

The results showed that 10 year olds use GPC rules more frequently than analogies (50 per cent vs. 40 per cent). For college students, the respective figures were 30 per cent and 59 per cent (the other pronunciations were predicted by neither strategy). Marsh *et al.* (1981) suggest that analogy is an optional strategy for adults, and that its use depends on whether or not obvious analogies are available.

SUMMARY OF SECTION 2

- An important aspect of early reading is learning to grasp the alphabetic principle: the way in which letters or groups of letters (graphemes) relate to the sounds of the language (phonemes).

- This principle is difficult for young children, partly because of irregularities in English, and partly because of the abstract nature of phonemes.

- Because of such difficulties, children usually begin reading by recognizing words as visual wholes, then move on to the application of spelling-to-sound rules before they develop more flexible strategies, including the use of higher-order spelling patterns and analogies.

3 READING-RELATED SKILLS AND TEACHING READING

Children who are beginning to read already possess a wide variety of relevant skills, and will acquire many others as their reading progresses. Some of these skills are prerequisites for reading, and others are related to it in less-direct ways. In this section, I discuss the various ways in which skills could be related to reading development. We need to start with an important methodological point: many of the findings about how the development of various skills relates to reading are only *correlational*. That is, they show a link between the age at which children develop the skill and reading ability, but do not necessarily indicate a *causal* link. And, even if there were a causal link, the correlation will not indicate in which direction it runs. Ehri (1979) has identified four kinds of relation. First, skills may be *prerequisites* for reading – they need to be acquired before reading can begin. Second, skills may be *facilitators* of reading – they may speed its progress, but are not essential for it to start. Third, they may be *consequences* of reading – skills that develop through practice at reading, rather than vice versa. Lastly, they may be *incidentally related* to reading ability, perhaps because each is related to some other factor, such as IQ or level of parental interest in reading. It is important to know the status of a particular skill. If it belongs to the third or fourth category, then it is not necessary for the child to acquire it before reading can begin; if it belongs to the first or second category, however, it may be beneficial to give children training in the skill to help their reading development. There are two main ways of trying to decide whether skills are causally related to reading, which complement each other. The first method is to use *longitudinal studies*, to see which abilities develop first. Since skills that a child develops later cannot, logically, cause earlier skills to develop, such studies can rule out a number of possibilities. But, of course, the converse argument does not hold. We cannot infer that there is necessarily a causal link between earlier and later skills – they might simply be related because of some other factor. Thus, longitudinal studies need to be supplemented with *training studies*. If training the skill that develops early has a specific effect on the one that develops later (e.g. improvement in the skill is accompanied by improvement in reading ability), then this is good evidence for a causal link. Let us now consider, in the light of the above considerations, some skills that have been linked to reading.

3.1 Reading-related skills

Children's ideas about reading and concepts of print.

Between the ages of 3 and 5 years, children's ideas about reading change quite a lot. Three year olds are much more likely to think they can read when they cannot but, by 5 years, children are more realistic about their own abilities. Studies by Jessie Reid (1966) and John Downing (1970) showed that children starting school often have problems with the essential vocabulary of reading. Downing provided a striking example of how perplexing things could be for a child who does not have this essential vocabulary, listening to a teacher trying to explain some of the fundamentals of reading.

ACTIVITY 3

Allow 5–10 minutes

READING-SPECIFIC VOCABULARY

Try making sense of the following short passage in which Downing replaced all the words that are used in a specific way in reading with nonsense words.

This is how you sove the zasp 'bite'. It is tebbed with the rellangs fly, ear, milk, wow. The last rellang is the silent wow. When you have a silent wow at the end of a zasp, the ear says ear not ook, like it does in the zasp 'bit'.

Can you guess what the passage is about?

When the original words are reinstated, it is clear that the passage is about the *silent e* rule. This is how you write the word 'bite'. It is spelt with the letters bee, eye, tea, ee. The last letter is the silent ee. When you have a silent ee at the end of a word, the eye says eye not i like it does in the word 'bit'.

But how impossible this passage would be for a child who did not have a grasp of the relevant terminology, like 'letter', 'word', 'write'! In addition, these words may be used in a sense that is different from the one with which the child is already familiar (e.g. 'letters' are things you get in the post, 'words' are things you hear and speak, not read).

Young children may lack other fundamental understandings, like *which parts* of the book one reads. In one study, two-thirds of the 5 year olds thought the pictures, not the words, told the story! Children's knowledge of such terminology has, not surprisingly, been found to correlate with later reading ability (Yussen, Mathews and Hiebert, 1982). But explicit understanding may not always be a *prerequisite* for beginning reading – children may learn many of these things once they start to read. Though, of course, some basic concepts, like the importance of reading the *words*, must be regarded as essential. Similarly, the print conventions of the language they are learning to read – the direction of the words, lines, pages etc. – will be important early on.

Letter recognition

Children's knowledge of letter names when they begin school is a good predictor of their reading progress in their first year. But children can start to read without the ability to name any letters, and teaching children the letter names does not improve their reading. It seems likely, therefore, that some common factor – such as interest in written materials – underlies both letter naming *and* reading. Knowledge of the letters' names could help children discover the link between letters and sounds because the names of most letters contain the phoneme to which the letter 'refers' (Adams, 1990).

Young children often also have problems with letter orientation – they confuse mirror images of letters, for example. This problem has nothing to do with their powers of visual discrimination. It is probably related to the fact that they have not, in general, needed to pay much attention to orientation before. Most objects do not assume a different identity when their orientation changes! A cup is still a cup regardless of which way its handle is pointing, a chair is still a chair whether it is standing up or has been knocked over (see Figure 1).

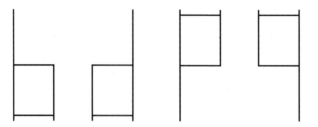

FIGURE 1 As chairs, each is labelled 'chairs': as letters, they are labelled b, d, p, q.

Word consciousness

This is the term used to describe the ability to recognize that both writing and speech are made up of distinct entities called words. This may seem very obvious to us as skilled readers, but is not at all obvious to young children. Their performance on a variety of tasks that measure word awareness is correlated with early reading skill. Examples of the tasks used are: saying whether a sound is a word, two words, or not a word at all; picking out the word or words that differ between two spoken sentences; tapping once for each word in a spoken sentence.

ACTIVITY 4

Allow 20 minutes

TESTING CHILDREN'S 'WORD CONSCIOUSNESS'

If you have access to a child of the appropriate age (4 to 5 years) you might like to try designing a short experiment to see whether they have these abilities by making up some materials for the tasks outlined above.

It is not clear, however, whether giving children training to improve their awareness of words will improve their reading skills. Some children do have such awareness before they begin to read, so it cannot simply be a consequence of learning to read. But there is no evidence that these skills are essential for reading to begin.

Phonemic and linguistic awareness

Very general phonemic awareness skills have been shown to be related to reading. Even very obvious features of words, spoken or written length, for example, may be difficult for children to perceive. For example, Rozin, Bressman and Taft (1974) showed pre-reading children two written words which differed dramatically in length, such as 'mow' and 'motorcycle', and asked the children to say which was which. Such children performed at chance level on this task: i.e. they were guessing.

What can be inferred from this poor performance? Obviously, the children could not read the words, but they should have been able to decide which was which based on the duration of the spoken words. It seems that they do not understand even this highly salient feature of writing – that longer words have longer pronunciations.

As we saw above, children may begin by recognizing words as visual patterns, more or less as logographs. But, once they have grasped the alphabetic principle, they will be able to work out unknown words for themselves. However, in order to do so, they must learn grapheme phoneme correspondence rules and, in order to use these rules, they will have to use segmentation (breaking the word into its component sound units) and blending (putting the parts together again once the sounds have been determined). Experiments with 4 and 5 year olds (Liberman *et al.*, 1974) have shown that they find the segmentation of words into phonemes virtually impossible, even though they are perfectly able to *perceive* differences at the level of phonemes (i.e. they know that words that differ by only one phoneme, e.g. 'cat', 'rat' and 'bat', sound different, and have different meanings). Children of around 5 or 6 years have difficulty in deciding whether two words begin or end with the same sound (Bryant, 1993), and perform poorly when asked to say what remains when a particular sound is removed from a word (e.g. /h/ removed from 'hill') (Bruce, 1964). Even young children, however, are much better at segmenting words into syllables. For instance, they can do a task that requires them to say 'cowboy' without 'boy': in one experiment, about 80 per cent of the 5 year olds tested could delete one syllable from two-syllable words. These findings show clearly that children beginning to read at about 5 years should find approaches to reading that demand explicit phonemic awareness very difficult.

Young children's difficulties in this area are probably related to the fact that phonemes are very abstract entities. Unlike syllables, phonemes do not have acoustic boundaries separating them in speech, so it is often impossible to say a phoneme in isolation. They overlap because of a phenomenon known as coarticulation. The way that the parts of the mouth move in speech production means that, for example, the articulation of the phoneme /d/ will depend on the vowel following it – how a phoneme sounds is dependent on context, particularly the vowels that precede or follow it. For instance, /d/ in 'dime' and 'dome' is pronounced slightly differently because the very first bit of the words contains information about the vowel as well as about the /d/. If you try to say /d/ by itself, you produce something like 'duh', which is not a component of either 'dime' or 'dome'. Thus, when a word is broken into its constituent sounds and these are said individually (e.g. 'cat' into /k/ /a/ and /t/) only approximations to the underlying phonemes can be derived. No matter how fast the consecutive sounds are spoken, they will not blend together to form 'cat' unless they are distorted. So, strictly speaking, 'one cannot teach a child that the letter p corresponds to the sound /p/ by showing the child the letter and saying the sound, because the sound cannot be said' (Harris and Coltheart, 1986, p. 86). However, although it is important to be aware of the potential problems, Adams (1990) argues that the advantages of encouraging children to articulate 'the sounds that letters make' will outweigh the disadvantages.

There are extensive data, from a variety of sources, that address the question of whether there is a *causal* link between phonemic awareness skills and reading (Goswami and Bryant, 1990; Morais, Alegria and Content, 1987) and the relevant findings will only be mentioned briefly here. Phonological skills (the ability to understand the sound structure of language) have attained such an important status in early reading because they provide children with the powerful self teaching mechanism inherent in an alphabetic writing system. Once the child knows the system, then he or she can, in principle, decipher new words and practise reading without help from an adult.

There are three main views on the link between phonological skills and reading, which we will consider in turn. The first is that phonological skills are *causally* related to reading acquisition. The second is that phonological skills are a *consequence of* reading acquisition (that they develop through learning to read), and the third view is that there is *reciprocal causation* – phonological skills are both *a cause and a consequence*. There is evidence for each of these views, which we will consider in turn.

Phonological skills help reading development

This first view is supported by various sources of evidence. First, strong positive correlations can be found between success in phoneme detection and reading level, even after IQ (an obvious mediating factor, see above) has been controlled. For example, in a study by Bradley and Bryant (1978), 10-year-old backward readers were compared not only with children of the same age, but with much younger children (6 year olds) who had the *same reading level as the backward readers*, but less experience of reading (the *reading age control group*). Such a group is important in reasoning about causal factors, in ways which will become clear below. The children were required to pick the 'odd one out' in sequences of four spoken words (either on the basis of alliteration, or of rhyme), and to produce words that rhymed with other words that were read out to them. For instance, in the odd-one-out task, they had to say which word was odd in sequences such as:

SUN–SEA–SOCK–RAG

WEED–NEED–PEEL–DEED

ACTIVITY 5
Allow 10 minutes

INTERPRETATION OF BRADLEY AND BRYANT'S RESULTS

Before reading on, you should think about the comparison groups that Bradley and Bryant used in their study, and try to work out what you might learn from particular differences between the groups. If there is any link at all between phonological skills and reading ability, we would expect the older good readers to perform better than the other groups, but what about the important comparison between the backward readers and the younger normal readers (remember that they have the same reading ability as the older backward readers, but less experience of written language)? What could you infer about the relation between phonological skills and reading if:

(a) The younger normal readers performed better than the older poor readers on the odd-one-out tasks?

(b) The older poor readers performed better than the young normal readers?

Write down the conclusions you would draw before you read on, then compare them with what was actually found in the study.

As expected, Bradley and Bryant found that the 10-year-old normal readers performed best, but the important finding was that the backward 10 year olds were poorer on these tasks than even the younger normal readers. Thus, these results support the idea that the phonological skills tested in Bradley and Bryant's study are *causally* implicated in reading ability, and do not just arise as a by-product of the development of reading ability, and familiarity with written material. If the 10-year-old poor readers had been better than the younger normal readers, it would have been impossible to come to any firm conclusions. We could not, for instance, conclude that experience with written language helps phonological skills, because the older children might have out-performed the younger ones for a variety of other reasons. The fact they performed *worse* makes the results of this study particularly striking.

In a later longitudinal study, Bradley and Bryant (1983) provided further support for their causal hypothesis. They showed that performance on the odd-one-out task at 4 or 5 years was a good predictor of reading achievement, but not of mathematical ability, three years later. They gave a large group of 4 and 5 year olds rhyme and alliteration tests before they had begun to read, and then followed their progress in both reading and maths over the next three to four years. There was a strong relation between the rhyme and alliteration measures and children's reading scores (but not their maths scores) when they reached 9 years. This relation was stronger than that between IQ and reading. Bradley and Bryant also included an element of intervention. Some children were given extra practice with rhyme and alliteration over a two-year period (when they were 6 and 7 years old). Their reading increased more than that of a control group.

A second source of evidence for this causal hypothesis comes from studies that show that children who are backward in reading are also poor at tasks that require the use of grapheme phoneme correspondence rules. Even if they are matched with children who have the same level of single word reading ability, they are still poorer than matched children at reading pronounceable non-words, for example, 'wef', 'slosbon' (Frith and Snowling, 1983). These findings suggest that poor readers are slower at learning to apply decoding procedures to reading.

Another source of evidence about causal links is training studies. An intervention study by Lundberg, Frost and Petersen (1988) showed that Danish children who were given extra phonological experience (breaking words into phonemes and constructing words from phonemes) learned to read more rapidly than a control group who were given non-phonological training. Bradley and Bryant (1983) also carried out a training study. However, they found that their phonological training condition – categorizing picture names by their initial sounds – did not improve reading and spelling abilities unless it was supplemented by teaching with plastic letters that showed children how words that have sounds in common have similar spelling patterns. This training showed, for example, how 'hand' could be changed to 'sand' or 'band' just by changing one letter. The improvement following this combined training was long-lasting. When re-tested at 13 years, those children given phonological training were still ahead of the control groups, but those trained additionally in the connection between sounds and letters were ahead of all other groups. One problem with Bradley and Bryant's study is that they did not test a group who were trained using the plastic letters alone – perhaps that was the vital ingredient in improving reading ability. However, a later study showed that training in sound categorization alone, or with plastic letters alone, was not as effective as the two sorts of training in combination.

Reading helps develop phonological skills

It is equally possible, and plausible, that there is a link in the opposite direction – perhaps children learn about phonemes *through learning to read*. A classic study that supports this viewpoint was carried out by Morais *et al.* (1979). They compared the performance of Portuguese people who had learnt to read only as adults ('ex-illiterates') with that of other adults who had never learned to read. Those who could read were much better at tasks requiring the segmentation of spoken words, e.g. remove the /p/ from 'purso' to give 'urso', add /p/ to 'alacho' to produce 'palacho'. The average scores were 19 per cent correct for the illiterate subjects, and 72 per cent correct for the literate subjects on the addition and deletion tasks. These findings were taken as evidence that learning to read and write makes one aware of the sound properties of language, rather than the other way round, and Morais *et al.* argued that explicit awareness is a product of being taught to read. A similar conclusion was reached by Read *et al.* (1986) who showed that it is learning to read in an alphabetic system which allows phonological awareness to develop. They compared two groups of Chinese readers on phoneme addition and subtraction tasks exactly analogous to those used by Morais *et al.* One of their groups of readers could only read the logographic script, whereas the other could read both the logographs and 'Pinyin', an alphabetic system which uses

Roman characters to represent the Chinese language phonetically. Those who had not learned an alphabetic system did very poorly in the segmental analysis tasks, getting only 21 per cent correct, whereas those who could read the alphabetic script did nearly four times as well, with 83 per cent correct. So, Chinese non-alphabetic literates, even though they are fluent readers of the logographic script, are similar to Portuguese illiterates in their inability to segment speech.

Reciprocal causation

Let us now turn to the third view: that there is reciprocity in the development of phonemic skills and reading. Work by Ellis and Large (1988) suggests such a relation. They showed that learning to read improves children's sensitivity to the sound properties of spoken words, particularly after the initial stages, and that the relation between reading and phonemic skills changes over the first few years of schooling. They tested a variety of phonemic skills: syllable- and phoneme-segmentation, and rhyming and blending. In a longitudinal study, they found that the phonemic skills of those children who were non-readers at age 5 years predicted their reading ability at age 6 years. However, once reading begins to develop, it seems to foster the development of phonemic skills. For those children who had begun to read, reading skill at 5 years, and again at 6 years, predicted phonemic skills one year later. Ellis has suggested that once children begin to read this 'makes sense of' sound skills, and fosters their development. Perfetti *et al.* (1987) also showed a reciprocal relation between phonemic skills and reading. They found that gains in reading led to gains in phonemic awareness which, in turn, resulted in further gains in reading.

A possible resolution

Peter Bryant (e.g. Goswami and Bryant, 1990; Bryant, 1993) has pointed out that, although pre-school children perform very poorly on tasks that require the explicit appreciation of phonemes, they are better with syllables, and enjoy rhyme and alliteration. Children of 3 and 4 years often play with sounds, and change the beginning sounds of words, just for fun. They love nursery rhymes and jingles and plays on words and, as we have already seen, there is considerable evidence that children's pre-school ability at rhyme and alliteration tasks is related to their later success in reading (Bradley and Bryant, 1983). Such studies provide clear evidence that there is a link between a pre-school, and largely untaught, phonological skill and learning to read. A reasonable conclusion might be that some aspects of phonological awareness (perhaps, in particular, the understanding of onset and rime, see below) may precede reading, and can be helpful in the beginning stages of learning to read, whereas other aspects are fostered by learning to read. However, whatever the precise relation between such skills and reading, it is clear that young children will find approaches to teaching reading that demand explicit phonemic awareness very difficult, and it is to this problem that we will now turn.

There is an apparent paradox here. On the one hand, considerable evidence now exists to show that a phonics approach to teaching reading (see later) produces the most rapid advances in early reading ability (e.g. Johnson and Baumann, 1984). In addition, a recent report by Her Majesty's Inspectorate found 'a clear link between higher standards and systematic phonics teaching. Phonic skills invariably formed a part of the repertoire of those children who showed early success in reading' (HMI, 1990). On the other hand, the evidence outlined above suggests that beginning readers will have considerable difficulties with such an approach because phonemic analysis is relatively hard for them, and they only become aware of phonemes as a result of learning to read. A possible resolution depends on a broader view of the role of phonological skills in learning to read. As Goswami and Bryant (1990) point out, there is no reason why phonological codes should operate only at the level of the phoneme. There are other regular correspondences between sound and print, and analytic approaches do not necessarily have to use segmentation into phonemes, at least in the initial stages. Since children usually already have a good sense of rhyme when they begin to learn to read, it might be useful to capitalize on this ability. Words that rhyme often also share spelling patterns. These shared rhyming sounds (e.g. *and, ing, ill*) are termed the *rimes* of the words. The onset is the opening consonant, or consonant cluster, and the rime consists of the vowel sound and any following consonants (e.g. s-and, str-ing). There is evidence from several sources that, within syllables, there is a natural distinction between onset and rime (speech errors, for example, respect this distinction). Rime is, of course, related to rhyme, and Goswami and Bryant stress the importance of harnessing children's natural ability with rhyme to help their beginning reading:

> They become adept at recognizing when words have common rimes or common onsets. So they form categories of words and when they begin to read they soon recognize that words in the same categories often have spelling patterns in common and that this spelling sequence represents the common sound. As soon as they realise this, they can make inferences about new words, and they do.

(Goswami and Bryant, 1990, p. 147)

Adams (1990), too, has pointed out how these speech units have been neglected in the teaching of reading. She demonstrated that, from only 37 rimes, nearly 500 primary-grade words can be derived.

ACTIVITY 6

Allow 5 minutes

GENERATING WORDS FROM RIMES

It is easy to see how useful a knowledge of the spelling patterns of a few rimes might be to young children if you try to generate words from them yourself. Here are some of the rimes suggested by Adams: '-all' '-ap' '-ell' '-oke' '-unk'. See how many common words you can produce from them, by adding a consonant or consonant cluster at the beginning.

Goswami (1986) has shown that even beginning readers can make analogies based on rime to help them read unknown words. The children in her study were shown 'clue words', such as 'beak', and were then asked to read a number of analogous and non-analogous words, on which they had previously been tested. The provision of clue words improved performance on words that could be read by analogy (e.g. for 'beak', words such as 'peak' and 'bean'), but not for other words (e.g. 'rain'). Even 5 year olds were able to make use of analogies to help them decode some of the test words. This, you will recall, contrasts with the idea that analogy is a late-developing skill, in terms of the stage models discussed above. Indeed, Goswami and Bryant (1990) question the need for positing discrete stages of reading development, and suggest, rather, that children just gradually get better at using strategies they use from the beginning. Perhaps phonics instruction works so well for beginning readers *not* because it teaches them GPC rules in the first instance, but because it fosters their awareness of speech units and the way in which these can be mapped onto written words, and gives children the general idea that words can be broken into smaller sound components.

3.2 Methods of teaching reading

The contribution of various skills to children's reading development may depend on their programme of reading instruction. Most, if not all, methods of teaching children to read are based on theories about how children can best learn to read, and some are based directly on research. Letter orientation, order and word detail will be important in programmes that emphasize sight recognition of words. Differentiation of letters, the associations between sounds and letters, and blending of sounds will be more important for phonics programmes. In the final part of this section, I outline the main approaches to the teaching of reading, and discuss in more detail how the various skills outlined above might be related to teaching procedures (for a fuller discussion of teaching methods, see Oakhill and Garnham, 1988). Until recently, there were two main approaches to teaching beginning readers to recognize words: the whole word (or look-and-say) approach, which teaches words as unanalysed visual patterns, and bases early reading on this sight vocabulary of learned words; and the phonics (or code-based approach), which teaches letter-to-sound correspondence and blending skills. The fierce debate about which is best has recently been complicated by another contender, the apprenticeship approach. The recent controversy about methods, and their relation to reading standards, has led to a reactionary return to phonics and basic skills teaching.

Whole word

In the whole-word approach, the overall shape and gross visual features of the word are stressed, not its component letters. Children are taught to recognize a small set of words, each of which is displayed singly on a card called a flashcard. Once children have built up an adequate sight vocabulary, they progress to the first reading books in the reading scheme, in which all or most of the words are ones they already know. The assumption behind this method is that children should be taught to read the way skilled readers do, by recognizing words 'directly' without having to analyse them into their component letters. However, as we shall see in the next section, such ideas are misguided. We saw earlier that beginning readers find analysis of words into phonemes extremely difficult. The whole-word method also circumvents the problem that, in English, there are numerous exceptions to any simple set of grapheme phoneme correspondence rules. Another advantage claimed for this approach is that it allows children to read for meaning early, presumably because it does not divert their attention away from meaning towards analysing words. However, equipped with only the ability to recognize words as visual patterns, beginning readers will be unable to tackle new and untaught words and, in any case, trying to remember the 50,000 or so words in the average adults' reading vocabulary, without capitalizing on the link between spelling and speech, would be highly inefficient. So, although the whole-word approach may get the reader off to a good start, and thus be beneficial from a motivational point of view, a more analytic approach to reading will be required at a later stage.

Phonics

Phonics approaches to the teaching of reading, of which there are many varieties, stress the importance of grapheme phoneme conversion rules. Children taught this way learn the sounds that the letters of the alphabet usually make, so that they can work out words for themselves. This approach provides children with a much more generalizable reading skill and, in principle, they should be able to 'sound out' any new words they come across. In practice, however, things are not so straightforward. Because grapheme phoneme correspondences in English are not regular, a letter may be associated with several different sounds, and the sound that a letter makes often depends on the context it is in.

A more serious problem for phonics methods arises from the difficulties that young children have with phonemes. As we saw earlier, most 5 year olds find it impossible to do the word-segmentation and blending that are fundamental to the phonics approach. Nevertheless, phonics seems to work. The evidence suggests that children taught by this approach do better in the longer term than those taught by other methods (Chall, 1979; Johnson and Baumann, 1984).

The apprenticeship approach

The apprenticeship, or 'story' approach to reading has been motivated by the ideas of the Americans, Frank Smith and the Goodmans. The links between learning to read and learning to speak are stressed, and there is little attempt at formal teaching of reading. Children listen to an adult reading to them while they follow the story in a book, then attempt to read along with the adult until they feel able to 'read' some or all of the book by themselves (Waterland, 1988). This approach has received a good deal of attention recently, much of it unfavourable (see e.g. Turner, 1990, who blames it for the fall in reading standards in the 1980s).

The basic tenets of the approach are derived from Goodman's 'psycholinguistic' approach to reading (e.g. 1970). This account assumes that young readers begin with expectations about the meaning and purpose of a text, and use the print only to confirm or disconfirm their predictions. It can be contrasted with an approach in which reading is primarily a process of decoding the marks on the page. Formal teaching of rules and reading-scheme books have no place in such approaches. However, despite their widespread appeal, there is no good evidence that such approaches are effective, and they have a very shaky theoretical background (Oakhill and Garnham, 1988). In particular, the acquisition of written language and spoken language differ in important ways, and context is not, in fact, a very helpful cue to a word's identity (Reid, 1993); skilled readers are much more dependent on the graphic information on the page than Smith and Goodman would have us believe.

Although the authors and advocates of reading schemes make many assumptions and claims about the way in which reading is best taught to young children, in practice teachers usually adapt the prescriptions to reflect their own experience and to accommodate the needs of the children they teach. Most teachers seem to use a mixture of the whole-word and phonics approaches, teaching some sight words first, and then going on to teach spelling-to-sound rules when they feel that the children are ready. The HMI (1990) report on reading found that nearly 85 per cent of teachers reported using a mixture of methods in early reading instruction. Indeed, it is often said that the good teacher is not a slave to a particular method, but has a wealth of knowledge and skills at his or her disposal, which can be drawn upon in a flexible manner according to the needs of individual children.

SUMMARY OF SECTION 3

- Children need to know at least some of the basic terminology and conventions of reading before they can begin, but many reading-related skills appear to develop as children begin to read, and are not necessary prerequisites.

- The precise nature of the relation between phonological skills and reading is equivocal, but most research points to the conclusion that each can influence the other. Some aspects of phonological awareness (perhaps, in particular, the understanding of onset and rime) can precede reading and can be helpful in the beginning stages of learning to read, whereas other phonological skills are fostered by learning to read.

- Children beginning to learn to read will find approaches that require explicit phonemic awareness very difficult.

- The two main approaches to the teaching of reading are the whole-word and phonics methods. In practice, teachers tend to use an eclectic approach, incorporating both these methods.

- A recent popular method has been the 'apprenticeship approach' to beginning reading. However, its theoretical basis is unsound, and its efficacy unproved.

4 CODING AND CONTEXT IN READING

In this section, I consider the information that children use during the course of reading development to help them decipher words. In particular, I address two issues. First, do words need to be recoded into their spoken form to be recognized, or can they be recognized more directly? Second, how does children's use of context change as their reading skill develops?

4.1 The role of phonological coding in reading

The first issue – whether children use phonological or visual information to access the mental dictionary (lexicon) and whether there is any developmental progression, has generated a great deal of research. Frank Smith (e.g. 1973, 1988) has argued that, since adults can derive the meaning of words *directly*, without recourse to phonological recoding, there is no reason why children should be taught to read by this 'unnatural' method, and that it may even be harmful. However, there are several sources suggesting that Smith's view of adult reading is incorrect (e.g. Oakhill and Garnham, 1988; Adams, 1991; Reid, 1993) and, even if it were correct, there is no reason to believe that the best way to teach children to read is to train them in the skills used by adults. As we have seen above, the ability to convert a written word to its spoken form is a useful tool for recognizing words, particularly in young readers whose aural vocabulary will be much larger than their reading vocabulary. The ability to carry out this so-called phonological recoding may be an important component of the development of reading. Phonological coding for word recognition requires the use of spelling-to-sound rules, such as the GPC rules discussed earlier. However, it must also be borne in mind that a word can be converted to its phonological form *after* it has been recognized, simply by looking up its pronunciation in the lexicon: this is called post-lexical phonology. Huey (1968) suggested why such coding might take place: phonological coding provides a more durable medium than visual coding for storing early parts of a sentence so that they can be combined with what comes later. Indeed, there is evidence that the most recently read portion of a text is retained in its exact phonological form. We shall consider both these types of phonological coding in more detail below.

Since the sight vocabularies of beginning readers are relatively underdeveloped by comparison with their aural vocabularies, phonological recoding will be particularly important for them in retrieving the meanings of words that they have heard, but never before seen in print. But it is not necessary to convert a printed word to a sound pattern in order to retrieve its meaning, and even beginning readers can recognize words directly from their visual appearance (see below). Indeed, as we saw above, children usually learn to read words as logographs before learning about GPC rules. Much of the work in this area was motivated by the idea of a developmental shift from using primarily phonological information, to using both visual and phonological information. Barron and Baron (1977) tested this hypothesis by asking 6- to 13-year-old children to make judgements about word meanings (saying whether words 'go together') while repeating the word 'double' over and over. This repetition was supposed to use up the children's phonological processing capacity, and thus prevent phonological recoding of the words whose meanings had to be judged.

ACTIVITY 7
Allow 5 minutes

EFFECTS OF REPETITION ON JUDGEMENTS OF WORD MEANING

Before you read on, stop to think about what pattern of results you would predict if younger children are more reliant on phonological information in judgements of word meanings? What effect would you expect having to say 'double' to have on their judgements?

If young children are dependent on phonological coding, then the repetition task should interfere with their ability to access the words' meanings. Barron and Baron found that the repetition task did not affect the extraction of meaning of individual words *at any of the ages* they tested. Even children who had less than a year of reading instruction were not affected by having to repeat 'double', demonstrating that even they were able to recognize words directly from their visual appearance. By contrast, the same repetition task affected the children's ability to make judgements about rhyme *at all ages*. Since judging whether a pair of words rhyme necessarily involves phonological recoding (not all rhyming words have the same spelling patterns) this finding provides evidence that the repetition task does affect performance when the use of phonological information is essential. Barron and Baron's conclusion was that even the youngest children in their study were able to go straight from graphemic information to the meanings of printed words, without phonological recoding.

However, more recent research in this area has produced conflicting results, and it now seems apparent that the strategies children use depend not only on their age, reading ability and type of word (high or low frequency, concrete or abstract), but also on the method of teaching reading that has been employed. In general, children move from using visual codes to access the lexicon, to using both phonological and visual codes. This fits in with the progression suggested by stage models of reading. Children rely initially on visual or graphemic cues, moving on to using phonological information, and then to a wider and more flexible range of strategies.

We will now turn briefly to the use of phonological codes *after* words have been recognized. It may be the case that, even though children can access word meanings directly, phonological coding of words plays some part in their reading strategies, as first suggested by Huey; it is not just some sort of unnecessary 'baggage' left over from being required to read aloud when they first learn. Indeed, there is evidence that older children and adults use phonological coding to store visually-presented letters and words in memory even when it is potentially disadvantageous to do so (for example, when the spoken forms of the letters and words would be highly confusable). In a test requiring children to remember a series of pictures, Conrad (1972) found that subjects older than about 6 years performed less well if the pictures had phonologically-confusable names (e.g. 'bat', 'bag', 'cat'). It seems, therefore, that phonological coding in memory is preferred by older children, and is not suppressed even when it affects their memory performance. Similarly, Japanese subjects reading Kanji seem to store the symbols in a phonological, rather than a visual or semantic, form (Erikson, Mattingly and Turvey, 1973: cited by Liberman *et al.*, 1977). In neither case – pictures or logographs – is the phonological code *necessary* to access meaning, and it cannot be produced by grapheme phoneme correspondence rules. The phonological form must be accessed from the visual pattern – picture or logograph – and its phonological form subsequently retrieved and used as a memory code.

4.2 Use of context in reading

The second major issue we will consider is the extent to which sentence context is used to help with word recognition as reading develops. The role that context plays in skilled reading and in learning to read has been much debated in theories about how reading should be taught (see e.g. Reid, 1993). However, in order to think clearly about whether increasing reading skill reflects increasing proficiency in using context, we need to distinguish between different ways of using context. First, context can be used to prevent or correct errors in reading – seeing whether a first guess at a word 'fits in' with the text. Second, context might be used to facilitate word recognition itself. In general, the evidence from research shows that older and more skilled readers are better able to use context to make predictions (e.g. guessing what the next word might be), but make less use of context to help them recognize words. These findings are in direct opposition to the ideas of Frank Smith who argues that because skilled readers read so fast, they could not possibly process words and letters thoroughly, but only sample the text sufficiently to confirm or disconfirm their predictions about what they think will be there (Smith, 1973). However, he ignores the fact that, when reading continuous text, more than one word is being processed at a time. In fact, skilled readers pay far more attention to individual words and letters than Smith allows (Just and Carpenter, 1987), and do not rely on context to help with word recognition in the course of normal reading – they don't need to.

Smith has argued that children will learn to read virtually by themselves, if exposed to enough meaningful and interesting language that will allow their natural hypothesis-testing talents to operate and that, like skilled readers, they should determine the meanings of new words from context, not by using rules to decode them. In fact, all the evidence from studies of word recognition shows exactly the opposite pattern – the use of context to help with the identification of words *decreases* as reading skill *increases*. The word recognition of skilled readers is so fast and automatic that preceding a word with a portion of relevant context does not help them, and neither are they slowed down when the word to be recognized is preceded by an incongruous context. For example, Schwantes, Boesl and Ritz (1980) tested 8 year olds, 11 year olds and adults in a task which required the subjects to say whether a letter string was a word or not (lexical decision). Thus, they should say, 'yes' to 'rain' and 'no' to 'roin'. Schwantes *et al.* varied the amount of prior context from, for example:

   the sky was dark and it started to
to
   started to

They found that the more congruous the context that was presented, the faster the youngest subjects (8 year olds) were able to respond to the word. Adults, however, were virtually unaffected by the amount of context supplied, i.e. they were equally fast to decide that 'rain' was a word, whether or not it was preceded by a relevant context. Similarly, increasing amounts of incongruous context (e.g. 'every fox has a white tip on the end of its – rain') interfered with word recognition only for the youngest readers. In a further study, West *et al.* (1983) used context sentences taken from children's reading primers, to try to make them as natural as possible. Their subjects' task was to name the final words as fast as possible. Once again, the younger the children, the more affected they were by prior context.

Stanovich (1980) has argued that, in reading, the contextual and perceptual information work together *(interact)*, and that the primary use of context in poorer readers is to compensate for the fact that they cannot recognize words from the perceptual information alone. Thus, for poorer readers, context can provide cues to a word's identity. The better ones, however, do not need to use context; it is quicker and more efficient for them to recognize words from their appearance, rather than going into time-consuming guessing and hypothesis-testing procedures. As we saw from the above studies, there is no evidence at all that better readers make more use of context in word identification: if anything, they make less.

This is not to say that skilled readers never use context, or that the ability to predict likely words from context, and to monitor the suitability of candidate words, is unimportant. Use of context can play an important role in beginning reading. It can also play a part in skilled reading when the text is somehow made hard to decipher (if the print is degraded, for instance), and is also important in monitoring comprehension (see below). However, common sense dictates that reading cannot just be some sort of sophisticated 'guessing game' (Goodman, 1970). The very nature of language – its creativity and unpredictability – makes such procedures very inefficient and error-prone (Reid, 1993). As Adams (1991) puts it 'Skilful readers are able to concentrate on meaning only because they have learned to process the words and their spellings very quickly and nearly effortlessly. But such automaticity grows from a history of having read words – not from skipping, ignoring or guessing at them' (Adams, 1991, p. 47).

SUMMARY OF SECTION 4

- The current consensus among researchers is that children progress from using a visual code to using a phonological code to access the meanings of written words, though their strategies may vary depending on the method of teaching reading, type of word and other factors.

- Phonological coding is important even after words have been recognized; it facilitates the retention of parts of the text in memory to help comprehension.

- In general, children become less dependent on sentence context to help their word recognition as their reading skill develops. At the same time, they become more adept at using context to monitor their word decoding and prevent or correct errors in their reading.

5 THE DEVELOPMENT OF COMPREHENSION SKILLS

It is usually, but not always, the case that once children have learned to decode words reasonably efficiently, comprehension will follow automatically. Since children who are beginning to read have been using and understanding their native language in its spoken form for some years, we would expect their existing skills to transfer to understanding language in its written form. However, although in general, reading comprehension ability correlates highly with word recognition ability, a small but substantial minority of children have a specific comprehension problem; they are able to read words accurately, and often read aloud fluently, but are poor at answering questions about what they have just read. In some cases, children who are poor at reading comprehension are also poor at listening comprehension, while in other cases, children may have comprehension difficulties that are specific to reading. In this section, I shall be discussing both of these possibilities.

An important point, which is sometimes overlooked specifically in relation to reading comprehension, is that writing is not simply speech written down. Children may not be familiar with the 'language of books' unless they have many books read to them in their early years; they need to be initiated into this book language. More generally, written language does not have all the supporting cues (stress, intonation, tone of voice, gestures, facial expressions and social context) that accompany spoken interactions.

A second problem that is specific to reading comprehension is that children may be so preoccupied with word decoding that they may not have the cognitive capacity to carry out comprehension processes at the same time. In addition, the rapid loss of information from short-term memory makes it difficult for very slow readers to hold information from earlier in a sentence so that they can relate it to what comes later. Since decoding skills will improve and become more automatic with practice, children will be able to devote more attention to comprehension as they become more skilled. However, the problem may be compounded by beginning readers' belief that the point of reading is 'getting the words right', and they may not necessarily connect this activity with deriving meaning from a text if it were read *to them*. Obviously, both word recognition and comprehension are important, and the two skills should be developed in parallel.

There is likely to be some overlap between the understanding of written and spoken language (though, of course, some of the common processes may be more difficult to carry out in the case of written text, for the reasons given above). Understanding a text – whether written or spoken – results in a mental representation of the state of affairs that it describes; a number of skills will be needed to construct such representations. First, the meanings of the individual sentences and paragraphs must be integrated with others. Inferential skills will be needed to help with this integration, and to go beyond what is explicitly stated in the text – a text that required no inferences to understand it would be extremely long and tedious, and authors necessarily leave some of the links between parts of a text implicit. Second, proper understanding of a text also depends on understanding the main point, and on sensitivity to the relative importance of other information in the text. Third, readers need to monitor their own comprehension – to be aware of whether or not they have adequately understood a portion of text – and to know how to remedy any breakdowns in comprehension.

5.1 Skills for comprehension

Inference making

Inferences are important for comprehension in many different ways. In particular, inferences are crucial to the process of connecting up the ideas in a text to build a coherent representation of the text as a whole. The developing mental representation of the text can be used to guide such inferences – it should help to indicate where the gaps are, and which of the many possible inferences need to be made. An example may help illustrate how much information in a text is left implicit and how readily we, as skilled readers, can fill it in.

ACTIVITY 8

Allow 5 minutes

IMPLICIT AND EXPLICIT INFORMATION IN TEXT

Read the following short text (taken from Charniak, 1972), and think about it for a moment.

> Jane was invited to Jack's birthday party.
>
> She wondered if he would like a kite.
>
> She went to her room and shook her piggy bank.
>
> It made no sound.

Now, write down all the things you understood by the text, but which were not stated explicitly.

On first reading, the text might seem very simple and straightforward, but to understand it in any real sense, we need some knowledge about taking presents to birthday parties, the conventions of saving money, and the need for money to buy presents. Someone who did not understand these conventions would find even this simple story impossible to understand. To take a couple of examples: in the second sentence, Jane is not simply *wondering* if Jack would like a kite, she is *thinking about buying him one* for his birthday. In the last sentence, the implication of the lack of sound is far from explicit, but we can infer what its likely consequences might be.

There have been numerous studies of primary school children's (5 to 11 years) developing ability to make inferences. In general, these studies show that younger children have the ability to make the same sorts of inferences as older ones (once differences in world knowledge are taken into account), but that the younger ones tend not to make inferences spontaneously; they only exhibit their ability when prompted or questioned explicitly (see Oakhill and Garnham, 1988, Chapter 5).

Understanding text structure

Many recent theories of comprehension point out that text is hierarchically structured, with one or more main ideas, each with subsidiary ideas and trivial details subordinated to them. Children's ability to pick out the main point of a text, and to judge the relative importance of other information in the text, increases markedly during the primary school years (Yussen, 1982). Children not only get better at selecting the main point, they change their minds about what the main point is. For example, Stein and Glenn (1979) found that 6 year olds usually picked the consequences of actions as the most important, whereas 10 year olds picked the goals of the main character(s). Such findings suggest that young children may have consistent ideas about what is important in a story, but that their ideas differ from those of older children and adults.

Brown and Smiley (1977) showed that children find it difficult to judge the importance of ideas in a text. They tested 8, 10, 12 and 18 year olds' ability to classify the ideas in folk tales in terms of of four levels of importance. The 8 year olds were almost completely unable to do the task, and even by the age of 12 years, children were only able to distinguish explicitly between the highest and the lowest levels of information (and not between intermediate levels). By contrast, children's *recall* of text was related to level of importance at all ages – even the youngest children remembered more of the important ideas. So, although children cannot explicitly identify which are the more important ideas in a text, they still pay more attention to those ideas. Even 5 year olds are likely to recall more of the important events in a text than the trivial details. The discrepancy between explicit awareness of importance levels, and the influence of importance on recall may be related to children's developing metalinguistic skills (see below).

Another important component of understanding text structure is seeing how the ideas in a text are related, and one way to assess children's understanding of the logical structure of texts is to ask them to tell stories themselves. Such research has shown that children's ability to produce coherent narratives develops gradually but that, like adults, they have certain expectations about the sort of information that should be present in stories, even from a very young age (see Baker and Stein, 1981, for a review of children's growing sensitivity to logical structure and knowledge of what makes a good story). The ability to understand how ideas in a story are related probably develops even before children learn to read, providing, of course, that they have been *read to* extensively.

Metalinguistic skills

Comprehension processes are more dependent than word recognition on meta-level knowledge (i.e. knowledge *about* knowledge). An important metalinguistic skill in comprehension is the ability to monitor one's understanding.

ACTIVITY 9

Allow 5 minutes

MONITORING YOUR UNDERSTANDING

Before you read on, think about the ways in which you have been monitoring your own understanding as you read this chapter. Did you have to look back to an earlier point, re-read a section which you didn't fully understand on first reading, look up a word or definition of a term, perhaps? Make a list of all the activities you have engaged in to check your understanding.

In general, younger readers are less likely to realise that they do not understand a portion of text, or know what to do about it even if they do realize (Garner, 1987). They are, for example, unable to detect that crucial information is missing from a text, or to spot even gross inconsistencies. However, the direction of the link between comprehension ability and metalinguistic skills is not clear. It may be that the process of learning to read increases children's language awareness, rather than the other way round.

5.2 Why do some children have comprehension problems?

Some recent research has identified children who have a *specific* comprehension problem, i.e. those whose comprehension is poor in relation to their word recognition ability and chronological age (see Yuill and Oakhill, 1991, for a review). Such children have been shown to differ from good comprehenders in their ability to make inferences and integrate information from different parts of the text, and in their metalinguistic skills. They could be characterized as superficial readers – they seem to process text fairly literally, without deriving the meaning of the whole. It has also been shown that such children do not have general memory problems, although they do have deficient working memory capacity. Working memory is utilized, for example, in complex mental arithmetic, where simultaneous demands are made on both processing and storage capacity. Since working memory is important in making inferences, and in the construction of a meaning representation from a text, it is not surprising that poor comprehenders are deficient in these comprehension skills. Poor comprehenders, like younger children, do not have a clear awareness of what comprehension is, and when it has been successful – they often fail to realize that they have not understood a text properly. There is evidence that their problems might arise, at least in part, because they fail to make use of comprehension-monitoring strategies (Garner, 1987). Once again, working memory may play a part in such processing. In general, we have found that children who are poor at understanding written text, and who do not have any problems at the level of single words, are also poor at listening comprehension, and even at understanding and narrating the main point of a *picture* sequence.

SUMMARY OF SECTION 5

- A substantial minority of children have comprehension problems. These may be either general language comprehension problems, or problems specific to reading comprehension.
- Efficient comprehension involves a number of skills: inference making, understanding the structure and main point of the text, and monitoring comprehension.
- Children may fail to comprehend adequately because of deficiencies in such skills, which may be related to underlying working memory problems.

6 CONCLUSION

The key to reading is learning the alphabetic principle of our writing system and, to do so, children need to learn about the correspondences that hold between spoken words and written symbols. There is an indication that some phonological skills can speed reading development (sensitivity to rhyme, for example) but, in general, learning to read and becoming aware of the sound system probably go hand-in-hand.

Stage models of reading development fit in with what is known about children's reading characteristics and abilities. In general, children progress from reading words visually (as unanalysed patterns) to using spelling-to-sound rules, and finally to reading by means of larger orthographic units.

In general, the research into children's use of phonological codes in reading suggests that children progress from using visual information to access a word's meaning to using phonological recoding. The work on children's developing use of context shows that proficient readers do not need to guess the identity of words; their word identification skills are so fast and automatic that they can recognize words from their perceptual properties far more quickly and accurately than they can guess them from context. Using context, however, can play a part in reading before word recognition skills become highly proficient.

Work on reading comprehension highlights the importance of recognizing that a significant proportion of young children may have a specific comprehension problem. Although, in general, children who are good at one aspect of reading will be good at others, comprehension skills do not necessarily develop automatically.

FURTHER READING

ELLIS, A. (1993) *Reading, Writing and Dyslexia,* second edition, Hove, Erlbaum.

GARTON, A. and PRATT, C. (1989) *Learning to be Literate: the development of spoken and written language*, Oxford, Blackwell.

GOSWAMI, U. and BRYANT, P. (1990) *Phonological Skills and Learning to Read,* Hove, Erlbaum.

HARRIS, M. and COLTHEART, M. (1986) *Language Processing in Children and Adults,* London, Routledge and Kegan Paul.

OAKHILL, J. V. and GARNHAM, A. (1988) *Becoming a Skilled Reader,* Oxford, Blackwell.

RAYNER, K. and POLLATSEK, A. (1989) *The Psychology of Reading,* Englewood Cliffs, N.J., Prentice Hall.

REFERENCES

ADAMS, M. J. (1990) *Beginning to Read: thinking and learning about print,* Cambridge (Mass.), MIT Press.

ADAMS, M. J. (1991) 'Why not phonics *and* whole language?' in ELLIS, W. (ed.), *All Language and the Creation of Literacy,* Baltimore, MD, Orton Dyslexia Society.

BAKER, L. and STEIN, N. L. (1981) 'The development of prose comprehension skills' in SANTA, C. and HAYES, B. (eds), *Children's Prose Comprehension: research and practice,* Newark (Del.), International Reading Association.

BARRON, R. W. and BARON, J. (1977) 'How children get meaning from printed words', *Child Development,* **48,** pp. 587–94.

BRADLEY, L. and BRYANT, P. E. (1978) 'Difficulties in auditory organization as a possible cause of reading backwardness', *Nature,* **271,** pp. 746–7.

BRADLEY, L. and BRYANT, P. E. (1983) 'Categorizing sounds and learning to read: a causal connexion', *Nature,* **301,** pp. 419–21.

BROWN, A. L. and SMILEY, S. S. (1977) 'Rating the importance of structural units of prose passages: a problem of metacognitive development', *Child Development,* **48,** pp. 1–8.

BRUCE, D. J. (1964) 'The analysis of word sounds by children', *British Journal of Educational Psychology,* **34,** pp. 158–70.

BRYANT, P. E. (1993) 'Phonological aspects of learning to read' in BEARD, R. (ed.), *Teaching Literacy: balancing perspectives,* London, Hodder and Stoughton.

CHALL, J. S. (1979) 'The Great Debate: ten years later, with a modest proposal for reading stages' in RESNICK, L. B. and WEAVER, P. A. (eds), *Theory and Practice in Early Reading*, Vol. 1, Hove, Erlbaum.

CHARNIAK, E. (1972) *Toward a Model of Children's Story Comprehension*, Boston (Mass.), MIT Press.

CONRAD, R. (1972) 'Speech and reading' in KAVANAGH, J. F. and MATTINGLY, I. G. (eds), *Language by Ear and by Eye: The relationships between speech and reading*, Cambridge (Mass.), MIT Press.

DOWNING, J. (1970) 'Children's concepts of language in learning to read', *Educational Research*, **12,** pp. 106–12.

EHRI, L. C. (1979) 'Linguistic insight: threshold of reading acquisition' in WALLER, T. G. and MacKINNON, G. E. (eds), *Reading Research: advances in theory and practice*, Vol. 1, New York, Academic Press.

ELLIS, N. and LARGE, B. (1988) 'The early stages of reading: a longitudinal study', *Applied Cognitive Psychology*, **2,** pp. 47–76.

ERIKSON, D., MATTINGLY, I. G. and TURVEY, M. T. (1973) 'Phonetic activity in reading: an experiment with kanji', *Haskins Laboratory Status Report on Speech Research*, **33,** pp. 137–56.

FRITH, U. (1985) 'Beneath the surface of developmental dyslexia' in PATTERSON, K., COLTHEART, M. and MARSHALL, J. (eds), *Surface Dyslexia*, Hove, Erlbaum.

FRITH, U. and SNOWLING, M. (1983) 'Reading for meaning and reading for sound in autistic and dyslexic children', *British Journal of Developmental Psychology*, **1,** pp. 329–42.

GARNER, R. (1987) *Metacognition and Reading Comprehension*, Norwood (N.J.), Ablex.

GOODMAN, K. S. (1970) 'Reading: a psycholinguistic guessing game' in SINGER, H. and RUDDELL, R. B. (eds), *Theoretical Models and Processes of Reading*, Newark (Del.), International Reading Association.

GOSWAMI, U. (1986) 'Children's use of analogy in learning to read: a developmental study', *Journal of Experimental Child Psychology*, **42,** pp. 73–83.

GOSWAMI, U. and BRYANT, P. E. (1990) *Phonological Skills and Learning to Read*, Hove, Erlbaum.

HARRIS, M. and COLTHEART, M. (1986) *Language Processing in Children and Adults*, London, Routledge and Kegan Paul.

HER MAJESTY'S INSPECTORATE (1990) *The Teaching and Learning of Reading in Primary Schools*, London, HMSO.

HUEY, E. B. (1968) *The Psychology and Pedagogy of Reading*, Cambridge (Mass.), MIT Press. (Originally published 1908.)

JOHNSON, D. D. and BAUMANN, J. F. (1984) 'Word identification' in PEARSON, P. D. (ed.), *Handbook of Reading Research*, London, Longman.

JUST, M. A. and CARPENTER, P. A. (1987) *The Psychology of Reading and Language Comprehension*, Newton (Mass.), Allyn and Bacon.

LIBERMAN, I. Y., SHANKWEILER, D., FISCHER, F. W. and CARTER, B. (1974) 'Explicit syllable and phoneme segmentation in the young child', *Journal of Experimental Child Psychology*, **18,** pp. 210–12.

LIBERMAN, I. Y., SHANKWEILER, D., LIBERMAN, A. M., FOWLER, C. and FISCHER, F. W. (1977) 'Phonetic segmentation and the beginning reader' in REBER, A. S. and SCARBOROUGH, D. L. (eds), *Toward a Psychology of Reading,* Hillsdale (N.J.), Erlbaum.

LUNDBERG, I., FROST, J. and PETERSEN, O. (1988) 'Effects of an extensive program for stimulating phonological awareness in preschool children', *Reading Research Quarterly,* **23,** pp. 263–84.

MARSH, G., DESBERG, P. and COOPER, J. (1977) 'Developmental changes in strategies of reading', *Journal of Reading Behavior*, **9,** pp. 391–4.

MARSH,G., FRIEDMAN, M., WELCH, V. and DESBERG, P. (1981) 'A cognitive-developmental theory of reading acquisition' in WALLER, T. G. and MACKINNON, G. E. (eds), *Reading Research: advances in theory and practice,* Vol. 3, New York, Academic Press.

MORAIS, J., ALEGRIA, J. and CONTENT, A. (1987) 'The relationships between segmental analysis and alphabetic literacy: an interactive view', *Cahiers de Psychologie Cognitive: European Bulletin of Cognitive Psychology,* **7,** pp. 415–38.

MORAIS, J., CARY, L., ALEGRIA, J. and BERTELSON, P. (1979) 'Does awareness of speech as a sequence of phones arise spontaneously?', *Cognition,* **7,** pp. 323–31.

OAKHILL, J. V. and GARNHAM, A. (1988) *Becoming a Skilled Reader,* Oxford, Blackwell.

PERFETTI, C. A., BECK, I., BELL, L., and HUGHES, C. (1987) 'Phonemic knowledge and learning to read are reciprocal: a longitudinal study of first grade children', *Merrill-Palmer Quarterly,* **33,** pp. 283–320.

READ, C., ZHANG, Y., NIE, H. and DING, B. (1986) 'The ability to manipulate speech sounds depends on knowing alphabetic spelling', *Cognition,* **24,** pp. 31–44.

REID, J. (1966) 'Learning to think about reading', *Educational Research,* **9,** pp. 56–62.

REID, J. (1993) 'Reading and spoken language: the nature of the links' in BEARD, R. (ed.), *Teaching Literacy: balancing perspectives,* London, Hodder and Stoughton.

ROZIN, P., BRESSMAN, B. and TAFT, M. (1974) 'Do children understand the basic relationship between speech and writing? The mow motorcycle test', *Journal of Reading Behavior,* **6,** pp. 327–34.

SCHWANTES, F. M., BOESL, S. L. and RITZ, E. G. (1980) 'Children's use of context in word recognition: A psycholinguistic guessing game', *Child Development,* **51,** pp. 730–6.

SMITH, F. (1973) *Psycholinguistics and Reading,* New York, Holt, Rinehart and Winston.

SMITH, F. (1988) *Understanding Reading,* New York, fourth edition, Holt, Rinehart and Winston.

STANOVICH, K. (1980) 'Toward an interactive-compensatory model of individual differences in the development of reading fluency', *Reading Research Quarterly,* **16,** pp. 32–71.

STEIN, N. L. and GLENN, C. G. (1979) 'An analysis of story comprehension in elementary school children' in FREEDLE, R. O. (ed.), *New Directions in Discourse Processing,* Norwood, (N. J.), Ablex.

TURNER, M. (1990) *Sponsored Reading Failure: an object lesson,* Warlingham Park School, Education Unit.

WATERLAND, L. (1988), *Read With Me: an apprenticeship approach to reading,* second edition, Lockwood, Thimble Press.

WEST, R., STANOVICH, K., FEEMAN, D. and CUNNINGHAM, A. (1983) 'The effect of sentence context on word recognition in second- and sixth-grade children', *Reading Research Quarterly,* **19,** pp. 6–15.

YUILL, N. M. and OAKHILL, J. V. (1991) *Children's Problems in Text Comprehension: an experimental investigation,* Cambridge, Cambridge University Press.

YUSSEN, S. R. (1982) 'Children's impressions of coherence in narratives' in HUTSON, B. A. (ed.), *Advances in Reading/Language Research,* vol. 1, Greenwich (Conn.), JAI Press.

YUSSEN, S. R., MATHEWS, S. R. and HIEBERT, E. (1982) 'Metacognitive aspects of reading' in OTTO, W. and WHITE, S. (eds), *Reading Expository Material,* London, Academic Press.

ACKNOWLEDGEMENTS

Grateful acknowledgement is made to the following for permission to reproduce material in this book:

Chapter 1

Text

Reading A: from *Theories of Developmental Psychology* by P. H. Miller, copyright © 1989 by W. H. Freeman and Company, used with permission; *Reading B*: Siegler, R. S. (1991) *Children's Thinking*, Prentice-Hall; *Reading C*: Butterworth, G. (1992) 'Context and cognition in models of cognitive growth' in Light, P. and Butterworth, G. (eds) *Context and Cognition*, Harvester Wheatsheaf; *Reading D*: Karmiloff-Smith, A. (1992) *Beyond Modularity: a developmental perspective on cognitive science*, MIT Press, © 1992 Massachusetts Institute of Technology.

Table

Table 1: Wood, D. (1991) 'Teaching and learning interactions' in Light, P., Sheldon, S. and Woodhead, M. (eds) *Learning to Think*, Routledge/The Open University.

Figures

Figure 2: Karmiloff-Smith, A. (1979) 'Problem-solving procedures in children's construction and representation of closed railway circuits', *Archives de Psychologie*, **1807**, pp. 37–59, Association des Archives de Psychologie, Geneva; *Figure 3*: Keil, F. C. (1990) 'Constraints on constraints: surveying the epigenetic landscape' in Ringle, M. D. (ed.) *Cognitive Science: a multidisciplinary journal of artificial intelligence, linguistics, neuroscience, philosophy, psychology*, **14**, pp. 135–68, Ablex Publishing Corporation, copyright © 1989, Cognitive Science Society, Inc.

Chapter 2

Text

Reading: Ferrier, L. J. (1974) 'Some observations of error in context', Language Development Project, University of Bristol, reprinted by permission of ESRC.

Table

Table 1: *Psychology Today*, 1979.

Figure

Figure 2: Bruner, J. S. (1976) 'Learning to do things with words' in Bruner, J. S. and Garton, A. (eds) *Human Growth and Development*, Oxford University Press, © Wolfson College, Oxford 1978, reprinted by permission of Oxford University Press.

Cartoons

p. 53: cartoon by P. J. Rigby, reproduced by kind permission of the Editor, *Education*, published by Pitman Publishing, 20 November 1992, p. 411; *p. 63*: reproduced by kind permission of Punch; *p. 66*: cartoon by Naylor, reproduced by kind permission of the Editor, *Education*, published by Pitman Publishing, 23 May 1986, p. 464.

Chapter 3

Figures

Figure 1: adapted from Conway, M. A. (1990) *Autobiographical Memory: an introduction*, Open University Press, copyright © Martin A. Conway 1990; *Figure 2*: Lachman, J. L., Lachman, R. and Thronesbery, C. (1979) 'Meta-memory through the adult lifespan', *Developmental Psychology*, **15**, pp. 543–51, American Psychological Association, copyright © 1979 by the American Psychological Association, adapted by permission; *Figure 5*: McClelland, J. L. and Rumelhart, D. E. (1985) 'Distributed memory and the representation of general and specific information', *Journal of Experimental Psychology: general*, **114**, pp. 159–88, American Psychological Association, copyright © 1985 by the American Psychological Association, reprinted by permission.

Chapter 4

Text

Reading B: Meadows, S. (1993) *The Child as Thinker*, Routledge, © 1993 Sara Meadows.

Figure

Figure 1: Mervis, C. B. and Crisafi, M. A. (1982) 'Order of acquisition of subordinate, basic and superordinate level categories', *Child Development*, **53**, University of Chicago Press, Inc., © The Society for Research in Child Development, Inc.

Tables

Table 1: Mervis, C. B. and Crisafi, M. A. (1982) 'Order of acquisition of subordinate, basic and superordinate level categories', *Child Development*, **53**, University of Chicago Press, Inc., © The Society for Research in Child Development, Inc.; *Table 2*: Bryant, P. E. and Trabasso, T. (1971) 'Probability of correct choices on tests for transitivity and retention' reprinted with permission from *Nature*, **232**, © 1971 Macmillan Magazines Limited.

Photograph

page 117: Barry Walker.

Chapter 5

Text

Reading A: selected excerpts from pp. 311–14 from *Psychology: the science of mental life*, by George A. Miller, copyright © 1962 by George A. Miller, copyright renewed, reprinted by permission of HarperCollins Publishers, Inc.; *Reading B*: Berger, M. and Yule, W. (1985) 'IQ tests and assessment' in Clarke, A. M., Clarke, A. D. B., and Berg, M. J. (eds) *Mental Deficiency: the changing outlook*, Methuen; *Reading D*: Dasen, P. (1984) 'The cross-cultural study of intelligence – Piaget and the Baoulé' in Fry, P. S. (ed.) *Changing Conceptions of Intelligence and Intellectual Functioning: current theory and research*, North-Holland.

Figures

Figures 6, 7 and 8: Richardson, K. (1992) 'Reasoning with Raven – in and out of context', *British Journal of Educational Psychology*, **61**, pp. 129–138, © 1991 The British Journal of Educational Psychology.

Chapter 6

The observations in Activities 7 and 8 were collected by S. Allen in a small-scale study for an Open University course and are reprinted with permission.

Figure 10: Driver, R. (1985) 'Beyond appearances: the conservation of matter under physical and chemical transformations' in Driver, R., Guesne, E. and Tiberghien, A. (eds) *Children's Ideas in Science*, Open University Press.

Chapter 7

Figures

Figure 1: figures from *Children's Drawings as Measures of Intellectual Maturity: a revision and extension of the Goodenough Draw-a-Man test*, by Dale B. Harris, copyright © 1963 by Harcourt Brace & Company and renewed 1991 by Dale B. Harris, reproduced by permission of the publisher; *Figures 3 and 7*: Piaget, J. and Inhelder, B. (1967) *The Child's Conception of Space*, Routledge and Kegan Paul; *Figure 6*: Piaget, J. and Inhelder, B. (1967) *The Child's Conception of Space*, Routledge and Kegan Paul, © The estate of Jean Piaget; *Figures 9, 10, 14 and 18*: Cox, M. (1992) *Children's Drawings*, Penguin Books Ltd, copyright © Maureen Cox, 1992, reproduced by permission of Penguin Books Ltd; *Figure 13*: Light, P. H. and MacIntosh, T. E. (1980) 'Depth relationships in young children's drawings', *Journal of Experimental Child Psychology*, **30**, pp. 79–87, copyright © 1980 by Academic Press, Inc.; *Figure 16*: Willats, J. (1977) 'How children learn to represent three-dimensional space in drawings', *Quarterly Journal of Experimental Psychology*, **29**, Lawrence Erlbaum Assoicates Ltd, copyright © 1977 Lawrence Erlbaum Associates Ltd.

Table

Table 1: Light, P. and Nix, C. (1983) ' "Own view" versus "good view" is a perspective-taking task', *Child Development*, **54**, University of Chicago Press, Inc., © The Society for Research in Child Development, Inc.

Colour plates

Plates 8, 9, 10 and 12: Jenny Oates; *Plate 11*: Lucy Dibble; *Plate 13*: Anna Oates; *Plate 14*: Charlotte Collis; *Plate 15*: Joe Dibble; *Plate 16a*: Victoria Collis; *Plate 16b*: Luke Collis.

Chapter 8

Figure 1: Garton, A. and Pratt, C. (1989), *Learning to be Literate*, Basil Blackwell Ltd, copyright © Alison Garton and Chris Pratt 1989.

NAME INDEX

SUBJECT INDEX